THE

# WORKING AND MANAGEMENT

OF

# AN ENGLISH RAILWAY

Yours faithfully
George Dudley

THE

# WORKING AND MANAGEMENT

OF

# AN ENGLISH RAILWAY

SIR GEORGE FINDLAY

**SIXTH EDITION**

REVISED BY

S. M. PHILLP

With a new introduction by
JACK SIMMONS
Professor of History, University of Leicester

EP Publishing Limited
1976

Republished 1976 by
EP Publishing Limited
East Ardsley, Wakefield
West Yorkshire, England
from the sixth edition of 1899 published
by Whittaker & Co.


New Introduction Copyright © Jack Simmons 1976


Copyright © EP Publishing Limited 1976

ISBN 0 7158 1149 5

**British Library Cataloguing in Publication Data**

FINDLAY, Sir George
  The working and management of an English railway
  . – 6th ed.
  Index.
  ISBN 0-7158-1149-5
  1. Ti 2. Phillp, S M
  DC. 385'.0942
  LC.HE3020.L/
  LCSH. London and North Western Railway
      Railroads–England–History

Please address all enquiries to EP Publishing Limited
(address as above)


Printed in Great Britain by
REDWOOD BURN LIMITED
Trowbridge & Esher

# INTRODUCTION

The London & North Western Railway was one of the greatest commercial corporations in nineteenth-century Europe, with a system not far short of 2,000 miles long in 1900 and a total capital of more than £120 million. Though, like all human undertakings, it had its points of weakness, the service it afforded, taken all round, was second to none. It had a marked character of its own, derived first from the great engineers who laid out almost the whole of its main line, Robert Stephenson and Joseph Locke; then from its chairmen, who were remarkable men too, notably George Carr Glyn and Sir Richard Moon; and no less from a series of exceptionally able officers, with Mark Huish and John Ramsbottom at their head. That character was compounded of caution, prudence, financial sobriety, and the most meticulous attention to detail. The Company was steeped in a profound conservatism, and yet its rivals often discovered to their chagrin that, however unenterprising it might appear, it was capable of providing a service as good as the most progressive of them, with much less noise and fuss.

The London & North Western abhorred all vulgar publicity. Its posters displayed no winsome maidens, such as the Great Western flirted with, still less the lush and alluring ladies of the Great Central or the Great Northern's bouncing fisherman of Skegness. They were sober and informative, but well presented and in the end, one may suspect, no less successful. The postcards

# INTRODUCTION

the Company produced in large numbers, of scenes on the line and of its trains, were highly appreciated; they have become collectors' pieces today. It is characteristic of the London & North Western—another example of its annoying capacity to succeed in business without really trying—that its work should have been carefully described in five books, none of them "official", that is to say commissioned as publicity material, yet all in their different ways serving that purpose excellently. The first two, Sir Francis Head's *Stokers and Pokers*[1] and its sequel *High-ways and Dry-ways*, belong to the 1840s. Next came this one, written by the Company's General Manager. The fourth was *British Locomotives* by C. J. Bowen-Cooke, a younger man on the staff of the Mechanical Engineer, published in 1893 and twice reprinted; and the series ends with the *Railway Reminiscences*[2] of G. P. Neele, the retired Superintendent of the Line, which provides a commentary on the Company's history from 1861 to 1895. As a result, we know more about the London & North Western as a working organism than about any other British railway company.

Findlay's book was the most successful of the five. It ran through six editions, from the first, which appeared in 1889, to the sixth ten years later, and the text was gradually enlarged from 263 pages to 383. The sixth edition, the one chosen for reprinting now, was extended beyond those limits with a biographical notice of the author (first prefixed to the fifth edition, which had appeared just after his death) and a supplementary chapter, recording some things that had taken place in the years 1894–99.

[1] Reprinted in 1968.   [2] Reprinted in 1974.

## INTRODUCTION

There is no need to say much here about Findlay himself. The introduction records the main facts of his life adequately, and there is little more that needs to be added. It ought, however, to be recorded that on Sir Richard Moon's retirement in 1891 the directors of the Company tried to persuade Findlay to succeed him as chairman: a signal and most uncommon compliment. He declined the invitation from a sense of duty, thinking that he should continue in the much more demanding office of General Manager while his strength lasted.[1] Unfortunately that was not for long. He died on 26 March 1893. He left a modestly comfortable estate, of a little more than £17,000.[2]

Findlay never lived much in the public eye. He is careful indeed to explain here (p. 70) how a man occupying an office like his should protect himself against all but the most necessary visitors. But this book provides clear evidence that he understood the importance of good public relations, and when he had to play his part in explaining his company's practice by word of mouth he could do so very well: in 1873, for example, when he was Assistant General Manager and gave evidence before the Court of Inquiry into the Wigan accident.[3]

In private negotiation he powerfully impressed those

---

[1] *The Times*, in its obituary (27 March 1893), recorded this as "an open secret". It may be mentioned that the other obituary notices, e.g. in the *Engineer*, *Engineering*, and Findlay's chief local paper the *Watford Observer*, add nothing to this good notice in *The Times*; for the most part they merely copy it word for word.

[2] One of the witnesses to his will was S. M. Phillp, a clerk in his office, who wrote the memoir and the supplementary chapter reprinted here.

[3] *Parliamentary Papers* 1874, lviii. 781–2, 789–90.

## INTRODUCTION

he had to deal with, on the opposite side of the table. A senior official of the Post Office—a body with which the railway companies' bargaining was often troublesome and sometimes acrimonious—paid him this tribute: "Sir George Findlay was an admirable General Manager, and a man of excellent judgment and rare decision. Familiar with every detail of the vast railway traffic which he regulated, taking broad and far-sighted views of every question, and being a man of transcendent fairness, he made negotiation an agreeable rather than a laborious effort".[1]

This book of Findlay's is primarily a work of description and analysis, and as such it is admirable. The task he had set himself before any other was to explain the way in which the London & North Western Railway was made to work: its technology, the structure of its administration, the framework of national politics and law that circumscribed it. As General Manager it was one of his chief functions to learn to understand the wishes and needs of his colleagues and to interpret them to the directors of his Company—with the corollary that he had often to explain in the opposite sense, to tell his colleagues why the directors would not accept their recommendations, or had decided to amend them. When he wrote the book he applied all the experience he had gained in these tasks since 1880, but in a new way: to interpreting the ideas and actions of his company—directors and officers alike—to the general public. And so, reading what he wrote, one is in chapter after chapter looking, as it were, over

[1] F. E. Baines, *Forty Years at the Post Office* (1895), ii. 203-4.

# INTRODUCTION

Findlay's shoulder at the papers he had to prepare for his directors' guidance, almost listening in to his voice when called upon to speak at their meetings.[1]

This faculty for the clear exposition of what is complicated is present throughout the book. Consider two examples of it: one concerned with technology, the other with law. In three chapters (x–xii), only sixty of his quite small pages, he gives an account of the actual working of the passenger and goods traffic of the railway that, in clarity and balance, could scarcely be improved on. Although conditions and techniques have greatly changed now, anybody who wished to depict the running of a railway in the 1970s would do well to begin by reading Findlay's account, and then to try matching his own against it. He has to perfection the mastery of the single example, which often tells more than generalised statement: the fog of 20 December 1891 (pp. 219–20), the big goods station at Holyhead, described fully on pp. 252–57, the little one at Daventry, illustrated with no waste of words but by means of a simple and sufficient plan (p. 260). Turn then to Chapter xvi, on the law relating to railways, and read his summary of the railway company's duties and rights as a carrier of goods (pp. 326–40). It is elegant, lucid, and saved from dryness by his deft attention to the minute. He tells us, for example (pp. 329–30), that under the Carriers Act of 1830 lace was considered an article so valuable as to be classed with jewellery, watches, bank-notes, and paintings, requiring special

---

[1] Findlay was in no sense a practised writer for the public. This is his only book. He also published privately a 48-page pamphlet, *Irish Railways and State Purchase*, in 1886.

(v

## INTRODUCTION

payment by the consignor, and that by a subsequent Act of 1865 this provision was amended so as to extend only to hand-made lace. We are observing here the very process of change in Victorian technology and fashion.

Perhaps the greatest difference between Findlay and a modern writer who attempted a similar task would arise from their treatment of the railways' employees. To give a truthful picture of a railway today, much of the available space would have to be allotted to the relations between labour and management, and especially to the part played by the trade unions. Though the railway unions we know now were all in existence, at least in embryo, in Findlay's time and growing in their membership, he does not mention them once in his book. The introduction spells this out for us: "he would never recognise the paid officials of the railway trade unions" (p. 33). He does not ignore labour relations: he devotes an early chapter, his third, to the staff of the Company and some of the conditions under which it was employed, and in his account of the works at Crewe and Wolverton he pauses to discuss the communities that the railway had called into being there. To say that he does this in a paternalistic spirit is true, but open to misinterpretation. No other way would have been conceivable, or indeed proper, in a man of his position at the time at which he was writing. The railway is to him a huge administrative machine absolutely dependent for its safe, efficient, and profitable working on a chain of command, understood and obeyed from the chairman to the young apprentice. He is describing for us a hierarchy such as could be found

# INTRODUCTION

nowhere else in Victorian Britain on this scale save in the armed forces.

But though the attitude towards command in all forms has wholly changed since, and deference has now become an obsolete concept, though the trade unions have assumed a power in the running of railways that would have been unimaginable—and profoundly shocking—to Findlay, things are not totally different here in all respects. The railway itself remains what it always was: a powerful and potentially dangerous device, whose running constantly requires close attention to rules imposed to secure safety. Most railwaymen recognise this today as well as their predecessors did in the 1880s. And so when Findlay is describing safety precautions like systems of signalling, he is dealing with things that in principle have not changed at all, however different their techniques may be now; and, to some extent at least, with attitudes of mind that remain constant.

It is when he looks at the railway's customers, at the society it served, that he is perhaps most remote from us. The public image of his company often seemed to be taken from its Mid-Victorian chairman Sir Richard Moon: inflexible, Puritanical, Olympian. By the nature of his office, Findlay had to be more supple, and one of the pleasant things about his book is that he avoids almost entirely the complacent and patronising tone that must have buzzed around him all day at Euston. The London & North Western Railway is a great public servant: that conviction shines out here from start to finish. But it is a servant, not a master. He rarely touches on matters of controversy, or finds it

## INTRODUCTION

necessary to enter even an oblique defence of his company against criticism. But when he does either of these things, he is judicious and urbane. At the time when he wrote, the railways were rapidly becoming unpopular in the country at large, and especially with manufacturers and traders, who complained loudly of the rates they levied. Findlay refers to this matter more than once (pp. 206, 225), quietly throwing out a brief answer to the critics' accusations. Another senior General Manager, James Grierson of the Great Western, had recently published what became a standard book on the subject, from the railways' point of view. By the time the later editions of Findlay's work appeared a young economist, W. M. Acworth, had offered a more independent analysis, *The Railways and the Traders*. Findlay does not attempt here any extended treatment of this complicated and explosive issue.

The tone in which he refers to it, and to all the other matters he touches on concerning the relations between the railways and those who use them, is always courteous, without being condescendingly patient. He seldom lays down the law, and his commentary is the more persuasive for that. Just occasionally he shows a touch of the over-certainty that we are apt to find disagreeable, and sometimes amusing, in the Victorians; and one of these occasions is important. Back in 1874 the Midland Railway, one of the London & North Western's chief rivals, had decided to abolish second-class travel on its system, to carry two classes of passengers only, first and third. In arriving at this decision it did not consult the other companies, and they were indignant. Some of them followed the Midland's

# INTRODUCTION

example, wholly or in part. Others—the great majority —stood their ground and maintained the old three-class structure intact. One of these last was, as we should expect, the London & North Western, and Findlay feels himself obliged to defend its policy here. He does so (p. 176) on two grounds. First, he takes leave to doubt whether in fact the decision has been profitable, though he does not develop the rather complex argument that is involved. But secondly he ventures into the field of sociology (the word was already current in his day) with this assertion: "The London & North Western Company maintained the belief that society in this country, for all purposes, naturally divided itself into three classes, and that the wants and tastes of the community were best served by their present practice". There is something comical to us in Findlay's magisterial statement of the immutability of a class structure, though it must be recognised that most of his contemporaries thought the same—as Matthew Arnold had done, when he talked of Barbarians, Philistines, and Populace in *Culture and Anarchy* twenty years before. Yet if this three-class structure of fares really reflected a social structure, how came it that on the German railways, in Findlay's time and far into the twentieth century, the classes were four? It would be hard to demonstrate that, in this respect, the society of Germany was different from that of Britain and her other neighbours.

If we sometimes remain dissatisfied with Findlay's explanations, as in this instance, it is a merit in him that he does at least try to explain. He is not content to say "here is what we do" without giving some reason

## INTRODUCTION

why it is done. This is, above all, what gave his book its value when it was new, and what makes it worth reprinting now. It might have been much longer, the explanations very much more elaborate; but then it would have missed the broad public for which he designed it, and it would be of interest to only a few specialists today. In fact, the book reached its audience; and in its quiet and reasonable tones it has the power to reach and speak to us still, eighty years later, in a very different world.

December 1975                                JACK SIMMONS

# NOTE

This is a photographic reprint of the sixth edition of *The Working and Management of an English Railway*, complete except for the half-tone photographic plates (nos. XVII–XXII, XXIV, and XXV), which are poor in quality and unsuitable for reproduction.

# PREFACE TO THE SIXTH EDITION.

In the world of railways, five years, which have elapsed since the above preface was penned, have seen many changes, and in order that these may not go altogether unrecorded in the pages of this book, a new chapter has been added to the present edition (page [377]) which gives a brief account of some of the more important developments which have occurred.

S. M. P.

EUSTON STATION
*March* 1899.

# PREFACE TO THE FIFTH EDITION.

No apology is needed for the production of a new Edition of this work. In the five years which have elapsed since its original publication it has come to be recognised, both in this country and abroad, as a handbook, or standard authority, on the working and management of railways, and it is of the essence of such a work that it should be periodically revised and brought—so to speak—up to date. In the world of railways, events move quickly, and history is so rapidly made, that what is perfectly true as a statement of fact to-day may be no longer true to-morrow, to say nothing of the fact that statistics, which are freely scattered throughout this book, are of little value unless they deal with recent periods.

Since the issue of the last Edition, its able author has passed away from our midst, and it has seemed to me that a new Edition of his work could not be more suitably prefaced than by a short biographical sketch of a career which was in many ways remarkable, and which as an illustration of the eminence to which an honest, upright, and able man can rise from the humblest origin, should serve as an encouragement and an example to all who come after him.

S. M P.

EUSTON STATION:
*May* 1894.

# CONTENTS.

| CHAPTER | | PAGE |
|---|---|---|
| | BIOGRAPHICAL SKETCH OF AUTHOR | 1 |
| I. | INTRODUCTORY AND RETROSPECTIVE | 37 |
| II. | MANAGEMENT | 58 |
| III. | THE STAFF | 71 |
| IV. | PERMANENT WAY | 84 |
| V. | SIGNALS AND INTERLOCKING | 116 |
| VI. | TELEGRAPHS | 137 |
| VII. | ROLLING STOCK.—I. ENGINES AND BRAKE POWER | 150 |
| VIII. | DO. II. CARRIAGES | 176 |
| IX. | DO. III. GOODS WAGGONS | 194 |
| X. | THE WORKING OF THE TRAINS | 201 |
| XI. | THE SHUNTING AND MARSHALLING OF GOODS TRAINS | 227 |
| XII. | ON THE WORKING OF GOODS STATIONS | 239 |
| XIII. | RATES AND FARES—DIVISION OF TRAFFIC—THE RAILWAY CLEARING-HOUSE | 262 |
| XIV. | ON THE RELATION OF THE STATE TO RAILWAYS IN ENGLAND, AND THE QUESTION OF STATE PURCHASE OF RAILWAYS | 278 |
| XV. | PASSENGER TRAFFIC | 297 |
| XVI. | ON THE LAW AS BETWEEN ENGLISH RAILWAY COMPANIES AND THE PUBLIC | 323 |
| XVII. | ON THE RAILWAYS AS A MEANS OF DEFENCE | 341 |
| XVIII. | RECENT PROGRESS IN WORKING AND MANAGEMENT | [377] |
| | APPENDIX | 377 |
| | INDEX | 399 |

# BIOGRAPHY.

THERE is always one broad line of demarcation separating into two distinct classes what are commonly called "public men," that is to say, men who, in one way or another, occupy prominent positions in the world of politics, or of commerce. There are, in the one class, men born to distinction, or who have it thrust upon them by no effort of their own, and in the other, those who achieve it in spite of all obstacles, and who climb the ladder of life step by step by dint of their own ability and force of character. It cannot be denied that the subject of this sketch comes within the second category, and he himself, so far from ever seeking to conceal the fact that he was a "self-made man," was always proud to relate that in his youth he worked as an artisan and used the tools of his craft. And surely such a reflection was a legitimate subject for honest pride in a man who, dying at the comparatively early age of sixty-three, had raised himself to the position of supreme command of perhaps the greatest joint-stock undertaking in the world, a position, indeed, which has been compared to that of commander-in-chief of an army of sixty thousand men, with a salary equal to that of a Cabinet Minister, and a social standing but little inferior. There is, in fact hardly any exhibition of snobbishness more deplorable or ill-judged than that which can prompt a man with a record of honourable achievement behind him, and who has won his way to distinction by his own talents, and by a lifetime of strenuous endeavour, to make it his constant aim to persuade the world that he was, after all, "born in the purple," and that there is nothing wonderful in his being where he is.

Certainly, the career of a self-made man must always be of far greater interest to the community—and especially to the younger portion of it—than that of one born, to use a familiar phrase, "with a silver spoon in his mouth," and this for a very obvious reason. Such a career is, to every young man who studies it, at once an incentive and an encouragement. He sees on the top of the ladder one who once stood, like himself, on its lowest rung, and, seeing this, he takes heart of grace to attempt the ascent in his turn. Few, it is true, may reach the summit, but none are the worse for trying, and out of much earnest effort some good must come.

Sir George Findlay, although born at Rainhill, in Lancashire, on the 18th of May, 1829, was descended from a family of small tenant farmers, who can be traced for some 250 years back as residing at Coltfield, or Caultfield, in the parish of Alves, in the county of Elgin, so that his family tree might be said to have been rooted in Scottish soil. There was, in fact, a George Findlay born in Alves as long ago as 1684, and as recently as 20 years ago, at any rate, there was still a George Findlay farming at Mosstowie, near the same place, in the county of Elgin.

Sir George Findlay's grandfather, James Findlay, was born at Alves in 1766; he married young, became **a** farm bailiff at Grantown, Inverness, and died there. A document which exists amongst the family records, relating to this James Findlay, throws a somewhat curious light upon contemporary customs in the Scotch Presbyterian Church, to which he belonged. When this young man, at the age of 22, left his native place to take a situation in another part of the country, he took with him a certificate signed by the minister and two elders of the church at Alves, testifying that:

> The bearer, James Findlay, a married man, was born and brought up in this parish of Alves, and lived in it till the term of Whitsuntide, 1788, always behaving himself soberly and honestly, nor is anything known to us to impeach his character, or prevent his reception into any Christian congregation or society where Providence may order his lot.
>
> Given at Alves, etc.

This James Findlay, whose character as a young man seems to have stood so high that even the elders of a Scotch Presbyterian Church could find no flaw in it, died at the age of 38, leaving his widow with a young family of seven children practically unprovided for. Her eldest boy was George Findlay, Sir George Findlay's father, who was only 12 years old when his father died. The widow, no doubt, must have had a hard struggle to provide for the wants of her young brood until they were old enough to shift for themselves, but in her efforts to keep the wolf from the door her great mainstay was her eldest boy. By his father's untimely death he was deprived of the advantages of the good education which doubtless he would otherwise have received, but he appears to have been of a sturdy and self-reliant disposition, and, even at that early age, he lost no time in finding employment during the summer months on the farms in the neighbourhood of Grantown, picking up what schooling he could in the winter months. The want of education was always his great stumbling-block, but he possessed much natural shrewdness and common sense, and of these he made such good use as ultimately to raise himself to a very fair position. As soon as he was old enough to be apprenticed, he learnt the trade of a stonemason, and when he was little more than 20 years of age he quitted Grantown, and went to Glasgow, where he worked for some years as foreman to several leading firms of builders, always with credit to himself and with the good opinion of his employers. In this groove he might have lived and died, but meanwhile great events were ripening elsewhere. The great engineer, George Stephenson, had overcome the early difficulties which beset the birth of his epoch-making enterprise, and was at length actively engaged in the making of the first railway, between Liverpool and Manchester. His great undertaking was talked of throughout the length and breadth of the land, and his strong personality drew around him many men whose energy and ability contributed materially to his ultimate success. Amongst these came George Findlay the elder, who left Glasgow about the year 1827, and from that time till the year 1835 was one of Stephenson's most valued helpers, being employed in superintending the construction of the Newton Viaduct, the Sankey Viaduct, the Bridge over the Irwell at Manchester, the Rainhill Skew Bridge (considered at that time a very remarkable work), and finally the Edge Hill Station and Tunnel at Liverpool. On the completion of the Liverpool Tunnel, he was engaged, still under George Stephenson, as inspector of masonry on the

London and Birmingham Railway, then in course of construction, and consequently had to remove his household from Liverpool to Coventry, so as to be near the scene of his new labours. We seem to a certain extent to realise the difficulties of locomotion in those early years of the present century, when we learn that his wife and children performed this journey by first taking shipping in a small steamer from Liverpool to Runcorn, thence travelling in a canal fly boat to Birmingham, occupying several days on the journey, and arriving there on a Saturday evening, and, there being no conveyance until the Monday, accomplishing the remainder of the distance on foot on the Sunday. Sir George Findlay was at that time a child only six years of age, but he must have been a sturdy youngster, for he trudged the journey of 18 miles with the rest of the party, and seems to have been none the worse for it.

While at Coventry, three years later, in 1835, his mother died; and his father shortly afterwards was engaged, under Stevenson, in the making of the Manchester and Leeds Railway, and in this work, and subsequently in the execution of masonry work on the Halifax Branch Railway, he was occupied until 1845. In that year, he accepted an appointment as inspector on the Trent Valley Railway, then in course of construction, and on the completion of that railway he remained in the service of the London and North-Western Company as inspector of permanent way until, in 1854, his health failed and he was forced to retire; while four years later he died, in his 66th year, leaving behind him the record of a long life of honest work, faithfully and diligently performed. His opportunities were always limited by his want of education, or he might have achieved a much higher position, for his natural abilities were considerable, and his character such as to inspire confidence and respect in all with whom he was connected. He was, too, of an extremely kind-hearted and generous disposition—as is sufficiently proved by the fact that, for some years, while his income was a very limited one and he had a tolerably large family of his own to provide for, he voluntarily undertook the support of two of his sister's children and two of his wife's sisters.

If we have thus dealt, at perhaps greater length than may appear to be necessary, with the life and work of the elder George Findlay, our justification for so doing lies in the fact that his character and career really form the key to those of Sir George Findlay, the subject of our present sketch. The latter was, in fact, the child of his surroundings, and was the worthy son of a worthy father. Born within sound of almost the first railway whistle, he lived to become one of the kings of that great world of railways then only in its infancy. Born the son of an upright, honest, and hardworking man, he did credit to his parentage, and by the aid of the education which his father lacked, he raised himself to a position which in his younger days he could have little dreamed of. He always had the greatest respect for his father's memory, and to the day of his death spoke of him with affection and admiration.

It is interesting to notice the fact that while Sir George Findlay's father was a Scotchman, his mother, Agnes Courtenay, was an Irishwoman; he himself was born in England, and much of his early business life was passed in Wales, so that, in one way or another, he was intimately connected with all the four parts of the United Kingdom. His connection with the world of railways may be said to have commenced in his cradle, for he was born at Rainhill while his father was engaged in the building of the famous Skew Bridge, already mentioned, near that place. His father, impressed with the value of the education from the want of which he had suffered himself, wisely took care that his boys should be better equipped for the battle of life, and young George Findlay was accordingly sent to the Grammar School at Halifax, his father being then employed on the Halifax Branch Railway. At the early age of 14, however, he left school and began to learn the practical work of masonry on the works of the Halifax Railway, while two years later, when he was a youth of sixteen, we find him working as an assistant to his brother James—his senior by ten years—who was then engaged under Thomas Brassey in the construction of certain of the bridges and viaducts between Shugborough Tunnel and Armitage, on the Trent Valley Railway. That railway was completed in May, 1847, but its opening was delayed for some months by a somewhat untoward circumstance, and one which showed that at that early period railway engineers were still new to their business, and had something yet to learn of the mighty agency they were assisting to develop. A compound cast-iron girder in a bridge over the river Dee, at Chester, gave way under the strain put upon it, and the makers of the Trent Valley Railway awoke to the fact that on their new and completed line there were several girder bridges of the same design as the one which had failed at Chester. These were now carefully examined and found to be faulty in design, so that they had to be strengthened and made secure before it could be considered safe to open the railway.

This work being completed, young George Findlay had now to find a fresh field for his labour, and he accordingly proceeded to London. Here he engaged in the service of Messrs. Bransome and Gwyther, contractors, and, by what would almost seem to have been a prophetic coincidence, was employed by them in building the new engine sheds of the London and North-Western Company at Camden Town, and what is known as the "Round House," a large circular building at Chalk Farm originally intended for an engine shed, but afterwards converted into a grain store. It was a matter of pardonable and legitimate pride on the part of the late general manager of the London and North-Western Railway that in their engine sheds at Camden Town he could point to the identical stones which he had cut and dressed for the buttresses and cornices of those buildings when he was employed as a young stonemason forty-five years ago, and when he little dreamed of ever becoming the chief officer of that vast undertaking.

During the latter part of his stay in London, which only extended to a period of less than a year, he was engaged under George Allen, the master mason to Messrs. Grissel and Peto, the contractors for building the new Houses of Parliament, and this also was a fact not without its subsequent significance. For the past twenty years much of his life was necessarily spent in the lobbies and committee rooms of these very Houses of Parliament, in promoting or opposing private Bills, and we may readily believe that it must have been with a certain justifiable complacency that he would frequently cast a glance at the great window at the east end of Westminster Hall, much of the stone tracery of which was fashioned by his own hands.

His next employment was under Mr. Brassey's agent Mr. Thomas Jones, in the construction of the Harecastle Tunnel on the North Staffordshire Railway. This work occupied him for two years, from 1847 to 1849, and although at this period he was only from eighteen to twenty years of age, his abilities had already found some recognition, for he was now employed, not on manual labour, but as chief inspector of mining and brickwork, his duty being to furnish the lines and levels of the tunnel, to prove the centres of the arches correct before they were turned, and measure up the work of the subcontractors.

On the completion of this important work, he undertook the contract for the building of the principal tunnel entrances, an enterprising proceeding on the part of a young fellow not yet twenty years of age, and after this for a short time, he had charge of the construction of the bridges on the Churnet Valley Branch of the North Staffordshire Railway, between Froghall and Alton.

The close of the year 1849 found him a step higher on the ladder, for Mr. Brassey appointed him, under his agent, Mr. Miles Day, as his assistant engineer in charge of the mining and brickwork of the Walton (or Sutton) Tunnel, on the Birkenhead, Lancashire and Cheshire Railway, then an independent undertaking, but since leased jointly to the London and North-Western and Great Western Companies.

In 1850 came what may be considered, without doubt, the turning-point of his career, for indirectly it had the effect of changing the whole course of his future life. In that year, Messrs. Brassey and Field commenced the construction of the first section of the Shrewsbury and Hereford Railway, between Shrewsbury and Ludlow, and Mr. Findlay was appointed engineer, and superintended the making of the line. On its completion, in April, 1852, Mr. Brassey decided to take a lease of it and work it himself, and he had then to look around him for a competent and trustworthy man to manage it in his interest. None seemed to him so suitable for the post as the young engineer who had helped to make the line, and it was accordingly offered to Mr. Findlay, who after some demur accepted it, and thus became a railway manager in his twenty-third year. It was doubtless a momentous decision for him to take—one affecting his whole future career—and it was not taken without some natural reluctance. He was thus abandoning the profession of an engineer, to qualify himself for which he had worked very hard from his boyhood upwards, and for which he had already evinced great aptitude, while he was entering on an entirely new sphere of duties, without the certainty of possessing the widely different qualifications required for their performance. But Mr. Brassey, as a judge of men and of what they were capable of, had few equals; he entertained no doubt that his young *protégé* would be the right man in the right place, and his judgment was fully borne out by results.

As a railway manager, of course, Sir George Findlay's success was far greater than he had ever dreamt of in those days, yet as a man has always a lingering regard for his first love, he was understood always to look back with a certain regret upon the career that he finally relinquished in 1852, and to entertain some doubt whether, if he had persevered in it, he might not have achieved even greater success as an engineer or contractor than in the new profession that he actually adopted.

However, for good or evil the choice was made, and he entered upon his new duties with characteristic energy and thoroughness. They afforded him a training such as he could hardly have obtained in any other position, for in his unique capacity as manager of a railway fifty miles in length, which practically belonged for the time being to a private individual, he was virtually entrusted with almost absolute power in all departments, so that he was the manager, the locomotive engineer, and the engineer for the permanent way, all—to use a familiar phrase— "under one hat." Mr. Brassey was a man whose practice it was, having chosen his instruments wisely and well, to leave them a wide discretion in matters of detail, so that the young manager, having entire responsibility thrown upon him, was forced to cultivate habits of self-reliance, and a readiness to meet all emergencies that might arise, which must have stood him in good stead in after life. Mr Brassey's only anxiety was that the railway should pay its way. "George," he would say, "have you got enough money in the bank to pay the rent?" and as long as the answer was in the affirmative he was content, and seldom troubled himself with the details of the accounts.

The railway was extended from Ludlow to Hereford in 1853. thus completing the railway communication throughout between Shrewsbury and Hereford; and, indirectly, this fact became Mr. Findlay's first point of contact, as a manager, with the London and North-Western Company—that great corporation whose fortunes he was one day to have so large a share in controlling. It came about in the following manner:—when the Shrewsbury and Hereford Railway got as far as Hereford, it there formed a connection with the Newport,

Abergavenny, and Hereford Railway, and this railway the London and North-Western Company had undertaken to work. Not being at that time themselves in the district, they contracted with Mr. Brassey to supply the necessary locomotive power for the line, and, of course, as Mr. Brassey's representative in the district, it became Mr. Findlay's duty to carry out the contract. In so doing, he necessarily came in contact with Captain Huish, the general manager of the London and North-Western Railway; Mr. (now Sir Edward) Watkin, the secretary of committees, who exercised a certain control over the policy of the North-Western Company; and Mr. Braithwaite Pool, then their general goods manager, who was a man of conspicuous ability and a great authority on all matters relating to railways, of which he was, indeed, one of the earliest pioneers. In conjunction with Mr. Braithwaite Pool, Mr. Findlay negotiated and carried out the first system of through rates for merchandise between South Wales and Liverpool, Manchester, and the whole of the North-Western system; in fact, the extension of the Shrewsbury and Hereford Railway to Hereford marked the advent of the narrow-gauge system of railways into South Wales from the North.

Mr. Brassey's contract for supplying locomotive power for the Newport, Abergavenny and Hereford Railway only continued for two years, when the policy of the North-Western Company changed, and, for the time being, they virtually abandoned the district of South Wales. The Newport, Abergavenny and Hereford Railway eventually fell into the hands of the West Midland Company, which was amalgamated with the Great Western in 1863, so that it is now an integral part of the Great Western Railway.

It was in the early days of his managership of the Shrewsbury and Hereford Railway that Mr. Findlay first came in contact with, and acquired the friendship of, several men who have since become well known and eminent in their respective spheres in the railway world. Amongst these may be distinguished Mr. J. S. Forbes, then the district goods manager of the Great Western Company at Gloucester, and now chairman of the London, Chatham and Dover Railway; Mr. Percy Morris, who was the manager of the Newport, Abergavenny and Hereford Railway, but who subsequently became manager, and is now secretary of the North Staffordshire; and, above all, the late Mr. James Grierson, probably one of the ablest railway officials we ever had in this country. He was at that time district goods manager for the Great Western Company at Birmingham, but he ultimately, as is well known, rose to the position of general manager of that undertaking, the fortunes of which, at the time he assumed the reins of power, were at a very low ebb, but which, under his wise and able administration, was rapidly improved and developed, until it became, as it is now, one of the greatest railway systems in the country. His personality was extremely winning, and Sir George Findlay attached a special value to his friendship, which in private life remained unbroken, in spite of many a tough and stubborn contest fought on behalf of their respective companies in Parliamentary committee-rooms, in conferences, and in arbitrations. Sir George felt it, therefore, an almost personal calamity when Mr. Grierson, in returning from a meeting of the International Railway Congress held at Milan in 1887, was attacked by typhoid fever, and died, in the midst of his active and useful career, at the comparatively early age of sixty.

It may be noticed, as a somewhat curious coincidence, that Mr. Grierson, like his great friend and rival, Sir George Findlay—one of his most formidable antagonists in the conflict of interests in the railway world—commenced life as an engineer, and deserted that profession to become a railway officer in the very same year (1852) which saw Mr. Findlay installed as manager of the Shrewsbury and Hereford Railway.

Mr. Brassey's lease of the Shrewsbury and Hereford Railway continued for ten years, but in 1862 the London and North-Western and Great Western Companies, who were both at that time pushing their way into South Wales, agreed to take a joint lease of the undertaking; and its young manager was taken over by the London and North-Western, as he jocularly put it, "as part of the stock-in-trade." They had about the same time purchased, on their own account, the Merthyr, Tredegar, and Abergavenny Railway, thus getting access to the great ironworks and coalfields of South Wales, so that, with an increasing interest in the district, which required active promotion, they appointed Mr. Findlay their district manager for Shropshire and South Wales.

The Shrewsbury and Hereford Railway, after being leased by the two great Companies, was made a double line, and a branch was constructed from Wooferton to Tenbury, but it speaks volumes for its able and energetic management under Mr. Brassey's lease that, on its transfer to the joint companies in 1862 this single line, 51 miles in length, passing through a sparsely populated country, which had formerly only supported a single coach running daily between Shrewsbury and Ludlow, was earning, on an average, £40 per mile per week. The joint companies guaranteed a dividend of six per cent in perpetuity, so that the ordinary share capital of the undertaking became at once worth upwards of 50 per cent. premium.

The transfer of the Shrewsbury and Hereford Railway terminated Mr. Findlay's connection with Mr. Brassey, which had continued for seventeen years, but there is no doubt that the success of his career was largely promoted by the fact that Mr. Brassey early appreciated his abilities and afforded him scope and opportunity for their display which otherwise he might have lacked. Mr. Brassey was, in truth, a very remarkable man, and though his peaceful warfare was waged against the forces of nature and his victories were bloodless ones, he may be truly called a great leader of men—more truly great, indeed, than many a master of legions who has gained his triumphs at the cost of countless lives and human suffering. Though his enterprises were vast, though in finance he dealt in millions as other men deal in hundreds, and though he was the great captain of a host of skilled and unskilled labourers all over the habitable globe, his manners were simple and unostentatious, and every one in his employ he treated with a courtesy and consideration which induced, not merely respect, but personal affection in all who were privileged to serve him. Sir George Findlay, who knew him intimately, always said of him that he was "the kindest-hearted man he ever knew," and one of his greatest pleasures was found in taking by the hand young men whose abilities his keen eye had detected, and promoting their success in life.

Sir George Findlay all his life looked back with peculiar interest upon the ten years he spent as manager of the Shrewsbury and Hereford Railway for Mr. Brassey, and even in his later days, when he had become eminent in the railway world, and to the ordinary caller he had become as inaccessible as a Cabinet Minister, any old officer or servant who could claim association with that period of his career was always sure of a patient hearing and every consideration at his hands. As long as he lived he carefully preserved the private letter-book he used in his correspondence with Mr. Brassey, and turning over the leaves of this volume it is easy to perceive how vigilant and able a lieutenant Mr. Brassey possessed in that district, at that time the battlefield of many rival interests, and one cannot but admire the shrewdness, foresight, and keen judgment displayed by the young manager, qualities which marked him out for the heavy responsibilities which were at a later period to devolve upon him.

In pursuance of the conflict at that time in progress between the London and North-Western and the Great Western Companies for predominance in Wales, the North-Western Company, in some degree, no doubt, as a set-off against the acquisition by the Great Western Company of the West Midland Railway, had, in the year 1861, entered into an agreement with the proprietors of the Oswestry and Newtown and Newtown and Llanidloes Railways, by virtue of which the latter were guaranteed a rebate or bonus mileage in return for running powers to the North-Western over their railways. The contractor for these railways, Mr. Thomas Savin, had leased them in the same way as Mr. Brassey had leased the Shrewsbury and Hereford, and at this juncture, seeing the close connection which was to exist between the North-Western Company and his railways, and that Mr. Findlay had just been appointed the North-

Western representative in the district, Mr. Savin invited him to combine with his new duties those of manager of the Oswestry, Newtown and Llanidloes Railways. Mr. Findlay accepted this appointment, of course with the full concurrence of the North-Western Board, and it was subsequently extended so as to embrace the Hereford, Hay and Brecon Railway, the Brecon and Merthyr, the Old Rumney Railway, and the extension of the Oswestry and Newtown Railway to Aberystwith and Towyn, all these lines being at the time under the control of Mr. Savin and Mr. Piercy, the contractor and engineer respectively, who had been engaged in their construction. Mr. Findlay's responsibilities extended to all departments on these lines, Mr. Savin leaving everything to him, including the arrangements in connection with the opening-up of new districts, very much in the same way as Mr. Brassey had been accustomed to do with regard to the Shrewsbury and Hereford Railway.

This kind of dual arrangement continued for a period of just three years, from January, 1862, to December, 1864, when Mr. Findlay began to realise that a change was desirable and indeed inevitable. Mr. Savin and Mr. Piercy, who had been jointly engaged in the promotion of what is now known as the Cambrian System of railways, were of an extremely sanguine temperament, which led them to be somewhat over-speculative in their enterprises. The extension of railways in this sparsely-populated district was altogether too rapid; they were constructed and financed at a very high cost, and Mr. Findlay's keen insight showed him, what has unfortunately been since made abundantly clear, that the undertaking could not possess the elements of commercial success, at any rate for many years to come. He reluctantly arrived, therefore, at the conclusion that it would be prudent, both in the interest of the London and North-Western Company and for his own sake, for him to relinquish his connection with Mr. Savin's railways, and his views to that effect were laid before Mr. (afterwards Sir Richard) Moon, the Chairman of the North-Western Company. The result was his transfer at the end of the year 1864 from Shrewsbury to Euston Station, there to take up the responsible position of General Goods Manager of the London and North-Western Railway.

Mr. Brassey, who had never ceased to follow with interest the career of his *protégée*, on this occasion wrote him one of his characteristically brief and cordial letters, as follows:—

Oct. 29, 1864.

My dear George,

I congratulate you most warmly and cordially on your well-earned promotion, and I hope you may be spared a long life to enjoy the prosperity you have attained.

Believe me, my dear George,

Yours very truly,

THOMAS BRASSEY.

But Mr. Brassey's were not the only good wishes he carried with him to his new sphere of duty. A committee, comprising representatives who were connected with the Welsh railways, gathered subscriptions, and at a banquet held at Oswestry in February, 1865, he was presented with a valuable gift of oil-paintings representing Welsh scenery. Two years previous to this, on the termination of Mr. Brassey's lease in 1862, the directors, officers and servants of the

Shrewsbury and Hereford Railway had presented him with a dinner-service in silver, as a mark of the esteem in which he was generally held in the district.

Once transferred to head-quarters his advancement was rapid. After he had held the position of General Goods' Manager for ten years, Mr. William Cawkwell, who had for many years been the General Manager of the North-Western, began to find his health failing with advancing age, and in 1874 he retired from the more active duties of his position, Mr. Findlay being appointed chief Traffic Manager; while, in 1880, Mr. Cawkwell's retirement became absolute, and, on his taking a seat at the Board, Mr. Findlay was fully gazetted as General Manager.

One important subject which largely engaged his attention for some few years after his transfer to Euston was the development of the through traffic between England and Ireland by the Holyhead and Dublin route, a development which, beyond doubt, has been of great advantage, both to consumers in England, and to agriculturists in "the distressful country." Previous to that time, the system of through rates was a very imperfect one, the cross-channel traffic was comparatively small, and the steamboat service between Holyhead and North Wall was a very poor one, being confined to one sailing daily in each direction. Under the auspices of the new Goods Manager a complete system of through rates was arranged and put in operation between the interior of Ireland and all the principal stations reached by the North-Western Railway, with the result that the through traffic rapidly increased and necessitated the running of additional trains and steamers and the improvement of the service generally. Since that time the new harbour at Holyhead has been constructed; the Company's fleet of steamers has been augmented; the accommodation at North Wall has been enlarged and improved, and, by means of the North Wall Extension railways, all the trunk railways leading to the interior have been linked together and brought into direct contact with the Harbour at North Wall. It is gratifying to add that the cross-channel traffic has, under this fostering care been, since 1864, a constantly-increasing quantity, its growth having been continuous and progressive from that time to this. At the present date there are no less than six sailings daily from Holyhead to Dublin, and in the reverse direction the same number.

In Parliamentary Committee rooms, and before Royal Commissions, Sir George Findlay was always a very familiar figure. His first appearance as a witness before a Committee was in 1854, when he gave evidence in support of Mr. Brassey's proposal to lease the Shrewsbury and Hereford Railway, and since that time there have been very few sessions of Parliament which have not found him engaged in private Bill legislation, affecting his own or other companies. He enjoyed the reputation of being an admirable witness, and his long and varied experience, mastery of detail, and perfect coolness, temper, and resource under cross-examination, rendered him a valuable supporter of any scheme which he was induced to interest himself in, and a formidable opponent where he threw his weight into the opposite scale. To the scheme for the construction of the Manchester Ship Canal he was strongly averse, and appeared as a hostile witness against the Bill on no less than six occasions during the years 1883, 1884, and 1885. On his examination before Mr. W. H. Forster's committee, which ultimately passed the Bill, he expressed a very decided opinion that the Canal, if it was ever constructed, could not prove a commercial success; that the enormous capital required would never be subscribed by the public, and that, to use his own words, the promoters, "When they got their Bill, would only be at the beginning of their difficulties." One portion of this forecast has been amply borne out by events, but only time can show whether the remainder was not equally justified.

At all royal commissions and parliamentary enquiries having relation to railways, his evidence was sought, and great weight was always attached to it. For instance, at the prolonged enquiry before the Board of Trade at the Westminster Town Hall in 1889, as to the revised schedules of maximum rates and charges proposed by the companies, under the Railway and Canal Traffic of 1888, after he had been under examination and cross-examination for no less than *eight days*, Lord Balfour of Burleigh, who presided, paid him, in the following words, a very high compliment on the manner in which he had passed the ordeal, and testified to the valuable assistance which his wide knowledge of the subject had enabled him to render to the Board of Trade in carrying their arduous and difficult enquiry to a conclusion. Lord Balfour said:—

"As this is the conclusion of Mr. Findlay's cross-examination, we think it right and just to say this: that we are impressed by the command of facts which Mr. Findlay has had at his disposal, his very great willing ness to give information, and the extreme patience with which he has endeavoured to answer all the questions put to him in cross-examination. I am quite certain from what I have gathered of the feeling here, that I am carrying with me a very large number of those who are here in giving that expression of our feeling."

Again, when a Select Committee was appointed in 1891, on the motion of Mr. Channing, to enquire into the hours of duty of railway servants, Sir George Findlay's able exposition of the case from the railway companies' point of view attracted much attention, and there can be no doubt that it was materially due to his efforts that the report of the committee was not, on the whole, unfavourable to the railway companies.

When Lord Salisbury's government, in 1891, appointed a Royal Commission to enquire into the many and complicated problems arising out of the relations between capital and labour, Sir George was one of the first persons who were invited to join the Commission, but not feeling at liberty to do so, he appeared before it as the chief witness on the part of the railway companies, and stated their case, as large employers of labour, so fully and so ably that there was little left for anyone to say on the same side.

Amongst other labours which occupied a long and busy life, Sir George found time to make his mark both as an author and as a lecturer. As far back as 1869 and from time to time up to 1878, a series of letters appeared in the *Times* under the signature of "A Railway Official," dealing with various important questions arising in connection with railways. These letters attracted a considerable amount of attention at the time, and were very generally noticed by the press, but it was not until 1886, when the General Manager of the North-Western Company published an interesting pamphlet on the subject of "Irish Railways and State Purchase," in which several of the *Times* letters were reproduced, that it became generally known that the author of this pamphlet and the "Railway Official" were one and the same person.

It may here be remarked that Sir George Findlay, for various reasons, always took a great interest in Irish railways, and when in 1888, the Royal Commission on Irish Public Works, of which the late Sir James Allport was President, presented its Report, in which certain proposals were made with regard to the Irish Railways, he ventured to disagree with some of their conclusions, and set forth his own views upon the subject in a memorandum which, it is an open secret, was brought under the notice of the Government of the day, and had some influence in shaping the policy they adopted in dealing with the question of light railways for Ireland.

What the Royal Commissioners recommended, was briefly (1) the compulsory amalgamation of all the railways in Ireland in the hands of a single company, (2) the constitution of a new Board or Railway Commission for Ireland with large powers of control, (3) the reduction of the statutory rates and tolls, and the guarantee from the State to the shareholders of the existing gross receipts for a term of years, and (4) certain amendments of the law relating to railway extensions in Ireland under imperial and local guarantees, and the application to certain specified works of the amount of guarantee available under the Tramways Act of 1883.

Sir George Findlay, in his memorandum, disagreed with the proposal to enforce compulsory amalgamation in the hands of a single company, and advocated, instead,

the division of Ireland for railway purposes, into four
territorial districts, the principal company in each district being empowered to absorb the smaller companies
on fair terms, to be settled by the Board of Trade or the
Railway Commissioners. He was opposed to the establishment of a new Board, which he thought would be
the setting-up of a cumbrous dual authority, sure to
come into conflict with the administrative boards of the
companies and produce constant friction without any
corresponding benefit, while he considered that the
existing Railway Commissioners, whose large powers
extended to Ireland, were quite competent to protect
the interests of the public. He quite agreed that it was
desirable to increase facilities and reduce rates and
charges, but he thought the shareholders' guarantee
should take the form of a minimum dividend based upon
the earnings of preceding years, and that, in virtue of
this guarantee, the Government should be enabled to
appoint a Chief Commissioner of Irish Railways, with a
seat *ex officio* at each of the railway boards, and with
powers somewhat analagous to those exercised by the
Government Director of Indian Railways. As regarded
branch railways or extensions designed to develop the
resources of the poorer districts of the country, he considered the right plan to adopt was for the Government
to find the money to construct the lines and for the
parent companies to work them at cost price, finding
their own advantage in the contributive value of the
new traffic to the trunk line. It may be added that Sir
George Findlay's views were generally endorsed by
some of the leading railway men both in Ireland and
England.

Sir George Findlay was the author of a book entitled
"The Working and Management of an English Railway,"

which deals with every branch of the subject in so comprehensive a manner that it has come to be looked upon as a recognised text book, or work of reference on railways. It has had a large sale, both in this country and abroad, and has already run through several editions.

As a lecturer, he made his *début* in 1875, when he delivered an address to his *confrères* at the Institute of Civil Engineers, and enlarged upon the difficulties to be encountered in conducting the traffic of our great railway systems. He afterwards lectured at the School of Military Engineering at Chatham, on the management of railways and their value in relation to any scheme of national defence (March, 1888); at the Society of Arts, on "Modern Improvements of Facilities in Railway Travelling," an interesting *résumé* of railway progress in fifty years (February, 1890); at the Royal United Science Institution (June, 1890), before Lord Wolseley and an audience composed chiefly of military experts, on "The Transport of Troops by Railway in the United Kingdom," and at the City of London Young Men's Christian Association (December, 1890), on railway work, and the qualities essential to success in life. He also submitted to the International Railway Congress, which met in Paris in 1889, a most able and valuable report on the mode of conducting passenger traffic in England; while at the Meeting of the Congress at St. Petersburgh, in 1892, he read (by proxy) a paper dealing with the regulation of the speed of trains in passing curves of various radii, facing points, swing bridges, etc.

In 1891, Colonel J. S. Rothwell published an article in the *United Service Magazine*, in which he discussed the capabilities of the railways in this country with regard to the transport of troops in the event of an invasion. He wrote somewhat in the spirit of an alarmist, and Sir George Findlay, as a railway expert replied to him in an article published in April, 1892, in which he clearly demonstrated that the railways of the country were so admirably laid out and equipped, and so well adapted to military purposes that they would be fully equal to the task of concentrating an army of 90,000 men upon any given line of defence within the space of forty hours.

In 1889, when the Government of New Zealand decided to reorganise the system of railways in the Colony and appoint a new Chief Commissioner of Railways, they consulted Sir George Findlay and derived much assistance from his wide experience and ripe judgment. This was acknowledged by a cordial letter of thanks from the Agent-General of the Colony, accompanied by a testimonial in the form of a handsome piece of plate.

One of Sir George Findlay's duties, as General Manager of the London and North-Western Railway, was, for many years, to organise and carry out the arrangements for the Queen's periodical visits to and from Scotland. Although in passing between Windsor or Osborne and Balmoral, Her Majesty's train has to traverse several different railways, the North-Western manager has always, by the Queen's command, taken the initiative in arranging the entire service; the North-Western Company's train is used throughout, and the North-Western manager, or some one representing him, travels with it from starting-point to destination. There have been times when the Queen's long railway journeys have been a source of great anxiety to those who were responsible for her safety, and special precautions have had to be taken to ensure it. During the troublous times between 1880 and 1883, when the Fenians were active, and dynamite outrages, one following another, were arousing some consternation in the country, it became of the utmost importance to guard in every possible way against the remotest chance of there being any attempt to interfere with the Royal train. In November, 1883, an anonymous communication was received by the Government, on the eve of one of Her Majesty's journeys, threatening an attempt to wreck the Royal train, and although there was the probability of its being nothing more than a hoax, Sir William Harcourt, who was then Home Secretary, did not feel justified in altogether disregarding the warning. The Queen, with her usual courage, was very reluctant to abandon or postpone her journey, and the railway authorities, on being put in possession of the facts of the case, were fully equal to the occasion. They called out literally an army of platelayers and other servants, some thousands strong, and these men, for some time prior to the passage of the train, were stationed along the line from Windsor to Ballater, a distance of nearly 600 miles, within sight of each other all the way, while every yard of the railway was narrowly inspected, and every bridge and every viaduct was watched and guarded until the train had passed over it. Under these circumstances, of course, any attempt at outrage was practically out of the question, and the Queen was enabled to perform the journey with her usual equanimity. On the following day the Home Secretary addressed to the General

Manager of the North-Western Company the following letter:—

"Home Office,
"Nov. 21st, 1883.

"MY DEAR MR. FINDLAY,

"I am much obliged for the prompt precautions that you took in regard to the Queen's train last night. These villains are so desperate in their attempts that it is not safe to neglect any warning, though I doubt not many of their schemes are devised more to frighten than to hurt.

"Yours faithfully,
"W. V. HARCOURT."

Three years earlier, in 1880, Her Majesty had expressed to Mr. Findlay, through her equerry, Sir H. F. Ponsonby, her appreciation of the precautions taken to ensure her safety in her journeys to and from Scotland.

In 1887, Sir George Findlay, in conjunction with Sir Henry Oakley, the General Manager of the Great Northern Railway, was engaged in negotiating the terms of a working union between the two great London dock companies, the London and St. Katharine, and the East and West India. These two great corporations had for some time been engaged in a ruinous competition, which had caused very heavy loss to both of them, and, in fact, for the East and West India, a receiver had already been appointed; but, after prolonged and difficult negotiations, the efforts of Sir George Findlay and Sir Henry Oakley resulted in an agreement, confirmed by parliament in 1888, which ended the long feud and paved the way for an improvement in the prospects of these great and important undertakings.

Sir George Findlay was an Associate of the Institute of Civil Engineers, a Lieut.-Colonel of the Engineer and Railway Volunteer Staff Corps, and an Alderman and

Justice of the Peace for the County of Middlesex. At
the Paris Exhibition of 1889, he acted as Vice-President
of a Committee formed for the purpose of exhibiting
a collection of appliances, past and present, used in the
conveyance of passengers and merchandise, and on this
occasion he was created, by President Carnot, a Chevalier of the Legion of Honour. His English knighthood
was conferred in May, 1892, and appeared amongst the
"birthday honours" of that year.

If the writer were called upon to define the qualities
which chiefly conduced to Sir George Findlay's undeniable success in life, he would place in the foreground a
certain element of strong, plain common sense, which
was probably his most distinguishing characteristic. It
is a well-known fact that many men of the greatest ability,
and even men of brightest talent, are lamentably deficient
in this homely quality, and for the lack of it they are
prone to be led away by prejudice, by enthusiasm, and
other disturbing influences, and miss their highest mark
in consequence. But Sir George possessed it in a high
degree, and made good use of it. When difficulties
arose and counsels were divided, it was this plain common sense that disentangled the question from all
extraneous matter, and perceived at a glance what was
the real issue and what was the right thing to be done.
He was, too, an eminently fair-minded man, with a
faculty for seeing both sides of a question, so that he
realised the spirit of compromise, and in this way conducted to a successful issue many a difficult and delicate
negotiation. Nothing surprised him more than the attitude of mind of men whom he occasionally encountered
at the conference table or elsewhere, who were only able
to see their own side of a question, wanted to have all

their own way in everything, and did not understand the principle of "give and take" which is really the essence of most business transactions.

He was at all times extremely anxious that the North-Western Company should pursue on every occasion a straightforward and candid policy, whether in dealing with other companies or the public, and nothing in the way of unfair competition or double dealing ever met with encouragement at his hands, or was anything but repugnant to his upright mind. He was proud of the great company of which he was the head and chief, and desired to see it always above reproach. The writer well remembers that on one occasion a mistake had been made in an account with another company, resulting in a credit to the North-Western of some hundreds of pounds. An official of the North-Western discovered the error, but the other company did not, and probably never would have done, and as it was a question of gratuitously refunding a considerable sum of money Sir George was appealed to, as to what should be done. He never hesitated a moment; "Put it right at once," he said, adding in his usual blunt way, "The North-Western is not so poor that we can't afford to be honest."

Another very distinguishing characteristic of Sir George Findlay—the more remarkable in so busy a man—was that he was never in a hurry, but preserved a cool imperturbability under all circumstances. Although he got through an enormous amount of work, he never allowed himself to be harassed or worried, and, in fact, acquired, or naturally possessed, the faculty of "hastening without hurrying." Railway work, as a rule, is performed at high pressure, and it is melancholy to recall the long list of well-known men of proved ability in the railway world who have failed in mid-career under the strain of anxiety and responsibility, and retired prematurely, broken down either mentally or physically, their place knowing them no more. It would be painful to mention individuals, though the writer has known of many such cases, but it might always have been predicted with the utmost confidence that Sir George Findlay's career would never end in that way, for he bore his vast weight of responsibility so easily, and got through his work so quietly and methodically, that he never appeared to be under the least strain. Even in the thickest of the fray in the parliamentary session, when he was sometimes wanted in two or three committee rooms at once; when fresh points and new difficulties were arising every hour and had to be met and encountered, when time pressed and everyone around him shared in the general excitement, his composure remained undisturbed, and he went from one committee room to another, from the House to his office at Westminster, and thence to his office at Euston, as occasion demanded, saying and doing the right thing at each place, all in the same quiet, methodical way, and always with the air of one who was master of the situation.

One thing he never would attempt, and that was to attend to two things or two people at the same time. When once his mind was bent upon a given subject, he steadily refused to be interrupted on any pretext whatever, making everything take its turn: and there is no doubt it was this concentration of ideas which enabled him to get through so much work so easily and so quickly. He once told a House-of-Commons Committee that he would undertake to manage all the railways in

Ireland and still find time for a day's fishing once a week, and although it was said in a jocular spirit, there is little doubt that he could have made his words good.

Like all men born to command, he was a good judge of other men, and chose his instruments well. He took an especial interest in young men, and most of the highest officials of the North-Western Company to-day are men whom he singled out for advancement at an early period of their career, when, to a less practised observer, there may have been little to distinguish them from their fellows.

Amongst the rank and file of the staff, it must be confessed, that he had the reputation of being at times somewhat austere, but this arose from the want of personal knowledge of him, for in reality he was an exceedingly kind-hearted man. He sometimes hid this kindness under a brusque exterior, but it was those who were nearest to his person and knew him most intimately who felt for him the greatest respect and affection. To evildoers he was a terror, it is true; he disliked those who fawned upon him and cringed to him, and held in some contempt those who appeared to fear him, but the self-respecting man, who knew his work well and did it conscientiously, and was not afraid to speak his mind, had nothing to fear in an interview with the dreaded "chief." To any old servant of the Company who had committed himself, and came in penitence to plead his cause, Sir George was kindness itself, and many such were, by his intervention, saved from dismissal and disgrace, and escaped with a fine or a reprimand. On one occasion, the late Chairman of the North-Western Company, in passing over the line had noticed a very old man at work as a porter, and, thinking him past active service, had told the District Officer, who accompanied him, to get rid of the man. Shortly afterwards, the same officer, being at the station with the General Manager, pointed the man out to the latter, and told him the instructions he had received. "Oh," said Sir George, "let him alone for this winter; perhaps the poor old chap may not live until next year." As a matter of fact, the poor old man remained undisturbed, and died at his post.

In dealing with bodies of men, he showed great tact and forbearance, and it was, no doubt, owing to his intimate knowledge of working-men and their ways, and his good judgment in knowing when to stand fast and when to make wise concessions, that in an age of labour troubles and disturbances, the North-Western Company, with its army of more than sixty thousand employés, was singularly free from strikes during the whole period of his management, and the two or three that did occur were quickly and easily put an end to without leaving any feeling of bitterness behind. He was, in short, a man of the times, and recognised the necessity of moving with the times, besides which he always had a great sympathy with working-men and never forgot, or was ashamed to own, that he had been one of them.

There was one respect, and one only, in which he opposed himself to the tendency of the age. He never would recognise the paid officials of the railway trades union. He fully admitted the great benefits that trades unionism had conferred upon the working classes, and he never objected to the North-Western men joining the union, but he always steadily refused to enter into communication with its officials, or to allow them to interfere between the men and their employers. He held that the railway service was unique; that for the efficient conduct of a great railway system, the state of discipline and obedience must be as high and as complete as in the army or the navy, and that any outside interference, by offering the men a divided allegiance, would be utterly destructive of such discipline. Questions of pay, hours of duty, or conditions of labour he was always ready to entertain and consider fairly, and his door was open to any man, or deputation of men, who thought they had a grievance to urge, but the secretary of the Amalgamated Society of Railway Servants he would never see nor correspond with, and he once told a Select Committee that there might as well be a trades union in the army, and the secretary dictating to the colonel of a regiment how long a soldier should be on sentry-go. Opinions may, of course, differ, as to whether his view was justified or not, but rightly or wrongly, he held it very strongly, and never wavered from it in the least.

His personality was a very striking one—in figure tall and of portly build, he had a large head and face with strongly-marked features, expressive of great determination and force of character. He looked, in fact, what he was, a man accustomed to bear great responsibilities, and to command and be obeyed without question or demur, notwithstanding which he could at times relax, and become extremely cordial and winning in his manner. He possessed a fund of anecdote, and to those with whom he unbent was a most interesting and agreeable companion.

In early life, possessed of a powerful and vigorous frame, he excelled in all athletic exercises, and rejoiced in the *mens sana in corpore sano*. On one occasion, while he was superintending the building of a bridge on the Shrewsbury and Hereford Railway, one of the men in his employ accidentally lost his balance and fell into the water, and, as he was unable to swim, he was in imminent danger of drowning. Without a moment's hesitation Sir George sprang into the river to his rescue, which he successfully effected, but the man, in his despairing efforts, seized him in so fierce a clutch that he bore the scar as long as he lived. Even up to the time of his death, at the age of sixty-three, he was a keen sportsman, and was never happier than when fishing the quiet waters of the Chess or the salmon streams of the Highlands, or enjoying a day's shooting at one of the many country houses where he was a familiar and welcome guest. But all men have a "hobby," and Sir George's hobby, in his later years, was fancy farming. Adjoining his pretty house at Edgware, on the borders of Middlesex, he had a few acres, admirably laid out as a sort of model farm, on which he took the greatest delight in rearing choice strains of cattle and poultry, and cultivating fruit and flowers—surely a charming relief to the prosaic details of railway management.

It was just before Christmas (1892) that he was seized with the illness which terminated fatally, and cut short his active and useful career. He had partially recovered, and attended the Board meetings in January, 1893, but subsequently serious symptoms developed themselves, and, although these were for a time attributed to the effects of gout, from which he had previously suffered, it was ultimately found necessary for him to undergo a difficult and dangerous operation for calculus. The operation was, in itself, successful, but it was followed by the lesion of an artery, when hemorrhage supervened, and to the effects of this he succumbed.

He was buried at Whitchurch (Little Stanmore), within half-a-mile of the charming residence which had witnessed the closing scenes of his life.

His death removed one of the most prominent figures in the world of railways, and created a gap which will not at once be filled up. It is indisputable that, in his later years he was looked upon as the foremost railway man of his time, and, after the retirement of Sir James Allport, and the death of Mr. Grierson, there was probably no one who would have denied his claim to be the doyen of railway managers, a distinction to which his long and wide experience, and calm and matured judgment clearly entitled him. His loss was keenly felt, not only by those who were intimately connected with him in business, and by a wide circle of personal friends, but by his contemporaries amongst the officers of other railways; all felt that the stoutest champion of the railway interest, and their foremost representative before Parliament and the public, had been suddenly removed from their midst.

Sir George was twice married. By his first wife, who was the daughter of Mr. Swainston Adamson, of Brereton, Staffordshire, he had a large family, of whom four sons and two daughters survive him. His first wife died in 1883; and in 1885 he married Miss Charlotte Jacob, daughter of Mr. Pryse Jacob, of Bridgend, Glamorganshire.

S. M. P.

---

NOTE.—It is eminently characteristic of the well-balanced mind and methodical habit of the subject of this memoir, that, foreseeing that after his death some account of his life and work would probably be of interest, at any rate to those connected with his own world of railways, almost his last act before his fatal illness was to set down with his own hand notes of the leading events of his career, giving dates and all necessary details. To the writer these notes have, of course, proved invaluable in preparing the foregoing brief sketch.

# AN ENGLISH RAILWAY.

## CHAPTER I.

### Introductory and Retrospective.

It may at first sight appear that the subject of "The working and management of an English railway," is one which is calculated only to enlist the attention of a limited class, namely, of those persons who are either directly or indirectly connected with the working of railways, in this country, or abroad; but a little reflection will probably suffice to show that the theme is one which should appeal to a much larger circle of readers, and, in fact, to almost every class of the community. If the attention of an individual is drawn to any new law, any fresh discovery, or social reform, calculated to promote his personal comfort or well-being, his interest is at once aroused; and the circumstance that, in this case, the revolution has been effected and the benefit is actually being reaped, should surely not suffice to rob the subject of its interest. At the same time, it is, of course, the merest common-place to say that people do not adequately value the advantages they possess, until they are threatened with the loss of them, and this is pre-eminently the case with regard to the best fruits of an advanced state of civilisation, such as that in which it is our good fortune to exist. We, or at any rate the younger portion of the community, were born into a world of railways, telegraphs, steam boats, daily papers, and the penny post, and we are apt to take these blessings very much as a matter of course, without a thought for the totally different circumstances in which even our immediate progenitors contrived to exist. The railway, however, in its present phase of development, enters so intimately into the social life of the community in its every detail, and has become so potent a factor in its every movement and operation, whether of business or of pleasure, that it must clearly be material for every individual to know something of the great agency which does so much for his happiness and welfare, and to realise fully what are its liabilities and obligations towards himself, and what he has a right to expect from it. Such knowledge, it is hoped this work may impart; but it has the further aim of constituting a practical guide or handbook for those who, whether in this country, or in our numerous colonies, may find it necessary, for whatever reasons, to acquire a knowledge of the principles upon which a great English railway is constructed and managed, and the methods and appliances by means of which its business is carried on.

It is not the intention of the present writer to enter into a detailed history of the conception and growth of the railway system from its earliest period to the present time. The story is one full of interest, but, having been recounted by other, and abler pens, may be said, in its main features, to be fairly well known. It may not, however, be out of place to allude briefly to the state of things which prevailed with regard to the means of locomotion before the genius of a great engineer and the courage and enterprise of a few Liverpool merchants inaugurated the enormous social revolution which has since displayed such extraordinary development, and has so greatly contributed to the happiness and prosperity of the human race.

In the middle ages, popularly known as the age of chivalry, and until about the middle of the sixteenth century, practically there were not any properly constructed roads—such as we should call roads at the present day—in the country, with the exception of a few, such as Watling Street, which were made by the Romans during their stay. Even such highways and bridle-roads as did exist were beset by lawless and desperate men; and, under these circumstances, locomotion, either for purposes of business or pleasure, except for armed men, was out of the question; while invalids and aged persons, belonging to the wealthy classes, could only travel in litters and protected by an escort. At this period, 20 miles a day was considered very fair travelling! Grain and produce and goods of all kinds could only be carried on the backs of horses or mules, or in heavy and cumbrous waggons, drawn by six or eight horses, and which often sank and were swallowed up, on roads which, in winter, became little better than morasses. Thus, for the want of the means of distribution, the fruits of the earth rotted where they ripened, while there might be famine in other parts of the country. One is apt to think that the glorious days of chivalry, of which poets still dream, may have been glorious, perhaps, for knights and nobles, but that the common people had little share in the glory, and that their lives must have been dull and colourless to a degree that it is difficult for us to realise.

Somewhere about the middle of the sixteenth century the people of this country began to bestir themselves in the matter of roads, a sure sign that they were awakening from the long slumber of the middle ages, and beginning to realise the hardship of not being able to move about more freely. Rightly considered, indeed, there is perhaps no more infallible index to the progress of civilisation in any country than the extent of the facilities for locomotion. Savage man, living in a state of nature, subsists by hunting and fishing; he roams on foot throughout the district in which he was born, and probably never wanders many miles from the hut or cave or wigwam where he first saw the light. He never dreams of making roads, for he has no necessity for them. But when he awakes to civilisation, his horizon widens, his wants are multiplied, and what nature does not supply him with at his own door, he must send for or fetch from farther afield, so that the necessity for making roads and constructing vehicles begins to dawn upon him. Thus, the most enduring mark which the Roman civilisation left upon savage Britain was the roads which our conquerors made and left behind them.

In the sixteenth century, by a Parliamentary enactment, the parish authorities were made responsible for maintaining the roads, which hitherto had been left to take care of themselves. The charges were levied upon the ratepayers, but every peasant was forced to give six days' labour upon the roads during the year, without payment, this being very similar to the *Corvées* or forced labour system of the French peasantry, which contributed as much as anything, it is believed, to the great Revolution, the difference being that while the English peasant gave his labour for the common good, his French prototype was forced to yield his to his seigneur, or feudal lord. This system continued during the seventeenth and part of the eighteenth century, but the roads were still very indifferent, as may be judged from the fact that at this period the carriage of goods by waggon between London and Exeter was as much as £12 per ton. About the middle of the eighteenth century, great efforts were made to improve the roads, so that by the year 1825, which saw the opening of the first railway, there was a network of splendid roads, in almost perfect condition, covering the whole kingdom.

It is now necessary to go back a little in the order of events, and to record the fact that, consequent, no doubt, on the gradual improvement of the roads, stage coaches were introduced about the year 1660, and in 1662 six of these vehicles were running between different points. They are described as dirty, clumsy, and lumbering machines, more like hogsheads on wheels than anything else, and vastly different to the handsomely built and splendidly horsed mail coaches of a later period. In 1669, a stage coach ran from Oxford to London in 13 hours. In 1706, stage coaches ran from York to London in four days, starting on three days in the week. In 1712, a coach ran from Edinburgh to London once a fortnight, occupying 13 days on the journey, and requiring the employment of 80 horses.

Only last summer a person with whom the writer is acquainted came across an old lady, in a small fishing village in North Devon, who was said to be nearly a hundred years of age, and who had never, in all her life, travelled farther than to Barnstaple, about ten or twelve miles distant, and such cases are not uncommon in remote country places. That they can exist, even in these days of railways excursions, and cheap travelling of all kinds will afford some idea of the kind of isolated lives that the population must have led in those days when the cost of a journey of any length represented what was a small fortune in the ideas of poor people.

In 1784, we come to an event which really effected a revolution in English locomotion, for in that year the first mail coach was put on the road between London and Bristol. Previous to that date, His Majesty's Mails were carried by mail carts, or by the post boys, riding on horseback, not always too safely, for, as may be read in Col. Corbett's "Chatter of an Old Coachman," on one occasion a post boy was robbed of his bags between Selby and York, and the empty bags were found 80 years afterwards, that is to say in 1878, in the mouldering thatch of a wayside inn. The bags, forming a curious memento of times long passed away, are now, it is said, in the Museum of the General Post Office.

The new mail coaches found great favour with the public, and rapidly multiplied in number, so that within two years from the running of the Bristol Coach, there were no less than twenty running out of London every night, in different directions, while within 50 years, that is, by the year 1834, there had been developed a perfect and complete system of road travelling by mail coaches, and by fast day coaches, running in competition with them. The vehicles were continually improved, keeping pace with the improvement of the roads, and they attained an average speed of 8 to 10 miles an hour, and even in some cases 12 miles. Travelling by them,

## INTRODUCTORY AND RETROSPECTIVE.

however, was very expensive and not within the reach of the working classes. A passenger travelling from London to Edinburgh in 1830 paid £10 if he travelled outside, or £14 inside, and the journey occupied 40 hours. He can now perform the journey in 8½ hours at a cost of 32s.

The coaches continued to run up to 1840, and in some parts of the country even some years later, and were only gradually elbowed out of existence by their rapidly growing rivals, the railways.

But if we go no farther back than the commencement of the present century, only a few years before the first railway was projected, we find that although the difficulties of earlier locomotion had been to some extent obviated so far as regarded communication between some of the more important cities in the Kingdom, by the introduction of the mail coaches, the only means of transit between the smaller towns and villages was by means of post-chaises or private carriages for the wealthy, and for the less well-to-do the humble carrier's cart, or the slow and ponderous stage waggon. Travelling was still so expensive a luxury that a journey was only undertaken under the most pressing necessity, and many of the roads were so ill-constructed that in bad weather they were almost impassable. Merchandise was conveyed from place to place by heavy and slow-moving waggons, and the cost of land carriage may be gathered from the fact that between Manchester and Liverpool, a distance of not more than thirty miles, the charge was forty shillings per ton. In those days a journey from London to Birmingham, if all went well and no mishaps were encountered, occupied ten or twelve hours at the least ; while now, a man of business may break his fast in London, be in Birmingham before noon, transact his affairs, and be back in town before dinner. At that time a journey from London to Scotland was something not lightly to be undertaken, for, apart from the heavy expense, dangers, difficulties, and fatigue to be encountered, it occupied several days; whereas now a traveller may leave London at 8 p.m. or 8.50 p.m., can retire to rest as comfortably as if he were in a well-appointed hotel, and awake in the early morning to find himself in Glasgow or Edinburgh, or even further north. Merchants are able to be in frequent personal communication with their correspondents in the most distant towns; young folks, exiled from their homes in pursuit of their various careers, are enabled to spend even the shortest holiday in the family circle; letters posted in the evening are read at breakfast tables hundreds of miles distant the following morning; every necessity of life is cheapened to the consumer; every branch of business is enormously stimulated and developed by the facilities thus brought to bear upon it, and in fact the speed and certainty with which the inland and import and export trade of the country is carried on is nothing less than marvellous. Goods are punctually collected, carried long distances between the most important towns in England, and delivered to their consignees within the day of twenty-four hours; while even between England and places in Scotland, and the seaport towns of Ireland, the transit is performed within forty-eight hours. The Yorkshire manufacturer, who attends the London wool sales to-day, can have the wool he purchases in his warehouse to-morrow. The Lancashire cotton-spinner will buy cotton in the Liverpool market one day, and it may be in actual

## INTRODUCTORY AND RETROSPECTIVE. 45

consumption in his mill the next. Dead meat from Scotland and abroad, poultry, butter and eggs from Ireland, vegetables, fruit and all perishable goods of the kind, are despatched by the growers with the narrowest possible margin of time to catch a particular market; and all this is done with the most absolute certainty and punctuality, making due allowance, of course, for trifling miscarriages, which will occur in every large business, often from circumstances that no foresight could control.

Such are a few of the advantages which have resulted to the community from the invention of railways, but the list might be extended indefinitely.

The first dawn of the idea of a railway was, no doubt, about the beginning of the seventeenth century, when some inventive genius hit upon the plan of laying down parallel blocks of timber to form tramroads in the vicinity of mines, to enable the mineral products to be drawn more easily by horses to the riverside. More than a hundred years later (about the year 1768), as we are told by Mr. Francis in his admirable "History of the English Railway," cast-iron rails were substituted for the wooden blocks, and this was a distinct step in advance. By the commencement of the nineteenth century, the application of steam as a motive power was no longer unknown, for it had been applied to the working of stationary engines in mines and elsewhere and, in fact, as early as 1804, a machine had been constructed at a Welsh ironworks, which moved upon rails, drawing after it a load of ten tons of bar iron, and which was, to all intents and purposes, a locomotive engine. The construction of the Stockton and Darlington Railway followed in 1821, but the first railway made with public money, and for the public benefit, and which marks the birth of the railway system as we know it to-day, was the Liverpool and Manchester. The conflict which was sustained by the promoters of that undertaking with the forces of ignorance and prejudice was really the decisive one, and when the struggle was over and the battle had been won, the floodgates of enterprise were opened wide and the era of railways had commenced.

About the year 1820, the relations between Manchester, as the great manufacturing town of the north, and Liverpool, as the nearest shipping port, had created a large traffic between the two places, for the conduct of which the road waggons and canal barges had proved to be totally inadequate. In the year 1821, therefore, a committee of merchants of Liverpool was formed to draw up a scheme for the construction of a railway or tramway between Liverpool and Manchester, the question of the motive power to be employed being left for a time an open one as between horses and the steam engine, with which Mr. George Stephenson was then experimenting. There was no idea at first of conveying passengers, but the scheme grew in importance as time went on, until at length it aroused a perfect storm of enthusiasm on the one side and of embittered opposition on the other. Much has been said and written as to the incredible lengths to which that opposition was carried by the enemies of the undertaking, and the story is one not without its painful, as well as its ludicrous features, but it need not here be enlarged upon. Suffice it to say that every weapon that the prejudice and narrow-mindedness of the many, or the alarmed avarice of the few whose interests were threatened by the impending change, could devise, was brought to bear without scruple, even to the length of personal abuse and calumny levelled against the promoters. The most absurd statements were gravely put forward and believed in; the smoke of the engines would kill the birds, cattle would be terrified, and cows would cease to give their milk; the sparks from the engines would set fire to the houses and manufactories on the line of route; the race of horses would become extinct, and many other direful consequences would ensue, amidst which the absolute ruin of the country would shrink to the insignificance of a detail! The first surveys had to be accomplished, in many cases, by stealth, and were, in some cases, resisted to the extent of the employment of armed force.

After the lapse of sixty years, we can afford to smile at the folly of those who seriously maintained such theories as these; but the opposition to be encountered was no laughing matter, we may be sure, to the earnest pioneers of the new movement, who had staked their means and their reputations upon the issue of the undertaking, and devoted themselves heart and soul to the effort to carry it to a successful termination. At length, in March, 1825, the survey, in spite of all difficulties, had been completed, and the Bill was in Committee; but, after a lengthened discussion, extending over thirty-seven days, and chiefly owing to the opposition of the landowners and canal proprietors, it failed, and its enemies were, for the time being, triumphant. The sequel, however, shows that their exultation was premature and but short-lived.

The simile of Dame Partington striving with her mop to keep back the waves of the Atlantic is one sufficiently trite and well-worn, but it recurs almost irresistibly to the mind in contemplating the futile and hopeless attempt of these enemies of progress to arrest the march of that tremendous social revolution which, within the span of a single generation, was destined to change the whole face of the earth.

Nothing daunted by their first failure, the great engineer and his courageous backers returned to the charge. A fresh survey was made, by which many of the difficulties which had been raised were overcome or circumvented; the Bill was re-deposited in the ensuing session of Parliament, and this time the enterprise of its promoters was rewarded by success. The Bill received the Royal assent on the 7th May, 1826; the works were at once vigorously proceeded with, and the railway was actually opened for public traffic on the 16th September, 1830. It was however, of a very different construction to the well-appointed and perfectly-equipped railways of the present day. It consisted, it is true, of a double line of rails; but those rails were of so light a description that they soon succumbed to heavy wear and tear, and large sums had afterwards to be expended in taking them up and replacing them with others of a more substantial character. Instead of the timber sleepers, now universally in use, the rails were laid upon huge stone blocks, soon to be found expensive and unsuitable. The passengers were conveyed either in open cars, unsheltered from the weather, or in covered carriages only a degree less comfortless, and presenting a strong contrast to the luxuriously-appointed vehicles in which the traveller of to-day is accommodated. The trains, at first, started at irregular intervals, and were few and far between, and it was not until after some time had elapsed that the time-table became a recognised institution. The journey between Liverpool and Manchester, which is now easily accomplished in forty-five minutes, occupied at that time an hour and a half. Of the engines employed, more will be said hereafter; but it will be readily believed that they were of an extremely primitive character compared with those of a later date. As first projected, the railway terminated at the Liverpool end at Crown Street, near Edge Hill, and omnibuses were employed for conveying the passengers to and from the City; but this was soon found to be a great hindrance to the development of the traffic, and in the session of 1832 powers were obtained for the construction of the tunnel under the City to Lime Street, which was completed and opened for traffic in August, 1836. Despite all its shortcomings, however, the undertaking was, from the very outset, a much greater success than even its authors had ever ventured to predict, and indeed their anticipations proved to have fallen almost ludicrously short of the results actually realised. They had expected to earn £10,000 a year from passenger traffic, whereas in the first year after the opening, the receipts from that source were £101,829. They had estimated the gross receipts from merchandise at £50,000 per annum, but in 1833 the actual amount received was £80,000. From the very commencement, the shareholders obtained a dividend at the rate of 8 per cent. per annum, afterwards rising to 9 and 10 per cent., and remaining at the latter figure for some years.

The great success of the Liverpool and Manchester railway, as might naturally have been expected, let loose a flood of railway enterprise all over the country. Lines were soon projected between all the towns of any importance in the kingdom, and even between remote villages. One enthusiast went so far as to propose a railway under the sea between Dover and Calais, and was no doubt looked upon by his contemporaries as a fitting candidate for a lunatic asylum ; but probably the distinguished promoter of the Channel Tunnel scheme of to-day may hold a different opinion upon that point. The most important result that immediately followed, however, was the revival of the scheme which had previously been mooted, but had been abandoned, for the construction of a railway between London and Birmingham. The Bill for this line, which was the parent of the London and North-Western Railway, was first deposited in November, 1831 ; but, after passing the House of Commons, was thrown out in the House of Lords on the 10th July, 1832. The opposition to this Bill was as unscrupulous, and of precisely the same character, as that which its precursor—the Bill for the Liverpool and Manchester Railway—had had to encounter ; but in the end it was overcome, and the line, having been sanctioned in 1833, was finally opened to the public in 1838.

For the purposes of this work, it is not necessary to follow, step by step, the gradual, yet rapid, development of the railway system throughout the country. It will be sufficient to record that by an Act obtained in 1846 the London and Birmingham, the Grand Junction (with which, under an Act obtained earlier in the same year, the Liverpool and Manchester Railway had already been incorporated), and the Manchester and Birmingham Railway Companies were amalgamated under the title of the "London and North-Western Railway Company." During the lapse of time since that period this Company has gradually absorbed the South

Staffordshire, the Chester and Holyhead, the Lancaster and Carlisle, and some forty smaller companies, many of which, for a time, were only leased, and retained their separate capitals, with varying rates of interest, and, in in some cases, their independent boards of directors. But in 1877 an Act was obtained, commonly called the "Consolidation Act," the effect of which was to weld all these separate companies into one homogeneous undertaking, the London and North-Western Railway, as it exists to-day, having a consolidated stock of upwards of £108,000,000, possessing more than 1,800 miles of railway, with nearly 650 stations, and employing a staff or an army, as it may be called, of 60,000 men.

So much having been said as to the origin and small beginnings of railways, it may be of interest to quote a few figures to show how mighty has been their development in point of magnitude within the short space of sixty years. There is nothing, indeed, more remarkable with regard to railways and railway enterprise than the extraordinary rapidity of their growth, for it is truly wonderful to reflect that there must be many people still living who can recollect the excitement that was aroused by the opening of the first passenger railway. At the present time the authorised capital of the railways in this country alone, that is to say the United Kingdom, amounts to considerably over a thousand millions of money, of which nearly nine hundred and fifty millions have actually been raised and spent in making railways. In 1892 the gross receipts of all the railways amounted to upwards of eighty-two millions, of which nearly forty-six millions, or more than one-half, were spent in wages and materials, while more than half a million of men are employed in connection with railways, either directly or indirectly, at the present time.

These are large figures, but, if we look beyond the limits of these islands, and come to enquire into the statistics applying to railway enterprise throughout the world, we arrive at figures so stupendous that they would be enough to take one's breath away if it were not that, like the astronomical distances we read of, their very magnitude prevents us from grasping their significance. However, they may be given for what they are worth. In the whole world the amount of money invested in railways at the present time is approximately *six thousand millions sterling*, and the receipts are nearly five hundred millions per annum. The total mileage of railways at the beginning of last year was 385,000 miles, of which about 135,000 miles represented the European railways, 167,000 miles those of the United States, and nearly 17,000 miles those of India. On these 385,000 miles of railway there are carried annually about two thousand five hundred millions of passengers, and about fifteen hundred millions of tons of goods. No figures are available to show the number of miles run by engines all over the world in a year, but we can make a fair guess at it, for there are fully 120,000 locomotive engines in steam at the present day, and if each one of these ran on the average from fifteen to twenty thousand miles in the year, we should get a train mileage of about two thousand four hundred millions of miles in a year, or twenty-six times the distance between the earth and the sun. Of course these figures are too vast for anyone to fully grasp, but imagine all this having sprung from the Liverpool and Manchester Railway, thirty miles long, and George Stephenson's little engine the "Rocket," and yet all to have been the growth of about sixty years.

It is perhaps a legitimate cause for pride that this little island was, beyond doubt, the birthplace and cradle of the gigantic conception which, in the short space of sixty years, has absolutely revolutionised the conditions of life throughout the habitable globe. Even our ingenious and "go-ahead" Yankee cousins, usually in the van of progress, and the pioneers of the world in the matter of inventions and discoveries, in this case had to borrow from us, and their engineers were glad to sit at the feet of our great countryman, George Stephenson, and learn from him how they might follow in our footsteps. A very interesting pamphlet reached the writer some little time back from America, being an account of the erection of a monument by the Pennsylvania Railroad Company, to commemorate the opening, in 1831, of the railway between Camden and Amboy, forming a link in what is now the trunk line between New York and Philadelphia. In this pamphlet, the fact is recorded that the introduction of railways in the United States was due to the energy and foresight of Col. John Stevens, a famous statesman and inventor, of New Jersey, whose son, Robert Stevens, afterwards invented the form of rail and spike fastening which is in use to-day upon most American railways. At the time the Stockton and Darlington Railway was opened, in 1825, John Stevens was connected with a Pennsylvanian Society for Internal Improvement, and at his instigation a member of the society, William Strickland, was sent to this country to investigate the new invention. On his report, the Camden and Amboy Railway was incorporated, and in October, 1830, Robert Stevens sailed for England to get the rails rolled to his own pattern, there being no rolling mills in the States competent to perform the work. In the following year, 1831, the first portion of the track was laid, and shortly afterwards an engine called the "John Bull," very much on the pattern of Stephenson's "Rocket," was brought over from England in parts, and set to work. It is interesting to note that Isaac Dripps, the first master-mechanic of the first American railway, who, as a young man, received the "John Bull" on her arrival, and put her together, is, or was, at any rate, a few months ago, still living, a hearty veteran, at the age of 82.

I will be seen that the Americans were not far behind us in the field, but other countries followed more slowly. In France it is believed that the late M. Thiers, when Minister of Louis Phillippe, was at the first opposed to the introduction of railways, and it was not until 1841 that the Paris and Rouen Railway—the first railway in France—was commenced, while the Rouen and Havre Railway was projected in 1843. It is interesting to recall that these railways were designed and surveyed by the late Joseph Lock, C.E., and constructed by another great countryman of ours, the late Thomas Brassey, and that he was compelled to take over with him, not only a staff of engineers and assistants, but a large number of English navvies, to carry out the work, Lock and Brassey being the engineer and contractor, respectively, who also constructed the Lancaster and Carlisle Railway. Brassey afterwards contracted for making railways in various parts of Europe and Asia, in Canada, and even in distant India, and he may almost be said during his time to have been the pioneer of railway enterprise throughout the world.

Having thus far dwelt on the great importance of railways as a factor in our social system, and as an indispensable element in that great commercial activity which has placed the people of these islands amongst the dominant races of the world, one is naturally led to consider what is the state of things which will result when our supplies of coal, upon which railways and our other important industries depend for their existence, become exhausted, as they must inevitably do at some period of time. A most interesting paper by Sir Robert Ball was recently published, in which he enlarges upon the alarmingly extravagant rate at which we are consuming our coal supply, a result to which the high rates of speed now demanded from railway trains and steamers is greatly contributing, and his calculation is that in all probability the coal in these islands will be exhausted in a century or two, while all the coal in the world will not last beyond a period brief in comparison with the ages of human existence. Sir Robert Ball believes, indeed, that the heat and light-giving powers of the sun upon which this planet depends for its existence, may endure for another five or six millions of years, but he predicts that the few centuries through which we are now passing will stand out prominently in the future history of the world as "the coal-burning age."

But let us consider for a moment what it will mean to England when her own coal deposits have all been worked out. For a time, no doubt, her industries might struggle on, and her railways be worked, by coal brought, at great expense, from other parts of the globe, but the struggle could not last for long. What has made England great, in disproportion to her size, is the happy accident of having large coal and iron deposits brought close together within her own narrow limits, so that she is able to supply the markets of the world with the products of her iron and steel foundries, to stock her mills with machinery and her ships with engines; the coal also supplying steam power for railways, ships, and every kind of machinery. If we had to import coal from abroad, it would be at such a cost that we could no longer compete successfully in foreign markets; our commercial supremacy must languish and die, and our very existence as a great European power would only be a question of time. We have become a manufacturing race, and our population has grown to such an extent, that the soil of the country does not now suffice to yield adequate food supplies for the people. At present, of course, our population is to a great extent fed by supplies drawn from abroad, bought and paid for by the products of our looms and iron foundries; but, when those products fail us, we shall have nothing left to buy with: we cannot go into the markets of the world with empty hands, and the end will be that our surplus population, finding no subsistence for them here, will have to migrate in large numbers to other shores, leaving only as many as can be supported by the tilling of the soil. This may seem to be a fancy picture, but really it appears to be logically correct, if Sir Robert Ball is right in fixing the duration of our coal supply at a comparatively brief period.*

---

\* It may be interesting to mention that the amount spent by this country in the purchase of food-stuffs during the year 1890 was, in round figures, £185,000,000, of which about £155,000,000 were paid to foreign countries, and about £30,000,000 to our own colonies. About £47,000,000, or nearly one-fourth of the whole, was paid to the United States alone.

It may be argued that electricity is only in its infancy, and that everything in future is going to be accomplished by that great agency, including locomotion on land and sea, but the fact must not be overlooked that electricity is not in itself a motive power at all. It is simply a marvellous vehicle for transmitting energy with the minimum waste of power, but the energy must first be developed by the combustion of matter, or by water power, or in some other way, so that, if you want to light your house with electricity, you must provide steam power to generate the current.

It may be, of course, that some day our descendants will find the means of storing up and using, by the aid of electricity, the great forces of nature, such as the flowing of the tides, the falling of rivers, and the force of the winds, and thus averting or postponing the results which we have ventured to apprehend, but as to this we will say nothing. As to the fate of this planet when its coal fields are exhausted, which Sir Robert Ball thinks will happen in a few centuries at the most, and when the sun has no longer heat and light to give us, astronomers may prophesy and theorise to their hearts' content, but the truth is known only to One mightier than they, and the future is in His hands alone.

It may here be stated that, although much of what follows may be taken as being more or less generally applicable to all the principal railways of the United Kingdom, yet the one, the working of which is more particularly described in the succeeding chapters, is the London and North-Western, with which the author has been connected for a great number of years, and with which he naturally, therefore, possesses a more intimate acquaintance than with any other.

## CHAPTER II.

### MANAGEMENT.

THE administration of the London and North-Western Railway is carried on by the Chairman, two Deputy-Chairmen, and a Board of thirty Directors, five of whom retire annually, but are eligible for re-election. Any shareholder may become a director by election, provided he possesses the qualification of holding ordinary stock to the value of one thousand pounds. The full Board of Directors meets once a month, viz., on the third Friday in every month, but the members are also organised in a number of smaller committees, called "Committees of the Board," which also meet once a month and deal with various branches of the business. For instance, there is a "Special Committee," consisting of sixteen members, which holds its meetings intermediately between the meetings of the full Board and devotes itself to much the same class of business; a "Finance Committee" of seven members; a "Permanent Way Committee" of ten members, at which the engineers attend, and which accepts tenders, approves contracts, orders relaying and repairs, and generally authorises all expenditure connected with the permanent works of the railway; a "Locomotive Committee" of ten members, which deals with all matters relating to the engine works at Crewe, the carriage works at Wolverton, the waggon works at Earlestown, and everything connected with the rolling stock of the railway and with the steamboats. There are also a "Fares and Rates Committee" of eight members, and a "Debts and Goods Claims Committee" of ten members, the titles of which sufficiently indicate their functions, and an important committee called the "Traffic Committee," composed of fifteen members, which approves changes in the staff and in the pay of the Company's servants, authorises expenditure upon new works, and deals, besides, with a variety of other matters connected with the discipline of the staff and the working and accommodation of the traffic. In addition to these there are smaller committees for the hotels and refreshment rooms, for legal and medical business, and for stores. At the meetings of the full Board, which are presided over by the Chairman of the Company, the minutes of all these various committees are submitted and approved or otherwise as the case may be, and the Board also deals with Parliamentary matters, questions of policy, proposals for new works involving large expenditure, and, generally, with all business of the first importance affecting the Company. The present Chairman of the Company, as is pretty well known, is an extremely hard worker, and has for many years devoted the whole of his time and his great talents for administration and finance to the service of the Company which he has done so much to place in its present position at the head of the railway enterprise of the country.*

The executive management of the line is carried on by a General Manager, a Chief Goods Manager with four assistants (two for the outdoor working, and two for the indoor work, the making of rates, etc.), and a Superin-

---

* Since the above was written, Sir Richard Moon, to the great regret of his colleagues, has been compelled, by failing health, to resign the Chairmanship, in which he has been succeeded by Lord Stalbridge.

tendent of the line with one assistant. These two last-named officials deal with the working of the trains, both goods and passenger, and all things pertaining to the movement of the traffic.

For administrative purposes, the entire system is divided into ten sections or districts, each of which is under the control of an officer of tried and practical experience, termed the "District Superintendent," having his offices at some central point, who is responsible for the train arrangements of his own district, the conduct of the traffic and the discipline of the staff. Each of these officers has under him an assistant and several travelling inspectors, who regularly visit every station and signal post and investigate and report upon everything that is going on in the district, these men being, moreover, encouraged to make suggestions for the improved working of the trains and the avoidance of irregularities, any such suggestions always receiving careful consideration. In some of the less important districts the District Superintendents are responsible for the goods work at the stations as well as the conduct of the passenger traffic, and in that case they are answerable both to the Chief Goods Manager and to the Superintendent of the line; but, in six of the more important districts, they are relieved of the management of the goods business (except as to the working of the trains) by district officers of equal rank with themselves, who are called "District Goods Managers," and who are responsible to the Chief Goods Manager at Euston. The same principle is followed out with regard to the management of the stations, at the majority of which a single agent is placed in charge of both the goods and passenger traffic, while at 180 of the most important stations there are two officials, one of whom, called the "Station-master," attends to the passenger work, and is accountable to the District Superintendent, and the other, styled the "Goods Agent," is responsible for the goods working, and is under the control of the District Goods Manager.

It will thus be seen that the chain of responsibility and of supervision is a very complete one, and, in fact, the secret of organising the management of a great service, such as this, is nothing more than a carefully arranged system of devolution combined with watchful supervision. It is not, of course, practicable for the General Manager to superintend in person the every-day actions of the porter or the signalman, but these latter act under the immediate direction of the Station-master, the Station-master is accountable to the District Superintendent, the District Superintendent to the Superintendent of the line, the Superintendent of the line to the General Manager, and the General Manager to the Chairman and Directors. If anything goes wrong, or any mishap or irregularity occurs, each of these has to bear his own share of the responsibility in turn, and thus all are kept on the alert, and each one has an interest in seeing that those subordinate to him are fit and capable in every way to discharge the duties placed upon them.

There are two "Conferences" held every month (so called to distinguish them as meetings of *Officers* from the meetings of the *Directors*, which are termed "Com mittees"). The first is called the "Officers' Conference," and meets monthly, the meetings being held usually, but not invariably, at Euston. It is presided over by the General Manager, and is attended by the chief officers at headquarters, and by the whole of the district officers, both goods and passenger. One of the most important functions of this Conference is to discuss and decide upon all alterations of the train service, but it also deals with mishaps and irregularities in working, and considers the causes that have led to them, and the means of preventing a recurrence. Proposals for the alteration of rules and improved arrangements for conducting the traffic are also debated, and, broadly speaking, all matters affecting the working of the line, or the running of the trains come within the purview of this Conference.

The second of the two Conferences is termed the "Goods Conference," which also meets once a month, usually on the day preceding the meeting of the Officers' Conference, its chairman being the Chief Goods Manager, and the members being confined to those district officers who are responsible for the goods working. This Conference takes no cognizance of train arrangements, which are dealt with entirely by the Officers' Conference, but concerns itself with questions relating exclusively to the conduct of the goods traffic, such as mileage and demurrage, outstanding freight accounts, the supply of waggon stock, ropes and sheets, claims for goods lost, damaged, or delayed, cartage and agency and kindred subjects.

The minutes of both these Conferences, which are printed for more convenient distribution to all concerned, are submitted for approval to the Board of Directors, and until they have been so approved, the recommendations contained in them are not valid and cannot be acted upon.

The fact of all the country officers being brought

together at headquarters once a month, primarily for the purpose of attending these Conferences, forms a very essential and valuable feature in the working of the line. They have thus the opportunity of meeting one another, comparing notes and exchanging experiences, besides which each of them in turn enjoys the advantage of a personal interview with the General Manager and with the other chief executive officers, in order to seek advice or instruction upon important and, perhaps, delicate matters which for various reasons can better be dealt with orally than by means of written reports. On the other hand, the chief officers themselves derive benefit from being brought in contact with the men who are engaged from day to day in supervising the actual working of the traffic, and are kept well posted in everything that is going on all over the system.

Another important feature is the system of periodical inspections. From time to time, some of the directors, accompanied by the chief officers, the engineers, and the district officers concerned, go over each district, visit the stations, and inquire into cases of alleged inadequate accommodation or other matters calling for attention. At other times, the chief officers, unaccompanied by the directors, visit the districts, inspect the stations, examine personally the principal stationmasters and inspectors, and satisfy themselves by careful inquiry that all the rules and precepts laid down for the efficient conduct of the traffic, and the safety of the line, are being scrupulously carried out throughout the system. Thus nothing is left to chance or to the possible carelessness of subordinates, but a jealous watchfulness is constantly exercised to ensure that all the necessary precautions that experience has dictated and authority has laid down are thoroughly and effectually observed.

Every servant of the Company, on his appointment, is presented with a copy of the "Rules and Regulations," and is expected to make himself master of its contents, but more especially of the section relating to the branch of the service to which he belongs. This book contains a complete *résumé* of the rules laid down for signalling, for the use of the block telegraph, and for the working of the line generally, and an intimate acquaintance with its contents is indispensable to any man who desires to make himself proficient in his duties. The book also contains the disciplinary rules of the service, and every *employé*, when on duty, is required to have his copy about his person, so that he cannot plead ignorance of his instructions as an excuse for neglect of duty.

The system of control over the expenditure of the Company's money is a very complete one. The general theory is that no expenditure whatever is incurred without the direct sanction of the Directors, expressed by a minute of some committee approved by the Board. The district officers are, indeed, allowed to make some small necessary payments, but even for these the vouchers are submitted monthly, and, after being carefully examined, are passed by the Finance Committee. No work is done by any of the engineering departments, except ordinary maintenance and repairs, without a minute of the Directors to sanction it, and, in like manner, no claim is paid, except those of very trifling amount, without the authority of the "Goods Claims Committee."

As might be expected, in an undertaking of such

magnitude, and with a constantly fluctuating but nearly always growing, traffic, the Executive at headquarters is daily inundated with suggestions and recommendations for alterations and increased accommodation at stations and depôts, but these undergo a very searching examination before any effect is given to them. We will suppose, for example, that a goods agent conceives it to be necessary for an additional siding to be laid down at a station. He makes a report to that effect to the Manager of the district; the latter inquires into the facts on the spot, and, if he concurs in the necessity, reports his recommendation to the General Manager. The latter consults, in the first instance, the Chief Goods Manager or the Superintendent of the line, as the case may be, and, if his report be favourable, authorises the Engineer to prepare a plan and estimate. The plan, when ready, is subjected to the criticism of the District Officer, the Chief Officer, and of the General Manager, and, if all are satisfied, the Directors are next asked to authorise the necessary outlay. But even this is not all, for, finally, the plan has to be signed by the Chairman of the Company before the Engineer commences operations, and that gentleman, who keeps a watchful guard over the Company's purse strings, has to be convinced that the expenditure is not only desirable, but actually unavoidable, before his signature is obtained. Thus the shareholders may rest perfectly easy in the assurance that their money is not dissipated in needless accommodation works.

One very important part of the management of a railway, as may be easily imagined, is the arrangement of the train service. The entire service is re-organised twice in the year, viz., in the spring, to provide for the summer months, when the passenger traffic is heavy and the goods and coal traffic light; and again in the autumn, with a view to the winter months, when, conversely, the passenger traffic is light and the goods and coal traffic heavy. As far as is practicable, the changes are confined to these two periods; but, owing to fluctuations of business, the growth of new neighbourhoods, and all kinds of local and special circumstances, there is really no month in the year when a number of train alterations do not have to be considered and decided upon. This is done, as before stated, at the monthly meetings of the Officers' Conference, held during the third week of every month, and between that time and the end of the month the time-tables have to be revised and reprinted. No one who has ever glanced with an intelligent eye at the time-table of a great railway will be surprised to learn that this operation is one of the most complicated nature, and involving great labour and considerable skill. This will be apparent if it be borne in mind that, supposing, for instance, a train running from London to Scotland is altered in its timing ever so slightly, it involves the necessity of altering all the trains running on branch lines in connection with it, and many other trains which are affected by it. A train service is, in fact, like a house of cards; if the bottom card be interfered with, the whole edifice is disarranged, and has to be built up afresh. Remembering all this, and the pressure under which the work must be done, the wonder is not so much that an occasional error creeps into a time-table, as that such marvellous accuracy is, on the whole, arrived at.

The time-tables of the London and North-Western

Railway are printed at Newton-le-Willows, where the contractors for printing and stationery, Messrs. McCorquodale & Co., have their headquarters. To that town, within a few days of the train alterations having been decided upon by the Officers' Conference, there repairs a clerk from each of the ten districts who is called the "time-table clerk," and with these ten clerks comes an official from the office of the Superintendent of the line to supervise their labours and assist them with his experience. Taking the minutes of the Officers' Conference as their guide, these clerks proceed to revise the timetable, each working out the times for his own section of the line, but all comparing notes as they proceed so as to ensure a harmonious result. As they progress, the results of their labours are placed in the hands of the printers who are on the spot, and the proof-sheets are afterwards revised and corrected by the clerks who have prepared them, and this is how the time-table of the North-Western Railway is produced.

It is extremely difficult to lay down any hard and fast rules for the efficient management of the whole or a section of a large undertaking. If the man who is called to the task has a talent for organisation and administration, he will be a law to himself, and if he does not possess these qualifications, no stereotyped rules will avail to supply their place. There are, however, certain maxims which are elementary and upon which it may be worth while to insist, and these may be briefly summed up as follows :—

(1.) Every man should be chosen with special reference to his suitability for the duties he is called upon to perform. To use a familiar aphorism there should be no "round pegs in square holes."

(2.) Care should be taken that every man entrusted with a responsible duty is thoroughly trained for its performance and competent, before the responsibility is cast upon him.

(3.) Every man should be fairly remunerated for his labour, and should be, as far as it lies with the management to make him so, a cheerful and contented servant. A discontented man makes a bad servant, for his mind is often pre-occupied by his own real or fancied grievances when it should be concentrated on his employer's business.

(4.) Every man should have his duties thoroughly defined and should know exactly what is required of him. To use another aphorism, "What is every one's business is no one's business," or, in other words, a piece of service which is equally the duty of two or three men is likely to be well performed by neither, for each will shift it on to the others if he can, and the one who ultimately discharges it, will do so grudgingly, thinking the others might have done it rather than himself. Moreover, if, after all, it is neglected, it is difficult to fix the responsibility for the omission on any one individual.

(5.) There should be, at all times, active and vigilant supervision in every branch of the service. It is not enough that every man should be fit for his duties and trained for their performance, but it must be the duty of someone to see that he actually does perform them, and that no slackness or carelessness is allowed to supervene in carrying on the working from day to day. The railway service is pre-eminently one requiring for its efficient conduct a high degree of smartness, alacrity, energy, and zeal on the part of every individual engaged in it.

To anyone who may be called upon to occupy the position of a chief official in any great undertaking, such as the one herein described, one or two hints, the result of the writer's practical experience of five-and-thirty years, may not be without their value. The first discovery that any man makes on his being appointed to such a post is that if the day consisted of forty-eight hours instead of twenty-four, and every hour were devoted to his office, his time would still be insufficient to meet the demands on it. It thus becomes essential to economise time as a most precious commodity, and this is best accomplished by acting strictly upon the following maxims:—

(1.) Choose your subordinates carefully and well, and let them be men you can thoroughly rely on. Do not concern yourself too much with points of detail, with which you must be fully conversant, but with which they are just as well able to deal as you are, and reserve yourself for such matters of moment as they are not competent to decide without your authority and experience.

(2.) Before any question is submitted to you for decision, insist upon having all the details filled in, and all the facts before you, so that you may not have to apply your mind to it a second time, but may decide it once and for all with a full knowledge of all its bearings.

(3.) Always decline steadily to attempt to do two things at once. If you are giving an audience to one person, be it a head of department, or any other, let your door be rigidly closed to everyone else for the time being. Let "one at a time" be always your maxim, and act upon it strictly. The man in authority who is seen continually surrounded by a throng of subordinates and striving to meet all their demands at once is the man who, by reason of excessive wear and tear, is most likely to break down in mid-career and fail either in health or intellect ; but the man who steadily concentrates his brain power upon one thing at a time, never wasting a moment, but never flurried or hurried, is the man who gets through the greatest amount of work with the least toil and harassment to himself and in the shortest possible time.

(4.) Always make a point of refusing (except, of course, in special circumstances) to see chance callers, who will otherwise occupy the best part of your time with trivial matters which could just as well be attended to by your subordinates. It is a good plan to make it a rule to see no one without an appointment made beforehand either in writing or through your secretary, or else without previously knowing their name and the nature of their business. It is very amusing, at times, to see the pertinacious attempts which are made to break through this rule, and it can only be maintained inviolate by the agency of a wily and imperturbable secretary, and an office which can only be approached through his. The man who has had a box delayed, the woman who conceives she has been overcharged in her fare, the discharged footman who seeks employment as a porter, will each and all insist upon seeing the general manager; each believes that no one else can or will give them a satisfactory answer, and it is often very difficult to get them even to disclose their business to another person.

## CHAPTER III.

### THE STAFF.

THE staff employed by the London and North-Western Railway Company (exclusive of the staff engaged upon lines owned jointly by the North-Western and other companies) consists at the present time of 61,005 persons of all grades, and these are made up as follows:—

| | |
|---|---|
| Salaried officers and clerks | 7,420 |
| Drivers, firemen, guards, breaksmen, and signalmen | 9,471 |
| Other servants working at weekly wages in the various departments | 44,114 |
| Total | 61,005 |

About 25,000 of these persons are engaged in one way or another in connection with the working of the traffic, the remainder being clerks, artificers, labourers, etc. A certain percentage are boys in training in the various departments, and the total includes about 180 girls and women who are employed at the principal goods stations in the performance of certain duties in connection with the accounts department, for which they are found to be peculiarly suitable. This experiment was first tried some years ago, and being found to be fairly successful, both on the score of economy and efficiency, is being gradually extended within certain limits.

To carry on the traffic of a great railway, one of the main essentials is a highly-trained and thoroughly qualified staff, and it may justly be said that the companies spare neither trouble nor expense in securing and maintaining this most important requirement. The practice adopted by the London and North-Western Company, and it is, in the main, the one which is observed by all English Railway Companies, is to appoint lads about fourteen years of age as boy porters, telegraph boys, and for other similar employments; these lads grow up in the service, and by the time they reach manhood they have become experienced in railway duties in their various branches, and are eligible for filling such posts as become vacant. The most scrupulous attention is paid to the training of signalmen, a class of men the difficult and responsible nature of whose enployment can hardly be exaggerated, and they are never entrusted with the sole charge of signals until they have received a specific course of instruction in the duties. The period of training varies according to the importance of the posts at which the men are to be stationed, but their appointments are not confirmed until the superintendent of the division has certified that he has examined the men, and finds them to possess every qualification for the posts they are to fill, including freedom from colour-blindness, which is a fatal defect in a railway servant. The guards of passenger trains are usually chosen from the ranks of the porters; and the goods train guards, or brakesmen, are selected from the goods porters, shunters, and men of that class; but all these men are subjected to a rigid examination before being appointed, and due regard is had, not only to their knowledge and experience, but to their general intelligence, capacity, and character.

For the superior positions of inspectors, foremen, station-masters, and the higher grades of the service, it is the invariable rule to select men from the lower ranks, solely on the ground of merit, the best man for a particular post being chosen, irrespective of seniority or any other circumstance. Thus it is no unusual thing for a station-master, by reason of special aptitude, to rise to the position of divisional superintendent, and even of General Manager.

As regards the highest positions, at the time when railways were a new feature in the social life of the country, and their promoters looked around them for men suitable to direct their operations and control the large number of persons engaged in working them, they found none who, in their opinion, at that time, were so suitable as officers who had retired from the army and navy, it being supposed that their acquaintance with discipline, and the habits of command they had acquired in the pursuit of their former avocations, would stand them in good stead in their novel career. Thus, in connection with the London and North-Western Railway, we recall the names of Captain Huish and Captain Bruyeres; the North Eastern Company appointed Captain O'Brien as their general manager; the Lancashire and Yorkshire, Captain Lawes, R.N., and the Caledonian, Captain Coddington, R.N., besides other officers of the two services, whose names might be mentioned. As time went on, and the strictly commercial character of these great undertakings became more evident and pronounced, it was perceived that the duties of the highest positions in connection with them required for their efficient performance men who had received a business training, and were thoroughly acquainted with all the details of railway working. It thus became gradually the practice to promote men of talent and capacity from the lower ranks of the service, from one post to another, through the intervening grades, until they reached the highest positions attainable, and the present writer can recall, within his own personal experience, many cases in which men have risen from subordinate posts to become general managers of some of the most important railways in the kingdom.

Thus the humblest railway servant, if he does not, like one of Napoleon's corporals, carry a marshal's *bâton* in his knapsack, may at least contemplate a field of possible promotion of almost as wide a scope.

It is scarcely necessary to say that engine-drivers are very carefully trained for their duties before being entrusted with the charge of a locomotive. They usually commence service as lads in the engine sheds, where they are employed as cleaners; after a time they are promoted to be firemen; then to be drivers of goods trains; next to be drivers of slow or local passenger trains, and, ultimately, the most experienced and intelligent men are selected to drive the express passenger, and mail trains.

The Company are very far from being unmindful of the material welfare of the men they employ, and indeed it is their constant study to maintain the most cordial and friendly relations with them, and to make them feel that their employers have a sincere interest in them and in their well-being at all times, apart from the mere buying and selling of their labour; in fact, they are taught to regard their employers as their best friends and advisers, as should be the case in every department of labour where proper relations exist between master and man.

Several funds or societies have been established in connection with the Company's service, in order to enable every member of the staff to make prudent provision against the results of accident, sickness, death, or old age, and a brief description of the working of these societies, which, judging from the success which has attended their operations, may to some extent be regarded as models of their kind, may not be without interest.

The first, and in some respects the most important, is the "Superannuation Fund Association," which was also the first established, having been in existence since 1853, and is for the benefit only of the salaried officers and clerks of the Company, its object being to provide each contributing member with a superannuation allowance on his retirement from the service at the age of sixty years, or at any earlier period should his health permanently fail, provided he has been at the time of his retirement a paying member for ten years.

There is also a payment to the member's representatives in the event of his death before superannuation. Membership is compulsory upon every servant of the Company receiving a monthly salary, and is in fact made a condition of entering the service, with the proviso, that no person is permitted to become a member after the age of 26 years.

The members' contributions amount to $2\frac{1}{2}$ per cent. per annum upon their salaries, deducted monthly from their pay, but the Company contribute, in respect of each member, an amount exactly equal to his own contribution. The accumulated balance is invested in the hands, and under the trust, of the Company, at such average rates of interest as the Company, from time to time, pay on their debenture bonds and mortgages, the interest being carried to the credit of the fund at the close of each half year. The fund is administered by a committee of six persons, three of whom are nominated by the directors, and three are elected by the members. In the event of the death of a member before superannuation, his representatives receive either the equivalent of half-a-year's average salary, calculated over the whole term of his contributions, or the sum of his own contributions and those of the Company in his behalf, whichever be the greater. Any member retiring from the Company's service before superannuation, *bonâ fide* of his own accord, receives back one half the amount of his own contributions to the fund. A member whose engagement is terminated by the Company from any cause other than fraud or dishonesty receives the whole of his own contributions, but if he is dismissed for dishonesty, he may, in the discretion of the Committee, forfeit the whole.

| Years of Contribution completed. | Superannuation in percentage of average salary. | Years of Contribution completed. | Superannuation in percentage of average Salary. | Years of Contribution completed. | Superannuation in percentage of average Salary. | Years of Contribution completed. | Superannuation in percentage of average Salary. |
|---|---|---|---|---|---|---|---|
| 10 | 25 | 19 | 36 | 28 | 46 | 37 | 56 |
| 11 | 26 | 20 | 37 | 29 | 47 | 38 | 58 |
| 12 | 27 | 21 | 38 | 30 | 48 | 39 | 60 |
| 13 | 28 | 22 | 39 | 31 | 50 | 40 | 61 |
| 14 | 29 | 23 | 40 | 32 | 51 | 41 | 62 |
| 15 | 30 | 24 | 42 | 33 | 52 | 42 | 63 |
| 16 | 32 | 25 | 43 | 34 | 53 | 43 | 64 |
| 17 | 34 | 26 | 44 | 35 | 54 | 44 | 65 |
| 18 | 35 | 27 | 45 | 36 | 55 | 45 &upwards | 67 |

The pensions of those members who remain in the service and claim them are calculated upon the foregoing graduated scale, to which, however, an addition of $\frac{1}{12}$ or $8\frac{1}{3}$ per cent. is made, in accordance with a supplementary regulation prescribed by the actuaries since the scale was laid down.

The fund has, at the present time, 6,547 members, its revenue amounting to £63,000 per annum, and its accumulated balance to more than seven hundred and forty-two thousand pounds. Yet, the actuaries who, in accordance with the Deed Poll, thoroughly investigate the position of the fund every five years, have hitherto advised that the benefits are the maximum that can safely be accorded, consistently with maintaining the association upon a sound financial basis.

The "London and North-Western Insurance Society" was established in 1871, its object being to provide for every member of the wages staff, except those in the Locomotive Department (of whom more hereafter), pecuniary relief in cases of temporary or permanent disablement, arising from accident occurring while in the discharge of duty, and also a payment in all cases of death, whether the result of accident or natural causes. Membership of this Society is compulsory upon all men on joining the service, and each man is called upon to sign an agreement under which the Company undertakes to contribute to the funds of the Society a sum equal to five-sixths of the premiums from time to time payable by the *employé*, and the latter agrees to accept such contributions, and any advantages to which he may be entitled under the rules of the Society, in satisfaction of any claim which he or his representatives might otherwise have had under the provisions of the "Employers' Liability Act" of 1880. By these means, for a small payment, the men, or their families, become entitled to a substantial sum in case of death or disablement, without any delay or any question being raised as to the circumstances of the accident from which they suffer, and this is far more to their advantage than being left with the questionable privilege of claiming under the Act, with all the delay, expense, and doubtful result of legal proceedings. Moreover, a state of good feeling is engendered between the men and their employers which could not be the case to an equal extent if each were taught to look upon the other as a possible opponent in litigation, and any legislation such as has from time to time been threatened in the direction of preventing the men from contracting themselves out of the provisions of the Act is justly viewed by the majority of the London and North-Western *employés* with dislike and dread, and is much to be deprecated alike in their interest and that of their employers.

The premiums payable by the members are as follows:—

CLASS 1.—Passenger Guards, and Breaksmen, and (optionally) men of other grades receiving wages of 22s. per week and upwards ... ... ... ... 3d. per week.

„ 2.—All other Wages staff, except those in Class 3 ... ... ... ... ... 2d. „

„ 3.—Boys and Persons whose Wages are under 12s. per week ... ... ... 1d „

The scale of benefits is as under :—

| Sum insured in case of death arising from accident whilst in the discharge of duty. | Allowance in case of permanent disablement and incapacity to resume employment arising from accident whilst in the discharge of duty. | Weekly allowance in case of temporary disablement by accident whilst in the discharge of duty. During continuance of disablement, not exceeding 52 weeks. | Sum insured in case of death from any cause not provided for in column No. 1. |
|---|---|---|---|
| £ | £ s. d. | s. d. | |
| Class 1 100 | 100 0 0 | 21 0 | £10 0 |
| ,, 2 80 | 80 0 0 | 14 0 | |
| ,, 3 40 | 40 0 0 | 7 0 | 5 0 |

The members elect delegates to represent them at the general meetings, viz., five for each of the twelve districts into which the line is divided, and the affairs of the Society are managed by a committee of 15 persons, 12 of whom are elected by the delegates from their own body, one representing each district, and three members are nominated by the Directors and are termed the " Company's nominees."

On the 31st December, 1892, this Society consisted of 46,549 members; its income for the year 1892 was upwards of £39,500, and it had an accumulated balance in hand of more than £25,000, the amount paid out to the members in the shape of benefits during the year being nearly £38,000

The London and North - Western Provident and Pension Society," an offshoot of the Insurance Society, was established in 1874 with the object of providing a weekly allowance in cases of ordinary sickness for the men composing the wages staff of the Company (other than those employed in the locomotive department) ; a retiring allowance for permanently disabled members ; and a sum at death in all cases not provided for by the rules of the Insurance Society. There is also an allowance to meet medical and funeral expenses on the death of a member's wife. Membership is compulsory as a condition of service. The Company contribute £800 per annum to the funds of this Society in addition to crediting the fund with the fines inflicted upon their servants, and the scale of payments by the members and of benefits is as follows:—

| Class. | | Weekly Payments. | Sum insured in case of Temporary Disablement for work owing to Sickness or to Accident incurred while not in the discharge of duty, or from any cause not provided for in the Rules of the Insurance Society. During Disablement, not exceeding 52 weeks. | Sum insured in case of Death from other causes than that provided for by the Rules of the Insurance Society under the head of accident on duty, the deceased having been a Member during the six months immediately preceding his Death. | Payment upon death of Member's wife to meet medical and funeral expenses subject to approval of Committee in each case. A sum not exceeding | Retiring gratuity to be paid to Members in the event of their becoming disqualified for duty, either through the infirmity of age, or earlier, upon a medical certificate from a doctor, approved by the Committee. | | | |
|---|---|---|---|---|---|---|---|---|---|
| | | | | | | After 5 & not exceeding 10 years' membership. | After 10 & not exceeding 15 years' membership. | After 15 & not exceeding 20 years' membership. | After 20 years membership. |
| | | | | | | £ s. | £ s. | £ s. | £ |
| 1st | Members receiving Wages of 12s. per week and upwards | 4d. | 12s. | £10 | £5 | 12 10 | 25 0 | 37 10 | 50 |
| 2nd | Members whose wages are under 12s. per week | 2d. | 6s. | £5 | | 6 5 | 12 10 | 18 15 | 25 |

The Society is managed in the same way, and by the same committee, as the Insurance Society. It has upwards of 31,000 members, with an income from all sources of £45,000, and an accumulated balance of upwards of £143,000, the amount paid to members in the shape of benefits, under the various heads, during the year 1892, being upwards of £34,000.

The "London and North-Western Pension Fund," for the benefit of the wages staff, was established as recently as 1883, and has therefore been in operation less than six years. Its object was to provide a retiring pension for members after they attained the age of 65, or for such members as, having reached the age of 60 years, were no longer able, by reason of failing health or impaired energies, to continue at work. There are two classes of members, and a man on entering the service may elect to join either one class or the other. First class members pay 2d. per week, to secure a pension on retirement of 10s. per week, while second-class members pay 1d. per week, and are entitled to a pension of 7s. per week.

The Company contribute upwards of £6,000 per annum to this fund, which is administered by the same committee as the Insurance Fund.

With a view to consolidate the two Funds, and thus enable them to be worked for the greater advantage of the members, arrangements were made, as from the 1st January, 1889, to amalgamate the Provident Society with the Pension Fund. New members entering the combined society, who were not previously members of the former Provident Society or Pension Fund, upon attaining the pension age will not, on leaving the service, be entitled to receive a retiring gratuity, but will in lieu thereof be allowed an increased pension of 2s. per week. To those who were members of the former societies it will be optional whether they take the retiring gratuity or the increase of pension.

It has been thought that the case of the men employed in the locomotive department differs in some degree from that of the men engaged in the traffic and permanent way departments, seeing that amongst a body of men who are continually coming and going, and constitute, in fact, a sort of floating population, no scheme which provides for a large surplus or reserve fund would be equitable, and therefore the following plan has been adopted :—

A society has been formed, or rather two societies—one for Crewe works and one for the engine drivers, firemen, and others comprising what is known as the "running department." These societies are managed by delegates elected by the members, assisted by representatives of the Company; and there is a scale of benefits ranging, according to the grade of the men, from £40 to £100 in the case of death or permanent disablement from accident on duty, with a weekly allowance in case of temporary disablement from any cause, and a payment in the event of death from natural causes. The expenses are met by calls upon the members from time to time throughout the year, as necessity arises, but averaging from five to ten calls per annum ranging from 4d. to 1s. per call, according to the men's pay, the Company supplementing these payments by liberal contributions. The number of men in these two societies amounts to upwards of 15,000.

By means of these twin societies, the men employed in that most important branch of the railway service, the Locomotive Department, are enabled, at an expense to themselves so small as hardly to be felt, to make a substantial provision against the results of illness and of death, either from accident arising in the discharge of their duties, or from natural causes.

## CHAPTER IV.

### Permanent Way.

WE have had occasion to remark in a former chapter that the permanent way of a first-class English railway of the present day represents a very advanced stage of development as compared with the rude methods of construction of the earlier railways, and perhaps this fact can most forcibly be illustrated by a brief retrospect of the various changes and improvements which have from time to time been introduced, and which have finally resulted in giving us the magnificent steel track of the present age, upon which a train weighing, with its engine, nearly 300 tons may travel with ease, safety and comfort at a speed of from fifty to sixty miles an hour.

As we have already seen (Chap. I.), the earliest conception of a railway or tramway found its embodiment in a wooden track consisting of oak rails laid upon blocks of wood about two feet apart, and upon which carts with flanged wheels were drawn. Tramways of this description are said to have existed in the neighbourhood of Newcastle-on-Tyne more than two hundred years ago. Nicholas Wood, in his "Treatise on Railroads," published in 1825, gives the Coalbrookdale Iron Works Company the credit of being the first to construct cast-iron rails, which they are said to have done in 1767, the rails being 5 feet long,

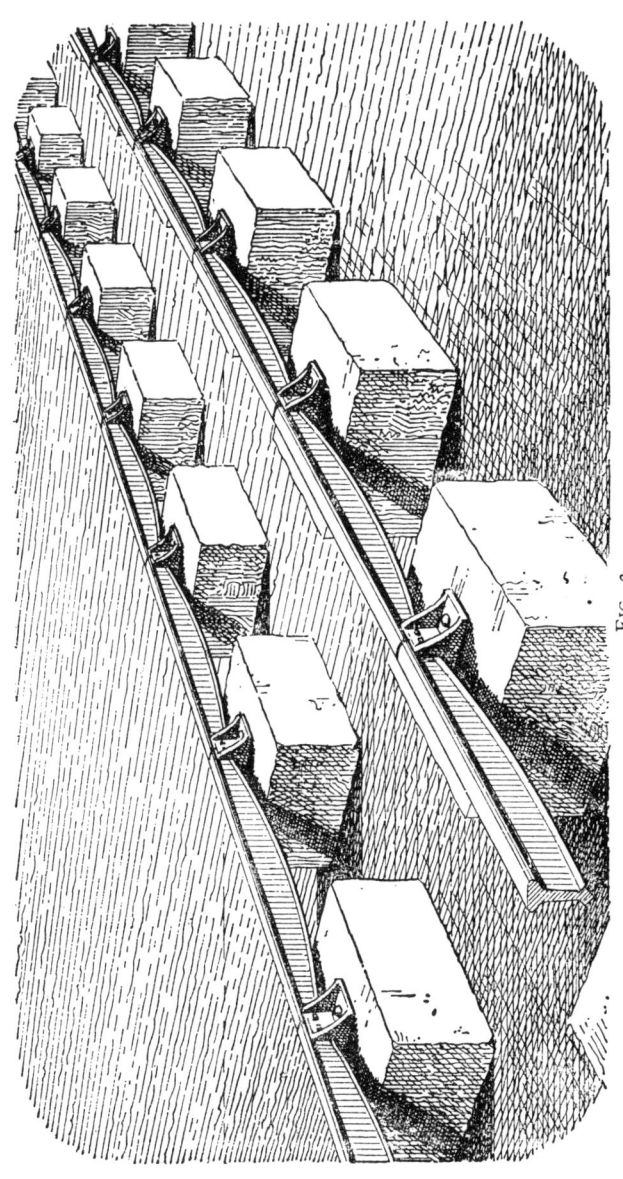

Fig. 2.

Railway with "Fish-bellied" Cast-Iron Rails laid on Stone Blocks—Constructed at Loughborough in 1789.

4 inches wide, and 1¼ inch thick, with three holes drilled in them, by means of which they were fastened to oak rails, these latter being in turn laid upon sleepers.

In 1776 we find in use, at the Sheffield Colliery, cast-iron rails of an angular section (Fig. 1), laid upon wooden sleepers, and which required no flanges to the wheels. Tramways constructed in this manner exist, and are in use in some parts of the country at the present time.

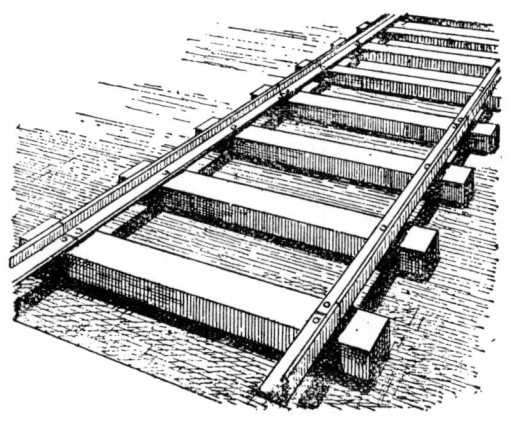

FIG. 1.
SHEFFIELD COLLIERY TRAMWAY OF 1776.

In 1789 a railroad or tramway was constructed at Loughborough, having cast-iron "fish-bellied" rails, from three to four feet in length, resting on stone blocks instead of wooden sleepers, and requiring flanged wheels (Fig. 2).

The first malleable iron rail was patented by J. Birkenshaw, in 1820, and this form of permanent way,

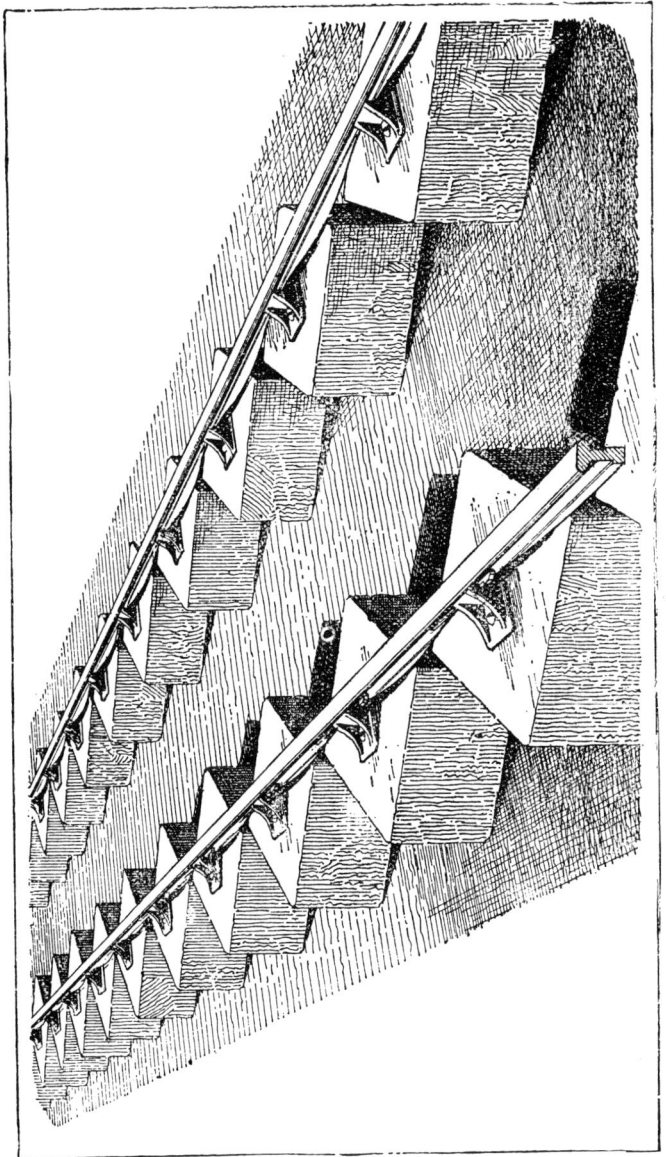

Fig. 3.

Permanent Way of Liverpool and Manchester Railway. 1830.

with rails weighing 28 lbs. per lineal yard, was used on the Stockton and Darlington Railway, and was subsequently adopted by George Stephenson when he constructed the Liverpool and Manchester Railway; but he increased the weight of the rails to 35 lbs. per lineal yard, their length being 15 feet. The rails rested for the most part on solid stone blocks, laid diamond fashion, but on embankments and on peaty ground oak sleepers were used (Fig. 3).

These rails, as will be seen from the illustration, were of the "fish-bellied" pattern, but in practice, and as the demand increased, these were found troublesome to roll, and this difficulty led to the introduction of the flat-bottomed or "flat-footed" section of rail, combining a solid head with a flanged base. This is known as the "Vignoles" rail (Fig. 4, No. 4), and, although still largely used in the colonies and abroad, it is very little in use in this country except in the case of lines laid down for temporary use by contractors.

Another form of rail, known as the "Bridge" rail (Fig. 4, No. 3), was introduced by Brunel contemporaneously with the "Vignoles" rail, and this section of rail, laid upon longitudinal instead of transverse sleepers, was adopted as the standard form of permanent way on the Great Western Railway.

In 1837 the double and equal-headed reversible rail, as shown by Fig. 4, No. 5, weighing 84 lbs. per lineal yard, was originated by Joseph Locke, and was adopted on the Grand Junction Railway. It was originally intended, when one head was worn out, to turn the rail and use the other, but it was found in practice that, unless the rail was turned very frequently, the lower head became indented, where

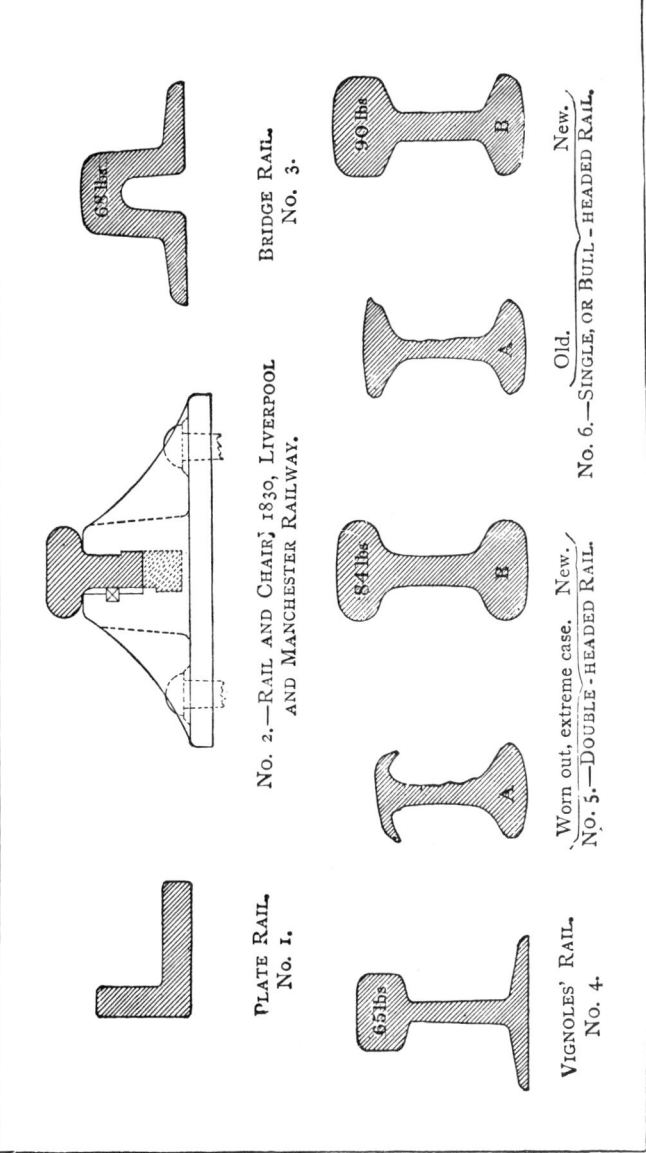

Fig. 4.

it rested in the chairs, to an extent which rendered it unfit for a running surface. This section of rail is still in use on some of the railways in this country, but it is being rapidly superseded by the "bull-headed" section (Fig 4, No. 6), which is simply a refined and enlarged copy of George Stephenson's single-headed rail, and was used in very nearly its present form on the Shropshire Union Railway some forty years ago.

Up to the year 1847 the ends of the rails rested in joint chairs, but in that year Mr. Bridges Adams introduced the suspended joint with fish-plates (Fig. 5, No. 1), by which a much greater degree of elasticity was imparted to the permanent way. The innovation was not adopted upon the London and North-Western Railway until the year 1853, but although, since then, many other plans have received a trial, and some hundreds of patents have been taken out, this form of connecting the rails is found to be the most simple and effectual, and, with one improvement, which is shown by Fig. 5 No. 2, is still used universally on the London and North-Western Railway.

Rails have gradually increased in length, in depth, and in sectional area, but perhaps the greatest improvement which has been effected in them is in the change of material from malleable iron to Bessemer steel. Steel is not only found to be more homogeneous, generally wearing uniformly from end to end, but its strength is half as great again as that of iron, and the rail may thus be reduced in weight by abrasion and corrosion to an extent that would be unsafe in an iron rail. On the other hand, it is only fair to add that steel corrodes more rapidly than iron (in the proportion of about five to four), and in tunnels, and in manufacturing districts

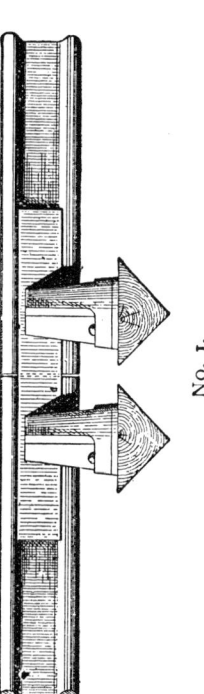

Fig. 5

where sulphurous and other acid gases are present in the atmosphere, the life of the rail is shortened to a material extent. On the whole, however, the balance of advantages is greatly in favour of steel.

Fig. 4, No. 5 (A), shows the section of a double-headed rail which has been in use for twenty years in the main line at a large station, and subsequently for five years in a siding, and one head of which is quite worn out. This is, of course, an extreme case, but it very forcibly indicates the possible reduction of sectional area in a rail constructed of first-class material. On the other hand, Fig. 4, No. 6, shows the section of a rail which is no longer fit for the main line, but might still be used in a siding; in both these cases it will be observed that corrosion has more or less had the effect of reducing the portion of the rail not in contact with the wheels, and that the original shape of the head of the rail is no longer recognisable, so great is its reduction and deformation under the heavy percussive and abrading forces to which it has been subjected.

The improved form of permanent way actually in use upon the London and North-Western Railway at the present time is seen in Fig. 6. It consists of wooden sleepers, laid transversely, and which are of well-seasoned Baltic timber, into which creosote oil has been forced under pressure to the extent of $3\frac{3}{4}$ gallons to each sleeper. The sleeper, which is 9 feet in length, 10 inches wide, and 5 inches deep, when creosoted, weighs 150 to 160 lbs. To each sleeper two cast-iron chairs, each weighing 45 lbs., are secured by two iron spikes and two galvanised iron screws, a layer of hair felt being interposed between the sleeper and the chair. The spikes are cup-headed, slightly tapered, 6 inches

FIG. 6.

PERMANENT WAY OF THE LONDON AND NORTH-WESTERN RAILWAY, 1894.

in length, and weigh 19 oz. each. The screws have a hexagonal head, are also slightly tapered, and weigh 20 oz. each, their length being $6\frac{3}{4}$ inches. A creosoted oak ferule or socket is inserted in each hole in the chair, through which the screws are driven, so as to obtain a mechanical fit by simple means. The steel rails, which are laid in the chairs, are of the single-headed section, 30 feet in length, and weigh 900 lbs., or 90 lbs. per lineal yard. It may be mentioned that over bridges, and for some other special purposes, about 10 miles of rails have been laid upon the London and North-Western Railway which are 60 feet in length.

Each 30 feet rail rests on ten sleepers, and is secured in its place by creosoted oak keys 6 inches long, $3\frac{3}{8}$ inches wide, and $2\frac{1}{8}$ inches thick, driven between the rail and the chair, outside the rail. The fish-plates by which the rails are joined (Fig. 5, No. 2) are 20 inches in length, $5\frac{1}{4}$ inches deep, and weigh 54 lbs. per pair. The four bolts by which they are secured to the rails are square-headed, with a Whitworth thread 9 to the inch, the nuts being hexagonal.

A certain number of iron and steel sleepers have been laid down on the London and North-Western Railway experimentally, the first step in this direction having been taken eight years ago. The results have been varied, a percentage of the sleepers having failed, while, on the other hand, a larger percentage appear to be standing well; but, on the whole, a sufficient time has not yet elapsed to fairly test their durability.

Permanent way engineers insist that the first and last requisite for the maintenance of a sound and good permanent way is a perfect system of drainage. The formation requires to be kept as dry as possible, and to this end, if the material is of a porous nature, retentive of moisture, it should be well drained by means of rubble or pipe drains; if it is not of a porous character, as, for instance, stiff clay or rock, the surface should be formed with a section similar to that of a well-constructed macadamized road, so as to throw the water quickly off its surface to the side ditches. Upon such a formation should be placed a layer of bottom ballast of uniform size and durable quality, free from dirt or any substance which absorbs and retains moisture. Upon the bottom ballast, the sleepers will be laid, and with a sufficient quantity of top ballast, which should be equally clean and durable, although, preferably, of smaller size, the line will be raised and adjusted to its intended level, the plate-layers, in laying the sleepers, taking particular care to obtain a uniformly solid and level bed for each sleeper, so that it may take precisely its proper share—no more and no less—of the weight of the passing trains. Skill and attention displayed at this stage meet with their due reward, and much subsequent trouble and anxiety is saved to the permanent way inspector, who has a length of road to maintain, if he takes care that his sleepers are not bedded on irregularly-sized lumps of stone, that his chairs are fixed to a uniform gauge, and that the sleepers are placed at right angles to the direction of the line, and well packed, or beaten up, as firmly under one rail as the other. He should see that his rails are not bent in unloading, that all crooked or defective fish-plates, spikes, and screws are rejected; that his curves are of uniform curvature, and with super-elevation proportioned to the radii, and that many other apparently insignificant precautions are not neglected, all of which contribute to the construction of a sound and perfect permanent way over which

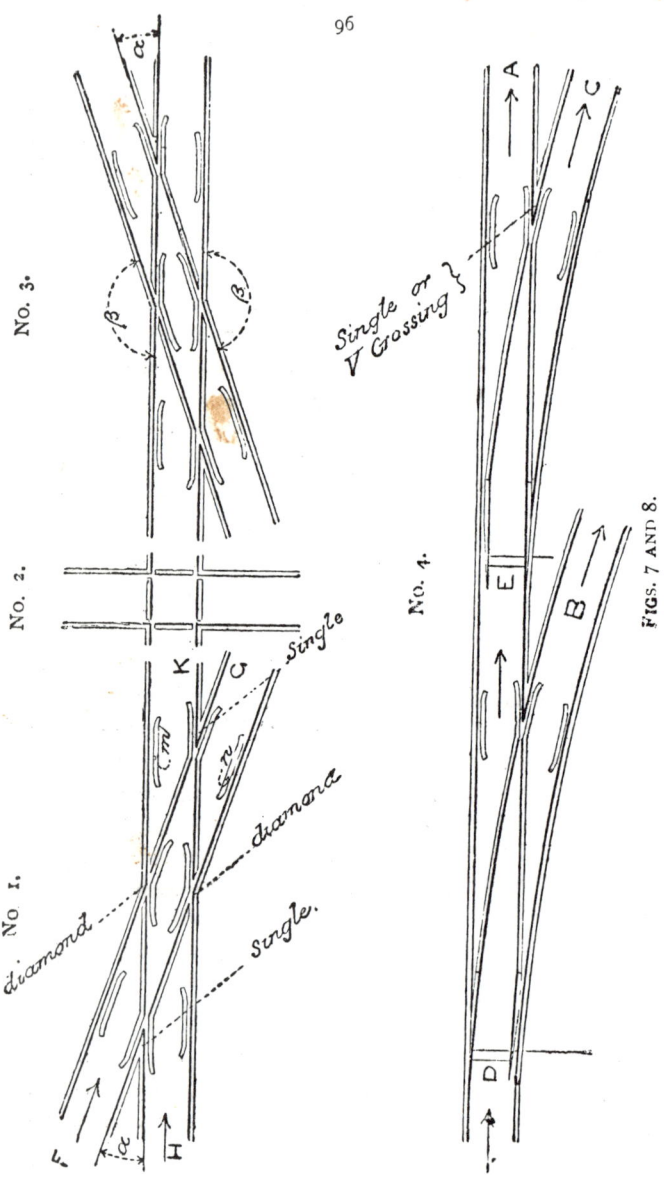

FIGS. 7 AND 8.

heavy trains may travel safely and smoothly at a high rate of speed, and with a minimum wear and tear and expenditure of motive power.

The intersection of one rail with another at any angle is termed a "crossing," and these crossings are so constructed with wing rails and check rails as to guide the flange of the wheel, and ensure its taking the required direction at the point of intersection. The simplest form of crossing is where the rails intersect each other at right angles (Fig. 7, No. 2), but such crossings are of rare occurrence. When the rails intersect at any other than a right angle, the crossings are of two types. When the external angle of intersection is acute (as at *a*, Fig. 7, Nos. 1 and 3), the crossing is known as a single or "V" crossing, but where the angle of intersection is obtuse (as at B, No. 3), it is called a "diamond" crossing. "Diamond" crossings occur only in pairs.

No one practically acquainted with diamond crossings can stand on the footplate of an express engine running through a large station, where there may be several diamond crossings, without his attention being drawn to them. The knowledge that there is a break in the continuity of both rails at the same point, over which there is nothing but the momentum of the train to carry him in safety, interests his mind as the fence does the rider when his horse is leaping over it.

The general regulation in England is that diamond crossings should not be more acute than 1/8, the break in the continuity of the rail being then about $3'\ 4''$ and the distance over which a wheel flange is uncontrolled being about $12''$ less, or $2'\ 4''$.

If the train is running smoothly at the time, and

H

the diamond crossing is in proper order, nothing can be more certain than that it will keep in its proper direction, and the faster the train travels, the shorter is the time during which any disturbing force can operate to divert it.

The safety is inversely as the length of the break, which varies with the angle, and, if the lines leading to the crossings are regular and straight, the safety increases with the speed.

In the majority of cases, derailments at diamond crossings are caused by anything which may set the vehicles oscillating violently, and by blows and jerks between them when the longitudinal centres of the vehicles are not in the same straight line; thus, an extremely unfavourable condition is when diamond crossings are on, or are approached by, curves or reverse curves traversed by loosely-coupled vehicles, violently buffered up in stopping by the sudden application of the engine-brakes, or jerked in starting, particularly if the vehicle on the diamond crossing be a light one between two heavy vehicles, or, when the driving-wheels of an engine commence to slip on the crossing, or vehicles are being propelled over it, as in shunting. In such conditions as these, vehicles are frequently derailed. Bent axles, and other defects in the rolling-stock tend in the same direction.

From this it will be seen that a passenger carriage is less likely to be derailed than a goods waggon, both because they are kept in a more perfect condition, and because they are far less frequently shunted; also when carriages form a train, they are less often propelled at stations and they are close coupled, which tends to diminish oscillation.

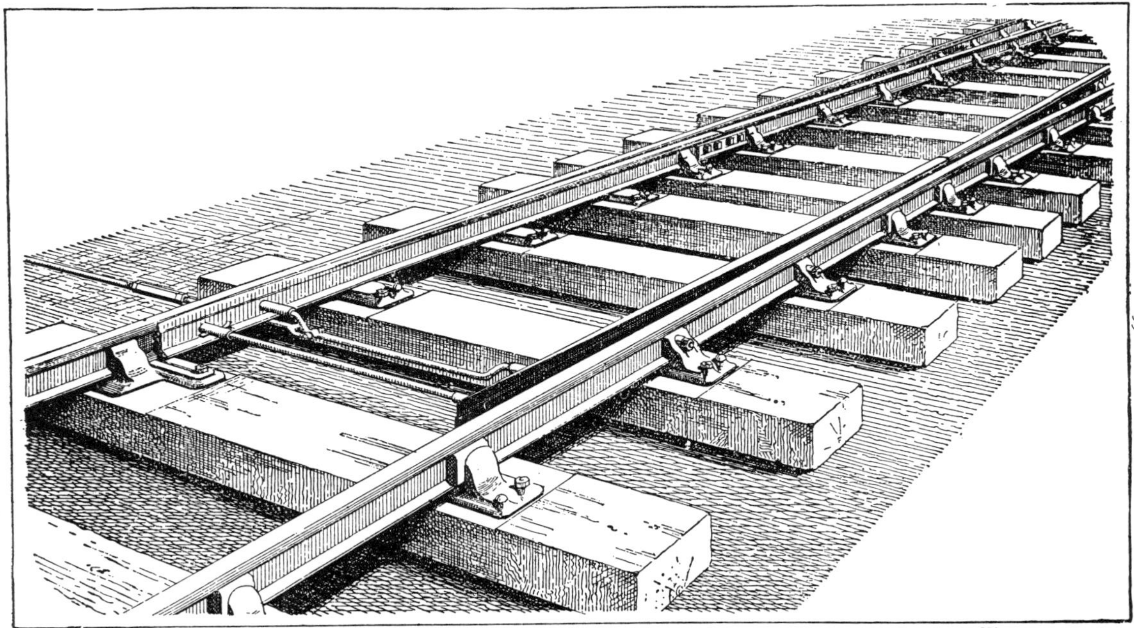

FIG. 9.—VIEW IN PERSPECTIVE OF A PAIR OF SWITCHES SHOWING THE MANNER IN WHICH THEY ARE WORKED.

There are 2,592 such crossings on the London and North-Western system of railways, 1,500 being in the main line, and there have been 625 cases of derailment in four years, 393 on crossings in running lines, and 232 in sidings.

Derailments take place twice as frequently on curved lines as on straight, the numbers being in the following proportion:—

|  | Inside rail of curves. | Outside rail. | Straight lines. |
|---|---|---|---|
| Vehicles | 17 | 25 | 21 |
| Engines only | 2 | 2 | 1 |

The number of each class of vehicle derailed has been nearly in proportion to the following numbers:—

| Carriages | 1 |
|---|---|
| Engines | 19 |
| Waggons | 156 |

Of the 625, 362 were propelled, 149 drawn, 110 no record.

Causes assigned: Defective vehicles, 48; long loads, 11; violent shunting, 51; slipping, 72; blows and jerks, 322; buffer-locked, 7; tail rope, 8; no record, 106.

For "V" crossings, check rails are provided ($m$ and $n$ No. 1, Fig. 7), which, by holding one wheel on an axle to its proper course, prevents the wheel at the other end of the axle from taking the wrong side of the point of the crossing between $m$ and $n$. The check rail $n$ guides the flange when a wheel is travelling from F to G, and the check rail $m$ guides it in the direction H to K.

From an inspection of these diagrams (Fig. 7) it will be easy to trace the course of the wheel flange, which is always on the *inner* side of the wheel.

To turn a train off one line of railway and on to another which connects with it, a pair of tapered movable rails, called "switches," or "points," are made use of (see Fig, 7, No. 4). These are connected by rods with a lever in the signal cabin, and worked by the signalman; the lever being so controlled mechanically that it is impossible for the signalman to lower the signals for a train travelling in the direction of the arrow on line "B," until the "points," or "switches," have been placed in their proper position, as at D. On the other hand, before the signal can be lowered for the line A the switches must be placed as at E.

Fig. 9 gives a view in perspective of a pair of switches, and shows the manner in which they are worked.

There is one important feature in the formation of a well-constructed permanent way, which is known as the super-elevation of the outer rail on curves. Any one who has witnessed the evolutions of a circus rider will have observed that both horse and rider, in order to maintain their balance, incline their bodies towards the centre of the ring, and the greater the speed, the greater is their deviation from the perpendicular. In order to enable a train to do by mechanical means what the rider does by muscular power—that is, to balance the centrifugal force of a train running round a curve—it is necessary for the outer rail on a curve to be raised somewhat above the inner rail, and the smaller the radius—that is, the sharper the curve—and the higher the speed of the trains, the greater must be the super-elevation. In practice it must be adjusted to the average speed of the fastest trains that are likely to run over it—that is, the express passenger trains.

Railway curves are invariably arcs of circles of greater or less radius, except for a short length, where they join or leave the straight line. Where the radius of the curve is uniform, an uniform super-elevation is given to the outer rail, but this elevation dies away gradually to the straight line, where the rails become level. As the super-elevation decreases, the radius of the curve increases until it becomes infinite, or, in other words, until the straight line is reached.

The various tables of super-elevation in use on all the principal railways in Europe are based upon the formula:

$$S = \frac{153 V^2}{R}$$

S = Super-elevation in metres;
R = Radius in metres;
V = Speed in metres per second.

If it be asked what is the steepest gradient a railway should have, the answer is, "The best that can be obtained under all the circumstances; or, in other words, the nearest to a dead level." There are cases in which the physical conditions of a country will only permit of a railway being constructed with sharp curves and steep gradients, except at a practically prohibitive cost. It is, nevertheless, a fact that the less the deviation from a straight line and moderate gradients, the greater is the safety and economy of working; and, in constructing a main line of railway, it is frequently worth while to incur heavy outlay at the outset rather than handicap the undertaking with difficulties of working, which will place it at a disadvantage in competing with other railways for the same class of

## PERMANENT WAY.

traffic, for which punctuality and speed are of the first importance.

In practice it is usually found that sharp and frequent curves are associated with steep gradients, and, upon railways which have to be constructed in this manner, the trains must necessarily be lighter, and the average speed must be considerably less than where the conditions are more favourable. Such lines are, therefore, in proportion to the traffic carried over them, more expensive to work and maintain; but as the weight of the train, the class of locomotive used, and all the other arrangements for conducting the business are specially adapted to the circumstances, such a line as this probably involves less trouble and anxiety in working than a railway which is generally level, but which has one or more long and steep gradients in its course. In the latter case, the steep gradient is the exception, and not the rule; all the conditions are adapted to the maintenance of the high rate of speed expected with heavy trains on fair gradients, and yet the engines must have sufficient adhesion and steaming power to surmount the difficulties of the exceptional gradient. In some cases, the plan is adopted of attaching an auxiliary engine (called a "bank engine") to the rear of the train at the foot of the incline; but this involves an additional stoppage and the loss of valuable time, and special precautions are required to enable the operation to be performed with certainty and safety.

The extent to which the average speed of trains is affected by the mode of construction of a railway is strikingly illustrated by the table on page 105, which gives particulars of the curves and gradients, and the speed of the trains, upon the main line of the

London and North-Western Railway from London to Carlisle, upon the Buxton Branch, the Central Wales line, and the Merthyr, Tredegar, and Abergavenny Branch.

It will be observed from this table that upon the Merthyr, Tredegar, and Abergavenny Branch, with its steep gradients and severe curves, the trains can only run at less than half the average speed that can, without difficulty, be maintained upon the main line, and it may be added that, while upon the main line the load drawn by a goods engine is five tons to every ton of engine, on the Merthyr Branch the load is only three tons to every ton of engine, notwithstanding the low rate of speed.

The following may be mentioned as instances of specially steep gradients for short distances:—The incline to the Fruit Market at Edge Hill, near Liverpool, is 1 in 24 for 173 lineal yards, and the load which can be drawn up it is only $2\frac{1}{2}$ times the weight of the engine. On the Hopton incline, on the Cromford and High Peak Railway, there is a gradient of 1 in 14 for a length of 440 lineal yards, and on this an engine is only able to draw its own weight of load.

On the other hand, on an easy gradient, a coal engine will draw from eight to ten times its own weight, and between London and Carlisle $2\frac{1}{2}$ tons of passenger train load can be drawn for every ton of engine at an average speed of from 45 to 50 miles an hour, and if this is compared with the same load conveyed over the Merthyr, Tredegar, and Abergavenny Branch at a speed of only 22 miles an hour, the effect of curves and steep gradients upon the working of a railway will be seen at a glance.

## TABLE OF GRADIENTS.

| Line | Length of Line. Miles. | Curves. Less than 20 chains radius. Percent. | Between 20 & 40 chains radius. Percent. | Between 40 & 80 chains radius. Percent. | Over 80 chains radius. Percent. | Straight Line. Percent. | Percentage of Level Line. Percent. | Gradients. Steepest Rising. | Steepest Falling. | Average Gradient both ways. | Average Speed. Miles per hour | Number of Stops. |
|---|---|---|---|---|---|---|---|---|---|---|---|---|
| Main Line. London and Crewe | 158 | ... | ... | 13 | 39 | 48 | 9 | 1 in 300 | 1 in 177 | 1 in 432 | 48½ | 3 |
| Crewe and Carlisle ... | 141 | 2 | 5 | 18 | 27 | 50 | 13 | 1 in 75 | 1 in 95 | 1 in 225 | 48¼ | 2 |
| Buxton Branch | 19 | ... | 34 | 32 | ... | 32 | 11 | 1 in 58 | 1 in 66 | 1 in 78 | 36 | 2 |
| Central Wales Line ... | 59 | 3 | 35 | 16 | 4 | 42 | 11 | 1 in 60 | 1 in 60 | 1 in 97 | 31 | 7 |
| Merthyr Tredegar and Abergavenny ... | 19 | 36 | 13 | 2 | ... | 49 | 5 | 1 in 38 | 1 in 35 | 1 in 44 | 22 | 3 |

Sharp and reverse curves add to the train resistance and increase the risks attending a high rate of speed, and they also largely contribute to the fatigue experienced by a passenger after a long railway journey.

The high speeds which now prevail on the principal railways, both in Great Britain and abroad, are, no doubt, the natural result of competition. Such speeds are admittedly not in the interest of the railway companies, for they involve greater expense in construction and working, while the passenger pays no more for travelling at fifty miles an hour than he would if the speed were half that rate. At the same time, the public like to travel fast, and in these days of high-pressure, the railway, which, in this respect, did not cater for its patrons to as great an extent as its competitors, would soon find itself distanced in the race for popularity and consequent profit. But the maintenance of high rates of speed very largely, though not entirely, depends upon the perfect design, construction, and maintenance of its permanent way.

One very important factor is the nature of the gradients of the railway, for the ideal railway for speed would be one laid on a dead level from end to end. This is in practice, of course, impossible, and every difference of level has its effect, greater or less, on the rate of speed, for, although it might be supposed that the time lost in mounting an adverse gradient would be balanced by the increase of speed in descending on the other side, this is not found to be the case in actual practice when the average speed is high and the gradients long. Moreover, caution dictates a limitation of speed in descending a steep gradient if there are any junctions or stations in the course of it, so as to keep the train under necessary control; and, while it is not customary in this country to lay down any hard-and-fast regulations for such limitation, the drivers of express trains, who are always careful and experienced men, are expected to use a certain amount of prudent discretion, based upon their knowledge of the line they are passing over, and have regard to the weight of the train, the brake power, the weather and consequent state of the rails, and the nature of the gradient.

The number and nature of the curves on the railway have a very material effect on the average rate of speed which can, with safety, be maintained. Probably no locomotive engines have, as yet, been constructed which are capable of hauling a train of average weight at a speed which would be incompatible with safe travelling, on a straight railway with a perfect permanent way; but where there are curves, especially reversed curves, of less than 20 or 25 chains radius, abnormal speeds are accompanied by such an amount of oscillation as to suggest caution and some abatement of speed, with a view both to safety and comfort.

Besides the friction between the wheel flange and outer rail, due to centrifugal force, the tendency of a wheel to become derailed when passing round a curve arises from the axles not being strictly radial, and to the inevitable sliding of wheels fixed on axles caused by the unequal length of the inner and outer rails. It is true that the more general use of bogie-frames and radial axles renders the wheel-base much more flexible, but speed-rates are only occasionally and accidentally in exact proportion to the super-elevation, and coned wheels on a line of normal gauge are only proportioned to the radii of the inner and outer rails of one particular curve, and soon become irregular by wear. On the most perfect permanent way, the radius and super-elevation of any curve, however skilfully adjusted at the outset, soon become sensibly irregular, while, at the best, they are only approximately exact.

| Radius. Chains. | Number of Curves. | Total Length of Curves. Feet. | Total Curvature in Degrees. |
|---|---|---|---|
| 8 | 2 | 192 | 19·50' |
| 10 | 1 | 97 | 8·26' |
| 11 to 17 | 2 | 366 | 18·54' |
| 18 ,, 22 | 10 | 2,803 | 123·38' |
| 23 ,, 26 | 7 | 3152 | 95·11' |
| 27 ,, 28 | 4 | 2411 | 74·39' |
| 29 ,, 34 | 18 | 13573 | 370·31' |
| 35 ,, 36 | 10 | 10,251 | 251·3, |
| 37 ,, 40 | 14 | 10,375 | 231·14, |
| 41 ,, 50 | 30 | 23,325 | 445·45, |
| 51 ,, 60 | 45 | 51,577 | 835·58, |
| 61 ,, 80 | 106 | 134,161 | 1,589·26, |
| 81 ,, 100 | 72 | 89,026 | 837·14, |
| 102 ,, 150 | 117 | 182,970 | 1,224·15' |
| 153 ,, 200 | 89 | 147.104 | 750·8, |
| 205 ,, 300 | 59 | 99,252 | 342·12' |
| 305 ,, 400 | 17 | 23,545 | 60·25' |
| 405 ,, 8,685 | 18 | 27,714 | 36·40' |
| Total. | 621 | 821,894 | 7,315·29' |
| Number of Curves per mile. | 2·48 | Average Curvature per mile. | 47·59 |

## PERMANENT WAY.

The foregoing list may be of interest, showing the number, length, and total curvature in degrees of the curves of different radii on the main line of the London and North-Western Railway between London and Carlisle, a distance of 300 miles.

In the following table are given all the places on the London and North-Western system where, by the working regulations, drivers are ordered to run at a more or less reduced speed :—

| Reduction of Speed laid down by Working Regulations at 93 places on the London and North-Western Railway. | Approaching Junctions at Stations. | Other Junctions and Connecting Lines. | Sharp Curves and Inclines. |
|---|---|---|---|
| Considerably reduced speed, and very slowly ... | 10 | 9 | — |
| Reduced speed ... | 15 | 36 | 7 |
| Speed reduced to 5 miles an hour | 1 | — | — |
| ,,    ,,    10    ,,    ,, | 1 | — | — |
| ,,    ,,    15    ,,    ,, | — | 9 | — |
| ,,    ,,    20    ,,    ,, | — | 1 | — |
| ,,    ,,    25    ,,    ,, | — | 2 | — |
| ,,    ,,    30    ,,    ,, | — | 2 | — |
| Total ... | 27 | 59 | 7 |

Nine of the above places are situated between London and Carlisle, one of them being a descending gradient of one in 87 for 55 chains, entering Euston, the terminal station in London. Down this incline, trains are required to run at such a reduced speed as will enable them to stop before reaching the platform if required.

It may be added that, on the main line between London and Carlisle no curves exist of less than 20 chains radius, except at important junction stations, where every train stops. There are, however, three junctions between the fast and slow lines with reverse curves of about ten chains radius, and five such junctions with reverse curves of about 20 chains radius. None of these curves can have any superelevation of the outer rail, and through all of them trains have to pass at reduced speed.

The question of "curves of adjustment" has received much attention, and some railways use such curves to connect the normal curve with the tangent; but it is remarkable that few railways which have the highest speeds adopt this refinement by direct measurement, but are satisfied with slightly flattening, or "easing," the curve at the junctions with the tangents by the experienced eye of the foreman-platelayer. However true a circular curve may be when first laid in, it is soon found (if tested by measuring the versines of short arcs) to have lost its exact uniformity of radius, and it would appear to be still less possible to maintain an exact parabolic or other curve—the principle of continuously varying radius is unimpeachable in theory, but unattainable in practice. In the construction of the works when a railway is made, care should be taken that the normal curves are ranged so as to admit of the subsequent "easing" at the tangent points, without lessening the radius of the normal curves a little further on.*

To maintain the permanent way of a great passenger

---

*It is only right to state that the facts contained in the foregoing paragraphs, relating to the effect of curves of various radii upon the speed of trains, are deduced from a Paper read at the Railway Congress held at St. Petersburgh in 1892, by Mr. Harry Footner, C.E., the principal permanent-way engineer of the London and North-Western Railway, for the late Sir George Findlay, who, at the time, acknowledged his large indebtedness to that gentleman for the technical details, upon which the paper was founded.—[ED.]

railway in perfect working order, a very careful and complete system of organisation becomes necessary, and this, upon the London and North-Western, is carried out in the following manner :—

Three men, with a foreman or ganger, form a gang, and have charge of the constant inspection and maintenance of about two miles of double line of railway, being an average of one man to each mile of single line ; but the exact number depends upon the extent of the traffic using the line, and the consequent wear and tear, and the number of junctions and sidings which have to be maintained. Every ten or twenty of these gangs are under the direct supervision of an inspector, who thus has a district of from 20 to 40 miles of railway. Every seven or eight of these inspectors are under the control of a chief inspector, who is therefore responsible for from 200 to 250 miles of railway, and who has also under him travelling gangs of ballasting men and relayers, who are employed in renewing the permanent way and carrying out alterations and additions. Each length has also a full complement of artificers, joiners, masons, bricklayers, painters, blacksmiths, etc., with their foremen and inspectors, and these men repair bridges, tunnels, stations, and all kinds of buildings which constitute the "works" of a railway. All these men, together with the Chief Permanent Way Inspector, and the men under him, are under the direction of a civil engineer of experience, who has also a staff of surveyors, draughtsmen, and clerks, with offices and workshops at the most important centre of traffic in his district. Such a section of the railway is called a "Division," and there are eight such divisions on the North-Western Railway, the eight divisional engineers being responsible to an "assistant engineer" who, together with another assistant engineer of equal rank who has charge of the construction of new railways and other important contract works, acts under the instructions of the engineer-in-chief of the Company.

The duties of the gangers comprise the daily inspection of every portion of the section of line under their charge, and the repairs of the permanent way, fences, drains, and roads. They have also to report anything they may observe to be amiss with the telegraph wires, the signals, or with passing trains more especially during storms, fogs, or heavy falls of snow. They furnish their inspectors with an account of all materials required and used, and are responsible for the work performed by the men under them, which is of a very miscellaneous character.

The inspectors of permanent way are responsible for the discipline of their men, and for keeping a correct account of the time they work, and the wages paid to them. It is their duty also to keep a record of all materials received and used, to see that every care is taken of the property of the Company, and to report to the chief inspector of the district, or to the divisional engineer, every circumstance of an unusual character which may come within their knowledge. They take charge of the renewals of permanent way, and of the operations necessary in case of floods, and of landslips of an ordinary character. In mining districts they keep careful watch, and see that the railway is lifted and maintained when subsidences occur; they daily visit portions of their districts, and are in constant personal communication with their gangers, acquainting them with all instructions issued from headquarters.

The chief inspectors of districts are responsible for the general condition of the main lines, and it is their special duty to see that a uniform standard of maintenance is kept up by each of their sub-inspectors, and that orders given by the engineer are duly observed and consistently followed out. They arrange the running of trains of materials, and provide for ballasting operations, and are in constant communication with the divisional engineers, to whom they report upon every matter affecting the permanent way.

A similar chain of supervision exists in the workshops in each district.

Periodical meetings of the divisional engineers are held, at which the various points which arise from time to time in connection with the maintenance and repair of the permanent way are discussed, and the engineers are thus enabled to compare notes and give each other the benefit of their respective experience.

The stability of the permanent way and works of a great railway is frequently threatened, and ceaseless vigilance has to be exercised to avert the dangers arising from circumstances which no human foresight can anticipate. Embankments and sea-walls are sometimes demolished by storms; landslips and the fall of rock from overhanging cliffs may cover the rails; sudden subsidences of the surface, due to mining operations, may take place; bridges and viaducts may be set on fire, or washed away by floods; dangerous compounds explode in transit, rails be torn up by collisions, or portions of tunnels may collapse. Instances of mishaps from all these causes have occurred in actual experience, and to repair the damage and restore the communication in the shortest possible time is the task which frequently has to be undertaken by the railway engineer, occurrences of the nature referred to frequently happening without the least previous warning. In such cases, the first difficulty the engineer experiences is very often in ascertaining, with any degree of accuracy, what has actually taken place, and the precise extent of the damage which has resulted, and he has next to determine what, with the time and means at his disposal, he is justified in attempting. It is often found that men, plant, and material can be more expeditiously obtained from some central depôt than from local resources, although the depôt may be a hundred miles or more from the scene of operations.

A notable illustration of what can be done in this way in an emergency by a company like the London and North-Western, possessing great resources, occurred when, in the great storm of Sunday, the 17th August, 1879, the Llandulas viaduct, on the main line of the Chester and Holyhead Railway, was undermined by flood, and washed completely away, interrupting, for the time being, the traffic between England and Ireland. For two days, until the flood subsided, nothing could be done, but within the space of five days afterwards the railway was deviated for about half-a-mile so as to strike the river at the narrowest point, and a temporary trestle bridge was erected, over which the first train passed at 2 p.m. on the 24th August, exactly seven days after the mishap occurred. The line was cut in the slope of the embankment leading to the old viaduct, and was everywhere placed upon solid ground, or upon stacks of old sleepers, so that there might be no settlement, and the line might be fit for the heaviest traffic immediately it was completed. The gradients were 1 in 23, dipping down to the river, and rising on the opposite side, and everything was finished off in the most substantial and careful manner; but of course great skill and attention were necessary on the part of the engine drivers, and the difficulty of working long and heavy trains, some of which required three engines, over these severe and changing gradients, without breaking the couplings, or heavily bumping the carriages together, can hardly be exaggerated, yet no mishap occurred, and the passengers in the trains were scarcely aware that they were travelling under unusual conditions.

The new permanent viaduct was meanwhile rapidly constructed, and was actually completed and opened for traffic on the 14th September, less than one month after the mishap. Its length is 224 feet, divided into seven spans of thirty-two feet each, and its height is fifty feet. Forty-two girders, each thirty-two feet in length, were required, and the plates and angles for each girder were rolled in one length. All these were made in the Company's own steel works at Crewe, and the whole of the material was turned out and ready for erection within seven days, the steel having been manufactured, rolled, and worked, within that short space of time.

## CHAPTER V.

### SIGNALS AND INTERLOCKING.

AN attempt will now be made to give some idea of the elaborate system of signalling the trains, which, in conjunction with the use of the electric telegraph, alone enables the traffic of a great railway to be carried on with safety and despatch, and which has grown up from the rudest beginnings side by side with the growth of the railway system itself.

There is, of course, a very obvious and primary necessity, on any railway, for some visible indication by means of which the drivers of the trains may be warned when they may proceed, and when they must come to a stand, and shortly after the opening of the Stockton and Darlington, which was the earliest railway constructed, one of the station masters is said to have adopted the simple expedient of placing a lighted candle in the window of the station-house when it was necessary for a train to stop. From this rude beginning to the complicated system of signals and interlocking which may be seen, for example, at Clapham Junction or Waterloo is a very long step in advance, and it has, of course, only been achieved by a gradual process of evolution. Thus when the Liverpool and Manchester Railway was first opened in 1830, the only arrangement made for signalling the trains was a flag by day or a

## SIGNALS AND INTERLOCKING.

lamp by night, held in the hand of the pointsman, as he was then called, and an old print from the "Illustrated London News" shows us the pointsman, or policeman, in the long-tailed coat and tall hat of the period, standing outside his hut, and making the prescribed motions with his flag; but this simple device was soon found to be insufficient, and, about four years after the line had been opened, stout posts were provided, upon which lamps were placed by the pointsman. This really marks the first step in the creation of the present system of signalling; but about the same time the Grand Junction Railway was approaching completion, and the necessity for some improved form of fixed signal seems to have been realised, since we find that the line, at its opening in 1837, was provided with station signals in the form of discs, carried on poles about 12 feet in height, with a lamp at the top, the disc and lamp being arranged to turn through a quarter circle by the pointsman actuating a lever at the base. If the disc was turned so as to face an approaching train, or the lamp showed a red light, it implied a signal to stop; while, if the disc was turned edgeways to the driver, or the lamp showed a white light, it meant "go on." These signals, which may still be seen in use in some remote country districts, were fixed on the platforms at stations, or outside the pointsmen's huts at junctions, and corresponded in position with the home signals of to-day, the "distant signal" being, at that time, a thing unknown.

Some five years later, about 1842, a semaphore signal, somewhat similar to those in use at the present time, was introduced, and it appears probable that this now universally-adopted type of signal very rapidly superseded the disc signals of the earlier period. The old semaphores showed three positions, "all right," "slacken speed," and "danger," the arms being actuated by the pointsman by means of a lever on the post. Up to this time, although the necessity must have existed, as it does to-day, for a driver to be warned as to the state of the line some time before actually reaching the point of obstruction, where he was required to stop, no attempt seems to have been made to meet the want; but at length accident proved once more the parent of design, for in the year 1846 a pointsman, who had to attend to two station signals, placed some little distance apart, in order to save himself the trouble of walking to and fro between them, procured some wire, which he attached to the levers of the signals, using a broken iron chair as a counter-weight, and by this simple expedient found himself able to work both signals without leaving his hut. Thus was demonstrated the possibility of working a signal at a distance, and this man's primitive contrivance doubtless hastened the introduction of distant signals, the use of which rapidly became universal. "Starting signals" were the development of a later period, the necessity for them having only been brought about by the application of the Block-Telegraph system some years after.

The next step in advance was the adoption, in a very elementary form, of the principle of interlocking, and this seems to have been forced upon the attention of railway engineers at a very early period, since, as early as 1843, we find that the levers for working the signals at a junction were provided with a simple mechanical device to prevent the main-line signal being lowered at the same time as that for the branch line; but, at that time, no attempt was made to extend the locking to the levers which actuated the points. In the following year Mr. C. F. Whitworth patented a scheme for locking points and signals on the ground by means of locks worked by wire, but there was no suggestion for *concentrating* the levers. The apparatus was complicated and difficult to work, and apparently it was never brought to bear, but there is no doubt that the proposal contained the germ of the interlocking system as we have it to-day.

In 1856 a successful attempt was made by Mr. John Saxby, at the Bricklayers' Arms Junction (London), to concentrate and interlock the levers working both points and signals, and although the apparatus employed was crude as compared with the perfect mechanism now in use, it represented the earliest practical application of the principle of interlocking. In 1859 the first interlocking frame was fixed on the London and North Western Railway, at Willesden Junction, by Mr. Austin Chambers, who patented his arrangement in 1860, and from this point the interlocking of the London and North Western system proceeded rapidly; for thirteen years later, in 1873, it is recorded that 13,000 interlocked levers were in use on that railway.

At this point it may be worth while briefly to describe the meaning and application of the different kinds of signals and locking appliances in use upon the principal railways at the present time.

The form of signal most generally adopted is the "Semaphore," which is no doubt familiar to most of my readers, and consists of a timber or iron pole varying in dimensions according to circumstances, but sometimes as much as 70 feet high, with an arm about 5 feet long, capable of assuming two positions when actuated by mechanical force. When this arm is horizontal and at right angles to the post it signifies "stop"; when it is nearly vertical it indicates "go on." As the arm cannot be seen at night, a lamp is provided on the post, and working with the arm is a frame containing coloured glasses, and termed "spectacles," which cause the lamp to show a red light to indicate "stop," and a white or green light to indicate "safety," or "caution."

The signals are distinguished as "home signals," "distant signals," "starting signals," "advanced starting signals," and "disc signals." The home signal, as its name implies, is placed close to the point at which it is desired a train shall stop. The distant signal is placed at varying distances behind the home signal according to the gradient of the line and other circumstances, but on a straight and level railway it would be about 1,000 yards back, and its function is to repeat the action of the home signal, so that if the latter is at danger the driver has timely intimation of the fact, and can at once reduce the speed of his train so as to stop at the home signal. Distant signals are distinguished by a notch cut in the end of the arm. In working a Military railway it would be quite practicable to dispense with visible signals altogether and rely entirely upon the use of the telegraph; or, at all events, the two simple signals, the home and distant, as described, would probably suffice; but for the purposes of ordinary railways the introduction of the block telegraph system has necessitated the provision of starting and advanced starting signals. Starting signals are usually placed at the end of the platform at a station, and they indicate to the driver, by the lowering of the arm, when he may start his train and enter the section in advance. The advanced starting signal is usually placed about 300 yards from the cabin, in front of the starting signal, and enables a train which has passed the platform starting signal for the purpose of picking up waggons from sidings, or to clear the section in the rear, to be brought to a stand without entering the section in advance. It may be explained that all semaphore signals are fixed in such a way that on approaching them the arm appears on the *left*-hand side of the post, and this arrangement enables the same post sometimes to be used for carrying both "up" and "down" signals.

The disc signal is used to indicate to a driver whose train is in a goods siding which joins the main line when he may leave the siding and pass out on to the main line. It is really a disc of metal, with a lamp, carried on a spindle fixed near the ground, and which turns on its axis. The position of the disc by day and the colour exhibited by the lamp at night furnish the required indications as to the state of the line.

Fig. 10 shows a simple arrangement of signals at a station, and Fig. 11 shows the ordinary signals required at a simple junction where there is no complication of lines.

At a small roadside station, where there are no sidings connecting with the main line, the signals are easily worked by detached levers, placed in any convenient position; but at larger stations, where there are many signals and points to be actuated, a means of concentrating the working becomes necessary, and this is done by means of the "signal cabin," which brings us to the question of interlocking. The signal cabin contains a most complicated piece of mechanism, called the "locking

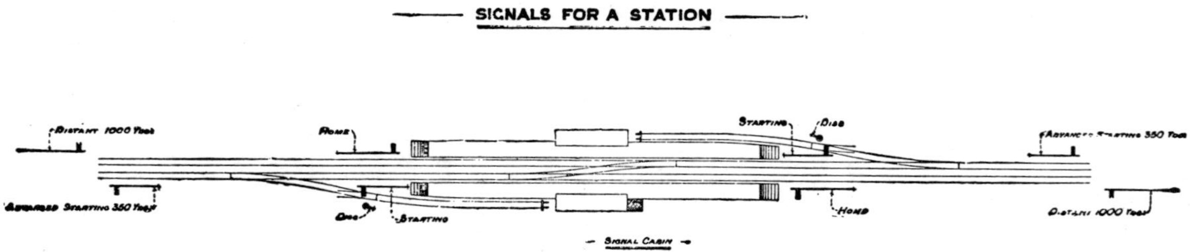

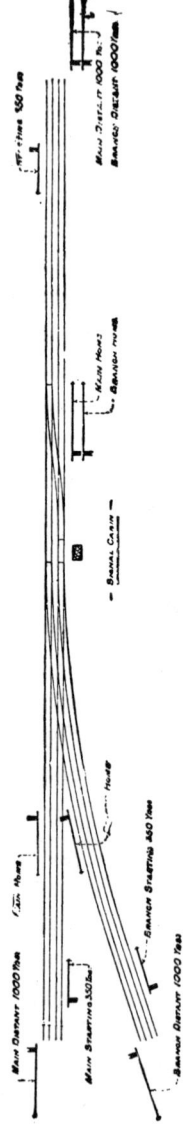

Fig. 10.—Signals for a Station

Fig. 11.—Signals for a Junction

## SIGNALS AND INTERLOCKING.

frame," consisting of a row of levers by means of which the signalman actuates every pair of points and every signal under his control. By a mechanical contrivance, the points and signals are interlocked—that is to say, supposing, for example, that the signalman has moved a lever that opens a pair of points, to enable a train to come out of a siding on to the main line, the home and distant signals must be at "danger" to stop any train from approaching on the main line, and it is physically impossible for the signalman to lower them. The manner in which this is accomplished was described some years ago in the *Engineer*, and that description is so complete and lucid that probably it would be difficult to improve upon it. The writer says:—

"Mounting by an iron ladder to the signal platform, we enter the glass-house. One side of this building is occupied by a row of strong iron levers standing nearly upright from the floor, and placed at equal distances along one side of the apartment; on the opposite side are many electric telegraph instruments, and the rest of the width forms a gangway or passage from end to end for two stalwart and serious-looking men, whose time is entirely occupied in looking through the glass sides of their cell, and pulling this way or pushing that way some of the levers which are arranged before them. These levers work all the points and signals, and their number is found to correspond exactly with the number of points and signal levers outside. Every lever is numbered, and on the floor beside it there is fixed a brass plate, engraved with its name and use. Sets of them are also distinguished in a way that readily catches the eye, by being painted in strong colours. Thus, for example, all the point levers may be black, the up signals red, the down signals blue and the distant signals green. The row of levers thus presents a diversified pattern to the eye, which is readily caught by the parti-coloured groups, and, having once got the key, distinguishes quickly and correctly between their different classes.

"On examining the levers somewhat more closely, we perceive that many of them have numbers painted on their sides, not one number only, but in some cases half a dozen or more; and one naturally asks what can be their meaning. These numbers involve the whole secret of the safety which is secured by the mechanism, as will be readily understood on examining the principles on which it has been devised.

"The keys and pedals of an organ, as every one knows, command numerous valves admitting air from a windchest to the pipes which it is desired to sound. The key-boards are sometimes double or triple, and are occasionally arranged so that the performer sits with his back to the instrument. The pipes are generally spread over a large space, and sets of them are sometimes enclosed in separate chambers. There thus arises considerable complexity in the mechanism by which the several keys are made to operate on their respective air-valves. Nevertheless, by means of rods, cranks, and levers, such a connection is effected that, on depressing a C key, not one C pipe only, but it may be twenty C pipes are made to sound, in whatever part of the instrument those pipes may be situated. And so it is with the point and signal levers. The whole row may be considered to form a key-board, every key of which is connected by suitable cranks and rods to some one of the points and semaphores which have to

be played upon. In the organ, a touch of the finger
serves to depress a key, for the movement has only to
admit a puff of air to certain pipes; but here the keys
require a strong and steady pull, for they have to move
ponderous point bars, or broad semaphore arms, and
their movements have to be conveyed round many
corners and over considerable distances. In both cases
the mode of communicating motion is the same, the
two mechanisms differing only in size and strength;
and thus far the organ and the signal instrument
exactly correspond. Now, however, we come to a
point in which they differ *toto cœlo*. A performer on
the organ can touch any keys he pleases in any order
or in any number; he can 'discourse most eloquent
music,' or he can rend the ears of his audience by
abominable discord. Not so the signalman. Concord
he can produce at will, but discord is utterly beyond
his powers. He cannot open the points to one line
and at the same time give a safety signal to a line
which crosses it; and the points must be properly set,
*close home to the stock, or fixed rail*, or the signal for a
train to pass cannot possibly be given, and the least
obstruction occurring to prevent the full and true
opening or closing of the points is at once discovered,
even with connecting rods of the greatest length
practicable. Moreover, while a train is actually travelling through the points, it is itself master of the
situation; not even the signalman can, either inten-
tionally or inadvertently, change their position or
disturb them until the whole train is safely passed.
When he gives a clear signal for a main line, he cannot
open a point crossing to it; when he gives a clear
signal for a crossing he must show danger for all the

lines which it crosses. And this is the meaning of the numbers marked on the different levers. No. 10, let us suppose, has 5, 7, and 23 marked on its side. He may pull at No. 10 as long as he pleases, but he cannot move it till Nos. 5, 7, and 23 have first been moved ; and so throughout the whole system. No signal lever can be moved to safety unless the point levers corresponding with it have first been moved, and no point levers can be moved while there stands at safety any signal lever that ought to stand at danger. Every lever is under lock and key, each being a part of the key which unlocks some of the others, and each forming a part of the lock which secures some of the others against possible movement, while each is at the same time subject to the control of all those which are related to it.

"This result, complex and difficult as it seems, is achieved by mechanism of great simplicity and beauty. Immediately under the floor of the platform, and just in front of the levers, are arranged several series of vibrating and sliding bars, somewhat like the tumblers of a lock, placed horizontally. These bars have projections here which stand in front of certain levers as obstacles to their motion, and notches there which permit certain levers to travel. Some of these have sloping faces, so that when a lever moves along them it edges them to one side, and this transverse motion being communicated to others of the series, brings the proper projections or notches in front of those other levers to which the moving lever is related. Thus by the movement of one lever some others are stopped, and some are left free, and this simple principle, carefully applied to all, combines them in a system incapable of discord."

There are several supplementary interlocking appliances now generally in use which may be briefly described. For instance, there is the " Facing-Point Lock," which is a bar of iron working in connection with facing points—that is, points by which one line diverges from another in the same direction. This bar, which is actuated by a separate lever in the cabin, works with, and securely locks, the points, and not until this has been done can the signal be lowered. The bar holds the points firmly in position, so that, even if the signal has been reversed, they cannot be moved while the train is passing over them. Then we have the "Locking Bar," somewhat similar to the facing-point lock, but actuated by the same lever that works the points. This is chiefly applied to siding points to prevent their being moved while a train is passing over them. " Detector Bars" are employed on parts of the line which cannot be seen by the signalman, to prevent the signals being lowered when the line is occupied by a train. " Detector Locks " are applied to facing points, and are worked by the wire that works the signals, and if the points should be injured or out of position the fault is at once detected, and the signal is locked at "danger."

Again, there is the " Point-rod Compensator," which automatically compensates for the expansion or contraction from heat or cold of the rods which actuate the points, and an " adjusting apparatus," which enables the signalman to adjust his signal wires without leaving his cabin, together with numerous other ingenious contrivances for working and interlocking with the signals the gates of level crossings, turn-tables, and canal drawbridges, and for many other purposes. There is, moreover, in use on some of the branch railways, a system of what is known as "Key Interlocking" for siding points, which merits a particular description, as it is both simple and effectual, and might prove valuable in the working of temporary or Military railways. By means of this system, while the large outlay required for laying down rods to work the points is avoided, all the security of interlocking is retained. A simple frame of levers is provided for working the signals, with a number of keys. If a certain siding is required to be used, the key which applies to that siding is withdrawn, and this has the effect of mechanically locking all signals for the road with which the siding connects. The key is then carried to the siding, and with it the points are unlocked, but when they are once opened the key cannot be withdrawn until they are closed and locked again, and the signals, of course, cannot be lowered until the key has been carried back and inserted in the lever frame, so that the security is complete.

During the interval between 1859, when the first interlocking apparatus was fixed on the London and North-Western Railway, and 1873, when, as before stated, considerable progress had been made towards interlocking the whole of the system, many alterations and improvements in the method, both of signalling and interlocking, had from time to time been introduced with the inevitable result that the signal plant and apparatus in use had come to be of very mixed types, causing great difficulty and unnecessary expense in maintenance and repairs.

This state of things led to the introduction of a new

## SIGNALS AND INTERLOCKING.

system altogether, with regard to signalling the railway, the organisation of which was entrusted to Mr. F. W. Webb, Mem. Inst. C.E., the Company's chief mechanical engineer. Up to this time, all signal work upon the railway had been provided and kept in repair under contract by the different firms of railway signal manufacturers, but chiefly by Messrs. Saxby & Farmer, of which firm Mr. John Saxby, before referred to as having been the inventor of the first effective system of interlocking, was an active partner. The Company now determined in future to make and keep in repair their own signals and interlocking apparatus, so as to secure not only efficiency and economy, but uniformity of pattern throughout the line. The scheme was brought to bear, and proved to be a success. The Company had already ample facilities in the locomotive works at Crewe for turning out all kinds of iron work; carpenters' and fitters' shops for making the cabins, signals, and other woodwork were added, a superintendent and a staff of artisans appointed, and the thing was done, the payment of royalties to inventors being soon dispensed with by the Company's engineers designing and patenting new systems of their own.

The signal-fitting shop at Crewe is 280 feet long, and 85 feet wide, the machine tools being driven by a fine Otto gas engine of 48 indicated horse-power. There is, of course, plenty of steam power available in the works, but the signal shop is often busy at a time when the other machinery is not working, and the gas engine is, for this reason, found to be a convenient and economical arrangement. One side of the shop is devoted to the preparation of the signal-posts, which are received from the saw-mill cut to the proper dimensions, and ready for fitting. The posts are of Baltic timber, varying in size from 9 inches to 15 inches square at the bottom end, and tapering to 6 inches square at the top, the length varying according to circumstances. About seven feet of each post, at the bottom, is left the full size of the timber from which the post is cut, and this portion is first charred in a furnace and afterwards well coated with gas tar, while upon the top of the post is placed a galvanised cast-iron cap. The arm of the signal is formed of a thin steel plate, stiffened by two corrugations running lengthways, and is riveted to a galvanised cast-iron centre, upon which is fixed an adjustable frame for the spectacle-glasses, made sufficiently heavy to counterbalance any accumulation of snow on the arm, and keep it in its "danger" position should any of the fittings fail. The arm works on a spindle squared to receive it at one end, and on the back light lever at the other end, except when the signal is electrically repeated, in which case a racked segment is substituted for the back light lever, and it is geared with a similar segment, in connection with the electrical contacts of the repeater apparatus. The spindle turns in a casting fastened to the post by four $\frac{5}{8}$-inch bolts, which also serve to secure the lamp bracket fixed at the back of the arm, this bracket being of sufficient width to form a "stop" for the arm when in its "danger position."

There are several other distinctive patterns of signals employed for special purposes, amongst them being the "disc" signals, previously mentioned, for controlling the exits from sidings, and the miniature semaphore signals placed low down on the post, which at certain busy parts of the line are used instead of a hand signal when it

## SIGNALS AND INTERLOCKING.

is necessary to call an engine cautiously past a signal at "danger," and which are termed "calling on arms."

On an average the fitting shop at Crewe turns out about nine signals per week, including composite or bracket and gantry posts, some of which have been constructed to carry as many as twenty-four signal arms.

On the other side of the shop are arranged a number of erecting frames, on which the interlocking apparatus is built up. The frame used by the Company is known as lever actuation, with horizontal and vertical bar locking. The horizontal bars are of Bessemer steel, rolled to a shallow channel section, the locking studs being squared to fit the channel and secured by riveting. The vertical bars are also of steel, notched, the notches being punched out cold. Each vertical bar is guided by a channel the length of itself, one wall of which is made deeper than the other; notches are cast in this to act as guides for the horizontal bars, these notches being faced by a special drifting machine at the rate of thirty-five notches per hour. The apparatus is characterised by great strength and simplicity, and, an unusual amount of special machine work being employed in its construction, a perfect interchangeability of parts is secured which is highly essential to economical maintenance. This is sufficiently demonstrated by the fact that, since the introduction of the present form of apparatus and methods of construction, the annual cost of maintenance has been largely reduced.

Signals are worked from the signal cabins by wires, but the points are actuated by rods. Trailing points are worked at a distance of 220 yards from the cabin, but in the case of facing points the distance is restricted by the Board of Trade to 150 yards, increased in some exceptional cases to 180 yards. At such distances as these, it is obviously of great importance to have a strong and thoroughly trustworthy means of connection between the points and the cabin, and for this purpose ordinary iron gas-piping was formerly used, but latterly it has been found that a steel channel section of rodding is far superior for the purpose, and the success attending this innovation has led to its adoption by several other railway companies. The chief advantage over gas-piping is that rods weakened by corrosion are readily detected and can be removed. Moreover, being manufactured to a standard in the works at Crewe, they are of uniform excellence, both in material and workmanship. About 6,000 yards of this rodding is turned out on an average every month, is sawn off to 18-feet lengths, and, when laid down, is jointed by means of fish-plates, secured by six $\frac{1}{2}$-inch bolts, the fish-plates being rolled to a section to fit the channel of the rod, and the bolt holes drilled by a multiple drill. After being laid down, the rodding receives a coating of red lead and a second coat of red oxide paint, which gives it a smart appearance, and is found to be a good preservative.

For lighting the signal lamps at night, gas is used in the neighbourhood of large towns, where it is readily obtainable; but by far the greater number are lighted with petroleum oil, a large number of spare lamps being kept always on hand to provide for cases of failure.

The signalling of the London and North-Western Railway as it exists to-day has involved the erection of 1,482 signal cabins, containing some 33,000 levers, and of 17,000 signals. The steel rodding used to actuate the points would form a continuous rod from the Land's End to John O'Groat's, while the wires which work the signals would stretch from Liverpool to New York. The largest interlocking apparatus ever constructed in the Crewe works is that at the entrance to Euston Station which contains no less than 290 levers.

The maintenance of all this complicated array of signals and interlocking apparatus, over upwards of 1,800 miles of railway, is in itself a work of great magnitude, and one requiring the closest and most anxious attention, having regard to the consequences that might result from a single point rod breaking or getting out of gear; or from a single signal arm failing to respond to the action of the lever. For the purposes of maintenance, the entire system is divided into eleven districts, each of which is in charge of an inspector, these eleven inspectors being assisted by twenty-one sub-inspectors and foremen, and having under their orders sixty-eight chargemen and 430 workmen. The districts are subdivided into lengths, and each length is placed in charge of a "chargeman" and an assistant, who visit every signal cabin on their length once a fortnight, clean and oil the fittings of each signal and point, execute any small repairs or renewals that may be required, and which it is possible to carry out during their visit, and report to the inspector of the district any repairs or renewals which they may find to be necessary, but which they are unable to deal with upon the spot. In every signal cabin the name and private address of the chargeman who is responsible for it is posted, and it is the duty of the signalman to report to him every failure or defect that may become apparent during the intervals of his visits, sending at the same time a duplicate of the report to the inspector of the district.

In addition to this, every cabin is visited once a month

by a fitter and his assistant, whose duty it is to carefully examine, clean, oil and, if necessary, repair the locking apparatus, particulars of the work done being entered in a monthly report, which is sent through the district inspector to the head office at Crewe.

Heavy repairs and renewals are executed by an extra gang, attached to each district, in charge of a responsible foreman, the most stringent rules being laid down as to the manner in which the work is to be carried out, so as to provide for the safe and uninterrupted conduct of the traffic during the time it is going on.

In order to secure uniformity in the sighting of the signals, the following rules are, as far as possible, adhered to, but these rules are always subject to modification so as to meet special circumstances such as, for instance, where bridges, trees, or other natural objects, or sharp curves, would otherwise obscure the sight of the signals.

*Home Signals.*—To be fixed within sight of the distant signal, and to be erected as near the signal cabin as possible, so that a driver, whose engine is standing at the signal, may be verbally communicated with, if necessary, by the signalman.

*Distant Signals.*—To be fixed at a uniform distance of 1,000 yards from the home signal, unless the gradient is a rising one, in which case a distance of 800 yards is considered sufficient. In special cases, a distant signal may be fixed a maximum distance of 1,200 yards from the home signal, where the circumstances admit of a sufficiently direct route for the wire connections to enable the signal to work freely.

*Junction Signals.*—The same rules apply to these as to home signals. They are to be fixed near the facing points to which they apply, and in no case at a greater distance from them than 200 yards, unless repeater signals or duplicate locking bars are provided.

Junction signals for protecting a junction in the trailing direction (*i.e.*, a junction formed by the connection of one line with another, not by meeting or facing points, but by trailing points) to be fixed a sufficient distance from the fouling point to afford some margin for a driver who may accidentally draw past the signal.

Junction signals are not in any case to be placed on the same post one above another, but a separate post is to be provided for each signal.

*Platform Starting Signals.*—These are sighted at a height of about 15 feet above rail-level, and so as to be seen by a driver the whole length of the platform. This rule, however, is not strictly applicable if the same post carries the distant or home signal for a cabin in advance, in which case the signals are sighted as home or distant signals, as the case may be.

*Advanced Starting Signals.*—These are to be sighted of a uniform height with platform starting signals, and are to be seen by a driver from the platform starting signal. They must not in any case be at a greater distance in advance of the cabin than 350 yards, and must be clearly in view of the signalman.

*General Rules.*—Bay starting and other subordinate signals are to be of a uniform height of 15 feet from rail level, and are to be provided with short arms and purple lights instead of red.

Lamps are never to be placed nearer together than 7 feet, except in the case of subordinate signals.

Signals elevated more than 45 feet above rail-level are to have a lower arm on the same post, 15 feet above rail-level, so as to be visible in fogs or thick weather.

Signal cabins are to be so placed that the signalman may have a good sight of all points and signals actuated from his cabin, more especially facing points.

All signals are to be fixed on the left-hand side of, and as near as possible to, the road to which they apply, no signal or cabin, however, being erected at a less distance than 4 feet 6 inches from a passenger line of rails.

A distant signal for a cabin in advance must never overlap a home or starting signal for a cabin in the rear, but must be fixed on the same post, 7 feet below the home or starting signal, and be controlled by the home or starting signal, to prevent the distant arm being "off" when the home or starting arm is at "danger." When a distant signal is placed below a home or starting signal, no other signal must be placed on the same post, excepting "fog" or "calling-on" arms.

When the distant signals for a junction have to be combined with the home or starting signals for a cabin in the rear, then the starting signal post must be nearest the line with the distant arm for the right-hand junction placed under it, and the distant signal for the left-hand junction must be carried by a separate post to the left of the home or starting post. Both distant arms must be controlled by the home or starting signal. This rule will not apply if the junction to the right is a goods loop or other subordinate line; in this case, the distant signal must be carried on a separate post to the right of the home or starting post.

## CHAPTER VI

### TELEGRAPHS.

TELEGRAPHY might not inaptly be termed "the handmaid of steam," for it plays an important part in almost every operation connected with railway working. By its means the trains are started from the stations and conducted safely from point to point throughout their journey; the signalmen who regulate their passage are placed in an unbroken chain of communication one with the other; the nature of the train and its destination, and the fact of its punctual running, or otherwise, are flashed ahead from signal cabin to signal cabin as it speeds on its journey; while the faithful telegraph warns the signalman if his signals are not acting freely or if his lamps are not burning brightly. By telegraph the marshalling of goods waggons, the loading of trains, and the movements of empty waggons are intelligently controlled, and the whole business of the railway is carried on with a promptitude and despatch that could not otherwise be attained. In short, the uses of telegraphy as applied to railways are so numerous, and so diversified, that it would be a formidable task even to catalogue them, and one still more formidable to attempt their description in detail.

In the earlier days of railways, and before electricity had been brought to bear upon their working, the only means for providing for the safety of the line was by erecting fixed signals at certain points, and keeping them at "danger" for a specified time after the passage of one train, before another was allowed to follow. Obviously, under a system of this kind, only a very limited number of trains could be dealt with within a given period of time, and as the traffic increased and trains were multiplied it was found quite inadequate, and some better plan had to be devised. The electric telegraph had already been utilised for transmitting from station to station the times of departure of the trains, and about the year 1853 Mr. Edwin Clark introduced the absolute block telegraph system, by means of which the number of trains which may be passed over a given section of line, with perfect safety, may, by the multiplication and shortening of the sections, be said to be almost unlimited.

Mr. Clark's apparatus took the form of what is known as the "three-wire" block telegraph for double lines, and this form has held its own up to the present time— that is, there is one wire with an instrument at each end of the section for the up line, the same for the down line, and one wire for the bell circuit, the latter being common to both lines. Besides this, there is in use a "one-wire" system, also for double lines, but which shows only two positions of the indicator instead of three. The advantages claimed for the "one-wire" system are (1) that on railways where there are four lines of rails only two wires are required, instead of the six that would be needed under the "three-wire" system; and (2) that where the sections are long, the "one-wire" system is less expensive, although in sections half a mile or less in length the "three-wire" proves to be the cheaper of the two, for the reason that, although the wires cost more, the instruments cost less. In addition to these, there is a single-line block telegraph, which is worked by two wires, one for the block instrument and one for the bell.

All the different kinds of block telegraph apparatus may be worked either on the "absolute" or "permissive" system, according to the requirements of the case

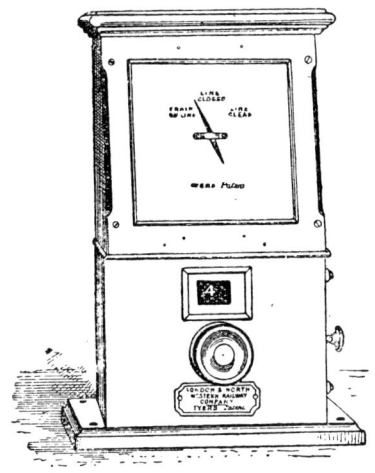

FIG. 12.
THREE-WIRE "TELL-TALE" BLOCK TELEGRAPH INSTRUMENT.

and the regulations in force; the meaning of the "absolute block" being that there can only be one train in a given section at the same time, while, under the "permissive" system, there may be more than one train in the section. Prior to the year 1879 it had not been found practicable to work with the block telegraph through busy station yards, and the passage of the train was, in such cases, regulated by a special code of electric bell signals, but this plan was very unsatisfactory, and the difficulty was at length met by the introduction of the "Tell-tale" instrument. This is really a form of block telegraph, worked under "permissive regulations"; but there is a special apparatus, by means of which a reminder is given to the signalman at a station of the number of trains there are in the section in the rear. (See Fig. 12.)

A block instrument of any kind consists of an indicating dial and a commutator or handle. The indicator is attached to an axle, on which a magnet is centred, being suspended either within, or in close proximity to, a coil of silk-covered wire, and deflected to the right or left according to whether a "negative" or "positive" current flows through the coil. The commutator is so arranged as to alter the direction of the current at will. The bells are generally of the single-stroke type, and are used for calling attention, and for giving the complete code of signals descriptive of the nature of trains, as agreed to by all the railway companies.

The normal state of the indicator of the three-wire block instrument is vertical ("Line closed") when no current is flowing; the deflection when a negative current is flowing is to the right, meaning "Line clear," and with a positive current to the left, indicating "Train on line." (A set of the three-wire apparatus is shown in Fig. 13.)

Briefly the *modus operandi* is as follows:—Attention is first called on the bell, and then station A will give to station B what is called the "Be ready" signal, consisting of a certain number of strokes of the bell, varying so as to indicate the nature of the train. The man at station

B, if the previous train has passed his cabin and he knows the section between A and B is clear, repeats this signal. The train is then despatched from A, the signalman at A gives the signal "Train on line," the signalman at B acknowledges this by moving his own indicator and the one at A to "Train on line," and at once gives the "Be ready" signal to C, and so on throughout. As soon as the train has passed B the man at B moves his own indicator and the one at A over to "Line clear," and

FIG. 13.
SET OF THREE-WIRE BLOCK TELEGRAPH INSTRUMENTS WITH BELL.

upon this being acknowledged by A the indicator is left vertical, signifying "Line closed," and thus the operation has been completed so far as that particular train and that particular section are concerned. Of course it will be apparent that if this system is properly carried out, it is an absolute impossibility for two trains to be between A and B at the same time.

A new form of instrument devised by Mr. G. E.

Fletcher, one of the Company's officials, has been recently introduced on the London and North-Western Railway, by means of which the whole of the apparatus shown in Fig. 13, viz., the indicating dials for both up and

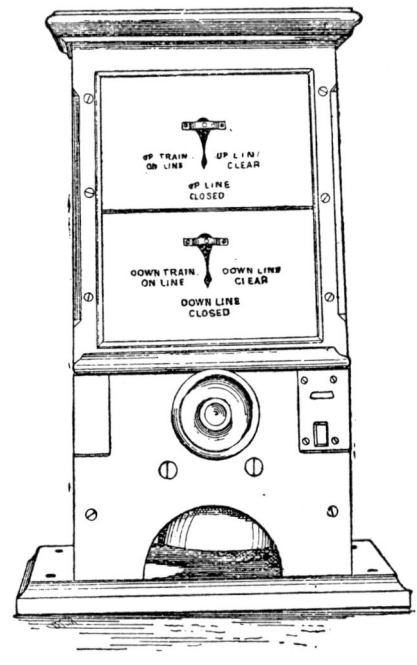

FIG. 14.
FLETCHER'S COMBINED BLOCK TELEGRAPH APPARATUS AND BELL.

down lines, and the bell, are combined in one instrument. (See Fig. 14.) The novelty lies, not so much in the combination, as in the mode of actuating the indicators, the advantages claimed for the invention being (1) a reduction in cost, and (2) considerable economy in space, which is a great desideratum in the smaller signal cabins.

The one-wire system differs from the three-wire, in so far as the indicator of the instrument is moved over to the different positions by a momentary current, and is

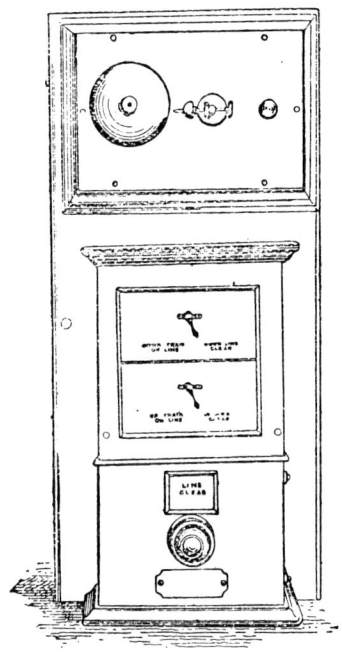

Fig. 15.
One-Wire Block Telegraph Instrument.

afterwards held there by induced magnetism, the wire being left free for any succeeding signals. The mode of working is about the same, only that there are but two positions, viz., "Line clear," and "Train on line," and no vertical position. (See Fig. 15.)

The "Tell-tale" instruments are somewhat similar in construction to the three-wire, the difference being that the commutator is provided with a revolving disc, lettered "line closed" (indicator vertical), "line clear," and "train on line," and Nos. 2 to 6 on the remaining five sections of the disc. Up to the point of getting one train in the section, the operation is exactly the same as with the ordinary three-wire instruments, but as each additional train is admitted into the section a corresponding disc is brought forward; and also as the trains pass out of the section the same disc is moved back, section by section, until the line is again clear, and the indicator is left at the normal position of "line closed."

It only remains to say that the single-line block telegraph is worked by a similar kind of instrument to the three-wire (absolute block), only there is a commutator at each end, which is blocked over by the station towards which the train is running, keeping the indicators at both signal boxes at "train on line" until the arrival of the train, when they are again released.

Important as the block telegraph is, it is, of course, only an auxiliary to the working of the outdoor semaphore signals, without which it would be impossible to conduct the traffic; and the maintenance of these in a state of perfect efficiency has much to do with the punctual running of the trains. It not infrequently happens that a train will run from London, say, to Liverpool or Manchester without a single "danger" signal being exhibited, or, in other words, that there is a clear road throughout. This efficiency is to a great extent secured by the application of electricity. As is well known, expansion and contraction of the signal wires take place owing to change of temperature, the

## TELEGRAPHS.

former preventing, by the elongation of the wire, the pulling of the signal "Off," and the latter, by shortening the wire, preventing the signal from getting properly "On." It is essential that the signalman should know the exact state of his signal, although, by reason of curves or other circumstances, it may be out of his sight, and, in order that he may be so informed, electric signal repeaters have been introduced, the function of which is to send currents from the signal-post, by means of

FIG. 16.
ELECTRIC SIGNAL REPEATER AND LIGHT INDICATOR

electric contacts, to a miniature signal-post fitted in the repeating instrument at the signal-box. Up to about three years ago the arm was only shown "On" by current, and "Off" by gravity, but since that time it has been found possible to show "On" and "Off" by current and "Wrong" by gravity; and, in addition to this, the apparatus now in use shows "Light in" and "Light out," one wire, only, being required for the five indications. (See Fig. 16.)

There are many other electrical appliances used in railway working, such as "Train-starting indicators," from platform to signal-box, to inform the signalman that trains are ready to start from certain platforms; "Route indicators" for junction cabins, by means of which signalmen are advised beforehand of the route an approaching train is required to take where the roads diverge; "Vehicles on line" indicators, to show the signalman when a line is fouled by a vehicle being detached from a train and left standing on the line; "Shunting indicators" for station yards, and a variety of other electrical apparatus of a similar character. There is, however, one special appliance which merits a somewhat more detailed description, viz., the " Electric lock" for sidings. This apparatus has been designed to lock and unlock sidings at a distance from the signal-box too far to be worked by rod and lever. There is an instrument at the signal-box, and another at the siding, each containing an electro-magnet capable of actuating an armature which constitutes the lock, fixed in connection with the locking bars of the signal frame. The normal state of the apparatus is "Signals at signal-box unlocked, and siding locked," by the constant flow of a current of electricity through the electro-magnets. If a train, arriving at the signal-box, has to call at the siding, the breakman, or person in charge, intimates the fact to the signalman, who, by the insertion of an ordinary carriage key into the electrical apparatus, disconnects the wire. This has the effect of locking the signals at the signal-box and unlocking the lever at the siding, and the key can only be inserted when the signals are at "Danger." There is a code of bell signals drawn up for the guidance of the men, but it will be sufficient to say here that when the train has finished its work at the siding and is ready to go forward, the breakman communicates this by bell signal to the signal-box, and at the same time, by the turning of a button in the front of the instrument at the siding, renews the flow of current, thereby again locking the siding lever and unlocking the signals at the signal-box. The security of the system lies in the fact that, whatever operation takes place at one end, it is only in the hands of the person at the other end to reverse it.

On all the more important main lines the signalmen are enabled to converse one with another, either by means of the speaking telegraph or of the telephone, which latter is found to be a great acquisition in facilitating the working of the line, more especially through busy station yards.

The mileage of telegraph wires upon the London and North-Western system for purely railway purposes is 12,566 miles, in addition to which there are 6,942 miles of wire appropriated to the use of the Post Office, making up an aggregate of 19,508 miles of wire, while the number of battery cells in work for carrying on the telegraphic business of the Company amounts to 120,808 cells. With such an extent of wires, and so large a number of instruments and batteries in use, it becomes of great importance to provide for a complete and perfect system of maintenance and supervision; but the staff which has to be employed for the purpose is not so extensive as may at first sight appear to be requisite. A line of telegraph has this advantage over a line of railway, that the person charged with the duty of maintaining it in a proper state of repair need not walk from end to end of it in order to detect any fault or weakness. A man can stand at one end of a line of telegraph, hundreds of miles in length, and, by exchanging signals with the other end, may satisfy himself that the entire circuit is in efficient working order. Thus the work of inspection and maintenance of the extensive system of telegraphs in operation on the London and North-Western Railway is carried on by nine inspectors, three sub-inspectors, and forty-eight "linemen." The line is divided for maintenance purposes into nine sections, each of which is in charge of an inspector; and the first daily duty of each inspector is, at a stated time previous to 8.0 a.m., to test all the more important circuits under his charge, and ascertain if they are intact and working efficiently, and the results of this inspection are telegraphed at once to the office of the chief telegraph superintendent, in Manchester, so that that officer has before him, by 9.0 a.m. each day, a condensed report of the exact state of the telegraphic communications over the entire system. By these means it is known where the services of the linemen are required, and some of them are told off to execute necessary repairs, while others undertake the duties of cleaning apparatus, and refreshing batteries. As a general rule, the batteries are cleaned, or refreshed, at fixed intervals varying from ten days to a month, according to the amount of work they have to perform; but it is the duty of any operator who perceives, by the failure or weakness of the indications, that his battery power shows signs of exhaustion at once to intimate the fact to the inspector in charge of the district, and to report any neglect or delay in attending to it to the chief telegraph superintendent.

Electricians are said to be somewhat divided in

opinion as to the relative advantages of iron and copper wires for transmitting the electric current, but for overhead wires the London and North-Western Company prefer galvanised iron wires, as having greater tensile strength and superior powers of elongation and contraction, so as to allow for a considerable variation in temperature. The gauges of wire used differ according to circumstances, but the wire chiefly employed has a standard diameter of ·171 inch with a minimum tensile strength of 1,200 lbs., and is subjected to a torsion test of 20 twists in 6 inches. The average life of the wire varies very much according to locality. For instance, in the vicinity of chemical works, as at Widnes and St Helen's, the wire corrodes and requires renewal in about three years, while, in the pure atmosphere of the island of Anglesey, there are wires that have been in use for five-and-thirty years, and which recent tests show to have been very little impaired, whether as regards conductivity or tensile strength; under ordinary conditions, however, the average life of the standard wire is about 10 years.

As regards battery power, the Company use, for speaking telegraph circuits, three wire block telegraph circuits, and electric locks, the Daniell Sulphate Battery; for bell wires the Leclanché Battery; and for signal repeaters, Fuller's bichromate battery.

## CHAPTER VII.

ROLLING STOCK (I.).—ENGINES AND BRAKE-POWER.

IN order to meet the locomotive requirements of modern times, and to draw long and heavy trains at the high rates of speed now demanded by the public, there has naturally had to be a great development in the engines employed for the purpose, and indeed nothing can be more striking than the contrast between the primitive machines which were regarded as triumphs of engineering skill in the early days of railways, and the magnificent engines which are produced in these modern times. This contrast is very forcibly illustrated by our reproduction in Plate XVII. of a photograph of the old "Rocket," the first engine made by George Stephenson for the Liverpool and Manchester Railway, in 1829, which is still preserved in the South Kensington Museum, and which the reader may compare with the representation in Plate XVIII. of the "Queen Empress," which embodies perhaps the highest form of development of the passenger train engine of the present day, and which was exhibited by Mr. Francis W. Webb, the locomotive superintendent and chief mechanical engineer of the London and North-Western Railway, at the Chicago "World's Fair" in 1893. Let none, however, venture to despise the humble "Rocket," with her wheels with wooden rims, her ungainly appearance, and as we are now told, her faulty construction, for she was the fruitful mother of a race of giants! It was reserved for the engineers of a later generation to clothe Stephenson's great idea in forms of beauty and of strength, and they are entitled to all credit for the perfection they have attained; but immeasurably greater must be the fame of him whose master-mind first gave the great conception to the world, with all its infinite possibilities of development for the advancement and happiness of mankind. His achievement can only be rivalled, and can hardly be eclipsed, by the genius of the man, perhaps yet unborn, who may endow the human race with a new faculty, by teaching them to navigate the air with the same ease with which they now traverse the ocean and the land.

It is extremely interesting to turn back to the reports of the directors of the Liverpool and Manchester Railway, in 1826, and for some few years after, when the plan for working railways by means of locomotives was still hardly out of the region of experiment, and was not yet freed from a great deal of hostile and sceptical criticism. Thus we find them writing on the 27th March, 1828, when the railway was under construction and the works were well advanced :—

"The nature of the power to be used for the conveyance of goods and passengers becomes now a question of great moment, on whatever principle the carrying department may be conducted. After due consideration, the engineer has been authorised to prepare a locomotive engine which, from the nature of its construction and from the experiments already made, he is of opinion will be effective for the purposes of the Company without proving an annoyance to the public. In the course of the ensuing summer it is intended to make trials on a large scale, so as to ascertain the sufficiency in all respects of this important machine. On this subject, as on every other connected with the execution of the important task committed to his charge, the directors have every confidence in Mr. Stephenson, their principal engineer, whose ability and unwearied activity they are glad of this opportunity to acknowledge."

It is, however, clear, from the perusal of these reports, that even while the works were in progress, and the railway was actually nearing completion, the directors were still somewhat doubtful whether steam engines were the best form of motive power to adopt. Stephenson was at this time continually experimenting, altering, and effecting improvements in his original conception, but the result was not yet conclusive, and in 1829 a prize of £500 was offered for the best engine that could be devised, when Stephenson's "Rocket" was entered for competition, and was successful. The circumstances of this trial, which took place at Rainhill, have been recounted in ample detail by Mr. Francis, in his "History of the English Railway," and by others, and they need not here be recapitulated; but the result was to complete Stephenson's triumph over all his rivals, and to establish the right, which he had so justly earned, to be considered the founder of railways.

The present writer may be excused for taking a special interest in the circumstance just related, inasmuch as he was born at Rainhill in the year 1829, just about the period of the famous trial, his father, who was then engaged under George Stephenson in the construction of the principal viaducts and bridges on the Liverpool and Manchester Railway, being at that time occupied in the building of the Rainhill Skew Bridge. This bridge, which is believed to be the earliest example of an oblique arch constructed in masonry, is still standing, and is a most remarkable work. George Stephenson at this time was so pleased at the result of the trial of the "Rocket," that he presented the writer's father with an English silver lever watch (then a scarce and valuable possession), which is still preserved in the family.

The Liverpool and Manchester directors now commenced to build engines of the "Rocket" type, although with continued improvements; but, as time went on, it was found in practice that the parts were too weak to withstand the heavy wear and tear. The directors were astonished and dismayed at the large expense incurred for renewals and repairs; the engineers were spurred on to tax their inventive powers for still further improvements, and it was thought that a great triumph had been achieved when, in February, 1831, an engine called the "Samson" carried 107 tons of merchandise from Liverpool to Manchester, a distance of about 30 miles, in two hours and a half. It was not, however, until five years later (1836) that the directors felt they could congratulate themselves upon having at length obtained engines upon which they could rely, and, although no model of the engines of this period has been preserved, so far as the writer is aware, there can be no doubt that they were vastly inferior to those in use at the present day.

The London and North-Western Company now employ, for the various purposes of their traffic, engines of fourteen distinct types, and an Appendix to this chapter gives, in a tabulated form, the details of construction of these different types, including their wheel diameter, cylinders, heating surface, weight, and other particulars.

Our illustration (Plate XIX.) shows an express goods engine with six wheels coupled, cylinders 18 inches by 24 inches, and wheel diameter 5 feet.

Plate XX. shows a special tank engine for goods trains, having six wheels coupled, 4 feet 3 inches diameter, and cylinders 17 inches by 24 inches.

Plate XXI. is an engine used for drawing coal trains having 6 wheels coupled, 4 feet 3 inches diameter, and cylinders 17 inches by 24 inches.

Plate XXIA. is a representation of the eight-wheeled side tank engine, having 4 wheels coupled.

It was formerly the practice to work the express passenger trains with single engines of the "Lady of the Lake" class (see Appendix), although, later, it was found better to work the heavier trains with four-wheeled coupled engines; but these are now being superseded by compound engines of a new construction, invented by Mr. Webb, of which the "Queen Empress" (Plate XVIII.) is an example, and which may be thus described: The engines differ from the compound engines in use on other lines chiefly in the number and disposition of the cylinders, there being two high-pressure cylinders fixed outside the frames, between the leading and middle wheels (the connecting rods working on to crank pins, set at right angles to each other, in the trailing wheels), and one low-pressure cylinder carried between the main frames at the front end of the engine, the connecting rod working on to a single throw crank in the middle pair of wheels. For the benefit of non-professional readers, it may be explained that the underlying principle of a compound engine is that the steam, instead of being allowed to escape after having once done duty, is compelled, by an arrangement of duplicate cylinders, to do duty again, and thus the maximum development of power is obtained, with the minimum expenditure of fuel. The advantages claimed for the improvement are :—

(1.) That the engine, being practically balanced, runs very steadily at a high rate of speed.

(2.) That the power of the engine is distributed over two axles instead of one, as in ordinary non-compound engines, and the strain on the various parts is thus very much reduced.

(3.) The adhesion of two pairs of driving wheels has been obtained, without the use of coupling rods, which become unnecessary.

(4.) The driving wheels may be placed further apart than would be advisable if coupling rods were used, and a larger fire-box can be introduced.

(5.) With independent driving wheels there is less friction in passing round curves, and, if more convenient for the working out of the general design, each pair of wheels may have a different diameter.

The first compound engine was set to work on the London and North-Western Railway in 1881, since which time eighty-three others of the same type have been built, and have run collectively nearly 17,000,000 of miles. On their first introduction they were met, like all innovations upon recognised methods, by a great deal of hostile criticism, but it is believed that they have lived this down, and are now pretty generally admitted to be a success. An actual trial has shown that with one of these engines and a train of 321 gross tons in weight, one ton of dead weight can be hauled one mile at a speed of twenty-four miles an hour, with an expenditure of 1·26 oz. of Welsh coal, while to haul the same weight one mile at a speed increased to forty-four miles an hour required 2·06 oz. of fuel—a striking testimony to the great increase in expenses which railway companies have had to incur to keep up the high rates of speed now demanded in railway travelling. The economy of fuel effected by these engines is very considerable, and the fact is not without importance to a Company whose engines consume in the aggregate an average of 3,000 tons of coal per day, or upwards of a million tons in a year.

The compound engines are fitted with "Webb's radial axle-box," which is described as follows:—The axle-box consists of a single casting, with brasses fitted in each end for the journals, and which works between two curved guides formed of flanged plates stretching from frame to frame, thus allowing a lateral motion of $1\frac{1}{4}$ inch to the axle on either side of the centre line of the engine. Underneath the axle, and within the box, are placed two horizontal helical springs, coiled right-hand and left-hand, and working one within the other, so that when the engine enters a curve the springs are compressed to one side against cross pieces connecting the axle-box guide-plates, and the shock transmitted from the rails through the wheels is minimised, while, as soon as the engine gets on the straight line again, the springs resume their normal position, and the engine is kept central. The axle-box, as originally designed, had two sets of controlled springs placed laterally on each side of the centre line of the engine, but as it was found that there was a tendency, in the case of a broken spring, or of one set being stronger than the other, for the wheels to be forced out of the centre line when running on the straight, the present arrangement was designed to overcome the difficulty. These axle-boxes were introduced in the year 1876, and there are now over 700 of them in use on engines, with the result that, in addition to the improved running, a considerable saving has been effected in the wear and tear of the flanges of the wheel tyres.

In addition to the various types of engines enumerated in the Appendix, Mr. Webb has constructed, for certain special purposes in connection with the railway, some small engines for narrow gauge lines, in which the usual link motion is done away with, and the engine is reversed by a pair of spur wheels, one of these spur wheels being keyed in the driving axle, and the other, equal in diameter, being fixed in a counter shaft, on each end of which is a crank driving the two valve spindles. The spur wheel on the driving axle is a broad one, occupying the space between the two bearings, and the spur on the counter-shaft is a narrow one, and held in position on the shaft by a skew-key, so that, by traversing the narrow wheel across the face of the broad wheel on this key, the relative position of the counter or valve shaft with the driving axle is altered, and so the engine is reversed, thus doing away with all eccentrics and link motion. The construction is simple, and there being so few parts, and those principally having a rolling motion, the engines are not likely to get out of gear, or, if they do, they are easily put right. These engines, of which Plate XXII. contains an illustration, can be driven from either end, and only require one man to work them.

It may here be mentioned that, in order to facilitate the working of the trains, and to avoid the necessity of their having to stop to take water at places where they are not otherwise required to stop, a number of narrow troughs have been laid down between the rails at convenient distances along the main lines, which, by an automatic arrangement, are kept always filled with water. The tenders attached to the engines have a "pick up" apparatus, provided with a scoop, which can be lowered into the trough while the train is passing over it at full speed, and the tanks are filled with water in a few seconds. Thus, not only is the time saved that would otherwise be spent at the stations in pulling up, obtaining a supply of water, and getting up speed again, but it is possible to use a smaller tender containing a less quantity of water, and consequently there is less dead weight to be hauled. These troughs were first introduced by Mr. Ramsbottom in 1857, and, having since been improved and developed, have now been laid down at eleven different places on the main lines; so that a train may run through, if need be, between London and Carlisle, or Holyhead, without once having occasion to pull up at a water column. Fig. 23 shows, by means of a diagram, the manner in which a tender picks up water from the feed-trough while in motion.

The Crewe works, where the locomotive engines of the London and North-Western Company are manufactured and kept in repair, constitute the largest railway works in the world, and have come, in process of time, to be looked upon as one of the most interesting sights to be seen by almost every Royal or distinguished personage who has visited our shores for many years past, as well as by engineers and railway officials from all parts of the world, who have visited England for the purpose of acquiring information as to the methods and

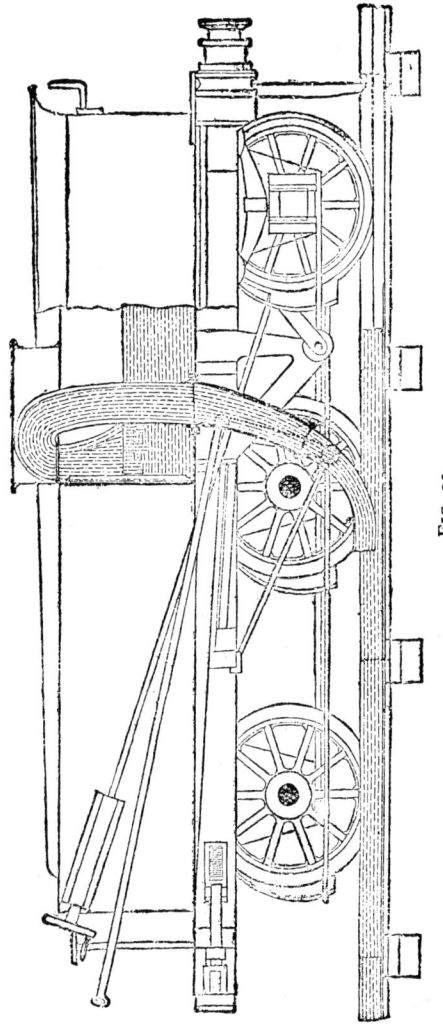

Fig. 23.

Diagram Showing a Tender Picking Up Water from a "Feed-Trough" while in Motion.

processes of railway working in this country. A brief description of the works, and of what is done there, will not, therefore, be out of place in a work of this character, which professes to give some account of the means and appliances which have resulted in causing a first-class English railway to be regarded as a model for the railways of the civilized world.

The works were originally established in 1843 for the purpose of repairing the engines, carriages, and waggons of the Grand Junction Railway, which was afterwards incorporated in the London and North-Western system, in 1846. As the locomotive requirements gradually increased, the carriage and waggon works were by degrees removed to Wolverton and Earlestown, respectively, and, since the year 1865, Crewe has been exclusively given up to the mechanical and engineering departments, and has become the chief centre of the London and North-Western Railway Company's works. In 1864 a very important addition was made to the establishment by the erection of works for the manufacture of Bessemer steel, and, as the whole of the space at that time available had been already occupied, these new works were placed a short distance from the junction, adjoining the Chester and Holyhead Railway. This railway had hitherto run through the works, but it was now thought desirable to divert it, and the land lying between the old line and the deviation was utilised for the new workshops, which thus came to be designated the "Deviation Shops," in contradistinction to the "old works." Other additions to the premises have been made from time to time as required, and the total area enclosed now amounts to about one hundred and sixteen acres; the covered shops and mills comprising thirty-six acres. It must be borne in mind, however, that at these works, not only are the engines used upon the railway made and repaired, but a number of other processes of the most varied description are carried on, including the manufacture of steel rails, signal work, the under-frames for carriages, cranes and machinery of all kinds for warehouses, girders for bridge-building, bricks, and joiners' work for houses, stables, and signal cabins, gas, water, and drain pipes, hydraulic machinery, and a multiplicity of other railway appliances far too numerous to catalogue.

The capabilities of the works are such that the Company is enabled to purchase the raw materials and to become the actual manufacturers of every part of the locomotive engines and other machinery constructed at Crewe, with the exception of brass tubes and copper plates.

In fact, it would be difficult to specify any way in which a person of enquiring mind, and with the least turn for mechanics, could spend a day more profitably, or more agreeably, than in making a tour of the extensive and multifarious workshops at the Crewe works. Here is to be seen the building of an engine, from the casting of the steel from which she is constructed, to the final coat of paint which completes her adornment; while the intermediate processes are so many and the innumerable parts pass through so many hands, no man seeing more than his own individual share of the work, that the visitor is filled with admiration for the master-mind that is able to combine all this bewildering and complicated mechanism and the work of all these busy hands and brains, into one perfect whole—a modern locomotive.

The total number of engines constructed at these works from their establishment up to the end of May, 1890, was 3,135, of which no less than 146 were constructed in one year, viz., the year ending the 30th November, 1872. In addition to constructive works, however, about 2,000 engines annually undergo repairs there being usually about 330 in the works for that purpose at one time.

The old works are now entirely devoted to the manufacture and repair of engines, and contain a shop for their erection, three repairing shops, a wheel shop, a fitting and turning shop, a smithy and forge, and a spring shop and copper smithy, as also the offices and general stores. With the exception of the light forgings and smiths' work made in this smithy, the various parts of the engines are brought to the old works in their rough state from other portions of the works; for instance, the frames and other wrought-iron plates come from the plate mill; the crank and straight axles, the tyres, the spring steel, the coupling and connecting rods, and other steel forgings come from the forge at the steel works; and the cylinders, wheels, horn blocks, axle-boxes, and other iron and brass castings come from the foundry. The different portions of the finished work ultimately find their way to the erecting shop, where the actual fabric of the engine is built up, and, as soon as the frame or skeleton is complete, the boiler is added. The engine is then grasped by two overhead travelling cranes, reaching down like giant hands, and is run bodily out of the shop in order that the boilers may be tested. This done, it is conveyed back to the shop, and the boiler is covered in, and all the remaining portions of the internal machinery and the external fittings are added, when the cranes again seize the engine and convey it to the paint shop. Meanwhile the tender has been constructed in another shop. It is now coupled to the engine, the two are painted, and, after receiving a trial, are ready for service. The usual time required in the erecting shop for building an engine is about four weeks, while the shortest time in which any engine has been built in this shop in the ordinary way of business is fourteen days. As an illustration, however, of what could be accomplished at these works in case of emergency, it may be mentioned that some time ago, as an experiment, the erection of an engine was commenced at six a.m. on a Monday, and at one o'clock on the following Wednesday, or within a space of twenty-five-and-a-half working hours from the time the frame plates were selected and laid down, the engine was finished, and in steam, and ready to work a train.

In the fitting shop, which, to the unaccustomed eye, presents a most bewildering appearance, with its endless ramification of pulleys, shafting, revolving wheels, and machinery of every description, all kinds of operations connected with the making of the various parts of an engine may be seen in progress. Here are turning lathes, planing, shaping, slotting, boring, and drilling machines. Here are made the cylinders, the pistons, the valves, connecting rods, injectors, axle-boxes, and a hundred other small fittings and castings, all these being adjusted to standard gauges suitable to the various *classes* of engines, without respect to the individual engine for which they may happen to be used. Thus, to a great extent, the interchangeability of parts is secured, so much so, that four of the standard classes of engines have many of their parts exactly alike, and any of these could be taken from one engine and fitted to another without difficulty, the result being to secure the greatest economy in effecting repairs. To such an extent is this principle carried, that when, as is sometimes the case, one of a pair of cylinders in an engine is damaged, a new cylinder can be straightway procured from the fitting shop and bolted to the remaining one, without any further fitting being required.

The nuts, bolts, pins, and a good many of the small parts are prepared by boys, who enter the works as apprentices, and remain at this work for some time before being drafted out as journeymen in the various branches.

The wheel shop, where the wheels and axles of the engines are constructed, is fitted with large and powerful machinery, suitable for the work which has to be carried on, some of the lathes being capable of turning a pair of wheels as much as 8 feet 9 inches in diameter. Interesting features in this shop are the "roughing lathe," in which seven cutting tools are employed at one time in "roughing out" the crank axles, and the "nibbling machine," designed for cutting out the "throws" in the cranks, and which has no less than 160 cutting tools arranged round the circumference of a large disc. An ingenious mechanical contrivance exists in this shop for lifting the wheels and axles into the lathes and other machines. It consists of a series of light jib cranes travelling on a single rail laid on the floor of the shop, parallel with the lathes, and worked by a cotton cord $\frac{5}{8}$ of an inch in diameter, running at the rate of a mile a minute, by which motion is transmitted to the various parts of the cranes. These latter travel along the shop, wherever they are required, at the rate of 80 feet per minute, and lift their loads at the rate of 9 feet per minute. Special light machinery of a similar type has been provided also in the erecting shop, and in the various repairing shops, and is found almost invaluable in facilitating the operations to be carried on.

One portion of the works which seldom fails to interest visitors is the steel works, which, at the time of their opening in 1864, consisted of a converting house with two converters, a cogging shop, and a small forge, but have since been greatly enlarged, the steel-making plant being now capable of producing 50,000 tons of steel per annum, besides which there have been added a large forge, iron, brass and steel foundries, rail-rolling mills, a boiler shop, and several repairing and other shops. To those who are not acquainted with the Bessemer process of converting iron into steel, a brief description of the operation may be interesting

The converting plant consists of four retorts or vessels, each holding 5 tons, and arranged in two groups, with the cupolas behind them. The pig-iron is first melted in a cupola, to which the air is supplied by a Root's blower, after which the liquid metal is run into a huge ladle moving on a line of rails, and is conveyed to the converting vessel. This latter is lined with ganister, and in the bottom of it are a number of small holes, through which air is injected upwards through the molten mass, the oxygen of the air combining with and eliminating the carbon of the iron, and keeping up a fierce combustion until the whole of the impurities are ejected. The blowing is continued for some fifteen or twenty minutes, until the metal is thoroughly decarbonized, when the process ceases, and a quantity, varying according to the quality of steel required, of "spiegeleisen," an iron highly charged with carbon and manganese, previously melted in a furnace, is run into the converting vessel, and combines chemically with the decarbonized iron. The vessel is now turned down and the liquid steel is poured out into a ladle carried at the end of a crane, the crane swings round, and the steel runs out through a small orifice in the bottom of the ladle into cast-iron moulds, and is thus formed into ingots ready to be used for making rails, or for any other purpose required. The air is supplied to the converting vessels by a fine pair of horizontal blowing engines of 450 horse-power, made by Hick, Hargreaves & Co., of Bolton. The steam cylinders are 36 inches in diameter and have a stroke of 5 feet, and the air cylinders are 48 inches in diameter with the same stroke. There are also three reheating furnaces, in which the steel ingots, as they come from the converter, can be reheated, and taken direct to the rolling mill.

The rail-making plant has an annual capacity of 45,000 tons, the rolling mill being driven by a Corliss condensing engine, developing, in ordinary working, about 700 h.p. The rails, while hot, are sawn off to the required length by a circular saw, and, after cooling, are drilled and straightened ready for use.

The powerful forge machinery consists of a duplex steam hammer of 30 tons, and one of 10 tons, together with eight vertical steam hammers weighing from 15 cwt. to 8 tons, tyre rolling, plate rolling, and merchant mills, saws, and shearing machines. The 30-ton hammer was designed by Mr. Ramsbottom, the late chief mechanical engineer of the Company, and consists of two huge blocks, each weighing 30 tons, moving upon rails, with eight small wheels. The blocks are actuated by steam cylinders placed behind them, and on steam being admitted to these, the blocks are propelled with enormous force against the mass to be forged, which is held between them.

An interesting machine to watch in operation, is the large circular saw, 7 feet in diameter, which is used for sawing off the crop ends of forgings, and which is driven by an engine at a great velocity, running at no less speed than 13,000 feet per minute. This will cut its way through an iron axle 9 inches in diameter in 30 seconds.

The tyre mill, plate mill, and merchant mills require no detailed description, as, although the machinery employed is powerful and admirable of its kind, it is analogous to what may be seen at work in other rolling mills, and possesses no features of special interest.

In the steel works there are fifty furnaces for heating the metal, all of which are Siemens' Regenerative Gas Furnaces. There are also seven for making steel by the Siemens'-Martin process, viz., five 20-ton, and two 10-ton furnaces. The gas for the furnaces is generated in a series of forty-nine gas producers, the gas being conveyed to the furnaces in underground pipes.

Steam is supplied to the various engines and steam hammers by two ranges of stationary boilers, each range consisting of eight boilers of the Lancashire type, 7 feet in diameter, and 30 feet long, with double flues, and constructed entirely of steel plates.

The engine repairing shops occupy an extensive range

of buildings, 993 feet long, and 106 feet wide, and are fitted with wheel lathes for turning the tyres of the engine wheels as they become worn, and with all kinds of machinery for effecting the necessary repairs to the various parts of an engine. They are also furnished with boiling pans for removing the oil and grease from the parts when they are taken to pieces for repairs, so that they are turned out well cleaned at very little cost, the grease removed being collected and converted into soap.

It may here be mentioned that up till about the year 1873, the attempts which had been from time to time made to introduce steel into the manufacture of boilers, had resulted in failure, but at the International Exhibition in Vienna, in 1873, a locomotive boiler and fire-box were sent from the boiler shop at Crewe, which were fine specimens of boiler work, and were constructed entirely of steel, and since that time no less than 2,863 locomotive, and 218 stationary boilers, have been made of that material without a single case of failure having occurred other than those due to ordinary wear and tear. The greatest care is taken to ensure the selection of reliable plates for the boilers, a piece being cut from each plate and subjected to the most severe tests of all kinds, and a register being kept of the result of the tests, and of the position occupied by every plate in each boiler.

Extensive brick-making plant exists at Crewe, consisting of two brick-making machines, and a large circular kiln, and drying sheds, the turn-out being some five or six millions of bricks in a year.

The "Deviation Works" previously referred to, consist of a range of shops built alongside the deviation of the Chester and Holyhead Railway, and comprise a chain and plate testing shop, a millwright's shop, devoted to the manufacture and repair of all the shafting and machinery in the works, shops for the making of cranes, warehouse machinery, and stationary engines, joiners' and pattern makers' shops, saw mills, &c.

The check upon stores of all kinds used in the works is very strict, and necessarily so; the stores are kept at the old works, and not the smallest article can be obtained from them without a written order signed by one of the foremen, none but the storekeepers being permitted to enter the stores.

A notable feature in the life of the Crewe works is the narrow-gauge railway, of which nearly five miles have been laid down, traversing every part of the works. The gauge of this railway is eighteen inches, and it is worked by small locomotive engines of the type shewn by Plate XXII., which draw trains of strong, low-wheeled trollies, conveying materials and finished work from one part of the premises to another. It also affords a ready means of locomotion for the workmen and officials from point to point, and visitors to the works seldom fail to make acquaintance with it.

Dining, or "mess" rooms, are provided at Crewe for the convenience of the artisans who live at a distance from the works, and here they can leave their food in the morning, and have it prepared and placed ready for them when dinner-time arrives.

The number of persons of all classes employed in these works is about 6,500, but in addition there are some 713 engine-drivers, firemen, cleaners, and others at the steam sheds at Crewe station, making a total of upwards of 7,200 persons employed in connection with the locomotive department at Crewe. Although the steam sheds referred to form no part of the Crewe works properly so-called, they yet contribute in no slight degree to the establishment of Crewe as the most important locomotive centre of the London and North-Western Railway. About 150 engines are kept in steam at this station daily, for the stabling of which suitable sheds have been provided, covering an area of nearly 3¾ acres. Here the waste and sponge cloths used for cleaning engines all over the London and North-Western system are washed and dried, and afterwards returned to the stations from which they have been received; the oil and grease collected from them in the process of cleansing being converted into soap, to be used in the various steam sheds.

The Company manufacture and supply gas, not only to their own works, but to the whole town of Crewe, and they also supply water to the works and to the town, the supply being derived from the red sandstone at Whitmore, about twelve miles distant, on the Crewe and Stafford Railway. The water is pumped from a large well into reservoirs, and descends to Crewe by gravitation.

Crewe, which previous to the establishment of the locomotive works was inhabited only by a few farmers and cottagers, has now developed into a flourishing town of thirty thousand inhabitants, composed almost entirely of the Company's workmen and their families, and the tradesmen who supply their wants. In 1877 the town applied for and obtained a charter of incorporation, and Mr. F. W. Webb, the chief superintendent of the works, was elected Mayor for the Jubilee year (1887), being re-elected for the year 1888. In commemoration of Her Majesty's Jubilee, and of the fiftieth anniversary of the opening of the railway through Crewe, the Company presented the town with a public park, about forty acres in extent, which was dedicated by Sir Richard Moon, Bart., chairman of the Company, on the 4th July, 1887, and was formally opened to the public by H.R.H. the Duke of Cambridge, on the 9th June, 1888.

The Company have built, and are the owners of, nearly 850 houses occupied by their workpeople, in addition to which a considerable number have been built by the workmen themselves. The town being almost entirely dependent upon the works, and constituting, in fact, a veritable railway colony, the directors have aided by their countenance, and by material support, every public movement deserving of their liberality. They have erected and endowed a church belonging to the Establishment, and have subscribed to the expenses of building several places of worship of other denominations; have established large schools for the education of the children of the men employed in the works, and erected public baths. They have also provided a Mechanics' Institute, which contains a library of more than 8,000 volumes, a comfortable reading-room, well supplied with newspapers, periodicals, and magazines; class-rooms, a smoking-room, a gymnasium, and a lecture hall seating 800 persons. During the winter months evening classes are held for the instruction, both in elementary and advanced subjects, of the young people employed in the works during the day, and these are largely attended, the fact that since 1871 no less than twenty-four of the students have been successful in gaining Whitworth scholarships, being a sufficient testimony to the character of the results accomplished at this institution.

The question of Brake-power is one which has an intimate relation to the locomotive department, since it is the great development in the speed and power of the engines employed, which has led to the imperative necessity of devising equally powerful means for bringing the trains quickly to a stand in case of need, and the Company has adopted a system of continuous brake known as the "Automatic Vacuum," with which the whole of their stock has already been fitted. This brake is applied to all the vehicles of a train, except the engine and tender, which are fitted with a separate steam brake. Each carriage carries its own length of train-pipe, flexible hose, and universal couplings; also a double vacuum "sack" combining the advantages of a brake cylinder and reservoir in one, the latter being supplied with a flexible diaphragm and connected through the piston rods with the brake rigging. The piston rods work through flexible stuffing-boxes attached to the bottom of the sack, and which adapt themselves to every movement of the rod, but prevent the air from leaking into the sack when it is not required to do so. Attached to the train-pipe, and in connection with the reservoir and the top and bottom of the sack, is an automatic cock, with a valve inside the plug through which the air passes to and from the train-pipe, so that when the air is being exhausted it is drawn from the reservoir, and the top and bottom of the sack, but when air is admitted to the train-pipe, the valve in the cock closes the connection to the reservoir, but leaves the ends of the sack open to the train-pipe. While the train is running a continual vacuum is maintained in the train-pipes and double vacuum sacks, by means of a small ejector or air pump on the engine, and in this condition the brakes are "off," but when it is desired to apply them, air is admitted into the train-pipe by the driver or guard; the valve in the automatic cock moves as previously described, and the pressure of the atmosphere, acting on the outside of the diaphragms, pulls in the piston rods and applies the brakes. The same result ensues if the train becomes separated or a coupling breaks, air being thus admitted to the train-pipe, and the brakes being applied automatically throughout the train.

When the brakes have been applied, and it is desired to take them off again, all that is necessary is to renew the vacuum by means of the ejector with which the engine is fitted, this being done while the engine is standing. The driver's brake valve on the engine is so arranged that both the steam and vacuum brakes can be applied simultaneously by one movement of a lever, and, in fact, when the engine is connected to a train, one cannot be applied by the driver without the other. The guards' vans are also fitted with a valve which enables the guards to apply the vacuum brake, but the valves on the engine are so arranged that, when the guard thus applies the vacuum brake, the air in the train-pipe causes the steam brake also to be applied on the engine. By means of the automatic cock previously referred to, the brake on each vehicle may be released while shunting is going on, and may also be shut off if the brake gear is out of order, leaving the train-pipe intact throughout the train.

## CHAPTER VIII.

### Rolling Stock (II.).—Carriages.

Mention has already been made in a previous chapter of the rude accommodation with which the earlier railway passengers of half a century ago had to content themselves, as compared with the luxurious conditions of modern travel. As illustrative of this wide difference, our illustration (Plate XXIV.) reproduces an old print showing two of the trains which were actually run upon the Liverpool and Manchester railway at, or soon after, its opening. One of these, which apparently represents the very earliest form of passenger train, is drawn by an engine which is a species of first cousin to the famous "Rocket." All the vehicles, as will be seen, are fully exposed to the weather, except for a slight awning overhead, and only a portion of the passengers are indulged with seats, the vehicles, being, in fact, not unlike an open goods waggon of the present day. The upper portion of the picture shows a train containing somewhat superior accommodation, for all the carriages are covered in, although we may be sure that the internal fittings of these ungainly vehicles were very different to the elegantly-furnished saloons of 1894. It will be observed, too, that the luggage of the passengers is piled on the roofs of the carriages, which elevated situation is also occupied by the guards, and that all the carriages have names, "The Traveller," "The Times," etc., like their predecessors, the stage coaches, which they have but recently superseded. Finally, a party of travellers are seen riding in their own family carriage, mounted upon a low truck without removing the wheels, and only dispensing with the horses. Modern advertisements of the running of excursion trains upon railways, frequently to this day announce the fares as "First class—Covered carriages"— and it is well understood that the term "Covered carriages," thus employed, is synonymous with "third class"; but not every one is aware that this expression is really a lingering survival of the period when railway companies, in announcing an excursion, held out the inducement of what was then the unwonted luxury of covered vehicles for the lower classes of passengers.

A striking contrast to the primitive conveyances of fifty years ago is the passenger carriage shown by Plate XXV., which is a specimen of the latest development of the art of carriage-building in these modern times. Forty-two feet in length, with accommodation for three classes of passengers, and a compartment for their luggage, provided with a lavatory for the first-class passengers, mounted upon the easiest of springs, well lighted by gas, and warmed during the winter, adorned with ornamental woods and the handsomest upholsterer's work, and replete with every convenience and comfort throughout, it embodies in fact in a high degree, the latest development of modern civilization as exemplified in railway travelling.

The London and North-Western Company possesses a stock of upwards of 5,000 passenger carriages, of which about 350 are forty-two feet in length, and the remainder vary from thirty feet to thirty-four feet in length. The whole carriage stock of the Company contains seating accommodation for 191,030 passengers in the following proportions:—

| | |
|---|---:|
| First class | 21,977 |
| Second class | 24,326 |
| Third class | 144,727 |
| | 191,030 |

these proportions being very carefully considered and adjusted from time to time in building additional carriages, or renewing old ones, so as to preserve the proper ratio of each class to the others. The Midland Company, as is well known, in the year 1875 decided upon abolishing second class compartments in their trains, and retaining only two classes, viz., first and third; but the wisdom of the experiment was believed by many of the companies to be open to serious question; whether upon financial grounds, or as a matter of public convenience. The London and North-Western Company maintained the belief that society in this country, for all purposes, naturally divided itself into three classes, and that the wants and tastes of the community were best served by their present practice, in which belief, apparently, they were supported by the great body of railway opinion in the country, since no other company has until recently followed the example of the the Midland Company. Within the last year or two, however, the North-Eastern, Manchester, Sheffield, and Lincolnshire, Cambrian, and some of the Scotch companies have adopted the Midland system and abolished the second class, while the Great Northern Company have done so to a great extent,

Although, nominally, the passengers who travel upon the London and North-Western Railway are divided into three classes, there are, in a manner of speaking, four classes, for the saloon passengers almost constitute a class in themselves, paying, in some cases, a slightly higher fare than first class, and enjoying superior accommodation. The North-Western have not seen their way to follow the example of their great rivals (the Midland Company) in introducing "Pullman Cars," as used in the United States, in their trains; but they have filled the places of these with saloon carriages of their own construction, which, in their belief, are quite equal, if not superior in some respects, to the Pullman Cars. These are run, as sleeping carriages, in all the night trains between London and Scotland, Holyhead (for Ireland), Liverpool, and Manchester; and, for the payment of a very moderate fee over and above the first class fare, the passenger can secure a berth in one of them, and accomplish his journey without any of the weariness and discomfort which, until some few years ago, rendered a night journey to the North an experience to be dreaded, and by all means, if possible, to be avoided.

The saloon is supplied with lavatory accommodation, and the passenger, being awakened by the attendant when nearing his journey's end, can make his toilet, enjoy a cup of tea or coffee, provided by the attendant, and alight at his destination refreshed and prepared to commence his business without losing time in repairing the fatigue of the journey. Saloon carriages are also available at all times for parties travelling by day trains, on payment of a certain minimum number of fares, and drawing-room carriages, luxuriously fitted up with couches, easy-chairs, and tables, are run by the principal express trains between London and Liverpool, seats in which can be obtained on application in advance by telephone or otherwise, without any charge over and above the first class fare.

Another great boon recently conferred upon railway travellers has been the introduction, by each of the three rival routes between England and Scotland, of corridor trains, having a communication throughout from end to end, and containing dining saloons for first and third class passengers. These trains are magnificently fitted up, and replete with every comfort and convenience that modern ingenuity has devised.

The London and North-Western Company have for many years built their own carriages at their Wolverton works, situated about midway between London and Birmingham. These works cover an area of about fifty acres, and are traversed by what was formerly the main line of the London and Birmingham Railway, but the line has since been deviated, and the old railway has been converted into sidings within the works. In the old days of the London and Birmingham Railway, Wolverton was a kind of "half-way house," and was fixed upon for that reason as the chief locomotive centre; but when the London and Birmingham became amalgamated with other undertakings, some of them reaching to the extreme North and West, and blossomed into the London and North-Western, it was found more convenient to remove the locomotive works to Crewe, and since 1877 the works at Wolverton have been devoted exclusively to the building and repair of carriages and other vehicles used in passenger trains, of parcel carts and vans, omnibuses, station furniture, office fittings, and many other requirements, both for trains and for stations. For all these various purposes,

## ROLLING STOCK—CARRIAGES.

the carriage department employs 2,234 workmen at Wolverton, besides 489 at other workshops which have been established at Euston and Crewe, and 731 men engaged at out stations in executing small repairs, and in cleaning, lamping, and examining the carriages. In the old days, when a journey of moderate length occupied a much longer time than it does now, the Wolverton passenger station was a very important place, having extensive refreshment and dining rooms, but the traveller of to-day is only on the threshold of his journey from London to the North when his train dashes through Wolverton without even deigning to stop there.

With the consent of our readers we will now pay a visit to the Wolverton Works, and endeavour to gain some insight into the method in which the rolling-stock of a great railway is built up and maintained. The smaller companies, of course, do not build their own carriages, but obtain them from one or other of the firms of railway carriage manufacturers in the country.

Entering at the main gateway, facing the old London and Birmingham Railway, and, for the moment, passing by the extensive ranges of shops devoted to various purposes, which meet the eye, we first visit (by way of beginning at the beginning) the timber stores, containing at all times a two years' supply of the raw materials of which the carriages are constructed. Here we find the spoils of the West Indian and American forests in the shape of huge logs of mahogany, baywood, pine, and Quebec oak, the East Indies being represented by teak, largely used in the framing and fittings of the carriages, while English oak and ash are not wanting. Overhead is a high-speed travelling crane which, as we are looking on, seizes one of the great logs in its powerful grasp, and lifts it on to two trucks, standing upon a miniature railway of two feet gauge, which runs throughout the works. The log is rapidly run into the saw mill, and is met on its entrance either by a large circular saw, which speedily converts it into planks, or by a frame saw, which cuts it into boards or panels as required. The planks are next cut into scantling of standard sizes, and are sent to the drying shed to season, or if they already consist of seasoned timber, they are at once marked out, and fashioned into the various parts of a carriage by some of the numerous machines of complex construction and bewildering variety which may be seen on all sides, performing the most complicated operations with the utmost apparent ease and rapidity. Meanwhile, however, we follow our log of unseasoned timber in its new form of planks, or scantling, to the drying shed, where we are shown timber of every description, and of all shapes and sizes, stacked symmetrically, and with the greatest neatness and exactitude, for seasoning, together with piles of mahogany panels, and of veneers of walnut, sycamore, ebony, and various other decorative woods, used for ornamental purposes. These are all labelled and dated, and receive, we are assured, as much anxious care and attention as a connoisseur would bestow upon his bins of choice vintages, for much depends upon the skilful selection and preparation of the materials from which the carriages are built.

The parts and sections, which we have seen cut out of the seasoned timber in the saw mill, are run by means of the small tramway into what is termed the "body shop," where they are put together by the coach-makers, and begin to assume the rough outline of the body of a carriage. This is raised by a crane, and lowered on to the under-frame already prepared for it, and which is constructed of channel steel, with Mansel wheels and radial axles. The vehicle, in its rough state, is next taken forward to another shop, where it undergoes long and tedious processes of rubbing-down, painting and varnishing; and meanwhile, the internal fittings, linings, and other upholsterers' work, which have been prepared in various shops devoted to such purposes, are put in, and the break gear and gas fittings are added. Finally, when the carriage is quite complete, it is placed in a cool airy shed, for the paint and varnish to thoroughly harden, before it is turned out for use in trains.

The making of the wheels for the carriages is a very interesting process, and will repay a visit to the wheel shop. The wheels are made without spokes, the centres being solidly built up by segments of teak compressed by hydraulic power. Passing the formidable double row of wheel lathes, which, with apparently very little attention from the workmen, are cutting long spiral shavings of steel from the tyres very much as one pares an apple with a sharp knife, or boring out tyres, and cutting the grooves for the retaining rings, which, when in position render it impossible for the tyre to leave the wheel, even if it is broken into several pieces, we arrive at the machinery by which the wheels are finally put together. A steel tyre, spun from a solid block of Bessemer steel, without a weld, is swung up by a hydraulic crane on to the press, the teak segments, already cut and shaped with the greatest nicety by an automatic machine in the saw mill, are placed in position within the circumference of the tyre; the press is closed up, and a handle is turned, which sets the hydraulic ram in motion. Soon we hear the solid teak blocks begin to groan as they are forced into the tyre, and with a few loud thumps they are driven home, when the press is opened, and the wood-centre is seen to be as compact as if it were fashioned out of one piece of timber. Nothing remains but to add the retaining ring and boss plates; another hydraulic press forces the wheel and its fellow on to the axle and keys them up; and one more pair of wheels is added to the many thousands that are ceaselessly rushing to and fro upon the iron highway.

Making a tour of the premises, we shall observe that there are special shops and rooms for almost every portion of the work which has to be carried on. Here for instance, is a shop devoted to the fine cabinet work required for the internal fitting and decoration of the carriages, and close at hand is a room where a staff of girls is employed in French polishing. The body shop, paint shop, and drying rooms, we have already seen; but here is a carpenters' shop, where furniture, ticket-cases, barrows, and similar articles are made; a smithy, where brawny workmen are wielding the heavy sledge-hammers, and fashioning all kinds of intricate ironwork; a spring makers' shop; brass and iron foundries, where casting is going on, and the molten metal is spurting from the cupola furnaces; a lamp shop, with its deafening sound of the ceaseless tapping of tinmen's hammers, and rooms where women are busily engaged in cutting out and making up the trimmings and linings of the carriages; while everywhere we cannot fail to be struck by the ingenious mechanical appliances which mimimise the labour, and secure uniformity in the work, although these are too numerous and complicated to be described.

Before leaving the works we must pay a visit to the laundry, where some half-dozen women are engaged in washing the linen and towels used in the saloon carriages, all of which are sent to Wolverton daily to be washed, in exchange for a clean supply, about 4,500 articles being thus dealt with every week. Most of the work is done by steam, supplied by a small vertical boiler, the linen being dried in a hot closet, and very scrupulously aired before being sent away, so that passengers never need have before their eyes the fear of damp sheets, in the sleeping saloons.

It is a somewhat interesting sight to watch the operation of paying the large number of men engaged in these works; and the method employed to facilitate the task, and avoid mistakes or disputes, is not without ingenuity. The whole of the men employed are numbered consecutively from one upwards, and at pay-time they arrange themselves in numerical order in a large yard, so as to form a *queue*, and pass the pay-window in single file. Each man, as he passes the window, hands in his pay check, and receives in return a tin box stamped with his number, and containing his wages. At the end of the passage is a receptacle, into which he throws the empty box, this being considered his receipt for the money; since any question as to the correctness of the amount must be raised before he parts with the box. The money is, of course, counted out and placed in the boxes beforehand, and so simple is the process, and so expert are the clerks employed, that the whole of the men, upwards of 2,000 in number, are paid and the business is at an end in less than half-an-hour.

The physical and moral welfare of the men are not lost sight of, but are promoted in many ways. There is,

## DESCRIPTION OF TYPES OF ENGINES IN USE C
### GOODS ENGINES.

PASSEN

| PARTICULARS. | 5 ft. Six Wheels Coupled Special D.X. Class. | 5 ft. Six Wheels Coupled 18 in. Goods Class. | 4 ft. 3 in. Six Wheels Coupled (Coal Trains). | 4 ft. 3 in. Six Wheels Coupled Coal Side Tank Engine. | 7 ft. 6 in. "Lady of the Lake" Class. | 6 ft. 6 in. Straight Link Engine. | 6 ft. Straight Link Engine. |
|---|---|---|---|---|---|---|---|
| Cylinders— Diameter | 17 in. | 18 in. | 17 in. | 17 in. | 16 in. | 17 in. | 17 in. |
| Stroke | 24 in. | 24 in | 24 in. | 24 in. | 24 in. | 24 in. | 24 in. |
| Diameter of Driving Wheels | 5 ft. | 5 ft. | 4 ft. 3 in. | 4 ft. 3 in. | 7 ft. 6 in. | 6 ft. 6 in. | 6 ft. |
| Wheel Base | 15 ft. 6 in. | 15 ft. 6 in. | 15 ft. 6 in. | 21 ft. 3 in. | 15 ft. 5 in. | 15 ft. 8 in. | 15 ft. 8 in. |
| Heating Surface Tubes | sq. ft. 980·0 | sq. ft. 980·0 | sq. ft. 980·0 | sq. ft. 980·0 | sq. ft. 981·4 | sq. ft. 980·0 | sq. ft. 980·0 |
| Fire Box | 94·6 | 103·5 | 94·6 | 94·6 | 87·3 | 103·5 | 103·5 |
| Total | 1,074·6 | 1,083·5 | 1,074·6 | 1,074·6 | 1,068·7 | 1,083·5 | 1,083·5 |
| Grate Area | 17·1 ft. | 17·1 ft. | 17·1 ft. | 17·1 ft. | 15 ft. | 17·1 ft. | 17·1 ft. |
| Weight in Working Order | tons. cwts. 31  0 | tons. cwts. 35  4 | tons. cwts. 29  11 | tons. cwts. 43  0 | tons. cwts. 29  6 | tons. cwts. 32  15 | tons. cwts. 33  4 |
| Weight on Driving Wheels | { 31  0 3 pairs coupled. } | { 35  4 3 pairs coupled. } | { 29  11 3 pairs coupled. } | { 33  11 3 pairs coupled. } | { 11  10 1 pair } | { 22  10 2 pairs coupled. } | { 22  17 2 pairs coupled. } |

CREWE WORKS, 9*th Oct.*, 1893.

# THE LONDON AND NORTH-WESTERN RAILWAY.

ENGINES.      COMPOUND PASSENGER ENGINES.

| . 6 in. Tank ngine. | 4 ft. 6 in. Side Tank Engine (Eight Wheeled). | 4 ft. 6 in. Side Tank Engine (Six Wheeled). | 7 ft. Compound Engine (Eight Wheeled) | 7 ft. Compound Engine (Six Wheeled) | 6 ft. 6 in Compound Engine. | 6 ft. Compound Engine. |
|---|---|---|---|---|---|---|
| 7 in. | 17 in. | 17 in. | 2 High Pressure Cylinders 15 in. diameter 24 in. stroke. | 2 High Pressure Cylinders 14 in. diameter 24 in. stroke. | 2 High Pressure Cylinders 13 in. diameter 24 in. stroke. | 2 High Pressure Cylinders 14 in. diameter 24 in. stroke. |
| 4 in. | 20 in. | 20 in. | 1 Low Pressure Cylinder 30 in. diameter 24 in. stroke. | 1 Low Pressure Cylinder 30 in. diameter 24 in. stroke. | 1 Low Pressure Cylinder 26 in. diameter 24 in. stroke. | 1 Low Pressure Cylinder 30 in. diameter 24 in. stroke. |
| . 6 in. | 4 ft. 6 in. | 4 ft. 6 in. | 7 ft. | 7 ft. | 6 ft. 6 in. | 6 ft. |
| t. 5 in. | 21 ft. 3 in. | 14 ft. 6 in. | 23 ft. 8 in. | 18 ft. 1 in. | 17 ft. 7 in. | 18 ft. 1 in. |
| . ft. 80·0 | sq. ft. 886·8 | sq. ft. 886·8 | sq. ft. 1,381·2 Firebox and Combustion Chamber. | sq. ft. 1,241·3 | sq. ft. 980·0 | sq. ft. 1,241·3 |
| 94·6 | 84·8 | 84·8 | 159·7 | 159·1 | 103·5 | 159·1 |
| 074·6 | 971·6 | 971·6 | 1,540·9 | 1,400·4 | 1,083·5 | 1,400·4 |
| 1 ft. | 14·2 ft. | 14·2 ft. | 20·5 ft. | 20·5 ft. | 17·1 ft. | 20·5 ft. |
| . cwts. 10 | tons. cwts. 45  18 | tons. cwts. 38  4 | tons. cwts. 52  2 | tons. cwts. 45  10 | tons. cwts. 37  15 | tons. cwts. 42  10 |
| 18 pairs pled | 26  16 2 pairs coupled. | 28  8 2 pairs coupled. | 31  0 2 pairs *not* coupled. | 31  0 2 pairs *not* coupled. | 27  7 2 pairs *not* coupled. | 30  0 2 pairs *not* coupled. |

for instance, a spacious dining-hall, with accommodation for 1,000 men, each seat being provided with a coffee can and cup, and a cooking tin. Adjoining the dining-hall are large kitchens fitted with ovens, boilers, and hot-plates, where the workmen can either procure their meals at a small cost, or can bring their own provisions, and have them cooked free of charge.

Near the works are schools, largely supported by the Company, where the children of the workmen are educated for a very small fee, while near the schools is a Science and Art Institute, a handsome brick building, in which so much good work is being done, that an extension of the premises will very shortly be necessary. The Company have provided also a spacious recreation ground near the station, and the men can boast of a promising amateur athletic club, cricket and football clubs, and a strong and efficient company of the County Volunteers.

Wolverton, to a great extent, resembles Crewe in being a railway colony, the inhabitants of which are all engaged in one occupation, and although a considerable number of young women are employed in the works, there were formerly a great many girls, the daughters of the workmen, who could find no occupation. Seeing this difficulty, Messrs. McCorquodale and Co., the Company's stationery contractors, considerately came to the rescue, and by erecting a large envelope factory in the immediate neighbourhood, have provided suitable employment for tne surplus female population.

Apart from the carriage works at Wolverton, the superintendent of the carriage department has under his orders, at what are termed "Out-stations," a staff of nearly 1,200 men, who are engaged in the repair, examination, greasing, lamping, washing, cleaning, and warming of the carriages throughout the system, and it may be useful to give some account of the manner in which these very necessary operations are carried on.

*Examination.*—About one hundred carriage examiners are employed, who are stationed singly or in small gangs at the most important stations and junctions from one end of the line to the other. Before any man is appointed to a post of this kind he must have had previous experience in the lifting and repairs of carriages in the shops, and it is his duty to carefully examine the wheels, springs, and other running parts of all carriages standing at, or passing through, his station, tapping every wheel-tyre with his hammer, so that his experienced ear may detect by the sound whether they are in good order and without flaw. Where no special staff of coach repairers is employed, the examiner has also to attend to slight repairs of internal fittings, defective locks, etc. At the more important stations pits are provided between the rails to enable the examiners to get beneath the carriages to inspect the under-gear.

*Greasing.*—This is attended to by men stationed at the principal stations and junctions under the orders of the examiners, their duty being simply to examine the axle-boxes of every carriage passing through their station, and replenish them with oil or grease when required.

*Washing.*—Every carriage is washed outside with water once each day, the water being usually obtained from cast-iron tanks let into the ground, with a self-acting ball-valve. The buckets can thus be filled instantaneously, without the loss of time involved in drawing water into them from a tap. At the large stations there are sheds specially provided for carriage washing, having wooden stages the height of the carriage floors, alongside each line of rails, with wrought-iron troughs running the whole length of the stages, which by the ball-valve arrangement are kept constantly full of water. Periodically, of course, the outsides of the carriages require something beyond the simple washing with water, and have to be thoroughly scoured with soap or some cleaning composition. The equipment of each "washer" consists of a bucket, a long-handled brush, with which he can reach from the ballast, if need be, the tops of the carriages, and a small spoke-brush for getting into corners, etc.

*Cleaning.*—The " cleaners," of whom a large number are employed, attend to the insides of the carriages. They are provided with a bass broom, a hard hand-brush, and a soft one, a wash leather and a linen duster. They are expected to shake each carpet, well brush the linings and cushions, clean the windows, and finally to dust the whole carriage throughout.

*Heating of Carriages.*—During the cold weather, that is to say generally from the 1st November to the 31st March in each year, every compartment of each class is supplied with at least two foot-warmers. The ordinary foot-warmer is an oblong tin, filled with water through an orifice which is then hermetically sealed, and the warmer is placed in a boiler until the water is heated. A patent foot-warmer has, however, been introduced, and is now in use on all the main lines, in which the water is replaced by acetate of soda. The utilisation of crystalised acetate of soda for this purpose is of comparatively recent introduction, the advantage consisting in the fact that the heat, before it has altogether disappeared, can be restored by merely shaking the receptacle, and that the heat is retained nearly three times as long as in the ordinary hot-water tins, viz., for about 8 hours, thus avoiding the inconvenience and annoyance to passengers of continually changing the foot-warmers on a long night journey. The acetate of soda used for this purpose should possess a slightly alkaline re-action to litmus test paper, and should be commercially free from sulphate-chloride and carbonate of sodium, as well as from acetate of lime. It should not possess any unpleasant odour of tarry matter, and its total impurities should not exceed 2 per cent. The warmers are charged in the following manner :—The acetate of soda is first placed in a large iron tank and reduced by heat to a liquid, of which seven quarts are placed in each warmer. Seven ounces of water are added, and two cast iron balls, each two inches in diameter, and weighing 20 ounces, are placed inside. The aperture at the end, through which the liquid has been introduced, is now covered by a cap, soldered down, with a small hole left in the centre. The warmer is placed in another tank, and the contents again brought to boiling point, when the receptacle is hermetically sealed, and is then ready for use.

The sleeping saloons in the through trains between London and Scotland, Holyhead, Liverpool, and Manchester, are warmed by means of high-pressure hot-water pipes, each saloon being supplied with a small heating apparatus for the purpose.

*The Lighting of Carriages.*—Until recent years the carriages upon the London and North-Western Railway were all lighted by means of oil-lamps, but this plan is being gradually superseded by the introduction of a system of lighting by compressed oil gas, about

26,000 oil lamps being, however, still in use. At all stations where the lamping of trains is performed, separate rooms are provided, as remote as possible from the station buildings, to lessen the risk of fire. These rooms are furnished with tables having iron frames and slate tops, with benches for cleaning and filling the lamps, wooden stands for cleaning the lamp cases, and racks affixed to the walls, in which the lamps are placed when cleaned, trimmed, and ready for use. The rooms are also fitted with iron tanks for the oil, waste bins, and sawdust bins. On the arrival of a train the lamps are removed from the carriages, placed on a truck specially constructed for the purpose, and taken to the lamp-room, where the cases are cleaned, the burners filled, and the wicks trimmed, when the lamps are replaced in the train, or placed in the racks, as the case may be.

The system of lighting by oil gas, previously referred to, is the patent of Mr. Pope, the gas being manufactured from shale oil. At the stations where this gas is made and supplied, the oil is brought to the works in barrels, and emptied into a large covered iron tank, let into the ground outside the gas-house, being afterwards pumped thence into a smaller tank, placed at a high level inside the gas-house. From this it is allowed to gravitate to red-hot retorts, through a small jet pipe, and is vapourised, afterwards passing through a hydraulic main to the condensers, thence to a coke scrubber, and, finally, through a registering meter to the gas-holder. The gas is stored in reservoirs about 18 feet long, and about 4 feet in diameter, built up of $\frac{1}{2}$-in. plates, to stand a working pressure of 150 lbs. to the square inch. The reservoirs are provided with gun-metal inlets and outlets, and also with a low-level outlet, to admit of drawing off the hydro-carbon which is thrown down owing to the compression of the gas. A combined engine and pump is employed to pump the gas from the reservoir to the receiver at a pressure of 150 lbs. to the square inch, whence it is conveyed by pipes to the cylinders attached to each carriage, each cylinder, as well as the main, being supplied with a pressure gauge, so as to show at a glance when they are sufficiently full.

The gas is conveyed from the works where it is made, to the station or shed where the carriages are charged, through an underground main of iron pipe, having an outside diameter of $1\frac{1}{4}$ in., and an inside diameter of $\frac{3}{4}$ in., connecting hydrants are then attached to the main, to which gas-hose is attached at distances of about 120 ft. for filling the cylinders in the carriages. The hose is of india-rubber and canvas knit together, and is capable of withstanding a pressure of 150 lbs. to the square inch; it has attaching unions and stopcocks at each end, so that it can be taken off the main without waste of gas, the main and the carriage cylinders having stop valves, so that all can be closed before detaching the hose. The gas in the main can also be drawn off into the gas-holder when it is desired, for any reason, to empty the carriage cylinders. Each carriage has one or two cylinders, which are filled to a pressure of 110 lbs. to the square inch, and are made of lined steel, with the seams welded, and two of these, 16 feet in length, with a diameter of 13 in., will carry a sufficient supply of gas to keep twenty lights burning on a journey from London to Aberdeen and back. Gas cannot be consumed under this high pressure, but has to be passed through a regulator, so as to reduce it to something like the pressure of coal gas as used for household purposes, and this is effected by a very simple contrivance. The gas passes from the high pressure cylinder through a small needle hole, with a pin valve and lever attached to a diaphragm, in a round box. As soon as 9·5 water gas guage pressure has entered this box, the diaphragm rises and closes the valve, which does not re-open until the lights are turned on, when it admits gas at the same rate at which it is consumed at the burners. Each jet can be regulated to a given size, so that it cannot blaze and cause waste, and all the lights in a carriage can be turned off or half-off by a key at the end of the carriage. Finally, each carriage has a pressure gauge to indicate the pressure of gas in the cylinders, and to shew when the supply is exhausted.

It must not be supposed that the London and North-Western Company, in their endeavours to secure an improved system of lighting their passenger carriages, have overlooked the question of electric lighting, or that they have been oblivious of the experiments which have been made in this direction upon various railways, but chiefly upon the Southern lines. They are, on the contrary, perfectly alive to the fact that in all probability the electric light is the light of the future for railway, carriages, as for most other purposes; and they have not been behindhand in making experiments with it on their own account. For some time past one of their trains running between Liverpool and Manchester has been lighted by electricity, and not without success; and although the directors, regarding the question as only in a transitional or experimental stage, have not yet seen their way to adopt the system to any large extent, a brief account of what has been done may perhaps be of interest.

It is tolerably well known that there are at least three methods in which a current of electricity may be obtained for lighting the carriages of a train. A primary battery may be used, or secondary batteries as on the

Brighton line, or the dynamo may be used direct. Each system has its own supporters, but the greatest consensus of opinion, at any rate amongst railway engineers, appears to be in favour of either the secondary batteries, or the direct action of the dynamo, while possibly the ultimate solution will be found in a combination of the two; that is to say, the train will carry both a dynamo and accumulators; but whether the dynamo is to be carried on the engine or driven from the engine direct, or is to be driven by a separate engine, or by the axle of the guard's van, are points not yet determined with any degree of authority. The train already referred to on the Liverpool and Manchester Railway, carries a Brotherwood's engine and a Siemen's compound shunt dynamo fixed on the tender of the locomotive, with an ammeter and switch on the engine, so that the driver may regulate the current, and there are two lamps in each compartment of the train with an automatic switch arrangement, so that in the event of one lamp failing, the second would be automatically brought into use. The system, which has been devised by the Company's chief telegraph superintendent, does not admit of the engine leaving the train without disconnecting the current, but this difficulty might be overcome by the use of secondary batteries or accumulators. The capital outlay required for the installation of this one train, including the Brotherwood engine and dynamo machine, was £286, and the working expenses for a year have amounted to £84 2s. 1d., which works out to about ·628 of a penny per lamp per hour, but this has since been somewhat reduced, and moreover, a portion of the working expenses would be no greater if there were three or four trains to attend to, working between the same points.

## CHAPTER IX.

### Rolling Stock (III.)—Goods Waggons.

Prior to the year 1881, the railway companies, generally speaking, only provided waggons for the conveyance of ordinary merchandise, and coal and coke, lime, salt, and some other commodities were carried in waggons belonging to the colliery proprietors and other traders, the companies making an allowance off their authorised tolls, for the use of the vehicles, and the owners performing all the services of loading and unloading. To a very considerable extent, this state of things still prevails, but in the year previously mentioned (1881) the Midland Company decided upon the new policy of becoming the owners of nearly the whole of the waggons running upon their railway. They accordingly obtained Parliamentary powers to raise a large sum of money for the purpose of buying up waggons from private owners, and building others for the conveyance of coal, and other traffic, and they now possess nearly 38,000 coal and coke trucks of their own.

The London and North-Western Company have also provided waggons for coal traffic, but not to so large an extent, as at the present time they have only some 10,000 coal waggons (including about 3,000 which are used for the conveyance of their own coal for locomotive purposes), and the bulk of the coal traffic upon their railway is still conducted by means of waggons owned by the traders. Of course, where the railway company find the waggons, they make a fair charge for their use, which charge varies from 6d. to 1s. per ton according to distance and other circumstances.

It must be confessed that the Midland Company's new departure was not without some justification in the fact that private owners' waggons are, always have been, and probably always will be, a fruitful source of trouble and anxiety. A railway company, in building its stock, has too much at stake to risk sacrificing efficiency to economy, and the vehicles are constructed with the utmost solidity and perfection of workmanship, without regard to cost; but the same considerations do not apply with equal force to private traders, and the companies are obliged to exercise the most stringent precautions, both in the matter of imposing a certain standard of construction and maintenance, and in keeping up a watchful system of examination, in order to guard against unsuitable waggons being run in their trains. The breaking down of a waggon may endanger the safety of a whole train, and cause the loss of valuable lives and property, and a very complete and elaborate system is adopted, with a view to guarantee that every private waggon shall be properly built and maintained. The system is as follows :—

A "Standard Specification," accompanied by drawings and dimensions, is drawn up, and private owners are required to build their waggons strictly in accordance with it, down to the minutest details, working drawings and descriptions of the waggons being first submitted for the approval of the Company's waggon superintendent before the work is commenced. When the waggons are complete and before they are permitted to run upon the railway, they are examined by the same official, and if he is satisfied that all the requirements of the specification have been faithfully complied with, he affixes to each side of each waggon a register plate, bearing the name of the Company, the registered number, the date of registry, and the maximum load to be carried. The waggon, with the plate so affixed, is free to work over the Company's, or any other, line of railway, the arrangement being a mutual one between all the railway companies in the Kingdom, agreed to at the Railway Clearing House.

The registration in no way affects the right of any railway company to inspect a registered waggon, and if found in any way defective, to stop or refuse it, and when a waggon, which has been approved, is repaired, or any of the parts renewed, the work must be carried out in accordance with the standard specification. The owners of the vehicles are required to keep them in a perfect state of repair, and to have them thoroughly greased and properly examined before each journey, any stationmaster being authorised to detain a waggon which appears to him to be unfit to travel.

Careful precautions are taken to see that every waggon, whether private or belonging to the Company, is in a fit and proper state of repair and efficiency while running in the trains, and the instructions issued to the men who are charged with this duty are of the most minute character. A staff of 240 examiners and greasers is employed, and these men are posted singly or in gangs at every important station and junction throughout the system. They are held responsible for seeing that every vehicle on commencing its journey from their station is in good and safe running condition, that the wheels, axle-boxes, springs, buffers, draw gear, brakes, and all other working parts are in perfect order, that the axle-boxes are well greased, and that any waggon in which a defect is discovered is promptly shunted out of the train, and a red card affixed to it to indicate that it is not to run until the necessary repairs have been attended to.

When a through train is standing at a station or junction, where it is required to stop, it is met by an examiner, whose duty it is to pass along each side of it and examine every wheel, not only by means of the tapping hammer, but by personal inspection. He also examines the axle-boxes, to see that they are well greased, and are not running "hot," and watches the revolving of the wheels, in order to detect a bent axle, stress being laid upon the fact that in the event of a waggon being stopped with a bent axle, no attempt is to be made to straighten it while cold, but the wheels are to be taken out and sent to a repairing shop where the axle can be heated, and thus properly and safely straightened.

The following are the minimum dimensions of axles to be allowed, which a long experience has dictated as representing the limits of safety, and any waggon found running with an axle of less dimensions is stopped and treated as a defective vehicle :—

|   | Wheel Seat. Ins. | Middle. Ins. | Journal. Ins. |
|---|---|---|---|
| For 6-ton waggons | $4\frac{1}{4}$ | $3\frac{1}{2}$ | $6 \times 2\frac{5}{8}$ |
| ,, 7-ton ,, | $4\frac{1}{2}$ | $3\frac{3}{4}$ | $6 \times 2\frac{3}{4}$ |
| ,, 8-ton ,, | 5 | 4 | $7 \times 3\frac{3}{8}$ |
| ,, 10-ton ,, | $5\frac{1}{4}$ | $4\frac{1}{2}$ | $8 \times 3\frac{1}{2}$ |

No tyres are allowed to run if they are less than 1 in. thick on the tread.

The London and North-Western Company possess in all upwards of 62,000 waggons of various descriptions, including the 10,000 coal waggons previously referred to, and the whole of these have been built, and are kept in repair, at their own waggon works at Earlestown. Of the total number nearly 34,000 are open goods waggons, 15 ft. 6 in. in length, and 7 ft. 8 in. in width, 20,000 of these having low sides only 9 in. in height, while the remaining 14,000 have sides 1 ft. 8 in. in height. There are 5,000 covered goods waggons, 15 ft. 6 in. long, 7 ft. 8 in. wide, and 5 ft. 8 in. in height, at side. The rest are vehicles of some forty different descriptions constructed for special classes of traffic, and having varying dimensions. The frames are all constructed of well-seasoned English oak, and the bodies of oak, teak, or red pine, the carrying capacity of the bulk of the waggons being 7 tons. The wrought iron work in the under frames is of the best Staffordshire iron, with the exception of the couplings, for which iron from the Low Moor furnaces is found to be the most suitable. The axle-boxes, buffer-shoes, and bearing spring shoes are of the best cast iron, and the wheel tyres and axles are of Bessemer steel.

The Earlestown works, although not quite so extensive as the carriage works at Wolverton, yet cover an area of thirty-five acres, and employ at busy times about 1,600 men, who are engaged in constructing and repairing, not only waggons, but the whole of the carts and vans required for cartage purposes throughout the Company's system. The works comprise a waggon-maker's and wheelwright's shop, 463 ft. long and 291 ft.

in width, a saw mill 200 ft. in length, two smithies containing over one hundred fires, a timber shed, turning and spring-making shops, foundries and forges, and numerous other shops devoted to various purposes, all fitted up with the most powerful and efficient machinery for minimising labour and ensuring accuracy of workmanship. The capacity of these works may be judged from the fact that when the full complement of some 1,600 hands is at work, they can turn out about eighteen finished waggons during the working day, or at the rate of one waggon every half-hour !

Most of the institutions which exist at Wolverton for the benefit of the men employed are represented by kindred institutions at Earlestown. Thus, there is a commodious dining-room, capable of seating 400 persons, where the men and boys employed in the works can have their food cooked free of charge. There is also a Mechanics' Institute, erected by the Company, where lectures on scientific and other subjects of general interest are given during the winter months, with free admittance for the workmen and their families. Five nights in each week are devoted to the classes held under the auspices of the Science and Art Department at South Kensington, and of the Lancashire and Cheshire United Institutes, preference being given to those subjects which have the most intimate relation to the avocations of the men. A circulating library with upwards of 5,000 volumes has been established, and a reading room has been provided, where all the leading newspapers and the best magazines are available for the use of the members. A spacious recreation ground, adjoining the Institute, and covering an area of six acres, contains three bowling-greens, lawn-tennis courts, and a cricket-ground, together with a miniature park tastefully laid out with flower-beds and trees, so that healthful recreation and manly sports are far from being neglected, and, by the liberality of the directors, all these advantages are secured to the men and boys engaged in the works in return for a payment of one penny per week by the men, and one halfpenny per week by the boys.

## CHAPTER X.

### THE WORKING OF THE TRAINS.

THE immense and continuous development of railway traffic during the last fifty years has taxed to the very utmost the ability and inventive faculties alike of those engaged in its management, and of constructive and mechanical engineers, in order to keep pace with it, and to enable it to be carried on with regularity and despatch, and with a minimum of delays and mishaps. In the foregoing chapters, some account has been given of the numerous mechanical and other contrivances which have been almost universally adopted by railway companies for this purpose; and the following pages will serve to afford an insight into the various administrative arrangements which alone enable the traffic of the chief lines in the country to be carried on. That traffic consists of varying elements. There are express and mail passenger trains, running at a speed of forty-five miles an hour, and, in some cases, more than that; others at a somewhat less speed, but still known as fast trains; stopping trains, calling at every station, and running at a rate of from twenty to twenty-five miles an hour; local suburban trains, running for short distances at a fairly high rate of speed, chiefly for residential purposes; express goods trains between the larger towns, attaining a speed of from twenty to twenty-five miles an hour; slow, stopping, goods trains, for serving smaller towns and villages; and, finally, the heavy coal trains, running out of the great colliery districts to every centre of population. All these various trains, heavy and light, fast and slow, some stopping at the stations and others dashing through them at high rates of speed, have to be accommodated to a great extent upon the same line of rails, yet all to keep their time and fulfil their appointed functions—and, briefly, this is the great problem which railway management has to solve. Such a service cannot be carried on under all circumstances, whether by night or day, in fogs, in snow-storms, in wind or rain, and under all other adverse conditions, without entailing hardships and dangers upon the men engaged in the working; yet it is gratifying to be able to say that the vast army of men of all grades employed in the service of the various railway companies exhibit at all times a state of complete discipline and cheerful devotion to duty, which could not be exceeded by any body of men whatever, and which, although perhaps not so well understood or appreciated by the public as might be the case, reflects the highest credit upon them as a class. Bearing in mind the vast importance of the interests entrusted to their charge, and the serious consequences that might easily arise from any carelessness or dereliction of duty on their part, it is a fact upon which the travelling public may well congratulate themselves, that their lives and limbs, their property and interests are confided to hands so trustworthy and reliable.

The train mileage run upon the London and North-Western Railway during the year ending the 31st December, 1892, was:—

Passenger trains ... ... 22,322,238 miles
Goods and mineral trains ... 20,914,461 ,,

Total 43,236,699 ,,

but this was exclusive of empty mileage and of shunting, and, as a matter of fact, the total engine miles run during the year amounted to 60,877,760. In other words, the engines of this one company ran more than two miles every second, or 121 miles every minute, and in effect they put a girdle round the earth once in every three hours and a half throughout the year; yet, such is the perfection of mechanism attained in the present day, that the engines were able to run a distance equal to twice round the world for every single case which occurred of a hot axle, the loss of a split pin or cotter, or anything tending to throw an engine out of gear.

During the year above mentioned, the number of passengers carried on the North-Western Railway was 67,231,603, and the number of tons of goods and minerals conveyed was 37,498,235. The revenue derived from all sources, except from rents, was £4,799,946 from passenger traffic, and £6,721,392 from goods and mineral traffic, giving a total of £11,521,338.

The accompanying illustration (Plate XXVI.) is a specimen on a reduced scale of the diagrams which are prepared for each section of the line, showing how the engine working is arranged, the time and speed of running, and the intersection of the trains at places where goods and slow passenger trains have to shunt into sidings for the fast express trains to pass them.

It will be perceived that the perpendicular lines divide the day of twenty-four hours into periods of hours, half hours, quarters of hours, and of five minutes; the horizontal lines dividing the railway into sections, while the slanting lines represent the engines or trains timed to run over the line. Thus the diagram offers, as it were, a visible picture of the state of the line, as to its being occupied or otherwise, between any two points at any minute of the day, and it will be easily apparent that such diagrams are invaluable, and in fact indispensable, in arranging train alterations or the running of new trains or special trains when required. The section of line chosen for illustration is that between Liverpool and Manchester, upon the major portion of which there is as yet only one up and one down line of rails, and on this portion one train cannot pass another proceeding in the same direction, unless the first one takes refuge in a siding. Over this Liverpool and Manchester Railway there are running at the present time, for greater or less distances, no fewer than 272 passenger trains, and 292 goods trains, or a total of 564 trains up and down within twenty-four hours. Of the passenger trains, 112 are expresses, fourteen of which travel at a speed of forty-four miles an hour, and the remainder at an average speed of thirty-five miles an hour ; and there are 56 express goods trains running at about twenty-three miles an hour.

Over certain busy portions of the North-Western system it has been found necessary, owing to the enormous development of the traffic, to lay down additional lines of rails, and there are now four lines (viz., two up and two down) between London and Roade, between Stafford and Crewe, and over some twenty shorter sections of railway, varying from half a mile to five miles in length, while, on other sections, a third line has been provided for goods traffic only. The advantages of the duplicated lines are obvious ; they admit of the fast and slow trains being kept separate, and thus simplify the working, lessen the risk of accident, and reduce delays and irregularities to a minimum.

If the theory of the Time Bill, with regularly appointed trains running at varying rates of speed, with specified places for them to pass each other, could be realised absolutely in regular practice, it would represent the perfection of railway working; but, owing to bad weather, the fluctuations of traffic, the running of special trains at short notice, and other uncontrollable causes, this ideal can never be absolutely attained. The most important thing, at all times, is to keep the line clear for the passenger trains, and, as a matter of fact, everything is made to give way to this, for there is nothing that adds so much to the reputation of a line, or redounds so much to the credit of the officers and servants, as a well-appointed and punctual passenger service. It pleases the travelling public, and brings both reputation and profit to the company.

On a line which is efficiently worked, the percentage of unpunctual trains is small, but at certain times of the year there will always be a considerable amount of late running, which cannot be avoided. For instance, in summer the passenger traffic is largely swelled by tourists proceeding to seaside resorts, the lakes, and Scotland, taking with them great quantities of luggage, which add to the weight of the trains and to the difficulty of getting them away from the stations promptly. Again, in winter, fogs, frosts, and snowstorms delay the progress of cross-channel steamers from Ireland, which run in connection with the trains, and these, in their turn, delay the trains. Those responsible for the working are thus constantly engaged in a contest against disturbing influences, and the arrangements have to be sufficiently elastic to enable trains to be run out of course, if necessary, as safely and well as at the specified times.

Goods trains, starting from terminal stations where the shunting and marshalling of the waggons take place, cannot always leave with absolute punctuality; nor can those having waggons to attach and detach at roadside stations, where a margin is allowed for the purpose, always accomplish their task within the specified time. The weight of the load, the capacity of the engine, the state of the rails and the weather, the varying gradients, and the more or less frequent running of special trains, are all disturbing elements which have to be reckoned with, and which tend materially to upset the calculations made in compiling the time bill, so that the arrangements for shunting goods trains off the running lines into sidings to allow passenger trains to pass them, have to be left very largely to the discretion of the station-masters and foremen. The most that can be done on the part of the management is to lay down certain rules and principles for the guidance of the men, and this is done. For instance, as a general rule, passenger trains take precedence of goods, cattle, and coal trains, and such trains are not allowed to be started from any station within a given space of time before a passenger train is due. This regulation is, however, subject to modification according to circumstances, and a light through goods or cattle train, on a clear day or night, may be started before a passenger train, if the latter has to call at all the stations. Again, if the station-master or foreman has been informed by means of the telegraph or otherwise, that a passenger train which is due, may not be expected for some time, he may despatch a goods train, taking care to inform the driver of the passenger train when it does arrive, what time the goods train was started, and where it was ordered to shunt. The same principle applies to a slow or stopping passenger train travelling in front of an express which is known to be late.

These are general rules, but on all the more important sections of the main lines it has been found desirable to fix an absolute margin of time within which a goods train is to leave a particular station in advance of a passenger train. This information is set forth, for each division of the line, in what is called the "Working Book," a compendium of general instructions and information issued every month for the guidance of the staff, and which gives also the locality of the various shunting or refuge sidings, and the number of waggons each of them will contain.

The following table (see page 208), as an example, gives these particulars for down trains on the line from London to Rugby; but, of course, similar arrangements exist with regard to up trains and for all the other divisions of the main line.

But this is not all. To ensure the principal station-masters and inspectors being kept well posted as to the working of the line and the movement of the trains, a most elaborate system is in force for telegraphing the progress of the trains from point to point. For instance, the telegraph clerk at Stafford will telegraph the time of departure of all trains from Stafford, to Crewe, to Chester, to Wolverhampton, to Tamworth, to Warrington, and to any other stations at which the information is useful, and this is continually going on all over the line, and from almost every station and signal cabin, so that everyone concerned is kept well posted as to what is going on.

DOWN FAST LINE.

| Distance from Camden. | STATIONS. | Siding capable of holding | Watford (Junc. from Fast to Slow). | Tring. | Bletchley. | Roade. | Blisworth (Gayton Loop). | Heyford South. | South end Kilsby Tunnel. | Hillmorton. | Rugby. |
|---|---|---|---|---|---|---|---|---|---|---|---|
| Miles. | | Wgns. | Mins. | Ms. | Ms. | Ms. | Ms. | Ms. | Ms. | Ms. | Ms. |
| 4¼ | Willesden Junction | ... | 30 | ... | ... | ... | ... | ... | ... | ... | ... |
| 16¼ | Watford (Junc. from Fast to Slow)... | ... | ... | 40 | ... | ... | ... | ... | ... | ... | ... |
| 30½ | Tring ... ... ... | 50 | ... | ... | 35 | ... | ... | ... | ... | ... | ... |
| 45½ | Bletchley... ... .. | ... | ... | ... | ... | 25 | ... | ... | ... | ... | ... |
| 58¾ | Roade ... ... ... | 50 | ... | ... | ... | .. | 15 | 20 | ... | ... | ... |
| 61¾ | Gayton Loop ... ... | 100 | ... | ... | ... | ... | ... | 15 | ... | ... | ... |
| 66 | Heyford (North) ... | 160 | ... | ... | ... | ... | ... | ... | 25 | 30 | ... |
| 75 | South end Kilsby Tunnel ... ... | 100 | ... | ... | ... | ... | ... | ... | ... | 20 | 25 |
| 79½ | Hillmorton ... .. | ... | ... | ... | ... | ... | ... | ... | ... | ... | 15 |

DOWN SLOW LINE.

| Distance from Camden. | STATIONS. | Siding capable of holding | Willesden. | Harrow. | Bushey. | Watford. | Boxmoor. | Tring. | Leighton. | Bletchley. | Roade. | Northampton. | Long Buckby. | Rugby. |
|---|---|---|---|---|---|---|---|---|---|---|---|---|---|---|
| Miles. | | Wgns. | Ms. | Ms. | Ms. | Ms. | Ms. | Ms. | Ms. | Ms. | Ms. | Ms. | Ms. | Ms. |
| | Camden ...... | ... | 10 | ... | ... | ... | ... | ... | ... | ... | ... | ... | ... | ... |
| 4¼ | Willesden ... | ... | ... | 15 | ... | ... | ... | ... | ... | ... | ... | ... | ... | ... |
| 10¼ | Harrow ...... | 45 | ... | ... | 15 | ... | ... | ... | ... | ... | ... | ... | ... | ... |
| 14¾ | Bushey......... | 45 | ... | ... | ... | 10 | ... | ... | ... | ... | ... | ... | ... | ... |
| 16¼ | Watford ...... | ... | ... | ... | ... | ... | 20 | ... | ... | ... | ... | ... | ... | ... |
| 23¼ | Boxmoor...... | 50 | ... | ... | ... | ... | ... | 25 | 35 | ... | ... | ... | ... | ... |
| 30½ | Tring ......... | 50 | ... | ... | ... | ... | ... | ... | 25 | 35 | ... | ... | ... | ... |
| 39 | Leighton...... | 80 | ... | ... | ... | ... | ... | ... | ... | 20 | ... | ... | ... | ... |
| 45½ | Bletchley...... | ... | ... | ... | ... | ... | ... | ... | ... | ... | 25 | ... | ... | ... |
| 58¾ | Roade ......... | 50 | ... | .. | ... | ... | ... | ... | ... | ... | ... | 15 | ... | ... |
| 66¼ | Northampton | ... | ... | ... | ... | ... | ... | ... | ... | ... | ... | ... | 25 | ... |
| 74½ | Long Buckby | 50 | ... | ... | ... | ... | ... | ... | ... | ... | ... | ... | ... | 25 |

## THE WORKING OF THE TRAINS.

In order that the different descriptions of trains may be the more readily distinguished one from another, especially at night, a system of distinctive head signals for the engines has been devised, which is as follows :—

1. Engines of Fast Passenger Trains, Fish Trains, and Break-down Van Trains ... — Two White Lights—one over each Buffer. Fish and Break-down Van Trains by day must carry a White Diamond Board over Right Hand Buffer.

2. Engines of Slow Passenger Trains and Light Engines — A White Light over Left Hand Buffer.

3. Engines of "Express" Goods and Through Trains of Cattle, Perishables, and Shipment Traffic ... ... — One Green Light over Right Hand Buffer, and one White Light over Left Hand Buffer. A White Diamond Board at Bottom of Engine Chimney during daylight. *See Note A.*

4. Engines of Fast Goods Trains not having to stop at intermediate stations and sidings; also Ballast Trains not stopping to do work on the road ... ... ... — Two Green Lights—one over each Buffer. A White Diamond Board over Left Hand Buffer of Engine during daylight.

5. Engines of Stopping Goods, Mineral, and Ballast Trains — One Green Light over Left Hand Buffer.

Where there are more than two lines (one Up and one Down) a Green Light must be carried at foot of chimney by Engines of all Trains travelling on the Auxiliary Lines.

Light Engines on the Auxiliary Lines must carry one Green Light at the foot of the chimney, the Light on the Buffer Plank being dispensed with.

*Note A.*—Urgent Express Goods, Cattle, Meat, or Vegetable Trains requiring unusual despatch, will, under special instructions from the District Superintendents, carry the following distinctive Head Signals :—

By day—A White Oval Board, with Green Cross on it, at foot of chimney.

By night—One Green Light over Left Hand Buffer, and one White Light over Right Hand Buffer.

These special Head Signals must only be used in cases specified by instructions from the District Superintendents.

There has been a very striking growth in the length and weight of the trains during the last five-and-twenty years, which has been rendered practicable by the gradual increase in the capacity of the engines employed The speed of the trains has also increased to almost as great an extent as the length and weight, and fast passenger trains now travel some fifteen per cent. quicker than they did even fifteen years ago. The increase of speed adds indirectly to the number of trains run, because, in order to admit of such a high rate of speed being maintained, but few stoppages can be indulged in, and additional trains must be run to serve the intermediate stations and to enable the passengers from those stations to reach the junctions where the important trains are timed to stop. This, of course, means an increase in the working expenses directly arising out of the greater speed which the public now demand.

The London and North-Western Company, however have not hitherto made it their principal object to run their trains at the highest possible rate of speed. In these days, journeys must be accomplished quickly in order to keep pace with the times, and meet the growing requirements of the travelling public; but the highest attainable speed is not always the most compatible with safety and punctuality, and these latter essentials are certainly not the least important to be secured in the working of a railway. Thus the London and North-Western, if it does not lay claim to the doubtful distinction of running the fastest trains in the world, is, it is believed, fairly entitled to the reputation of being the most punctual line in the kingdom. Still it can, on occasion, achieve notable records in the way of fast travelling, and an illustration of its ability to do so, occurs to the writer in connection with what happened some years ago, at the commencement of the civil war in America. It was at the time when the British Foreign Secretary had sent a despatch, in the nature of an ultimatum, to the Federal Government, with respect to the case of Messrs. Mason and Slidell, the Confederate Envoys, who had been forcibly taken out of a British ship by a Federal cruiser. There was no Atlantic cable in those days, and although all England was on the tip-toe of expectation to know the terms of the reply which would govern the issue of peace or war between two great nations, there was no quicker means of communication than by steamer to Queenstown, thence by rail to Dublin, then again by steamer to Holyhead, and by rail again to London. During this anxious period from the 2nd to the 9th of January, 1862, an engine was kept constantly in steam at Holyhead, and when at length the long expected despatch arrived, it was brought from Holyhead to Euston, a distance of 264 miles, in five hours, or at an average speed of 53 miles an hour throughout, including one stoppage at Stafford for the purpose of changing engines. It may be added that although at that time the Company had not adopted the block telegraph system, and the working was carried on by the ordinary telegraph signals from station to station, the entire journey was performed without the slightest stoppage or interruption of any kind.

For the working of single lines of railway, most companies adopt what is known as the "Train Staff and Ticket System," which is carried out in the following manner:—Supposing the line, or the section of line, extends from A to B, and there are three trains at A wanting to proceed to B. The first one is despatched with a ticket, and the second also, but the third, or last, must carry on the engine what is known as the train staff, a straight piece of wood somewhat resembling a constable's staff, but coloured and lettered in accordance with the particular section of line it refers to. The box containing the "tickets" can only be unlocked by means of the train staff, which is really the key, and no train can enter the opposite end of the section until the train staff itself arrives at that end, so that it is impossible for two trains to meet in opposite directions, and the proper distance between trains proceeding in the same direction is maintained by fixed signals and the block telegraph, the same as on double lines. Where the branch is a long one, it is divided into sections, with crossing places at convenient intervals, and each section has its own staff and set of tickets, and is worked separately in the manner described.

This system of working single lines, although it has been altered and improved upon in many ways, until it may now be considered to be almost perfect, both as to safety and convenience, was originally devised by Mr. Henry Woodhouse, until lately one of the engineers to the London and North-Western Company, for the working of a long tunnel, called the "Standedge Tunnel," on the Huddersfield and Manchester railway, of which he had charge nearly forty years ago, and was authorised generally by the Board of Trade, and included in their requirements in 1860.

Some single lines of short length, and where the traffic is light, are worked by a single engine in steam, and this fact, of course, supersedes the necessity for any special precautions such as those already described.

## THE WORKING OF THE TRAINS.

Another method of working single lines which has been introduced within a comparatively recent period is what is known as the "Train Tablet System," which is now in operation on a section of the line at Cockermouth, on the Callander and Oban railway in Scotland, and elsewhere. Although the train staff system, as described above, combined with the block telegraph, has answered its purpose well, it has one drawback, which is that the sections have of necessity to be short in order to avoid serious delays, and under any circumstances it may occur that the train staff may be at one end of the section while a train is waiting for it at the other. This fact led one of the officers of the Caledonian Company to set his wits to work to devise an arrangement by which a train staff, or its equivalent in the form of a tablet, or circular disc of metal, could be electrically controlled from the other end of the section, so as to constitute in point of fact a train staff and block telegraph system combined.

The apparatus has been since improved and perfected, and has been patented by Messrs. Tyer & Co., the well-known electrical engineers. Although the working is, in practice, very simple, a detailed description of the instruments used, and the way in which they are manipulated, would appear extremely complicated, but the essential features of the system are as follows:—
Supposing A and B are the two ends of a section of single line and a train is waiting at A to proceed to B. The signalman at A gives a signal to that effect on an electric bell to the signalman at B. If, according to the block telegraph regulations, the train may proceed to B, that is to say if the line to the knowledge of the signalman at B is clear between A and B, the signalman

at B draws out a slide in his instrument, and depresses a plunger, which, by means of an electric current, has the effect of enabling the signalman at A to draw out a corresponding slide in *his* instrument, and remove from it a train tablet, which he hands to the driver of the train as his authority to start and enter the section in advance towards B. On arrival at B the driver delivers up the tablet to the signalman there, who inserts it in his instrument, *and until this has been done, the apparatus is automatically locked, and a second tablet cannot be obtained from the apparatus at either end.* Thus it is impossible for two trains to be in the same section at the same time, proceeding in opposite directions, although trains may follow one another in the same direction at the proper intervals without intermission or delay.

An apparatus very similar to this, and designed to attain the same objects, has recently been devised and constructed at the Crewe works, and is now in use on the Bedford and Cambridge and several other branch lines, having been approved by the Board of Trade. In this case train staffs of the ordinary type take the place of the tablets, and these are made in such a form that they will serve to open any of the intermediate sidings within the section, which in their normal state are locked. Although the apparatus differs in form, the manipulation is almost identical with that of the train tablet system, it being physically impossible for a staff to be withdrawn without the concurrence of the signalmen at the two ends of the section.

The experimental trial of this system has proved so successful as to justify its more general adoption, and there being, both in this country and abroad, so many railways and branches having only a single line of rails, and a perfectly safe and efficient method of working such lines being beyond doubt an important *desideratum*, it is perhaps worth while to give here a description in some detail of the "Webb and Thompson Electric Staff System":—

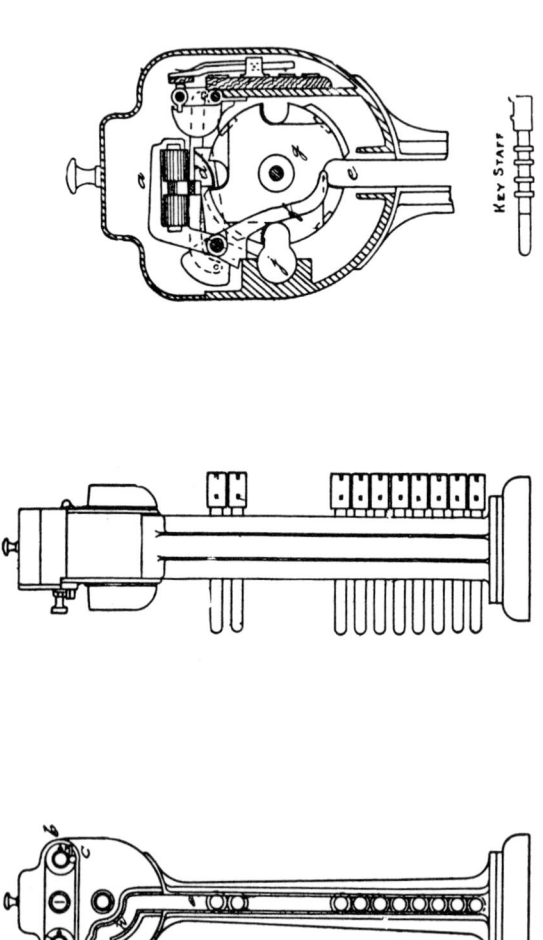

PLATE XXVII. WEBB & THOMPSON'S ELECTRIC STAFF APPARATUS. [*Page* 215.

The line, if it is more than two or three miles long, is divided into sections, and it may be assumed that A and B are stations, at each end of a section. Each station is provided with an apparatus, consisting of a pillar or standard, as shewn in Plate XXVII., having a number of slots for the reception of the train staffs, the apparatus being connected by an electric circuit; and supposing that a train is at A and requires to travel to B, the following is the mode of precedure: In accordance with a pre-arranged code of signals, the signalman at A telegraphs on an electric bell to B, and asks for permission to withdraw a staff from the apparatus. If the man at B knows that the line between A and B is clear (that is, that the preceding train has passed B) he sends an electric current to A which unlocks the apparatus there, and enables A to withdraw a staff and hand it to the driver of the waiting train. On the train reaching B, the driver hands the staff to the signalman there, who places it in his apparatus, and until this has been done it is not possible for a second staff to be withdrawn from the apparatus either at A or B. These results are brought about by the following mechanical arrangements:—

In Fig. 3 (Plate 27) the letter *a* indicates an electro-magnet, provided with four coils, and when A has asked for permission to withdraw a staff, as described above, he turns the dial handle *b* (Fig. 1), which sends an electric current through two of the coils; when station B wishes to give the permission asked for, he does so by pressing the key *c* (Fig. 1), which sends an electric current through the other two coils, thus establishing a current through all four coils. Now, if these currents are in unison, *i.e.*, of the right polarity, the magnet becomes energised and firmly grips the armature, or lock *d* (Fig. 3), enabling the man at A to lift one of the staffs to the top of the slot *e* and, when at the top, a projection on the staff strikes, and lifts the tail piece $f$ (Fig. 3), which is attached to the magnet. The magnet is thus lifted also, and as it grips the armature or lock, the lock is lifted with it, so that the drum $g$ (Fig. 3) is released and is free to turn, as the man draws the staff through the segmental slot $h$ to the opening $j$, where it is finally withdrawn.

It remains to show how the withdrawal of one staff prevents either A or B from withdrawing a second until the first has been placed in the apparatus at B. The turning of the drum "$g$" by the withdrawal of the staff, reverses the direction of the current from B, so that it now passes through the two coils of A's apparatus, in a reverse direction to the current passing through the other two coils, and, the one current neutralising the other, there is no power to energise the magnet. Another effect of the turning of the drum $g$ is to reverse the direction of the current sent from A to B, so that this current has no longer any effect on the magnet at B. In order to bring the currents sent from A and B respectively again into unison, the staff withdrawn must either be replaced in the apparatus at A, or carried to B, and placed in the apparatus there. Assuming that the latter is done, the effect is to turn back the drum $g$, in the apparatus at B, which alters the direction of the current sent from B to A, and also that sent from A to B, and brings the two currents again into accord, so that permission may now be given to withdraw a staff at either end.

In addition to the electric lock, each instrument is provided with three mechanical locks, as safeguards against any tampering with the mechanism, and there is also a detector lock which acts automatically, and prevents the use of the apparatus if the electric lock should become deranged.

There is one element which causes, perhaps, more **difficulty, and** entails more anxiety upon those engaged

## THE WORKING OF THE TRAINS.

in the management of a railway than all others put together, and that is the prevalence of fogs in this country. When one of these unwelcome visitations descends upon us, although the telegraph still remains, the whole system of visible signals is, as it were, blotted out, and it is easy to realise how extremely difficult this must render the working. The greatest caution has to be observed, the speed has to be reduced, and more or less delay is inevitable in the interests of safety, which, after all is, of course, the first and last consideration. To admit of the trains running while the signals are invisible, a system of what is called "fog-signalling" has been devised, and a brief description of this system, which is as simple as it is perfect, may do much to reassure any of our readers who may chance to find themselves performing a journey by an express train during a fog. At such a time the platelayers are perforce idle, since the permanent way is not allowed to be interfered with until the weather clears, and these men for the most part furnish the ranks of the fog-signalmen. Directly a fog comes on, a man is stationed at the foot of each distant signal, and becomes, in fact, a living signal-post. As soon as the signal-arm is raised to "Danger," he places upon the rails two detonating signals, which are exploded by the engine of a train passing over them, and the driver of the train is thus apprised that the signal, although invisible to him, is at "Danger," and he must act accordingly. If the signal is lowered to indicate that the line is clear before any train approaches, the fog-signalman at once removes the detonators, but replaces them as soon as the signal is again raised to "Danger."

Each man is provided with a hut to shelter him, a fire

and a thick warm overcoat, which is supplied by the Company for his use. As soon as he has been on duty three hours he is supplied with refreshments at the Company's expense, and again six hours later if the fog continues so long; and, after twelve hours, if the fog still continues, he goes off duty, and his place is taken by a relief man. The refreshments supplied consist usually of bread and meat, and tea or coffee.

During the week ending the 14th January, 1888, as may perhaps be remembered, occurred one of the most severe visitations of fog within living memory. It was general throughout the country, and, in fact, was not confined to England, but extended over some portions of the Continent. In most parts of the country it commenced either on Sunday night or Monday morning, and, with brief intervals, and in some places with, practically, no interval whatever, it continued until Friday night. It may readily be imagined that to carry on the working of the railway under such circumstances, and for such a lengthened period, became a matter of great difficulty, and imposed a very severe strain upon all the men engaged.

Delays, more or less, were naturally inevitable, but it is gratifying to state that, with the exception of one or two trifling mishaps with goods trains, involving no serious results, the whole of the traffic was carried on during this trying week without any actual interruption, and without accident or injury to a single passenger. This result was entirely due to the efficient carrying out of the system of fog-signalling above described, and probably there could not well be a more searching test of the efficiency of the system employed. Enquiries have shown that during the week in question on the

## THE WORKING OF THE TRAINS.

London and North-Western Railway alone, fogmen had to be provided at 2,462 signal posts; 2,375 men were employed, in addition to 1,377 relief men, making a total of 3,752 men. During the week scarcely any express train was more than half-an-hour late, and some of the trains actually ran to time.

Another very trying period of fog for those engaged in working railway traffic in and near London occurred at Christmas, 1891, and will not readily be forgotten by those whose business it was to encounter and overcome the difficulties it entailed. About 10 a.m. on Sunday, December 20, in that year, a dense fog descended over the metropolis and lasted, practically without intermission, until 8 o'clock on the evening of Christmas Day. The fog at times was so intense that a man standing at the foot of a signal-post 15 or 20 feet high could not see the light in the signal lamp, and men standing but a few yards apart could not see each other. A shunter, standing on a pair of rails, could not tell whether it was a main line or a siding, and could only ascertain this by following the rails and seeing where they led him Under such conditions as these, it seems almost incredible that it was possible to carry on the working of a railway at all, much less to cope with the exceptionally heavy traffic of Christmas week, and yet it was done, and done successfully, for, during these four days, at Euston station, alone, three hundred trains were made up and dispatched, and 15,000 passengers, with their luggage, besides 40,000 parcels, were got away, all this being accomplished in the blinding fog without the smallest mishap of any kind occurring. At such a time, it is not too much to say that every man engaged in the service incurred great risk whenever he went on duty, and it speaks highly for the courage, discipline, and devotion of the staff that the work was carried on at all in such a state of things, and did not absolutely come to a stand.

Various plans have from time to time been suggested for dispensing with the fog-signalmen, and conveying to the drivers the requisite warning as to the state of the signals during a fog, by mechanical means, either in connection with electricity or otherwise, and it appears probable that sooner or later some efficient system of this kind will be devised, but, so far, none has been developed which has been thought to be sufficiently reliable, and the matter is still within the region of experiment.

A great deal of difficulty was formerly experienced in getting the fog-signalmen to their posts, especially if the fog came on during the night, as is frequently the case. In remote country districts the men often found it impossible to obtain dwellings near their work, and even in the vicinity of large towns the only houses available were sometimes those of a type unsuited to the means of men of the class to which they belonged. Thus the signalman, confined to his cabin, perhaps in some lonely cutting, far from any station or town, during the solitary hours of the night, would see a fog approach and blot out his signals, and, not daring to leave his post to call assistance, and knowing that the nearest fog-signalman lived a mile, or perhaps more, from the spot, he was frequently placed in a position of great anxiety and perplexity. This difficulty is being gradually met by the expedient of the Company themselves building in the neighbourhood of every station or signal-post where the circumstances are such as to give rise to the necessity, a number of workmen's cottages sufficient to accommodate the platelayers and others who are required for fog-signalling at that particular station or post. These cottages are specially designed for the convenient occupation of a single family; they are of uniform construction, all the wood-work, iron-work, and other fittings being turned out in quantities at the Company's works at Crewe, where the bricks are also made; and owing to this, and to the buildings being erected by the Company's own workmen, they can be completed at a comparatively moderate outlay, each pair of cottages costing from £350 to £400. There is usually an electric bell communication between the signalman's cabin and the bedroom of one of the men, generally the ganger, whose duty it is, on the alarm being given, to call out the other men, so that within a very few minutes of the first warning, every man is at his appointed post, and ready for duty. Both the Company and the men are the gainers by this arrangement. The Company attain their object of having the men concentrated on the spot, and easily accessible at all times, and the rents paid by the men, which range from 2s. 6d. to 3s. per week, ensure them a certain return, although a small one, for their outlay. The men, on their part, reap the benefit of occupying, at a small rental, a commodious and convenient dwelling, near to their work, constructed under proper sanitary conditions, kept in a good state of repair, and in every way infinitely superior to the best accommodation which their small means would otherwise enable them to obtain.

Besides the cottages for fog-signalmen, the Company provide houses for their station-masters, foremen, signalmen, engine-drivers, brakesmen, and others, who cannot easily obtain suitable dwellings near the stations to which they are attached, the houses owned by the Company and occupied by their servants, being in all nearly 4,500 in number.

It is only during the passage of the Royal train to convey Her Majesty and suite to and from Scotland twice a year, that the ordinary arrangements for working the line are suspended. The exceptional nature of the regulations then adopted may be considered as affording the nearest approach to perfection in railway travelling that has yet been arrived at. The train is lighted with gas, and fitted throughout with the Westinghouse and vacuum brakes, with an electrical communication between the compartments of each saloon and carriage, and the guards, and with a communication between the front guard and the driver. A pilot engine is run fifteen minutes in advance of the train throughout the entire journey, and in order to guard against any obstruction or interference with the safe passage of the train, no engine, except the pilot, or any train or vehicle, is allowed to proceed upon or cross the main line during an interval of at least thirty minutes before the time at which the Royal train is appointed to pass. All shunting operations on the adjoining lines are suspended during the same period, while, after the Royal train has passed, no engine or train is permitted to leave a station or siding upon the same line for at least fifteen minutes. In addition to these regulations, no engines or trains, except passenger trains, are allowed to travel between any two stations on the opposite line of rails to that on which the Royal train is running, from the time the pilot is due until the Royal train has passed. For instance, supposing the Royal train is to run on the down line from Stafford to Norton Bridge, and the pilot is due at Norton Bridge at, say eight o'clock, if a goods train or light engine required to travel on the up line from Norton Bridge to Stafford, and it was ready to start at eight o'clock, it would be kept back until the Royal train had passed.

The precaution is also taken of specially guarding every level crossing, farm crossing, and station, to prevent trespassers, and of securely bolting all facing points over which the Royal train must pass. Platelayers are also posted along the line to prevent the possibility of any obstruction or impediment occurring; and all level crossing gates, where gatekeepers are not kept, are locked an hour before the train is due, and kept so until it has passed. Special arrangements are made for telegraphing the passage of the train from point to point as it speeds along its journey, and an instrument is conveyed by the train by means of which a telegraphic communication can be established at any place on the journey in case of need. The train is accompanied by a staff of fitters, lampmen, and greasers, who keep a vigilant watch on each side of it, so as to notice any irregularity in the running of the carriages, and who, upon the train stopping at the appointed stations, examine it throughout and grease the axle boxes. The average speed of the train does not exceed about thirty-six miles an hour excluding stoppages.

The working of a railway is, at times, not altogether devoid of picturesque features and scenes of great animation, and, for example, anyone who has ever paid a visit to Euston Station on the 10th of August, the night on which the great exodus takes place to the Scotch moors on the commencement of the grouse shooting on the 12th, is hardly likely to forget the scene. The spacious courtyard blocked with cabs and carriages incesssantly arriving and departing, the long lines of people waiting their turn at the numerous booking offices, the extensive platforms, crowded with passengers from end to end, and so blocked with mountains of heavy luggage that it is difficult to move a yard, the great engines noisily blowing off steam as if they were bellowing their impatience to set off upon their long journey, and, to make confusion worse confounded, the Post Office Mail vans dashing up every five minutes and discharging into the thick of the fray tons of parcels and mail bags— all go to make up a scene which might well daunt the courage of the perspiring officials, who know that they are responsible for getting all these excited and bewildered passengers, these mountains of luggage and these tons of mails and parcels into the right trains, the right carriages, and the right vans;—in short, for evolving ultimate order out of this chaos, and all within a short space of time. The task would appear to be almost an impossible one; but such is the power of system, and of careful organisation of means to an end, that after all it is triumphantly accomplished, and soon after ten o'clock at night the vast station is again silent and all but deserted, while the huge crowd that lately thronged it is packed into the many heavily loaded trains speeding fast through the darkness to their destinations in the distant North.

On the 10th of August last year, between five and six thousand passengers left Euston Station, most of them travelling long distances and having large quantities of luggage with them. During the day, 94 trains were made up and dispatched, many of the most important trains being run in two and even three parts to accommodate the traffic, while by the night trains, no less than 450 beds were made up in the sleeping saloons.

Another interesting feature of railway working is presented by the operations connected with the carriage of the mails and parcel post. Every night, at half-past eight, a long and heavy train leaves Euston Station, carrying no passengers and made up entirely of vehicles devoted to the purposes of the Post Office sorting carriages, bag tenders, and vans for parcel-post hampers. This train carries the mails from London, and other places on the line of route, to Scotland and for other places passed on the way, and although, of course, there are many other trains which carry mails, this is the Postal train *par excellence*. The huge bags of letters brought in by the mail vans and carts are thrust pell-mell into the sorting carriages, where they are seized upon by the clerks whose duty it is to travel with the train, to sort the letters *en route* and hand out the bags at the stations on the journey, taking in, in exchange for them, the bags containing letters from those stations for the North. This operation of taking in and handing out mails while the train is at full speed is a very interesting one, and merits a few words of description. The mail bags to be taken on board the train are hung upon standards erected by the side of the line, and when the train approaches the spot, a net is outstretched from the mail carrriage and, by a clever arrangement of mechanism, sweeps the bag from the standard, and, with the same motion, and in an instant, flings it on the floor of the carriage. In much the same way, and by a reversal of the process, the bags to be handed out are hung upon an arm or standard protruded from the carriage and caught by a net erected by the side of the line. A recent writer upon the railways of England, who was privileged to travel by the Postal train from Euston to Scotland, has given what is certainly a most graphic picture of the manner in which the mail service is conducted, of the innumerable cross country trains which join the great trunk mail routes at the appointed junctions in the dead of night and safely and punctually exchange their precious freight; of the ingenious apparatus already described, and of the busy interiors of the brilliantly lighted mail carriages where the clerks perform their duties of sorting and making up the bags while the train is speeding on its way, and he appears to have been greatly impressed by the interesting nature of the operations he witnessed.

## CHAPTER XI.

### THE SHUNTING AND MARSHALLING OF GOODS TRAINS.

IN working the goods traffic on a line such as the London and North-Western, the trains are so arranged as to run with full loads between the most important points, as from London to Birmingham, Liverpool, Manchester, Scotland, and so on; but the traffic at the intermediate stations is collected by a service of local stopping trains, and conveyed to the large junctions, such as Rugby, Crewe, and Stafford, where the waggons are properly classified and marshalled for transit by the through trains. This operation of marshalling and classifying the goods and mineral traffic into district and station order, as will be readily believed, is one of immense magnitude and difficulty, and the work at the terminal stations, and at the important junctions, is extremely complicated, and carried out at a great cost. It is obvious that, unless the trains were properly marshalled for their various destinations, and the waggons arranged in station order, it is not enough to say that the traffic could only be carried on with the most serious interruption and delay; but it would, in fact, be impracticable to carry it on at all, now that it has attained its present dimensions. As it is, any neglect or omission on the part of the men employed in this duty results in great confusion and difficulty at the junctions and stations, as the train proceeds on its journey. The extent of the operations required may be gathered from the fact that the London and North-Western Company alone have no less than 300 engines constantly employed in this work of marshalling and classifying the trains in the sidings, and that the total number of hours of shunting performed last year by these engines was estimated at 900,000, representing a cost to the Company, at 5s. per hour (including wages), of £225,000.

The great importance of performing this work in an effectual manner, and with the minimum expenditure of time and money, has led to the subject being studied and debated perhaps to a greater extent than any of the other problems which railway management has had to deal with. Many plans have been suggested and put in operation, as, for instance, at Camden, where the sidings are laid in parallel lines, with a double line of turn-tables across them, worked by hydraulic capstans; at Willesden, Stafford, and other places, where there are sets of sidings in the shape of a fan, with a shunting "neck," or siding, which represents the handle of the fan; and at other stations where the fan-shaped sidings are adopted, but with a falling gradient, utilised so as to economise power. The "fan" arrangement, either with or without the aid of gravitation, is the one most commonly in use, and its utility is sufficiently apparent if the nature of the operation required to be performed is borne in mind. By its aid a miscellaneous collection of waggons for different destinations can be broken up into sections, each section being placed either by gravitation, by a shunting engine, or by horses, in a separate siding. All the sidings running into a common departure line, it is obvious that the sets of waggons can then be drawn out in any order in which they are required to be marshalled in the trains.

At certain important places throughout the country, as at Shildon, on the North-Eastern Railway; at Chaddesden, near Derby, and at Toton, near Trent, on the Midland Railway; and at Blaydon, near Newcastle, on the North-Eastern, and elsewhere, schemes of marshalling sidings of elaborate construction and great extent have been laid down, and these have in each case their own distinctive features, but they have for the most part been devised to meet the special circumstances of a particular traffic or locality, and probably it is not necessary to enter into a detailed description of them. The most successful experiment which has been tried upon the London and North-Western Railway, and possibly also the most successful in the kingdom, whether with regard to efficiency or economy, has been an ingenious plan devised by Mr. Harry Footner, M.I.C.E., one of the Company's principal engineers, for marshalling the waggons in *district* and *station order* by one operation, and by means of gravitation. This plan has been put in operation on an extensive scale at Edge Hill, near Liverpool, and as it is one which would be applicable to any large station or junction where a great number of waggons required to be sorted and marshalled, and where a suitable gradient either naturally existed, or could be easily obtained, a description of the method in which the work is carried on and the results obtained, may not be without value.

Edge Hill, as is no doubt well known, is a place on the outskirts of Liverpool, and is situated on the Liverpool and Manchester Railway, which, as we have seen in an earlier chapter, was the first railway constructed by George Stephenson, nearly sixty years ago. At this point the Liverpool and Manchester Railway, which has its passenger terminus at Lime Street, a mile and a quarter from Edge Hill, is joined by a branch railway running round the city, to the docks at the north end, and also by branch lines running through tunnels, under the city, to the various goods depôts at Wapping, Waterloo, and Crown Street, so that it will be easily perceived that as regards goods traffic, Edge Hill is a very important and busy place indeed. This is sufficiently proved by the fact that, at the present time, no less than 534 trains of all descriptions are running in and out of Edge Hill within 24 hours, viz., 273 in, and 261 out, and that it has been found necessary to build there a steam shed or engine-house, which holds eighty engines.

Of course, all goods trains arriving at Liverpool have to be broken up at Edge Hill, and the waggons have to be sorted out for the several depôts, whence they are distributed to the various docks and warehouses. On the other hand, the trucks loaded at all the depôts have to be sent, in the first place, to Edge Hill, where they are classified and marshalled in trains for despatch in all directions. These comprise what is called the "outward" traffic.

It was about the year 1873 that the Company began to have strongly impressed upon them the urgent necessity for making provision on a very much larger scale than they had, up to that time, contemplated, for the shunting and marshalling of trains at Edge Hill, and that they commenced to carry out, as an experiment, and, to a limited extent, the system which has since been elaborated and extended with such beneficial results. In that year (1873) they found themselves in presence of this state of things—that, while the outwards traffic at Edge Hill had grown from 257,025 tons in 1850 to 1,032,853 tons in 1873, the siding accommodation had only been increased from 1,782 waggons to 3,215 waggons; in other words, the business had quadrupled, while the facilities for dealing with it had only been doubled. It may here be said, that, at the present time, the area occupied by shunting lines and sidings at Edge Hill is 200 acres, and that there are 60 miles of running lines, and siding room for nearly 7,000 waggons.

At the period mentioned it became necessary to consider seriously how the difficulties were to be met, for, in addition to the want of room, the main passenger lines had to be crossed every time waggons were moved from one group of sidings to another (and there were a great many groups), so that there were serious obstacles to be encountered in carrying on the working, and as the safety of the passenger trains always had to be the first consideration, the goods traffic had often to suffer delay.

The Company had, at that time, about 70 acres of spare land on the north side of the railway, and available for extension, but to reduce this to the level of the main lines would have involved a stupendous amount of excavation, and the fact that the surface of the land rose from west to east, and that, for a comparatively reasonable outlay, sidings could be laid upon it on a uniform gradient which would enable them to pass *over* the branch line running round to the docks, which branch line intersected the land, suggested to Mr. Footner a scheme for marshalling by gravitation. In considering a scheme of this kind two things appeared to be essential—first, that in the passage of the trucks from the top to the bottom of the incline, all the necessary changes in their relative positions should be effected, so that when they reached the bottom they should be ready to go away as properly marshalled trains; and secondly, that there should be some means of stopping, without injury to them or their loads, any trucks which might get beyond the control of the shunters. The mere principle of shunting by gravitation was no new thing, as it had already been successfully adopted for coaling ships on the Tyne, and for sorting mineral trains at Darlington on the North-Eastern Railway; but Mr. Footner claims as his own the idea of an inclined plane specially constructed in such a way as to *sort and marshal* a mixed goods train by gravitation alone, without any assistance from locomotive or horse power.

The arrangement he devised is shown by the accompanying diagram (Fig. 28 B). The sidings consist of, first, the six upper reception lines at the summit of the incline, holding 294 waggons; secondly, the sorting sidings, 24 in number, and capable of holding 1,065 waggons, into which the waggons, when separated, first run, each siding receiving the waggons for a particular *train;* thirdly, two groups of marshalling sidings, which owing to their peculiar formation have been christened "gridirons," through which the trucks are filtered so as to make them take their proper order of precedence in the train; and, fourthly, the lower reception and departure lines, which receive the trains in their complete state, and where the engines are attached to take them away. All these, it may be remarked, are laid out in such a manner, with a view to future requirements, that without altering any of the existing lines

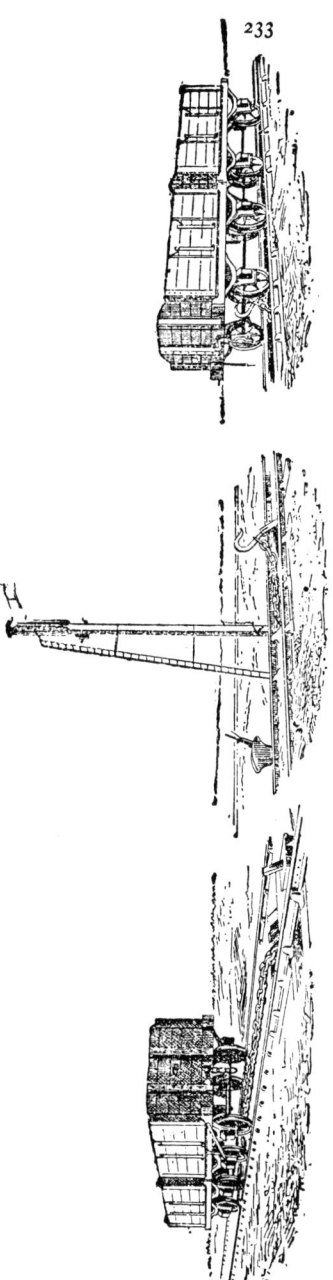

SKETCH OF CHAIN DRAG AND HOOK.

FIG. 28 A.

EDGE HILL MARSHALLING SIDINGS.

## SHUNTING AND MARSHALLING OF GOODS TRAINS.

the accommodation can be increased, when necessary, by 50 per cent.

The *modus operandi* is as follows:—On the arrival of a set of waggons in the upper reception lines, the rear brakes are put on, the engine is detached, and then on each waggon is chalked the number of the sorting siding it has to enter. One man carefully inspects the brakes of each waggon, and calls out the chalked number to a second man standing below him, who has to regulate the speed of the descending waggons. This second man passes the number on by hand signal to the shunter lower down who has charge of the points, and who, by moving a lever, turns the waggon into its proper siding. The shunters are provided with brake sticks, which they insert between the wheel and the waggon-frame to steady the waggons in going down, and they also use these implements for letting down the brake levers when required. By the process thus described, each sorting siding now holds a separate train, although the waggons composing it are in indiscriminate order, but by a repetition of the operation, the waggons of each train are separated in the gridirons, and are lowered, one by one, into the departure lines, in the precise order in which they are required to be sent away.

Fig. 28 A also shows the apparatus known as the "chain drag," devised by Mr. Footner for arresting runaway waggons, which may occasionally get beyond the control of the shunters. This consists of a heavy iron chain cable, placed in a wrought iron tank between, and below, the level of the rails ; a steel hook attached to the cable is fixed in a loose socket, at the height of a waggon axle, and is worked by a lever which also works a signal.

When a train is intended to pass, the hook is lowered by the lever, but if it is desired to stop a waggon, the hook is raised by the lever, and catches the axle of the waggon, and the heavy cable attached to the hook, being drawn out of the tank, by its weight, when dragged over the ballast, soon stops the runaway. During the last twelve years this apparatus has come into use 135 times, and in no case has it failed to stop the waggons, without injury either to them or to their loads, or to the apparatus itself. At the present time there are six of these chain drags in use at Edge Hill, the cables varying in weight from 86 cwt. to 109 cwt.

The gradient of these sidings varies, according to requirements, from 1 in 60 to 1 in 115. For instance, through points and crossings, and round the standard curve of seven chains radius, the gradient is from 1 in 70 to 1 in 100, but on straight lines, where waggons have to start singly, and enter curves, as, for example, at (1), the lower end of the upper reception lines; (2) the lower end of the sorting sidings; and (3) the lower end of each siding in the gridirons, the gradient is one in 60. Again, on straight lines, where many waggons move together, and good "runners" compensate for bad, the gradient varies from 1 in 100 to 1 in 115. All the curves are of the same radius (seven chains), so that a shunter, in determining the speed necessary for any particular truck, may concentrate his attention upon it, knowing that the resistance of every curve it encounters will be the same. Speaking generally, the gradients are so regulated that the greatest momentum is imparted where the trucks are required to start quickly, and where there is the greatest amount of resistance to be overcome.

In practice it is found that in shunting by gravitation, no two trucks run exactly alike, some railway companies and private owners keeping their stock in better order than others, and much depending upon the precise condition of the tyres and axle-boxes, the length of the wheel base, the nature of the load, and the description of brake gear employed. Strong winds also affect the running, especially of covered vans lightly loaded; severe frost offers an impediment, while, on the other hand, warm and moist weather renders the rails slippery, and heavy concentrated loads on a narrow wheel base will often run too freely; but there are simple appliances which are found in practice easily to overcome all these difficulties. The shunters, during the day-time, use various recognised gestures to indicate in advance to one another the numbers chalked on the trucks passing down the incline, and during the night, similar information is communicated by the movement of the coloured lenses of their hand-lamps.

During the year 1890, 545,000 loaded waggons were passed through these sidings, in addition to 101,000 empty waggons, making a total of 646,000 waggons, or a daily average of about 2,000, equal to fifty average trains.

There are seventy-eight men employed to work the sidings, including nine foremen and inspectors. The various foremen's offices are connected by telephone circuits, and, finally, the whole of the sidings are lighted by lofty and powerful lamps of the Siemen's type, in addition to smaller lamps fixed near each pair of points.

One special advantage claimed by its inventor for this system of marshalling waggons, is that it can be carried out by any active man without previous training, the operations being so simple that the work can be learnt in a week or two, and the only man who is really required to be possessed of geographical knowledge and experience being the one who chalks the numbers of the sidings on the waggons.

## CHAPTER XII.

ON THE WORKING OF GOODS STATIONS.

To the uninitiated, it may possibly appear that when a package or a consignment of merchandise is handed to a railway company for transit, it is a very simple operation to place it in a waggon and convey it to its destination, but it is only necessary to bear in mind the vast extent of the operations carried on at a large and important goods station, the multitude of consignments that have to be simultaneously dealt with, their varied description, and the many destinations to which they have to be conveyed, in order to realise that to enable a vast business of this kind to be conducted with promptitude and certainty, to provide securities against goods being mis-sent or wrongly delivered, and to ensure a reliable means of tracing them in the event of their, after all, going astray, a most complete and careful system of organisation is indispensable. It may be premised that the methods and appliances employed by different railway companies, as a means of securing these results, are not precisely identical in practice, nor are they absolutely uniform at all the stations of one company, it being frequently necessary to be guided by physical circumstances, the mode of construction of the premises, and the special nature of the traffic at particular stations, but from a description of the mode of working certain of the goods depôts on the London and North-Western Railway, the reader will be able to gather a fair idea of the nature of the operations to be carried on in working a large merchandise traffic, and of the arrangements which, with more or less variation, are adopted at the most important goods stations.

A goods station which possesses certain features of interest, chiefly on account of its somewhat unique mode of construction, is Broad Street, which is the City Depôt of the London and North-Western Company, in London. The North London Railway, which is connected with the North-Western, passes round the Northern suburbs of London to Dalston Junction, where it trends almost due South to its passenger terminus at Broad Street, in the very heart of the City. Land in the City of London being, of course, extremely valuable, the line is carried during the latter part of its course by means of bridges and viaducts at a high elevation, in some cases over the tops of the houses, and it thus reaches its terminus at a point considerably above the level of the surrounding thoroughfares, the passenger station having accordingly been built on arches. Advantage has been taken of this fact to enable the London and North-Western Company to provide themselves with an extensive goods station without incurring the enormous expense of taking land for the purpose in the busiest part of the City, and the goods traffic is, as a matter of fact, conducted in the arches under the passenger station, the waggons of goods being transferred one by one from the upper to the lower level and *vice versâ*, by means of powerful hydraulic lifts. All along the front of these arches, which are fourteen in number, and, including some space beyond them, which has been covered in, each measure 340 feet in length, and 32 feet in width, a roomy stage, or unloading bank, has been erected, 430 feet long and 45 feet deep, and from this, at right angles, narrow stages 240 feet in length, and 12 feet in width, with a line of rails on each side of them, extend through each arch, the lines of rails being at the further end connected with a cross-line, by means of which the waggons can be turned upon turn-tables, and taken to one or other of the hydraulic hoists, each of which will raise a weight of fourteen tons.

On the further side of the arches some additional space has been taken in on the street level to form an open goods yard, on one portion of which a lofty warehouse has been erected for the storage of goods waiting delivery, or goods for forward transit.

Before attempting to describe the manner in which this station is worked, it is necessary to explain that traffic arriving from the country for delivery in London is called "up traffic," while "down traffic" means traffic sent from London to the country, and these two elements in the business of the station are in practice kept perfectly distinct.

The inwards or "up" traffic at Broad Street, consists very largely of provisions for supplying the early markets with fish, meat, poultry, butter, eggs, and other perishable commodities, which have to be delivered in time for sale to the retail buyers who attend the markets as early as four o'clock in the morning, and also of general merchandise, purchased from manufacturers in the provinces one day, and expected to be in the City warehouses by nine o'clock on the following morning; and to effect deliveries at such an early hour is a work which demands for its accomplishment the most perfect organisation and attention to detail. For instance, in the Metropolitan Meat Market there are no less than 230 stalls or shops, all of which receive meat from the provinces, and the railway companies are expected to deliver and *hang* the meat in these shops before the arrival of the salesmen. Thus, a waggon will arrive, say, from Scotland, with thirty sides of beef for delivery to as many consignees, in as many different parts of the market, while other meat will arrive simultaneously from other stations for the same consignees, and, with a view to speed and economy, the different consignments have to be brought together, and the vans loaded in such a way that, as far as possible, two vans will not be delivering at the same time to one shop. This is effected by sorting the meat into districts, according to the position of the stalls in the market, on the stage at Broad Street before it is loaded on to the vans.

Speaking more generally, the mode of dealing with "up" goods is as follows :—This part of the business is conducted, not in the arches previously described, but in the warehouse of which mention has already been made, the ground floor of which is staged, so as to form a deck, or platform, upon which the goods can be sorted and transferred from the railway waggons to the street vans. This platform is open on both sides, so that vans can be backed up to it on one side, while a line of rails extends along the other side, on which the railway waggons on arrival are placed, after being lowered from the upper level by means of the hydraulic hoists. The invoices which are received with the waggons, and which are documents containing a description of the goods, their marks and addresses, the weight, and particulars of the charges, are passed into an office called the delivery office, where each invoice is entered in a book, stamped with a progressive number, timed as to arrival, checked as to correctness of rate and charges, and is then passed to a "marking clerk," whose duty it is to mark against each entry on the invoice the position on the platform or sorting bank in which the article to which the entry refers, is to be placed. On the platform, by means of letters and numbers painted on the columns which support the roof, the whole of London is mapped out into districts with great care and precision, and the numbers inserted by the marking clerk on the invoice correspond with these divisions, and are for the guidance of the checkers in unloading the goods from the waggons, and loading them into the vans for delivery. The marking clerk having discharged his office, the invoice passes on to another set of clerks, each of whom extracts from it, and enters on the carman's delivery sheets, such of the entries as refer to the particular section of the City with which he is appointed to deal, and by this process of exhaustion, the whole of the entries for delivery to a particular district are brought to a focus, although the goods may have arrived from hundreds of different stations, and be entered on as many different invoices. The same set of clerks enter the charges in the carmen's delivery sheets in cases where they are to be paid by the consignees.

The next step is to pass the invoice out of the delivery office to the platform, where a gang of men unload the goods from the waggons, checking them with the invoice as they do so, and wheel them away on hand-trucks to the different positions on the platform, according to the numbers marked against the entries. Next, the carmen's delivery sheets are passed out to the platform, and the delivery foreman directs the loading of the vans from the different sections on the bank, the goods being carefully checked against the entries on the delivery sheets as they are placed in the vans. Finally, the cartage department take possession of both vans and delivery sheets, the vans are horsed and started away to their respective destinations, all the processes being carried out with the utmost care, but at the same time, with the greatest rapidity.

There are, however, many contingencies which arise in the working of the traffic, and must be promptly met, in order to prevent delays occurring, and the chief of these may be classed under four heads, as follows :—(1) Goods arriving without invoice ; (2) discrepancies between the invoice and the goods actually received in the waggons ; (3) invoices arriving without the goods ; and, (4) goods accidentally trucked to the wrong position on the platform.

If the waggon arrives without invoice it is unloaded in its turn, an account of the goods contained in it is entered on a special form provided for the purpose, and, where the addresses of the consignees appear on the goods, they are trucked away to their proper position on the platform, the number of the section being marked on the form by the checker. The form is then passed into the delivery office, and, as far as possible, delivery sheets are made out from it in the same way as if it were the missing invoice. Such goods as are found in the waggon merely under mark and not addressed, are taken to a particular position on the platform to wait further orders on the arrival of the invoice. Meanwhile the sending station is applied to for a copy of the invoice, and the goods which remain on hand are dealt with on its arrival. A similar course is adopted in the case of goods found in a waggon without there being any corresponding entry on the invoice.

When the invoice arrives, but not the goods, which usually results either from the waggons having been wrongly labelled or having missed their proper train, the telegraph is set to work to ascertain their whereabouts, and the invoices are held over until the goods make their appearance.

The most troublesome errors arise from the porters misunderstanding the directions given by the checkers, and wheeling goods to a wrong section on the platform. In a case of this kind, when the delivery sheet for that section arrives from the office, it, of course, contains no entry of this particular package, and it is consequently left on the bank. On the other hand, the checker for the section to which it should have been taken finds he is short of it, and makes a remark to that effect on the sheet which he passes back to his foreman, and the latter employs every means in his power to discover the whereabouts of the missing package. Failing to do so, he calls in the services of two men, who are called "searchers," and are employed upon this duty all day, but if their efforts prove fruitless there is nothing for it but to wait until the "bank list" is taken, that is, when at four o'clock each afternoon a complete list is made of all goods remaining on the bank after the morning's deliveries, by means of which most errors can be rectified.

The "down," or outward traffic is dealt with in the arches before described, the "runs" or lines of rails alongside the stages being gradually filled during the day with rows of empty waggons, ready to receive the goods as they come in during the afternoon and evening. This is effected by transferring to the "down" arches the waggons which have come in with "up" goods and have been emptied during the morning. As the loaded vans come in at the gates they are stopped at an office placed at the entrance, called the "weighbridge office," and the consignment notes are impressed with an official stamp, which alone renders them authentic. The consignment note plays an important part in the manipulation of the outwards goods, and it may be explained, for the benefit of the uninitiated, that it is a document which the sender of goods hands to the carman or other agent of the Company, to whom he delivers the goods, and in which is described their nature, their marks, and addresses, and sometimes their weight. Business firms who are in the habit of forwarding goods use for this purpose printed forms supplied by the Company, or provided by themselves, but where ordinary members of the general public forward isolated packages without a consignment note, the Company manufacture one from the address, or the entry in the carman's book, the principle acted upon being that there must be a separate consignment note provided for every distinct package or parcel of goods for the same destination. The object of stamping the consignment notes at the entrance gates is to checkmate a very ingenious system of fraud which was found to be in operation some time ago, when some dishonest servants of the Company hit upon the plan of obtaining possession of valuable goods, by simply destroying the original consignment notes and addresses, and substituting false documents, by which the goods were consigned to confederates in some other town. Under the present system, as the fraudulent note could not bear the weighbridge stamp, its character would at once be detected.

Large firms frequently enter a whole van load of goods for various addresses, on one consignment note, and therefore the first step is for all such notes, containing more than one entry, to be taken to an office called the "Shipping office," where a separate note is made out for each separate consignment, these manufactured notes being officially stamped to shew that they are "extracted" from an authentic note.

Meanwhile the vans, as they arrive, are placed in position for unloading on to the large stage or platform, previously described as running along the front of all the arches; the consignment notes relating to each load are handed by the unloading foreman to the various checkers who are in charge of the unloading gangs, and the goods are removed from the vans, checked against the entries on the consignment notes, and weighed on the weighing machines, which are stationed at regular intervals all along the stage. On the wall in each of the arches is painted a number, and the name of the place or district for which goods are loaded in that particular arch; for instance, one will be "Liverpool," another "Manchester," a third "North Staffordshire," and so on, and in each arch, also, there is displayed a copy of a table, corrected from time to time, and which shews in more detail the stations to which goods are loaded in each arch, and the times of departure of the trains made up and despatched each night to the various destinations. The experienced checker, however, has all this in his head, so that when a package is taken out of a van, and the marks or address is called out, he is able at once to check the entry on the consignment note and to shout "No. 5," or "No. 6," as the case may be, when the package is forthwith placed on a hand truck and, accompanied by its consignment note, is wheeled away to the particular arch to which it belongs, and deposited on the stage there, ready for loading into the waggons. Here one of the loading gangs, each of which consists of a checker, a loader, a caller-off, and two porters, take it in hand, and deposit it in a waggon destined for the station to which it is addressed. When the goods are in the waggons, the consignment notes are taken to the shipping office, and the clerk in charge sorts them out to the different clerks whose duty it is to make out the invoices for the various destinations. These clerks enter on the invoices the names and addresses of consignees, the nature and description of the goods, the weight and the charges; and the invoices, if they are ready in time, are handed to the brakeman in charge of the train by which the waggons are despatched; if not ready at the time the train departs, they are sent afterwards by fast passenger trains, so as to arrive at the same time as the goods, or before. The consignment notes, having been marked with a progressive number in such a way as to identify them with the corresponding entries on the invoices, so as to facilitate the tracing of goods which may go astray, are carefully filed for future reference.

The waggons of goods when loaded, sheeted, and labelled, are run out at the further end of the arches, turned on to the hydraulic hoists by means of the turntables and capstans, and emerge on to the upper level, where in a group of ten long sidings adjoining the North

London Railway, and still by the aid of hydraulic capstans, they are marshalled into trains, and sent away to their various destinations.

This process is, however, very much facilitated beforehand by the fact that the waggons have been arranged in the runs or arches in *train order*, *i.e.*, a separate train or portion of a train has been loaded in each arch and in station order, so that the waggons emerge from the lifts on the high level in the order in which they are required to go away.

Goods intended for large centres such as Liverpool, Manchester, etc., to which many waggons are loaded on the same night, are dealt with in two of the arches which are laid out in a somewhat different manner from the rest. In these arches, there is a roadway for carts throughout, and the goods are loaded direct from the carts to the railway waggons without any hand trucking being needed.

If, through extra pressure, or by oversight, goods are left on the stages when the loads have been made up, and the night's work is over, the consignment notes found with them are taken into the shipping office, and stamped with the letter "S" (Stage), to indicate that the goods have been left over, and that special attention must be given to their despatch by the first available train.

When goods are found left on the stage without consignment notes, if the names and addresses of consignees are apparent, they are entered on new consignment notes, and dealt with in the usual way. If, on the other hand, there is nothing to indicate their destination, they are kept on hand, and a record of the fact is made in a book set apart for the purpose, and which is referred to whenever there is any enquiry with regard to goods not delivered, every available means being meanwhile taken to discover the owners, by a number of clerks specially employed on this duty.

There are many other arrangements in operation, both with regard to "up" and "down" traffic, with a view to guard against irregularities, and to rectify mistakes; but perhaps enough has been said to give an adequate idea of the amount of method and organisation required to conduct such a business with order and despatch.

The warehouse, already referred to, which occupies one side of the yard, and rears its imposing height far above most of the surrounding buildings, consists of four storeys, besides extensive cellarage in the basement, and the different floors are reached from the stage by means of two 25-cwt. hydraulic lifts. Packed closely from top to bottom with goods of every possible description, it would at first sight appear that an individual package once deposited here, would be to all intents and purposes lost, but a brief examination will correct this error, and reveal order in the apparent chaos, for the numerous iron pillars which support each floor divide it into small sections, each of which bears a number, while every article which comes into the warehouse, either waiting for delivery, or for forward transit, is entered in a book with the number, against the entry, of the floor and section in which the article is deposited. Amongst a great deal of curious flotsam and jetsam, which has drifted into this capacious repository, perhaps one of the most interesting features is a huge wooden case, fashioned after the manner of a coffin, and which contains what are alleged to be the fossilised remains of a gigantic specimen of the human race, upwards of twelve feet in height, and of colossal proportions. It is said to have been excavated near the Giant's Causeway (surely an appropriate spot for such a *trouvaille!*), some years ago, during some prospecting operations for the discovery of iron ore, and was for a time exhibited at Liverpool; but a dispute arising as to its ownership, the grim relic was thrown into Chancery, and has remained "on hand" at Broad Street ever since the year 1876, the Railway Company having a very considerable lien on it for warehouse charges. Whether it be, as stated by its original owner, the petrefaction of a human being, or merely a specimen of very antique sculpture, it is beyond doubt one of the most curious consignments ever warehoused by a railway company.

The total area embraced by the Broad Street Goods Station, including three and a half acres on the high level, is seventeen acres, the lines affording, in all, standing room for 820 trucks, of which 487 can be placed in position for forward loading on the low level at one time. On the average, 456 loaded waggons are received daily, and 508 are forwarded, making a total not far short of a thousand waggons a day.

The crane power employed is as follows:—

> Nine 30-cwt. hydraulic cranes, and twenty-seven manual cranes, for loading from vans to waggons and *vice versâ.*
>
> Eleven 30-cwt. hydraulic cranes, and five manual cranes, for loading from vans to platforms and *vice versâ.*
>
> Twenty 30-cwt. hydraulic cranes, and sixty-nine manual cranes, for loading from waggons to platforms and *vice versâ.*

Besides which there are twelve hydraulic and twenty-eight hand cranes used for special purposes, and one 5-ton and one 10-ton hydraulic crane in the yard, for dealing with exceptionally heavy articles.

A goods station of the London and North-Western Company, which has excited the attention, and, to some extent the admiration, of foreign engineers and railway managers who have visited this country for the purpose of comparing their own methods and appliances with ours, is Holyhead. The Company have devoted a great amount of attention to cultivating and encouraging the trade between England and Ireland, and one means to this end has been the provision of very complete and admirably adapted accommodation at Holyhead, for the transfer of traffic between the railway waggons and the fleet of steamers belonging to the Company, fourteen in number, and having a gross tonnage of 14,308 tons, by means of which a daily service is established between Holyhead and the North Wall, Dublin.

Holyhead Harbour, the entire quay frontage of which is about 3,760 feet, has an area of twenty-four acres, and an average depth at high and low water of thirty feet and twelve and a half feet respectively, the transhipment of the goods being carried on in two large warehouses, each about 750 feet in length, erected on the quays on the east and west sides of the harbour, of which the one on the east side is devoted exclusively to the export traffic, or traffic going from England to Ireland, and the one on the west side to the traffic from Ireland to England. Lines of rails, conveniently connected with the railway, run right through both warehouses, with a platform or loading deck, fifteen feet wide, running throughout between the lines of rails and the quay. In each warehouse there are six hydraulic cranes, having a rake of twenty-five feet, and a capacity of three tons, so fixed that they can lift goods from the railway waggons to the platform, or to the hold of a vessel, or *vice versâ*. With screw steamers, of which the Company possess four, it is practicable by one operation to take a package from the waggons and deposit it in the hold of the vessel, but with paddle-wheel steamers, owing to their greater width, the hydraulic cranes are worked in connection with a winch which raises or lowers the goods between the hold and the deck.

The harbour and quays are illuminated at night by five powerful electric lights, one being fixed at each end of each warehouse, and the fifth at the south end of the harbour.

The mode of carrying on the working is as follows:— Waggons containing export traffic for shipment, having been brought by the train engines, and deposited close to the entrance of the export warehouse in reception sidings provided for the purpose, are drawn up by hydraulic capstans, and placed in exact positions opposite the berths, where are moored the vessels into which they are required to be unloaded. The goods are taken from the waggons, checked with the invoice, and lowered into the vessel, full particulars of the goods shipped by each boat being recorded in a "Transfer-book." The clerkage is carried on simultaneously with the actual handling of the goods, so that almost as soon as the hatchways are closed, and the gangways removed, the invoices are sent on board, and the vessel is ready to leave. Specially heavy articles, such as furniture vans or machinery, are loaded on the quay by means of 18-ton hydraulic cranes, or, if necessary, by a pair of shear legs, which will carry eighty tons.

With regard to import traffic, as soon as the vessel is berthed alongside the quay, the invoices are passed to a checker, who, for the guidance of the men on the platform, first makes out a "card," or list, of the urgent, or "perishable," traffic, showing the loads which have to be made up for different destinations, so that as the goods are landed from the boat, the ganger in charge of the men on the platform is enabled to direct the loading into waggons. By the time the urgent, or perishable, traffic has been dealt with, the checker has prepared another "loading-card" for the general cargo, and thus the discharging and loading-up of the goods is enabled to proceed without interruption, until the whole have been despatched.

Ireland being to so large an extent an agricultural country, an important feature in her exports to England is live stock, and for the transfer of this from the vessels to the waggons at Holyhead, the arrangements are very complete. There is accommodation for the unloading of the animals from the vessels at any height of the tide all along the front of the import warehouses, and this operation can be carried on at the same time as the unloading of parcels and the perishable goods traffic from the same boats, while, close at hand, is a covered pen set apart for the reception of lame and distressed animals who are unfit to walk to the cattle yard, such animals being loaded up and taken by an engine to the yard. The animals who are fit to walk are conducted by a convenient roadway to the yard, which contains covered accommodation for upwards of 180 cattle, 800 pigs, and fifteen horses, together with open pens capable of holding 230 head of stock. There are also pens erected alongside a siding, upon which twelve waggons can be placed in position for loading the animals up for forward transit. The sidings appropriated to the cattle traffic hold in all 140 waggons, and there are ample facilities for cleaning and disinfecting them after each journey, including twelve hydrants for the supply of water. During the year 1890, 55,730 cattle were transhipped at Holyhead to the various towns in England, in addition to 118,238 sheep and lambs, 9,823 horses, and last, but not least, 200,000 pigs. The live stock shipped to Ireland from England is not considerable, but in one recent year it included two lions and two elephants, although what these strange denizens of the far east were to do in the "distressful country," can only be a matter of conjecture.

When import goods are loaded into waggons, a kind of inventory is made of them, which is termed a slip, and as soon as the load is completed, these slips are compared with the invoices, so as to discover and rectify any mistakes, as for instance, goods loaded in the wrong waggon. A transfer book is also kept, as in the case of the export traffic, and in this is recorded the date and number of the invoice, particulars of the traffic, the weight, the name of the vessel by which the goods are received, and the number and destination of the waggon in which they are loaded for forward transit.

As the waggons are loaded, they are turned over turntables on to adjoining lines of rails, where they are marshalled in proper order, labelled, and sheeted, and within a few minutes of the loading of the last waggon being completed, the train is ready to start. In discharging a vessel, as already mentioned, preference is always given to perishable and urgent goods, and these are despatched by express passenger trains within an hour after the boat is berthed, but within two hours and a half of the arrival of the vessel, a full train load, of sometimes upwards of thirty waggons, is despatched, while a second and a third train follow at intervals of not more than an hour, a striking proof of the excellence of the arrangements, and the energy and skill with which the operations are conducted.

There is a large fish traffic at Holyhead, and in dealing with this, speed is, of course, of the utmost importance, especially in hot weather. In order to accommodate the fish brought to the harbour by steamers and sailing vessels direct from the fishing grounds, the Company have constructed a fish jetty, 440 ft. long and 50 ft. wide, on the import side of the harbour, with two platforms and two lines of rails, each line being capable of holding twenty-five waggons. The loading from the vessels to the waggons is performed by means of three hydraulic cranes, each lifting 30 cwt., and having a sufficient rake to cover both platforms, so that two train loads of fish may be loaded simultaneously. To save time, the empty waggons are placed in proper station order, so that there shall be no delay in marshalling them, and the labels and way-bills being prepared while the loading is proceeding, the train can start on its journey as soon as the last load is completed.

At all the Company's large goods stations, ample provision is made for the prevention or extinction of fire, fire brigades composed of members of the staff being organised, drilled, and frequently called together by signal for exercise, and these precautions are not omitted in the case of Holyhead. The fire appliances here are of a very complete description, and water is supplied from no less than sixty-three powerful hydrants.

The total traffic handled at Holyhead during the year 1889, in addition to live stock, was about 270,000 tons, including coal; of this total about 135,000 tons was cross-channel traffic with Ireland.

It has always been a question involving some amount of controversy, as to what is the best and most convenient manner of laying out the accommodation in a large goods warehouse, so as to enable the business to be carried on in the most expeditious and economical manner. Many different arrangements have been tried, and, of course, in building a warehouse at any particular station, there may always be special circumstances to be taken into consideration, such as the nature of the traffic, and the available space; but our illustrations (Figs. 29, 30 and 31) shew the ground plan, first-floor plan, and section, of a large goods warehouse of the first class, built upon the most modern principles, and laid out in the manner which is believed to be the best adapted to the needs of an important goods station (Chester), where three different classes of traffic have to be dealt with, that is to say (1), local traffic, or traffic which commences or ends its journey at the station; (2), transfer traffic, or traffic loaded to the station, for the purpose of being transhipped into other waggons, and forwarded to destination; and (3), warehouse traffic, or goods which are required to be stored, awaiting orders for forwarding or delivery. It will be perceived that this is what is termed a "dead-end" warehouse, or, in other words, the waggons come in and go out the same way, and cannot be taken *through* the warehouse, and out at the other end. There are five platforms, or stages, and six lines of rails, so that every platform, as will be seen, has a line of rails alongside it, and three of them

S

have a line on each side. There is also a stage running transversely along one end of the building, to which access is given by a roadway for carts. To facilitate the handling of the heavy goods, there are in all twenty-four cranes, each carrying thirty cwt., four of which are power cranes, and the rest are worked by hand. The upper floor is devoted to storage purposes, and to enable grain to be conveniently delivered from this storey, slides are provided, down which the sacks can be passed to the ground floor; there are also a number of shoots for transferring loose grain from sack to sack. Grain in sacks can be hoisted direct from the waggons or carts below to the upper storey by means of cranes, but if required to be stored in bulk, it is lifted by crane to a gangway, or gallery, erected *over* the upper storey, and supported on the principals of the building, and then is shot out of the sacks into bins below, through shoots provided for the purpose.

Under the stages of the warehouse are capacious cellars for the storage of ale, bacon, and such commodities, which can be lifted or lowered direct between the cellars and the carts, or railway waggons, by means of suitable cranes.

Waggons containing goods arriving by train for delivery in the town, are placed on the outer line of rails, next to one or the other of the side stages, nearest the walls, and as carts can approach either of these from the side of the warehouse, where they stand sheltered by a projecting awning, the goods can be transferred by the cranes direct from waggon to cart, or light goods can be handed across the platform. Other town goods can be unloaded in the second line of rails on either side and trucked to the platform at the end of the warehouse where carts can approach them. Outward goods, collected in the town for forward transit, are brought in by carts, unloaded on the transverse stage, and trucked thence to the various stages alongside which the waggons have been placed for their reception. The narrow centre platform, having a line of rails on each side, and cranes suitably arranged, is appropriated to transfer traffic which can thus be easily removed from one waggon and placed in another.

A warehouse of this description and dimensions will accommodate upwards of forty waggons at one time, and in this particular warehouse about eighty are loaded daily, and ninety are discharged. Warehouses designed upon this plan are in use at Liverpool (Edge Hill), Bolton, Blackburn, Leicester, Derby, Chester, and other stations.

Fig. 32 is an illustration of a small wooden goods shed, suitable for a roadside station, where the traffic to be dealt with is purely local, and not of an extensive character. The arrangement, in this case, is so simple and obvious, as to speak for itself and to require no detailed description.

In goods warehouses where a small amount of machinery requires to be actuated, and the business to be conducted is not sufficiently extensive to justify the application of steam or hydraulic power, a gas engine is found to afford very satisfactory results, both as regards economy and convenience, as a means of actuating the cranes. For a machine of this kind no special attendant is required, as one of the ordinary warehouse porters can start and stop the engine when necessary, and clean and oil it in his spare time. The peculiar advantage of the gas engine is that it can be

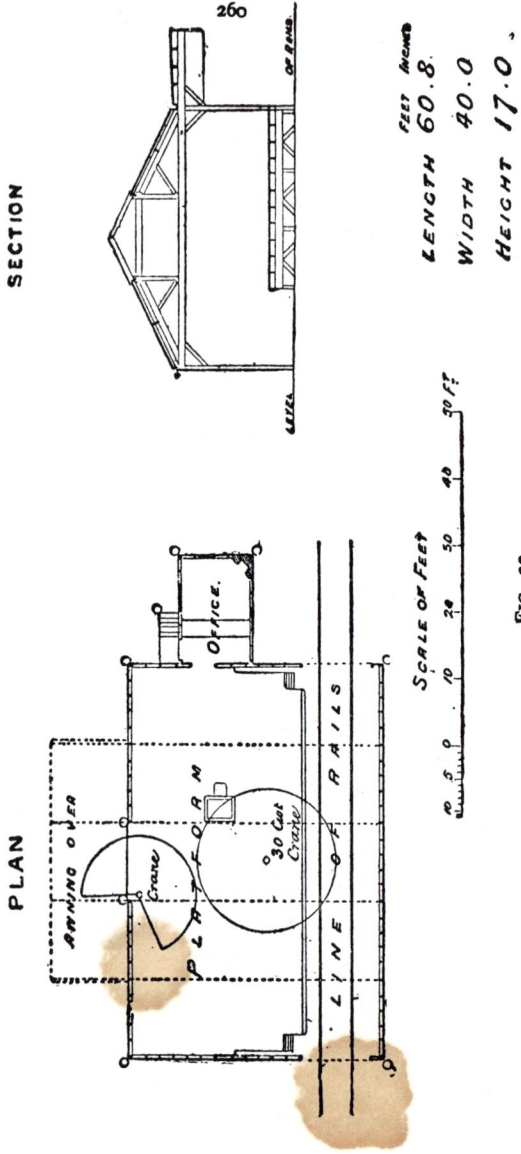

Fig. 22.

started and stopped at a moment's notice, and there is accordingly no waste of fuel whatever, besides which the first cost of the machinery is very moderate compared with that of hydraulic power on a small scale, and the average cost of gas for an eight h.p. gas engine is not more than from threepence to sixpence per hour, according to the price of gas in the locality, and the work required of the engine

The London and North-Western Company have at the present time thirty warehouses in which the machinery is actuated by gas engines, varying from one and a half to eight h.p., according to the size of the building, and the number of cranes and lifts required. A good example of this class of machinery is found at the Northampton warehouse, erected by the North-Western Company, in 1881. In this warehouse there are two cranes of thirty cwt. capacity, and two 10-cwt. friction jiggers, worked by a gas engine of eight h.p., the first cost of the installation having been £950. The cost of gas consumed (about 108,300 cubic feet) averages £10 10s. per annum, in addition to about £3 10s. for maintenance and repairs, and £3 5s. for oil and waste, etc.

## CHAPTER XIII.

### RATES AND FARES—DIVISION OF TRAFFIC—THE RAILWAY CLEARING-HOUSE.

IT is not the intention of the present writer to enter very deeply into the thorny and much debated question of railway rates, and the many controversial points arising out of them. The late Mr. Grierson, General Manager of the Great Western Railway Company, in the work published shortly before his lamented decease, and entitled, "Railway Rates, English and Foreign," has so completely exhausted this subject from almost every point of view, that, from the stand-point of the railway companies at least, there remains very little to be said. In a work of this character, it will be sufficient to give merely a brief account of the manner in which rates and fares are made, and the way in which the different railway companies share the receipts amongst themselves, where those receipts are derived from "through" traffic, *i.e.*, traffic which has to be carried over more than one railway before its transit is completed.

The rates and fares to be charged upon a railway are, in a sense, regulated by Act of Parliament; that is to say, that, until recently, the Act which authorised the making of the railway fixed the *maximum* tolls, which were not to be exceeded for any traffic using the line.

In practice, however, the maximum tolls were rarely charged, and a great deal was left in the discretion of the railway companies—moreover, it is impossible for an Act of Parliament to fix the precise charge to be made for each particular commodity which may be conveyed over a railway, and, as a matter of fact, the articles specified in the Acts were comparatively few in number, the remainder being summed up in the comprehensive phrase, "other articles, matters, and things." In fixing its rates, therefore, a railway company had to classify these "articles, matters, and things," as nearly as might be with relation to the commodities which were actually specified in the Act. This necessity was met by the companies meeting in conference at the Railway Clearing-house, and drawing up a comprehensive list of the articles usually carried on railways, classifying them under eight different heads, according to their weight, bulk, value, and destructibility, in what is called the "Clearing-house Classification;" for instance: minerals, sand, and such matters, would be in the lowest class, while fresh fruit and fish, furniture, china, and other valuable or fragile articles would be in the highest. Each company then fixed its rates between each pair of stations for each class of goods in the classification, having due regard to its *maximum* powers; but in addition to these "class rates," there were always a number of special rates for particular descriptions of goods.

But the old order of things has been totally changed since the passing of an Act in the last session of Parliament, entitled "The Railway and Canal Traffic Act of 1888," the provisions of which will be more particularly described in the succeeding chapter. The general effect of it, however, has been to place upon the railway companies the obligation of submitting an entirely new classification and schedule of maximum charges, which, after running the gauntlet of all objectors, and securing the approval of the Board of Trade, has been embodied in an Act, and received the sanction of Parliament.

The rates are governed by the nature and extent of the traffic, the pressure of competition, either by water, by a rival railway route, or by other land carriage; but, above all, the companies have regard to the commercial value of the commodity, and the rate it will bear, so as to admit of its being produced and sold in a competing market with a fair margin of profit. The companies each do their best to meet the circumstances of the trade, to develop the resources of their own particular district, and to encourage the competition of markets, primarily, no doubt, in their own interest, but nevertheless greatly to the advantage of the community.

The fixing of passenger fares is a comparatively simple process. Between local stations on the North Western Railway the fares are made up, roughly speaking, on the basis of charging twopence per mile travelled for first-class passengers, three half-pence per mile for second-class, and one penny for third-class, the amount of the passenger duty being added to the first and second-class fares; but where there are competing routes, or where, in suburban districts, the opposition of omnibuses or tramways has to be encountered, the fares are often considerably reduced. Railway companies are sometimes very unfairly assailed when they reduce their rates or fares in order to meet competition, and it is somewhat hastily assumed that, if they were able to reduce their charges on compulsion, it was incumbent on them to have done so before. Thus, it is not uncommon to hear the remark, "The —— Company have had to reduce their fares at last, thanks to the opening of the —— line." This is, however, unjust. So long as competition does not exist, the companies are only discharging their duty to their shareholders in obtaining what Parliament has sanctioned as a fair rate of remuneration for the services they perform, but when there is a rival in the field, they are justified in concluding that "half a loaf is better than no bread at all"; although it by no means follows that their previous charges were unfair or excessive.

In days gone by, it cannot be denied that railway companies incurred great losses and sacrificed a considerable portion of their revenue by extreme competition amongst themselves, but in this matter, as in many others, they have gained wisdom by experience, and "profited by the uses of adversity." A certain amount of healthy competition will always exist; but the companies now mitigate its severity by agreeing amongst themselves what the rates between competing points shall be by all routes. The competitive rates between most places in Great Britain are, in the main, governed by two Conferences, "The English and Scotch Traffic Rates Conference," and the "Normanton Conference." The English and Scotch Conference is composed of representatives (who are usually the Chief Goods Managers) of all the companies, both English and Scotch, who are interested in the carriage of goods between places in England and places in Scotland by the various routes. These representatives meet once a month, and deal with all questions arising in connection with the making of new rates or the alteration of existing rates for competitive places between which more than one company can carry. The Normanton Conference, which was originally established to control the rates for a certain district of which Normanton, where its meetings were formerly held, was a convenient centre, has gradually so much extended its scope that it is now composed of representatives of nearly every company of any importance in England, and governs almost the whole of the competitive rates which are not dealt with by the English and Scotch Conference. The cross-channel rates between England and Ireland are controlled by an "English and Irish Traffic Rates Conference," and, besides these three, there are some minor Conferences which have been established in connection with the traffic of particular districts, but have not the importance of those which have been already alluded to.

In addition to the system of agreeing the rates between competing points, there is another plan which railway companies sometimes adopt, in order to avoid the losses arising from competition, which is known as "Percentage Division of Traffic," and which is carried out in the following manner. Supposing that there is a certain traffic to be conveyed between two towns or districts, and that there are two or more railway companies, each having a route of its own by which it is enabled to compete for the traffic. An agreement is come to that the receipts derived from the whole of the traffic, carried by all routes, shall be thrown into a common fund, and that each company shall be entitled to a certain percentage of the whole—say, for example, 50 per cent. to the company having the best route, 30 per cent. to the second, and 20 per cent. to the third. The percentages are usually adjusted on the basis of past actual carryings, but in settling the terms of the agreement due weight is accorded to any prospective advantages which may entitle one company to claim a larger proportion than it has carried in the past. An agreed allowance for working expenses is made to any company carrying more than the percentage allotted to its route, but, as this allowance is fixed with due regard to the actual cost of the service, it will be perceived that there is no very great inducement for any company to carry more than its share.

Let it not be hastily concluded that an agreement of this kind is opposed to the interest of the general public, for it may safely be asserted that in the long run it is a mistake to imagine that the public are the gainers by an extreme course of competition between two railway companies. If the contest is waged to the bitter end, the public may enjoy low rates for a time, but the result must be the "survival of the fittest"—or, rather, the strongest—and the latter, becoming masters of the situation, will naturally seek to recoup themselves for the severe losses they have sustained during the progress of the struggle. Meanwhile, neither of the competitors will have been in a position to perform the services they have undertaken in as efficient a manner as would have been the case if they had been working with a fair marign of profit. The only competition from which the public can reap a real and lasting advantage is that of two companies carrying at fair and remunerative rates, and each seeking to attract business to its own railway by performing the service to the public in the most efficient, safe, and expeditious manner.

It must be admitted that railway companies set a good example to the community at large in the method they adopt of settling disputed claims and other matters of difference between themselves instead of having recourse to expensive litigation. By the terms of an Act passed in the year 1859, and entitled the "Railway Companies' Arbitration Act," it was provided that any two or more companies might, by writing under their Common Seal, agree to refer to arbitration any differences or disputes in which they were mutually concerned, and which they might legally settle by agreement between themselves. This Act is incorporated in all modern Acts of Parliament and in most agreements entered into by railway companies, and the effect is to reduce litigation between them to a minimum, with a consequent great saving in expense. Under the Act, the arbitrators have power to call for the production of books and documents, to administer oaths, and hear evidence, and their decisions are final and binding upon all concerned, and may be legally enforced in any of the Superior Courts of Law. Two companies may agree to appoint a single arbitrator, or each company concerned may appoint one, in which case the arbitrators appoint an umpire to decide between them in case of difference. In the event of either company failing to appoint an arbitrator after having agreed under seal to do so, or of the arbitrators failing to appoint an umpire, the Board of Trade may be called upon by either of the other companies concerned to name an arbitrator or an umpire, as the case may be.

A very complete machinery exists for the settlement of cases of disputed liability for claims arising on through traffic in which two or more companies are concerned. A tribunal has been constituted which is termed the

"Claims Arbitration Committee," and which holds its meetings at the Railway Clearing-house in London once each quarter. It consists of twelve members chosen by election from their own body by the Goods Managers of the companies who are parties to the Railway Clearing-house, the members holding office for three years, and one-third of them retiring annually and not being eligible for re-election until after the lapse of a year from their retirement. When two or more companies fail to agree as to the liability for a claim arising upon traffic in which they are jointly interested, either party to the dispute may, by giving due notice, appeal to the decision of the Claims Arbitration Committee. Statements of the facts are drawn up and submitted on either side; and, after examining these, the Committee hears the evidence and arguments of the parties concerned, and gives its decision, which is held to be final.

For claims arising upon through passenger-train traffic there is a similar committee, having the same functions and constituted in the same manner, but which, in this case, consists of twelve Passenger Superintendents, elected by the members of the Superintendents' Conference. There can be no question as to the great advantages of a system of this kind; for not only are railway companies saved a vast expense which would otherwise be incurred in litigation, but the cases are adjudicated upon by able and experienced railway men, who are perfectly conversant with the facts, and incomparably more competent to arrive at a satisfactory decision than any other tribunal which could be selected. It should be mentioned that in order to secure the complete impartiality of the Committee, no member is permitted to take part (except as an advocate) in the proceedings upon any case in which the company he represents is in any way interested.

In cases where traffic, in being conveyed from its starting point to its destination, has to be carried over the railways of two or more companies, the receipts are divided between the companies concerned in proportion to the mileage travelled over each railway. In the case of merchandise traffic, before this division is made, a certain fixed sum is allowed (according to the nature of the traffic) to the forwarding and receiving companies respectively, for terminal expenses—that is to say, for the use of the stations, and for the services of loading and unloading and clerkship. A simple illustration will perhaps best serve to show the working of this arrangement.

We will suppose that a ton of goods has to be forwarded a distance of 100 miles, and in completing its journey has to travel 60 miles over one railway (**A**) and 40 miles over another (**B**). We will assume that the freight amounts to 23s. and that the terminal allowance at each end is 4s.:

Company **A** will receive—
$$\frac{60}{100} \text{ of } 15s. = 9s. + 4s. = 13s.$$
Company **B** will receive—
$$\frac{40}{100} \text{ of } 15s. = 6s. + 4s. = 10s.$$
$$\text{Total} \quad \ldots \quad \overline{23s.}$$

The question of division of traffic brings us to the consideration of one of the most important features of the railway system, which is known as the Railway Clearing-house. In the early days, when railways began to multiply and to run in connection one with another, it was necessary for a passenger who had to travel over two railways before his journey was completed, to change carriages on the termination of the first one and to take a fresh ticket; and similarly every consignment of merchandise had to be transhipped from one company's waggon to that of another at the point of junction, and to be re-invoiced. As the business increased, this was soon found to be a perfectly intolerable system, and a demand arose from the public that they should be enabled to travel between any points by paying the fare for the whole journey at the place of departure, and that in the same way merchandise and live stock should be forwarded throughout without sustaining the delay and possible damage involved in frequent transhipments. The difficulty to be overcome in giving effect to this demand was twofold; for not only would one company be receiving money part of which was due to another company, but each would be obtaining a service from the carriages and waggons of the other for which, clearly, some payment must be made. For a time the companies attempted to meet the case by a system of keeping accounts and exchanging returns of the receipts of each from through traffic; but this plan was open to many objections. Different companies had different modes of keeping their accounts, and no one had any authority to impose uniformity; so that there were mutual difficulties in agreeing the figures, and the consequent disputes engendered ill-feeling, recriminations, and charges of unfair practice. At length, in the year 1842, it occurred to Mr. Morison, who was at that time an audit clerk of the London and Birmingham Railway, that the true remedy for the unfortunate state of things which prevailed was to establish a central office, founded somewhat upon the lines of the Bankers' Clearing-house (which had then been established more than half a century), and which should receive the returns of through traffic from all the companies, impartially make the apportionments, and declare the balances due to each. The scheme thus outlined met with the warm approval and support of Mr. Glyn, who was at that time the chairman of the London and Birmingham Railway, and, after sharing the fate of every innovation or reform in encountering a great deal of opposition from various sources, it was finally brought into operation. Like most great institutions, the Railway Clearing-house had a very humble commencement, for it began its operations with a staff of only four clerks, and dealt with the traffic of only four railways, controlling an aggregate mileage of 418 miles; but its growth has only been paralleled by the growth of the railway system itself, and the magnitude of its operations may be judged by the fact that it employs at the present time a staff of upwards of 2,100 persons, and deals with the traffic of all the railway companies in Great Britain, having, in the aggregate, nearly 17,000 miles of railway. If we add that during the year 1892 the number of traffic settlements made was 13,270,444 and the value of the receipts dealt with exceeded £20,000,000, we shall have said enough to give a fair idea of the extent of the business carried on in the vast building in Seymour Street, Euston Square, where the Railway Clearing-house has found a home.

Since the year 1850 the proceedings of the Railway Clearing-house have been regulated by Act of Parliament

(13 and 14 Vic., cap. 33), and its authorised functions are thus defined : " To settle and adjust the receipts arising from railway traffic within, or partly within, the United Kingdom, and passing over more than one railway within the United Kingdom, booked or invoiced at throughout rates or fares." The management is conducted by a Committee of Delegates appointed by the boards of the several railway companies, parties to the system, each company, however great or small, having the power to appoint one delegate, and the expenses being borne by the companies in the ratio of the amount of business done on their behalf. Any railway company not a party to the clearing system may apply under seal for admission, and if the Committee of Delegates assent to the application, the company is at once received on an equal footing with all the other companies already parties to the system. Any company may withdraw at will by giving one month's notice under seal, or a company may be expelled by the vote of two-thirds of the delegates present at a meeting specially convened for the purpose. The Committee meets four times a year, or oftener if needful, and its chairman is elected annually, but is eligible for re-election indefinitely.

The accounts of the clearing system, and the balances due to and from the several companies, are settled and adjusted by the secretary, who also determines the amount to be from time to time contributed to the funds of the Clearing-house by each company. In case of any difference arising with respect to the accounts, the decision of the Committee that a certain balance is due and payable by a particular company is final and conclusive, and such balance is recoverable in a court of law, upon simple proof that the committee have declared the amount to be payable.

In earlier days, the operations of the Clearing-house were limited to dealing with passenger and parcel traffic, and the mileage and demurrage charges for the use or detention of carriages, waggons and sheets, when travelling upon railways other than those belonging to the owners of the stock; but since the year 1847 the system has been extended to merchandise and live stock traffic, including a considerable proportion of the through coal traffic. The general principle upon which the receipts arising from through traffic are apportioned between railway companies has already been described, but two or more companies frequently enter into agreements for special modes of division of certain traffic, and the Clearing-house gives effect to these on receiving "joint instructions," mutually agreed between the companies concerned, the system being sufficiently elastic to meet every kind of agreement that can be devised for the apportionment of traffic receipts. In any case in which one company claims a larger share of the receipts from a particular traffic than its partners are prepared to concede, the Clearing-house reserves, in making the apportionment, a sufficient amount to meet the claim, until the difficulty can be adjusted by agreement, arbitration or otherwise, and amounts thus reserved are said to be "in suspense."

Having described the results achieved by this admirable organisation, it may be worth while to glance briefly at the machinery by which those results are attained.

In the first place, the Clearing-house have accounts from the stations of all through passenger tickets issued, and these accounts are corroborated by the last ticket issued each month between given points being forwarded to the Clearing-house, so that if a passenger journeys from London to Inverness he pays the full fare at Euston, and the Clearing-house take care that the Caledonian and Highland Companies are credited with their proper share of the receipts. A similar course is adopted with regard to the invoices of merchandise traffic, accounts being sent in by the receiving, as well as the forwarding, stations; and in addition to this, every station makes a return to the Clearing-house of all parcels booked through, and of carriages and waggons, either loaded or empty, received and despatched. Then, scattered all over the country, at every junction of two railways, the Clearing-house have number-takers stationed, who record the number and description of every vehicle that passes a junction going from one line to another, and these men forward returns to the head office in Seymour Street. All these returns are examined, analysed, and checked, one with another, and thus, with enormous labour, but with the most marvellous accuracy, the accounts are made up and the balances declared. The advantages of such an institution as this, which has had such great results in facilitating intercourse and the trade of the country, can hardly be over-estimated, for it is only by means of this system that the produce of remote districts has been brought to the door of the consumer; while, as for Ireland, if the facilities thus afforded for her cattle, poultry, butter and eggs to command the English markets had not existed, it is certain that the social condition of her people must have been much worse than it is.

The Clearing-house, however, discharges other functions besides the division of traffic receipts, and the adjustment of mileage and demurrage accounts. It affords a convenient neutral ground where the various companies, whatever their conflicting interests or differences of policy, can meet on friendly terms, can agree upon measures of concerted action, and afford one another the benefit of their mutual experience in devising measures for the common good. Three important conferences are held at the Clearing-house every three months, one attended by the general managers of the different companies, another by the goods managers, and a third by the passenger superintendents, all these dealing with the subjects specially germane to their respective departments. Thus the Goods Managers' Conference deals with such questions as the charges for the use of waggons, the classification of goods traffic, terminal allowances, etc.; the Superintendents' Conference deals with the speed and signalling of trains, rules and regulations for the working of railways, the block telegraph system, excursion trains, and subjects of like nature; the General Manager's Conference reviews the recommendations of the Goods Managers and Superintendents, and, in its turn, frames proposals to be submitted to the Committee of Delegates for adoption by the companies.

To the Clearing-house is also entrusted the apportionment of the gross amounts accruing to the railway companies under the Post Office (Parcels) Act of 1882, in remuneration for their services in conveying the Parcels Mails from station to station within the United Kingdom. This apportionment is made half-yearly in ratio to the receipts of the various companies from parcels traffic proper, interim distributions, based on their parcels receipts for the corresponding half of the previous year, being meanwhile made of the sums received quarterly from the Post Office. For the purpose of the apportionment, the companies render to the Clearing-house certified monthly returns of their receipts from local parcels traffic, and these are supplemented with their earnings from through traffic, as ascertained from the Clearing-house accounts. The Clearing-house also, as representing the railway companies, undertakes the auditing of the Parcel Post accounts of the Post Office, besides placing a check upon the accuracy of the companies' returns on which the apportionment is made. Since the institution of the Parcel Post in August, 1883, the business of this department of the Post Office has enormously increased, the railway share of the Parcel Postage amounting now to over half a million per annum, and probably there is no better instance of economical administration than is afforded by the distribution of this fund amongst some 130 companies.

Since the year 1847 the Railway Clearing-house, as a central establishment well adapted for the purpose, has been employed to facilitate the recovery of lost luggage, a duty which it discharges in the following manner:—A description of every article lost or found is forwarded daily to the Clearing-house, who, in turn, furnish the information to the different stations, and anything found on hand at a station which answers to the description of an article lost is forwarded for identification. During the year 1892, nearly 600,000 articles were reported to the Clearing-house as being lost or found, and in the majority of cases, thanks to the machinery employed, the owners were traced and their property restored to them.

## CHAPTER XIV.

### ON THE RELATION OF THE STATE TO RAILWAYS IN ENGLAND, AND THE QUESTION OF STATE PURCHASE OF RAILWAYS.

As is well known, the relations of the State to railways differ in various countries to a very wide extent. For instance, in Belgium, practically the whole of the railways have been purchased by the State, and are worked by a department of the Government for the benefit of the public, very much as the Post Office is in England.

In Prussia, Bavaria, Wurtemburg, and most of the other German States, nearly the whole of the railways have been acquired by the Government and are worked as a Department of State; while in Austria, with the exception of one line, which is a State railway, the whole of the railways have been made and are worked by private companies, the Government merely exercising a certain power of control over the fixing of the rates and charges.

In France, some of the railways have been constructed and are worked by the State, and others have been made by private companies, but on a system of territorial concessions, by which these companies are secured against competition, and the Government, in consideration of this fact, exercise a complete control over the fixing of the rates. In India, the railways have been constructed under various conditions, some of them by joint-stock companies, as in England, but guaranteed by the State, while others have been built absolutely by the Government. In the United Kingdom, all the railways have been constructed by joint-stock enterprise, under the sanction of Parliament, without any subsidy or guarantee whatever; but Parliament, in granting the powers to buy land and make a railway, fixes the *maximum* tolls to be charged, and the Government, under various Acts of Parliament which have been passed from time to time, retains certain powers of inspection and control which will be more particularly detailed hereafter.

It may be said that, *prima facie*, anyone has the right to construct a railway on their own land and for their own use, and, similarly, a joint-stock company can be formed for any purpose by complying with certain formalities and by the process of registration; but when a number of individuals desire to form themselves into a company for the purpose of making a railway for public traffic, they require to obtain from Parliament compulsory powers for the purchase of land, whether the owners are willing to sell or not, to cross highways, divert roads and footpaths, to bridge rivers, and to make legal bye-laws, the breach of which shall be penal. Therefore, the first thing to be done by any group of promoters who desire to construct a new railway is to deposit a Bill, together with plans showing the course of the line and the limits of deviation. The Bill, if opposed, is referred to a Select Committee of the House of Commons, and subsequently to a like Committee of the House of Lords, and both these Committees sit and hear all the evidence that can be adduced, both on behalf of, and in opposition to, the Bill, as well as the arguments of the counsel employed on each side. The opposition usually proceeds from private landowners, from Corporations and Town Councils, and from other Railway Companies who foresee competition from the new comers; but where a good case can be made out, and the Committee can be fairly satisfied that the construction of the new railway is required and will be for the advantage of the public, the powers sought for are usually granted, and the opposition is satisfied as far as may be necessary by the insertion of accommodation or protective clauses in the Bill.

The Bill having been sanctioned by Parliament, the company next proceed to purchase the land, and here they find the advantage of the powers they have obtained; for if they find a landowner unreasonable and exorbitant in his demands, they can serve "notice to treat," and claim to have the merits of the case investigated either by a sheriff's jury or by arbitrators, who will hear evidence and decide what is a fair price to be paid, which price the landowner is bound to accept. The case was widely different with the promoters of the early railways, who had to submit to the most excessive demands on the part of the landowners as the price of their consent to sell their land for the purposes of the railway, and we are told, for instance, that the land for the London and Birmingham Railway, which was liberally estimated to cost £250,000, actually cost three times that amount, or about £6,300 per mile, the most extravagant sums having to be paid for compensation, for consequential, damages for fancy prospects, and other unreasonable demands, in order to buy off the opposition of the landowners. Claims such as these are not heard of in these days, or if they were, they would at once be scouted by any jury or arbitrator before whom they were brought.

The growth of the traffic on the principal railways has brought about the necessity of widening or laying down additional lines of rails upon the principal trunk railways, and as this usually involves the purchase of additional land, and more or less interference with public roads and bridges, the operation has to be sanctioned by Parliament very much in the same way as if an absolutely new line of railway were contemplated, although there is not, as a rule, so much serious opposition to be encountered.

Another point of contact between the railway and the State is the power of control, within certain limits, possessed by the Board of Trade. Before any new railway or branch line can be made use of, it must be examined by the Inspecting Officers of the Board, and the permanent way, bridges, stations, and signals must be certified by them as being satisfactory and in accordance with a schedule of requirements laid down by the Board, and to which all railway companies are bound to conform. The same applies to any new line, or siding, or any interference, however slight, with the lines upon which passenger trains run. All accidents involving the least injury to life or limb, whether of passengers or the servants of the company have to be reported to the Board of Trade, who, in every case where they consider it necessary, appoint one of their Inspecting Officers to view the *locus in quo*, and hold an enquiry upon the spot into the circumstances of the mishap, hearing evidence, and reporting to the Board of Trade. A summary of these reports is submitted to Parliament annually.

The Board of Trade have also power to compel the

companies to make use of a proper system of communication between passengers, guards, and drivers, to impose regulations as to the use of level crossings, to order bridges or subways to be constructed in lieu of level crossings, to insist upon the running of workmen's trains where they consider it necessary, and to call for various statistical returns from the railway companies.

In 1873, an Act was passed entitled the "Railway and Canal Traffic Act," which contained provisions of great importance as affecting the railways in this country. Divested of various minor enactments and of all unnecessary verbiage, the essential principles of this Act were as follows:—

(1) A new tribunal was constituted consisting of three "Railway Commissioners," one of whom was to be of experience in the law, and another of experience in railway business, who were to decide all questions of difference between any two railway companies, or between a railway company and a canal company or between any individual and a railway or canal company, upon the application of either party to the difference.

(2) It was ordained that where two railways formed part of a throughout route between two given points, one of the said companies might call upon the other to afford facilities for the conveyance of through traffic over the lines of the two companies, by giving written notice of the through rate to be charged and the route to be travelled. If the company receiving the notice objected to the rate or the route, the matter was to be referred to the Railway Commissioners for decision.

During the twenty years that this Act has been in force, the Railway Commissioners have had a considerable number of cases submitted to their judgment, and although their decisions have not at all times escaped severe criticism, it cannot be denied that they have dealt fairly and equitably, on the whole, with the questions which have been brought before them.

During the last few years a demand has arisen from certain quarters for fresh legislation in a spirit apparently hostile to railway companies, although mistakenly supposed to be in the interest of the general public. The promoters of this agitation have assumed that the rates and charges of the companies were too high, and that the commerce of the country would benefit if the State were empowered to fix the rates, instead of leaving the companies to do so within the limits of their toll powers. The companies have strenuously opposed this demand, on the perfectly logical ground that Parliament, having sanctioned the existing railways, with power to take certain tolls for their use, upon the faith of which the capital for their construction had been subscribed, had no just claim to deprive the shareholders of a portion of their profits, unless it was prepared to compensate them for their loss. It is also argued, and is easily susceptible of proof, that the railway companies, so far from having unfairly taxed the trade of the country, as is asserted by their assailants, have been its best friends, and have done everything in their power to foster and encourage it; treating the public fairly and liberally, and keeping well within their powers as regards tolls. They would, indeed, have been suicidal in acting otherwise, for their course is shaped by men of business, who are well aware that the prosperity of trade means the prosperity of the railway companies, and that, in short, the welfare of each is dependent upon the other.

The public, however, it is to be feared, are far from realising how much the companies have done for them, or how the conditions of railway transit, both for passengers and merchandise, have been revolutionised in their favour in these modern times, without the companies reaping any additional remuneration, the maximum tolls being now precisely what they were when the railways were first authorised, while in every other respect the scene has entirely changed. The stations, which were once of the most primitive description, consisting of little more than a platform and an office, have been replaced by costly and elaborate structures, replete with every kind of accommodation, and erected at a large expense; the trains are luxuriously fitted up with every modern appliance for comfort and convenience, and run at a rate of speed never dreamt of in the earlier days; the merchandise is carried in express goods trains from one end of the country to the other within the twenty-four hours; vast sums have been spent in providing warehouses and depôts, machinery and appliances, where, in the old days, the companies simply took their tolls for the use of the rails and left others to find the accommodation; and yet, for all these advantages, they exact no increased payment. On the contrary, during the last few years great concessions have been made to the traders in the matter of rates; and wherever it has been shown that a particular industry could be developed or created by the quotation of low rates, or the granting of any other facilities, the companies have always been willing to meet the case in a liberal spirit recognising the fact that in so doing they were consulting their own best interests as well as those of the public.

## THE RELATION OF THE STATE TO RAILWAYS. 285

There is no doubt that the agitation against the railway companies has arisen in consequence of the depressed state of trade which has existed during the last few years, not only in this country, but all over the world, many of the largest undertakings in the coal and iron industries having been carried on in fact with little or no margin of profit to those interested in them ; but, whatever the cause of the agitation, it has had sufficient force to induce two successive Administrations to attempt legislation in order to satisfy it.

In 1886 Mr. Mundella, the then President of the Board of Trade, introduced a "Railway and Canal Traffic Bill," which met with vigorous opposition on the part of the railway interest, but Mr. Gladstone's Government fell before any decision was arrived at with regard to it. In the session of Parliament of 1888, however, a bill was introduced by Lord Salisbury's Government, and with some modifications in Committee became law, under the title of the "Railway and Canal Traffic Act, 1888," containing, *inter alia*, the following provisions :—

(1) The Railway Commissioners' powers, as defined by the Act of 1873, are renewed, and their body is re-constituted so as to consist of two appointed members (one of whom is to be of experience in railway business), and three ex-officio commissioners, one for England and Wales, one for Scotland, and one for Ireland, these latter being judges of a superior court, each of whom will preside in cases only which are heard in that part of the United Kingdom for which he is nominated.

(2) Town councils, county authorities, urban and rural sanitary authorities, harbour boards, chambers

of commerce, trade associations, and, in short, almost every constituted body may become the plaintiff to the Railway Commissioners in any matter in which that tribunal has jurisdiction.

(3) The new Commission is invested with jurisdiction over disputes as to the legality of tolls, rates, and charges, and may enforce payment of them, may order traffic facilities to be granted, notwithstanding agreements between companies to the contrary, unless the agreements are confirmed by Act of Parliament, by the Board of Trade, or by the Commissioners themselves, and may award damages to aggrieved parties.

(4) Every railway company within six months of the passing of the Act, is to submit to the Board of Trade a revised classification of merchandise traffic, and a revised schedule of maximum rates and charges applicable thereto proposed to be put in operation, and is to state the nature and amount of all terminals proposed to be authorised in respect of each class of traffic. The Board of Trade are to consider the classification and schedule of charges, to hear any objections made by any parties whom they consider entitled to be heard, and on coming to an agreement with the company as to what the classification and schedule of charges are to be, are to embody them in a Provisional Order, submit them to Parliament, and bring in a Bill for an Act to confirm the order. If the Board of Trade cannot agree with the railway company, they (the Board) are to determine for themselves what they consider fair and reasonable, and report to Parliament, calling attention to the points of difference; certain machinery is then provided, by means of which

Parliament will, in the end, decide between the Board of Trade and the railway company.

(5) Where complaint is made that a railway company unduly favours one trader or body of traders, or the traders of a particular district, by charging them less than they charge other traders or districts for similar services performed, the burden of proving that the difference in treatment does not amount to undue preference is cast upon the railway company. In deciding cases of alleged undue preference, however. the Commissioners may consider whether the lower charge or difference in treatment is necessary for the purpose of securing in the interests of the public the traffic in respect of which it is made ; no difference, however, is to be sanctioned in the tolls, rates or charges for home and foreign merchandise in respect of similar services.

(6) Any person receiving or sending goods by any railway who believes he is being charged an unfair or excessive rate may complain to the Board of Trade, who, if they think there are reasonable grounds for the complaint, may appoint a competent person to communicate with both parties and endeavour to bring them to an arrangement.

Such are the leading provisions of an Act which the railway companies, it need hardly be said, opposed so long as there was any utility in opposition ; but seeing that the majority was against them, they have recognised the wisdom of bowing to the inevitable, and loyally accepting this Act as a compromise of propositions of an even more extreme nature. They feel, however, that the railway interests have been hardly dealt with, and, in particular, that the introduction of the clauses providing for a revision (which may imply a reduction) of the tolls fixed by the Acts of Parliament authorising the construction of the railways, constitutes an extreme measure not warranted by the circumstances or by any failure in their duty to the public on the part of the railway companies. On the contrary, the Railway Rates Committee of 1882, after going very fully into the subject and hearing an immense mass of evidence, mostly offered in a spirit hostile to the railway companies, have recorded their conviction in the following words, which will be found in their report :—

"Your Committee, in conclusion, report that on the whole of the evidence they acquit the railway companies of any grave dereliction of their duty to the public. . . . . . Your Committee find that the rates for merchandise on the railways of the United Kingdom are, in the main, considerably below the *maxima* authorised by Parliament."

But there are not wanting those who are advocates of measures of a much more sweeping nature even than those involved in the legislation of the session of 1888, and who go so far as to propose nothing less than that the Government should become the purchasers of all the railways in the United Kingdom, and work them as a department of State for the benefit of the public, the assumption being that by the concentration of the management, the absence of competition, and the appropriation of the profits reaped by the existing railway companies to the reduction of the present rates and charges, great benefits must accrue to the public at large. This proposal is one which has been more or less the theme of discussion from a very early period, and indeed it is a fact not perhaps generally known that an Act was passed as long ago as 1844 empowering the Government to acquire the whole of the railways on certain terms, and that the Act in question has never been repealed. In the House of Commons on the 5th May, 1888, Mr. Watt moved a resolution to the effect:—

"That in the opinion of this House the time has arrived when the Government should appoint a Committee or Royal Commission to take into consideration the question of acquiring the railways of the United Kingdom in accordance with the provisions contained in the General Railway Act of 1844."

The motion was, however, negatived.

It is to be feared that supporters of this proposition have not fully realised the magnitude of the operation they recommend, and nothing is more probable than that, if it ever came to be carried out, the sanguine anticipations of its advocates, as to its financial success, would prove to have been based upon fallacy. The Act of 1844 authorised the transfer of the railways to the State at 25 years' purchase of their average profits for the three years antecedent to the purchase, and this sum would be represented by about *eight hundred and twenty-five millions sterling;* but if ever a scheme of the kind comes within the region of practical legislation, it will certainly not be carried out on the basis of an old and obsolete Act of Parliament, passed at a time when the railway system was in its infancy. To commend itself to the legislature of the present day, and to overcome the strenuous opposition it would undoubtedly encounter, it must proceed upon the principle of equitable treatment of the shareholders of the existing companies, who would have to receive not merely the capital they had sunk in the undertakings, but some reasonable compensation for its prospective value. We believe that if the principle of State purchase were decided upon, it would ultimately have to be carried out somewhat in the following manner :—

As regards the lines that are now earning a profit, Government should guarantee a rate of dividend, which might be taken at the average of, say, three years preceding the purchase, and this would certainly not be putting too high an estimate on their prospective value, which would have a tendency to increase in view of the Government guarantee.

As regards capital invested in railways constructed, but paying no dividend, the question is more complicated. Each case would have to be considered on its merits, but for our present purpose we may assume that the justice of the case would be roughly met by taking this capital at half its nominal value, the Government paying say, $2\frac{1}{2}$ per cent. per annum upon the reduced amount in consideration of their obtaining the possession and control of these lines.

Lines under construction and paying no dividend at the time of purchase might be taken at their nominal value, the Government paying $2\frac{1}{2}$ per cent. per annum upon that amount.

A perpetual Government railway consolidated stock might be created, and the stocks of the different companies be converted into this Government stock on the principle of equivalents ; that is to say, that, for example, supposing the Government consols to bear interest at $2\frac{1}{2}$ per cent. per annum, a company whose invested capital was five millions, and who, during the preceding three years had been paying a dividend at the rate of 4 per cent., would receive eight millions of Government bonds.

The following calculation is only an approximate one, but it will afford some indication of the probable financial result of an operation of this kind, supposing it to have been undertaken at the close of the year 1892.

The total amount of capital (including both share and loan) invested in the railways of the United Kingdom was in December, 1892 . . . . . . £944,357,320

The gross revenue earned in the year 1892 was . . . . . . . . . . £82,092,040

At the present time the capital is earning dividend at various rates, from nothing at all up to 10 per cent.; but the bulk is earning from 3 to 7 per cent., and the amount thus distributed to the shareholders in the year 1892 was . . . . . . . £36,374,075

The capital invested in railways constructed, but paying no dividend, is £56,098,854, upon one-half of which, say £28,049,427, the Government would pay 2½ per cent. . . £701,235

The capital of railways under construction on which no dividend is paid

|   |   |
|---|---|
| amounts to £2,197,482, interest on which at 2½ per cent. amounts to . | £279,236 |
| Total interest payable . . . . . . | £37,354,546 |
| Add working expenses of the railways, which in 1892 were . . . . . . | 45,717,965 |
| Total outgoings . . . . . | £83,072,511 |
| As against the gross receipts of . . . | 82,092,040 |
| Deficiency . . . . . . . | £980,471 |

There would thus be, instead of the large gains anticipated, an actual loss of nearly a million sterling per annum; but this calculation proceeds upon the assumption that the rates and charges and the gross receipts would be the same as they are at the present time, whereas one of the principal avowed objects of those who recommend State purchase is that, as the profits of the shareholders would be reaped by the Exchequer, the Government would be enabled to reduce the rates and fares for the benefit of the public. Yet if the Government ventured to do this even to the very moderate extent of ten per cent., they would, even after making every allowance for any economy of working that might be effected by the concentration of management, at once find themselves with a deficit of several millions sterling per annum, on the working of the railways, to be made up out of other sources of revenue.

But apart altogether from financial considerations, there are many and grave objections to the scheme, the most important of which may be briefly summed up as follows:—

The State purchase of railways would involve an objectionable amount of interference with the industries of the nation, and with the character of the people. The Government would become the direct employers of a vast army of men of all classes, from labourers to highly trained artisans, clerks and officials; they must come in contact with trades unions, face the question of employers' liability, and all the other difficult labour questions which from time to time agitate the industrial community, and at times they would even have to deal with strikes. In all matters of this kind, they, as a Government, would occupy a very invidious position as compared with the railway companies, who are merely mercantile bodies, dealing with labour as a marketable commodity, under the ordinary laws of supply and demand.

Trade would suffer from the absence of the efforts now put forth by the different railway companies, by granting low rates, constructing branch lines, and by other facilities to develop the competition of markets and to open up new districts.

The Government would be invested with a large amount of patronage, not only in the appointment and promotion of the staff, but in the placing of contracts for coal and iron and other materials, in granting railway facilities, and in many other ways, and they would always be open to the accusation of making use of this patronage for political purposes.

The policy of the railway administration, instead of being guided by one consistent principle, as at present, viz., the improvement and development of the traffic, with which the prosperity of the country is necessarily bound up, would, in all probability alter from time to time, as one party or the other succeeded to office, and this want of continuity would prejudicially affect the management of the railways, and the commercial interests so largely dependent upon them.

All experience of the working and of the scale of expenditure of Government departments is strongly opposed to the belief that so vast and difficult an undertaking as the administration of the railways of the country could be carried on economically and upon sound commercial principles by a department of State. Complaints would be innumerable, and the House of Commons, already overburdened with matters of detail, would, by the multitude of questions to be asked and answered, find its labours so much increased that the business of the country would be seriously interfered with. The traders, who have now the advantage of free access to the officials engaged in the management of the railways—men trained to understand their business and their needs, and willing and anxious to meet their views and assist their operations—would find themselves confronted by the attitude of a Government official, bound inflexibly by hard and fast rules, with no personal discretion, and with, above all, a great disinclination to incur any responsibility.

It only remains to add that in France, where the experiment of ownership of railways by the State has been tried for many years past on a very considerable scale, an agitation is now growing up, as may be gathered from recent debates in the French Chambers, for the absolute sale of the State railways to private companies, on the grounds that the present system involves a very heavy annual loss to the Exchequer, and that any advantages which might be expected to result from the ownership of the railways by the Government are not reaped by the public, but are applied to the furtherance of political objects.

In Belgium, where, as before stated, the railways are worked as a department of the State, and the appointment of Minister of Railways is a political one, the patronage which lies in his gift is well known to be largely exercised for party purposes. Promotion in the service is entirely governed by consideration of the political tendencies of the individuals concerned, and when the Minister is a "Liberal" he will systematically refuse to appoint or promote officials who are known to belong to the "Clerical" party; while, on the other hand, if a "Clerical" Minister is in office, there is no hope of advancement for "Liberals" until their friends, in turn, succeed to power.

In Germany, where there has been considerable experience of the plan of working the railways as a Government Department, the financial result does not appear to be too encouraging. The Railway Department, it is true, figures in the Budget with a large annual profit, but this is only apparent, for the Landtag is every year called upon to vote supplies to be expended on the railways far in excess of the so-called profit, notwithstanding which loud complaints are heard of the want of sufficient plant for carrying on the working in an efficient manner.

The inference drawn from what is taking place in the older countries of Europe is in nowise contradicted by the experience gained from the result of the experiments tried in the new world at the Antipodes. The Victorian State Railways, which, until recently, were managed as a branch of the Government, somewhat on the plan adopted in Belgium, have now been committed to the charge of three commissioners, who are to be freed from all political influences, and to have absolute powers of control, as if the railways were the fruits of private enterprise, as in Great Britain. The same plan is about to be adopted by the Government of Queensland.

## CHAPTER XV.

### PASSENGER TRAFFIC.

A CONSIDERABLE amount of controversy has taken place during recent years amongst those engaged in the management and working of railways, and also amongst statisticians and others who, as *amici curiæ*, have taken an interest in the subject, upon the question of the relation of the classes one to another, and their relative productiveness from a revenue-earning point of view, and a great deal of diversity of opinion has been shown to exist, even amongst experts, as to the number of classes into which passenger traffic should be divided, the fares which should be charged, and as to what should be the composition, the speed, and the weight of trains, so as to reduce the amount of unprofitable haulage to a minimum, and, while accommodating to the fullest extent the requirements of the travelling public, to secure the best paying load, and preserve a reasonable margin of profit for those whose capital is embarked in the business of conducting railways.

This question—or group of questions—formed one of the subjects of debate at the meeting of the International Railway Congress at Paris in 1889, and as the writer accepted the honour of acting as reporter on that occasion for the English railway companies, and has consequently had occasion to consider the topic with some care, it may be of interest not only to those professionally engaged in the working of railways, but to the public whose interests are largely concerned, to give here some of the conclusions to which he has been led. It is only fair, however, to premise that although the views expressed in the following pages are fully endorsed by some of the leading English railway managers, there are others with whom they find less favour, and they must therefore be taken merely as representing the result of the writer's own experience.

There can, at least, be no question as to the great importance of the subject to all who are engaged in conducting railway traffic, whether in Great Britain or upon the Continent of Europe, since it is a fact that in these modern times the demands made upon railway companies on behalf of the public, not only for the reduction of fares, but for increased speed, more frequent trains, and improved accommodation, have increased, and continue to increase, in such ratio as to render it exceedingly difficult for the companies to keep pace with them without altogether sacrificing the interests of their shareholders. There is, in fact, a great tendency to regard railway companies as monopolists—a reproach to which, in these days of unrestricted competition, few of them are open—and to bring to bear every sort of influence to exact new concessions without any regard to the profit derived, or the loss incurred, in carrying on the business. Thus, while the travelling public benefit, the railway shareholder finds himself filling the doubtless honourable, but not always profitable, *rôle* of a philanthropist, investing his capital for the advantage of the community at large. It may be, perhaps, that on the Continent, where the railways are more or less under

State control, the case may somewhat differ from that of Great Britain, where all the railways have been constructed by private enterprise; but, in the main, the pressure of public opinion will no doubt operate in the same direction, and there will be a constant tendency to require greater and still greater facilities, and thus continually to diminish the revenue-earning powers of the railways. The facts and figures which are here adduced will probably suffice to convince any impartial student of the subject that this process has continued upon the principal railways of Great Britain, to such a degree as to bring about a state of things which can scarcely be defended on sound commercial principles—at any rate from the shareholder's point of view.

Prior to the year 1872 the general practice of all English railway companies was to convey by the mail, and principal fast passenger trains, only first and second class passengers, third class passengers being compelled to travel by less important trains calling at a greater number of stations, or by the Parliamentary trains, so-called, which stopped at every station, and which the companies were bound by statute to run over their lines at least once a day in each direction. For example, in 1872 the Parliamentary train from Euston to Liverpool, a distance of $201\frac{3}{4}$ miles, started at 7.40 a.m., stopped at every station on the route, and reached its destination at 6.35 p.m., thus occupying nearly eleven hours on a journey which the more fortunate third class passenger of to-day is enabled to perform in four and a half hours. The fares charged at that period averaged 2d. per mile for a first class passenger, $1\frac{1}{2}$d. per mile for second class, and 1d. per mile for third class by Parliamentary trains, while fares at a fraction over 1d.

per mile were charged for third class passengers conveyed by a few fast trains of a secondary character, to which third class carriages were beginning to be attached. At this time the third class carriages, although they were covered in as a protection from the weather, were not upholstered in any way, and contained nothing more than plain wooden seats.

Taking a period of thirteen years, from 1860 to 1872, during which the traffic was conducted under these conditions, a table which has been prepared showing the gross receipts of the London and North Western Railway from each class of traffic, and from the three classes combined, per passenger, and per passenger train mile run, from year to year, gives the following averages for the whole period :—

|  | Average Receipts per Passenger. | Average Receipts per Train Mile. |
| --- | --- | --- |
|  | PENCE. | PENCE. |
| First Class ... ... | 64·18 | 16·69 |
| Second Class ... | 23·92 | 17·99 |
| Third Class ... ... | 13·15 | 17·62 |
| All Classes combined. | 22·17 | 52·30 |

Space would not admit of the details of this table being given, but an examination of it shows that from about the year 1869 third class traffic began to assume greater importance, and that the receipts per train mile from this class were gradually increasing; the fact being that the companies about that time commenced to extend the practice of attaching third class carriages to some important trains—other than express trains— while the receipts per train mile from the first and second class had begun to fall off. For instance, in 1868 the first class earnings were 16·05d. per train mile, and the second class 18·05d., while in 1872 they were only 13·21d. and 10·82d. respectively. On the other hand, the third class receipts, which in 1868 were only 16·99d. per train mile, in 1872 had risen to 24·63d. The same causes, however, had led to an increase in the train mileage, which had the effect of reducing the average earnings per train mile, from all classes combined, from 51·09d. in 1868 to 48·66d. in 1872.

In April, 1872, the Midland Company adopted the practice (immediately and necessarily followed by all the other leading railway companies) of conveying third class passengers by all the trains, while nearly three years afterwards—viz., on the 1st January, 1875—they introduced the further innovation of abolishing second class in their trains altogether, and running only two classes, which they termed, rather paradoxically, perhaps, first and third, at the same time reducing the first class fares to about 1½d. per mile. The London and North Western Company did not follow the Midland Company's policy as regards abolishing second class, for the reasons which have been already set forth (see page 125), nor with one or two exceptions, and then only to a limited extent, have any of the other leading railway companies done so, but all were compelled by the exigencies of competition to place themselves on an equality with the Midland Company so far as regarded the re-adjustment of their fares, which was effected by reducing the first class to about 1½d. per mile, and making the second class about 1¼d. and the third 1d.

The striking effect of these changes upon the passenger earnings of the London and North Western Company is very clearly shown by a table which has been drawn up, and which gives the same particulars in respect of the period from 1873 to 1888 inclusive as are given in the table previously referred to, for the period from 1860 to 1872, viz., the gross earnings from each class of traffic per passenger and per train mile. Comparing the average gross earnings of each class for the two periods, we arrive at the following results:—

|  | AVERAGE RECEIPTS PER PASSENGER. | | AVERAGE RECEIPTS PER TRAIN MILE. | |
| --- | --- | --- | --- | --- |
|  | During period of 13 years—1860 to 1872 | During period of 16 years—1873 to 1888. | During period of 13 years—1860 to 1872. | During period of 16 years—1873 to 1888. |
|  | D. | D. | D. | D. |
| First Class | 64·18 | 54·70 | 16·69 | 8·46 |
| Second Class | 23·92 | 23·05 | 17·99 | 6·35 |
| Third Class | 13·15 | 11·59 | 17·62 | 28·27 |
| All Classes combined | 22·17 | 14·97 | 52·30 | 43·08 |

The average receipts per passenger were thus reduced in something like the ratio of the reduction of fares, but the increased mileage consequent upon the greater weight of the trains, coupled with the reduction of the fares, had the effect of reducing the average receipts per train mile from all classes, comparing the two periods, from 52·30d. to 43·08d.

Taking the classes separately it will be seen that while the average receipts per passenger train mile from first class passengers fell in the later period to about one-half what they were in the earlier period, and the second class to about one-third, the receipts from third class traffic were nearly doubled.

But it must not be forgotten that during the last fifteen years other causes, besides the conveyance of third class passengers by all trains, and the reduction of the fares, have been at work in the direction of increasing the cost of the service, and reducing the profits from the conveyance of passengers.

In the first place, there has been a great increase in the speed of the trains generally, and particularly in that of the express passenger trains. For example, in 1872 the fastest trains between London and Liverpool, $201\frac{3}{4}$ miles, performed the journey in $5\frac{1}{4}$ hours to 6 hours, while now it is accomplished in $4\frac{1}{2}$ hours. Between London and Manchester, $188\frac{3}{4}$ miles, the shortest time occupied was 5 hours, while now the distance is covered in $4\frac{1}{4}$ hours. Between London and Birmingham, 113 miles, one train ran in $3\frac{1}{4}$ hours, but the others were much longer on the road, while to-day the fast trains all perform the journey in $2\frac{3}{4}$ hours. But the most remarkable development in the rates of speed is found in the running of the express trains between London and Scotland ; and as regards these it will be a sufficiently striking illustration to mention that the 10.0 a.m. Scotch Express from London which, in 1872, reached Edinburgh at 9.10 and Glasgow at 9.30 p.m., now starts from London at the same time but is timed to reach Edinburgh at 6.30 and Glasgow at 6.45. The journey to Edinburgh is thus performed in $8\frac{1}{2}$ hours, and to

Glasgow in 8¾ hours, but even this rate is sometimes exceeded, and during the tourist season of 1888 the journey to Edinburgh was accomplished in less than 8 hours, the distance being 401 miles, giving a speed throughout of 50 miles an hour, including all stoppages.

The 8.50 p.m. train from London to Scotland, well-known for many years as the "Limited Mail," and which formerly ran to Aberdeen in 14 hours and 50 minutes, conveying, under contract with the Post Office, a limited number of passengers as well as mails, has been superseded in its functions as the principal mail train from London to Scotland, and since the 1st July, 1885, a special train, conveying no passengers, but only the mails and postal parcels, has left Euston at 8.30 p.m., and reaches Aberdeen at 9.55 a.m., thus performing the journey (540 miles) in only 13 hours and 25 minutes, and travelling at the rate of about 40 miles an hour, throughout, including all stoppages. Between London and Carlisle, this train travels at an average speed of 46 miles an hour.

These exceptionally high rates of speed add to the cost of working in more ways than one; in fact they have a tendency to increase almost every item of expenditure. In the first place, there is a greater wear and tear of the engines and vehicles, and more frequent repairs and replacements become necessary. Secondly, the engines must be worked at much higher pressure, and be of greater capacity, and the increased consumption of fuel, as has already been shown (see page 104), is a very serious item. Then again, to permit of heavy trains being run at such high rates of speed the permanent way must be proportionately strengthened, and becomes more expensive to provide and maintain in the perfect condition which is essential. It is also in a great measure the high rate of speed at which the trains have to be run that necessitates the elaborate and complicated system of signalling and interlocking which has been described in Chapters V. and VI.

Again there has been a very striking increase in the size and weight of the carriages employed for the conveyance of passengers, arising from the popular demand for improved accommodation, and the extent to which that demand has been met.

The standard third class carriage of 1872, for example, was $30\frac{1}{2}$ feet long, and weighed 10 tons, but the standard third class carriage of 1889 is 42 feet in length, and weighs upwards of 18 tons. The carriage of 1872 was capable of seating 50 passengers, but that of 1889 only seats 20 more, or 70 in all, so that while the weight of the vehicle has increased by 80 per cent. the seating capacity has only increased by 40 per cent.—in other words, the weight has increased in double the ratio of the accommodation provided. To take another illustration, the standard composite carriage built by the London and North Western Company in 1872, 30 feet 5 inches in length, weighed 10 tons 8 cwt., but those of the latest type, built recently, measure 42 feet in length and weigh from 18 to 19 tons. These contain lavatory accommodation for the first class compartments, and a cupboard for luggage, and they only provide seats for 44 passengers, as against 36 who could be conveyed in the smaller vehicle of the earlier period.

To keep pace with the increased weight of the vehicles, the power and weight of the engines employed to draw them has also had to be correspondingly augmented. The most powerful passenger engines in use on the

London and North Western Railway in 1872, having driving-wheels 7 ft. 6 in. in diameter, weighed, without tenders, 27 tons 1 cwt.; but the compound engines now being made by Mr. Webb at the Crewe Works, having triple cylinders, and driving-wheels 6 ft. in diameter, weigh $42\frac{1}{2}$ tons; while an even more powerful type of engine on the compound system, having 7-ft. driving wheels, weighs no less than $45\frac{1}{2}$ tons, or, with the tender attached, $70\frac{1}{2}$ tons.

The effect of this increase in the weight and dimensions of the vehicles employed is to cause a very serious augmentation of the length and weight of all the most important trains on the principal railways during the past five and-twenty years. All the principal trains have been affected in the same way, and of course when trains, under ordinary circumstances, are of such great weight and length, they cannot easily be strengthened to meet any abnormal increase of traffic or sudden pressure, and it becomes necessary, instead, to run extra, or duplicate trains, thus adding in another way to the working expenses. The increased speed has also indirectly had the effect of adding very considerably to the number of trains run, and to the amount of train mileage. In order, for instance, to enable a train to run last year from London to Edinburgh in eight hours, it became not only necessary to maintain a high rate of speed throughout, but very few stoppages at intermediate places could be permitted, and other trains had to be run to serve the stations where the stoppages were omitted, and to enable the passengers from those stations to get on to other stations at which the train did stop.

Another cause which has tended greatly to increase

the weight and bulk of the trains is the introduction of saloon carriages of various descriptions, to which allusion has been made in Chapter VIII. (page 179) since these vehicles, although of exceptional weight and dimensions, and extremely expensive to build and maintain, yet accommodate but a very limited number of passengers. For instance, a sleeping saloon 42 feet in length, weighing $22\frac{1}{2}$ tons, and costing £1,300, only contains berths for 16 individuals. A family carriage measuring 32 feet, weighing 15 tons 4 cwts., and costing £820, accommodates eight first class passengers (sleeping) and six second class passengers. The ordinary first class carriages have also lost part of their seating capacity from the fact that no first class passenger in these times is satisfied unless he is provided with lavatory accommodation, and this requirement is being met in building all new stock, so that practically nearly all first class carriages used on the main line are furnished with lavatories. If we take, for example, a first class carriage of the largest size, 42 feet in length, which under ordinary circumstances would provide seats for 40 passengers, with a luggage compartment, we find that, when the necessary space for lavatories has been abstracted, we have only accommodation left for 28 passengers; so that nearly one-third of the accommodation is lost, and the weight of the train is correspondingly increased. It may be added that some of the companies are now commencing to provide lavatory accommodation, not only for first class, as hitherto, but for second and third class passengers also.

Another cause which has a tendency to increase the length and weight of the trains, especially in the busy tourist season, is the growing desire on the part of the travelling public to secure the exclusive use of compartments for a small number of passengers. The companies very generally offer this facility to any one who desires it, subject to the payment of fares as for a minimum number of passengers, viz., four first or second class, or six third class. Great numbers of people, however, seek to obtain the privilege on one plea or another without the payment of the minimum charge, and where the traffic is highly competitive there is a disposition on the part of the companies to make the concession somewhat freely, and often without adequate grounds.

Having thus briefly touched upon the principal causes which have operated during the past fifteen or sixteen years in the direction of reducing the profits derivable from the conveyance of passengers, and more especially of those of the higher classes, it will probably be of interest to refer to certain calculations which have recently been prepared showing (1) a comparison of the receipts from passenger traffic of the three classes carried by the London and North Western Company in the years 1871 and 1888 respectively; (2) the number of *passenger miles* run (*i.e.*, taking the unit of one passenger conveyed one mile, which is arrived at very simply by dividing the gross receipts of each class by the assumed average fare per mile); (3) the cost at which each class has been worked in the two periods; and (4) the net profit derived from each class.

It is found, then, that during the two years mentioned the gross receipts of the London and North Western Railway from passenger traffic (including season tickets) were as follows:—

## PASSENGER TRAFFIC.

| Year. | First Class. | Second Class. | Third Class. | Total. |
|---|---|---|---|---|
| 1871 | £758,665 | £903,627 | £990,051 | £2,652,343 |
| 1888 | 550,535 | 366,552 | 2,487,532 | 3,404,619 |
| Increase | ... | ... | 1,497,481 | 752,276 |
| Decrease | 208,130 | 537,075 | ... | ... |

So that the first class receipts decreased 27 per cent., and the second class 59 per cent., while the third class *increased by* 151 *per cent.*, the total increase from all classes being 28 per cent., while within the same period the capital invested in the undertaking increased to the extent of about 46 per cent.

The *passenger miles* (not to be confounded with *passenger train miles*) calculated in the manner above described by assuming the average fares to have been:—

|  | First Class. D | Second Class. D | Third Class. D |
|---|---|---|---|
| In 1871 ... | 1·80 | 1·35 | ·90 |
| In 1888 ... | 1·50 | 1·25 | ·90 |

give the following results:—

| Year. | First Class. | Second Class. | Third Class. | Total. |
|---|---|---|---|---|
| 1871 | 101,155,333 | 160,644,800 | 264,013,600 | 525,813,733 |
| 1888 | 88,085,600 | 70,377,984 | 663,341,867 | 821,805,451 |
| Increase | ... | ... | 399,328,267 | 295,991,718 |
| Decrease | 13,069,733 | 90,266,816 | ... | ... |
|  | 12·9%  | 56·2% | 151·3% | 56·3% |

So that while the total receipts from all three classes shew an increase of only 28 per cent., the work done, measured by passenger mileage, has increased by just twice that amount, viz., by 56 per cent.

If the reader will now refer to the figures given at page 125, he will find that the number of seats provided in the company's carriage stock at the present time is :—

|  |  |
|---|---:|
| First Class | 22,375 |
| Second Class | 24,426 |
| Third Class | 130,173 |
|  | 176,974 |

In 1871 the numbers were :—

|  |  |
|---|---:|
| First Class | 19,462 |
| Second Class | 28,768 |
| Third Class | 44,960 |
|  | 93,190 |

Thus the accommodation has in the aggregate been increased by 90 per cent., while the gross receipts, as stated above, have only been augmented by 28 per cent., which shows—assuming that the carriage stock provided in 1871 was proportionate to the requirements of the traffic—that under present conditions the trains are not so well and fully occupied as under the old state of things, and that unprofitable mileage of carriage stock is being run.

It has always been a somewhat vexed question amongst railway statisticians as to what is the most reliable method of arriving at an estimate of the relative net profits derived from the various classes of passenger traffic; that is to say, that, having ascertained the total cost of working the traffic as a whole, the difficulty is to find a sure basis upon which to apportion it between the three classes. The number of passengers carried is obviously not a safe guide, because it is necessary to take into consideration the wide difference in the conditions under which they are conveyed. To divide the amount in proportion to carriages employed is impracticable, because a great number of the carriages contain accommodation for all three classes in varying proportions. The number of seats provided in the carriages employed is a somewhat more reliable basis; but even this leaves something to be desired, because a first class seat occupies more space in a train, and adds more to its weight than a second class seat, while even a second class seat occupies more space than a third. In addition, the lavatories for first class, and the great size and weight of the saloons of various descriptions have to be reckoned with.

After very careful consideration of the subject, the writer has arrived at the conclusion that the nearest approximate results are to be obtained by apportioning the total passenger working expenses betwen the three classes in the ratio of the *seat space* occupied in the entire carriage stock of a company, and a calculation made upon this basis, with regard to the passenger traffic of the London and North Western Railway in 1888, and in 1871, the last year before the introduction of the changes which have been enumerated, gives the following results:

| Year. | First Class. | | Second Class. | | Third Class. | |
|---|---|---|---|---|---|---|
| | Working Expenses per cent. | Net profit per cent. | Working Expenses per cent. | Net Profit per cent. | Working Expenses per cent. | Net Profit per cent. |
| 1871 | 53·00 | 47·00 | 51·55 | 48·45 | 36·35 | 63·65 |
| 1888 | 92·05 | 7·95 | 72·55 | 27·45 | 42·25 | 57·75 |

If it be assumed that these figures are approximately correct, and that the principle adopted in arriving at them is theoretically sound, which there is probably not much reason to doubt, their significance can hardly be exaggerated. It will be seen that the net profit on first class traffic, which, in 1871 was nearly half of the gross receipts, has by reason of the reduction of fares and the greatly enhanced cost of working (from causes which have already been dwelt upon) diminished until in the year 1888, it represents not quite eight per cent. of the gross receipts. The profit upon second class traffic, which, in 1871 was also nearly half the receipts, has now, from the same causes, dwindled to little more than a quarter, while even the profit on third class traffic has fallen off to some extent, although not so seriously, owing to the fares remaining practically undisturbed.

Another calculation shows that the net earnings per passenger per mile, after payment of working expenses, for the two periods under comparison, were approximately, as under:—

| | First Class. | Second Class. | Third Class. |
|---|---|---|---|
| | D. | D. | D. |
| 1871 | ·85 | ·65 | ·57 |
| 1888 | ·12 | ·34 | ·52 |

So that, under the old state of things, the first class traffic paid best, but the second class paid better than the third ; while, under present conditions, the third class is the most remunerative traffic, the second class comes next, and the profit on first class appears to be very small indeed.

During the period of eighteen years which elapsed between the years 1870 and 1888, although the mileage of railways owned and worked by the London and North-Western Company only increased to the extent of forty-five per cent., the passenger train mileage increased by sixty-one per cent., and the gross amount of fuel consumed per annum by passenger engines was augmented by no less than 142 per cent., or in more than double the ratio of the increase of train mileage, showing the unmistakable effect of the increased speed, and the heavier weights to which motive power has to be applied. The total number of passengers carried increased, it is true, by eighty-seven per cent., but the earnings were only improved to half that extent, or by forty-four per cent., while the number of passengers conveyed for the expenditure of one ton of fuel decreased by 22 per cent.—that is to say, that the amount of fuel, which in 1870 was sufficient to convey 100 passengers, in 1888 only sufficed to convey about seventy-eight, owing to the greater amount of dead weight to be hauled, and the higher speed to be maintained.

Mr. Price Williams, Mem. Inst. Civil Engineers, who has achieved a considerable reputation as an indefatigable statistician, and an authority on most questions relating to railways, submitted to the writer, about four years ago, some very interesting calculations which he had prepared with the view of demonstrating what he believed to be the unproductive character of the first and second class traffic upon the principal railways, consequent upon the altered policy which had been brought about since 1873, and to which reference has been made. These calculations assumed the form of an analysis of the passenger receipts and working expenses of the London and North Western Railway during a long period of years, viz., from 1860 to 1884, and as they impressed me very much at the time as showing striking results, and bearing out to a great extent the conclusions at which I had already arrived, it may be worth while to give a brief abstract of them in this connection.

Mr. Williams' figures, which were most carefully prepared, showed that from 1860 to 1871 the net profits from first and second class continued to be over 50 per cent. of the gross receipts, although the average gross receipts per passenger and per train mile were gradually reduced. In 1873, the first year in which the policy of attaching third class carriages to all trains was brought fully to bear, although the gross receipts from first-class traffic continued to increase, there was a larger growth in the working expenses, and the first class net receipts therefore fell off from 2s.9½d to 2s. 3¼d. per passenger, and from 7⅓d. to 5¾d. per train mile. The second class suffered to an even greater extent, the number of passengers of that class having decreased from 8,281,366 in 1871 to 5,418,494 in 1873, and the gross receipts from £867,099 to £557,200. The second class net receipts fell from 1s. 3d. per passenger to 9d., and the net receipts per train mile from 10d. to not quite 4d. The third class receipts, as might have been expected, were very largely increased.

Coming to the year 1875, the year in which second

class was abolished on the Midland Railway, and the fares were consequently reduced, as previously described, we find that, although the number of first class passengers conveyed by the London and North Western Company reached its maximum of 3,288,661, the net receipts were, owing to the reduction of the fares, only 1s. 6½d. per passenger, and 4d. per train mile, as against 2s. 3d. per passenger, and 5d. per train mile in 1873. The second class net receipts, from the same cause, were similarly affected.

From 1875 to 1881 the number of first and second class passengers and the receipts continued rapidly to decrease, and the third class to increase, in a remarkable degree. The net receipts from first class fell from 1s. 6½d. to 1s. 2d. per passenger, and from 4d. to 2d. per train mile, and in the second class, although the gross receipts per passenger were slightly increased, the net receipts were reduced from 5d. to 4d. per passenger, and from 2½d. to less than a penny per train mile.

The figures for the last period compared, from 1881 to 1884, continue to show the same tendency, but in an accelerated degree, the effect of the decrease, year by year, in the first and second class gross receipts, combined with the increase in the working expenses, being to still further diminish the slender profit upon these classes of traffic, until we find that in the year 1884 the net profit per first class passenger has come down to 5·71d., as against 3s. 5d. in 1860, and from 11d. per train mile to ·68d. The net profit upon each second class passenger, which in 1860 was 1s. 2d., in 1884 has fallen to 2d., and the net profit per train mile has been reduced from nearly a shilling to less than a halfpenny.

It will be seen that the tendency of these figures,

although they have been compiled by a different hand, and arrived at by a different process, is to confirm the conclusions based upon the more recent calculations prepared under the writer's directions, and which have already been quoted, and to show that the altered conditions under which the business is carried on have contributed to render the profits derived from first and second class very small indeed, and that the companies must now look chiefly to the third class traffic for their revenue. In fact, in contemplating the returns for a series of years, nothing is more striking than the enormous and uninterrupted growth in the number of third class passengers from year to year, no matter how the other classes may fluctuate. The companies, in short, have spent and are spending large sums of money in providing the most luxurious accommodation, and every facility and convenience for the benefit of the superior classes, but they are doing this practically at their own expense, and it is really the humble and once despised third class traveller who furnishes the sinews of war. It must be borne in mind, moreover, that although the figures show a profit, however small, upon the carrying of first class passengers, this result is only arrived at as an average, by treating all first class passengers alike, and while it may still be a profitable business to carry first class season-ticket holders, or passengers by local and suburban trains, it may well be doubted whether, under present circumstances, upon first class passengers carried long distances by express trains—say between London and Scotland—there is any profit at all.

On the whole, therefore, it would appear that the revenue to be derived from the conveyance of passenger traffic upon English railways is a diminished and diminishing quantity, and that it is only the fall during recent years in the value of materials, especially of coal, and other favourable circumstances, that have enabled the principal companies to fairly maintain their dividends; while if the present conditions with regard to passenger traffic remain unaltered, and there should be any material rise in prices of stores, or loss upon the working of the goods traffic by reason of bad trade, or if there should be any considerable reductions of the Parliamentary powers of the companies, which are now undergoing revision at the hands of the Board of Trade in conformity with the Railway and Canal Traffic Act of last Session, then the outlook for railway shareholders would be a serious one for them to contemplate.*

There seems to be no reason to doubt that the state of things thus described, so unfavourable from the railway shareholders' point of view, has been brought about chiefly by reason of the lengths to which the companies have gradually proceeded, under the pressure of competition, in making concessions without adequate remuneration for the privileges bestowed. These concessions have certainly been very great, and they have had the effect of placing railway travellers in Great Britain in an extremely favoured position as compared with the public who use the Continental railways, since there need be no hesitation in saying that although the methods of working in France, Belgium, Germany, and Austria may be sufficiently well adapted to the circumstances of those countries respectively, they are not such as would commend themselves to the British public. On most Continental railways the express trains carry, as a rule, only first and second class passengers, and the fastest trains travel, on an average, ten miles an hour less than the

* This was written in 1889, since which time the revision has been completed, but there has scarcely been time to judge of its effect upon the revenue of the companies.—ED.

express trains in England. The permanent way—constructed with Vignoles, or flat-bottomed rails bolted to the sleepers, without chairs, and weighing considerably less to the yard than the rails commonly in use in this country—is not adapted to bear the enormous strain which would be imposed upon it by long and heavy trains running at the high rates of speed which prevail upon English railways.

It is evident that the readiness of English railway companies to yield to the demands of the public, and to proceed from one concession to another, has arisen from the peculiar nature of the traffic of a country of limited extent like Great Britain, and where the business is so extremely competitive. Most of the railways in Germany, Austria, and Belgium are either State railways, or are controlled more or less by the State, and are worked not only for the benefit of the travelling public, but with an eye to the improvement of the State revenue; and in France, although the principal railways have been constructed by private Companies, it has been done upon a system of territorial concession for a period of time, the State reserving a control over the fixing of the rates and charges, so that the question of competition seldom arises. In England, on the contrary, the Legislature has fostered the principle of competition by sanctioning the construction of railways forming alternative routes between most points of importance. For instance, between London and Manchester there are three routes open to the intending traveller; between London and Liverpool there are three, between London and Edinburgh, Glasgow, Perth, or Aberdeen, three; between London and Leeds, three, between Liverpool and Manchester three, between London and the principal places in the West of England two ; and so on throughout the country.

From London to Manchester the London and North Western Company are running 16 trains daily, the Great Northern Company are running 8, and the Midland Company the same number. From London to Liverpool the North Western Company are running 13 trains daily, the Midland Company 9, and the Great Northern Company 6. From London to the principal places in Scotland, the North Western Company run 8 trains daily, the Midland Company 6, and the Great Northern Company 6. Between Liverpool and Manchester the London and NorthWestern Company run upwards of 20 express trains a day in each direction, the Cheshire Lines Committee run about 25, and the Lancashire and Yorkshire Company will shortly be running about an equal number. Many of these trains run at the same times, or nearly so. For example, both the North Western and Great Northern Companies have trains leaving London for Scotland at 10 a.m., and the Midland Company have a similar train only half-an-hour later. By three different routes a train leaves Liverpool for London at or near 4.0 p.m., and such instances might be multiplied indefinitely, the trains in most cases performing the journey in about the same time, and at precisely the same fares. The traffic is thus acutely competitive, and the conditions being so equal, it requires but a trifling inducement to influence the travelling public in the choice of route, so that there is a constant temptation to the competing companies to make fresh concessions so as to attract the business from their rivals ; and as any new departure by one company is immediately followed by its competitors, it becomes at once stereotyped, and merely forms a basis for still further concessions.

It may be, of course, that during the busiest season —extending over four or five months of the year—there is sufficient traffic to utilise the whole of the trains run by the various routes; but there is no doubt that during the remaining seven months the accommodation provided is, in the aggregate, far in excess of the requirements, and that, as a matter of fact, the trains are frequently run with very few passengers in them, doing little more than paying their expenses.

So far as the public are concerned there is, of course, in all this nothing to be complained of; but if it be asked from a railway shareholder's point of view, what is the remedy for the loss of revenue which has been indicated, although it is not impossible to find an answer to the question, the solution of the problem is one involving many difficulties. As regards increasing the traffic greatly beyond its present volume, there is probably not much to be hoped for, the country being limited in extent, and the possibilities of expansion being circumscribed by the amount of the population, although it will, naturally, always fluctuate with the prosperity of the country. The only thing to be done in this direction is to follow out the policy which has already been adopted by most of the companies, of granting low fares and season ticket rates between all the large centres of population and places within a radius of about twenty miles, so as to build up a residential traffic, by encouraging the people to live in the healthier suburbs instead of in the large towns in which they pursue their avocations. As regards long distance traffic it is very doubtful whether the reduction of fares, or any other concessions, tend to materially increase the volume of business; as a rule people do not take long journeys unless they are called upon by actual necessity to do so, and in that case they will travel, whatever the fare may be, within reasonable limits. Of course, however, this remark is not intended to apply to the traffic between large towns and seaside or other holiday resorts, which all the companies encourage by granting return tickets at low fares during the summer months, this being a case in which, by judicious concessions, a traffic is created which would not otherwise exist to anything like the same extent.

A return to the earlier practice of conveying third class passengers only by secondary trains, combined with a general reduction of speed, is practically out of the question, for if anyone were sufficiently bold to propose any such retrograde policy, it would encounter the strongest tide of public opinion in opposition to it, and it would be impossible to get all the companies to adopt and adhere to it in the face of the pressure which would be brought to bear upon them. For good or evil these concessions have been granted and cannot now be withdrawn, and it only remains for the railway companies to make the best of the situation as it exists, and to endeavour to protect themselves against further losses. In the end, it seems probable that the companies, if they are wise, will achieve this object by some kind of combination amongst themselves by which excessive competition may be obviated, and two or more companies carrying between common points may be enabled to reduce their train mileage, to curtail the running of unprofitable trains and a great deal of unnecessary expenditure, and to keep the speed of the trains within reasonable limits, so as, without lessening the accommodation afforded to the public, to preserve conditions under which the business of carrying passengers may again be conducted with a fair margin of profit to those whose capital is engaged in it.

## CHAPTER XVI.

### ON THE LAW AS BETWEEN ENGLISH RAILWAY COMPANIES AND THE PUBLIC.

IT is not the writer's intention, under this heading, to enter upon a minute examination of the whole body of what is known as "Railway Law." The limits of the present work would not indeed admit of this, nor is it necessary, for books of reference already exist, edited by competent hands, and affording the widest information upon all the legal questions which can arise in connection with railways. These are, however, for the most part overlaid with legal formulæ, references to case law and Acts of Parliament, and contain a great deal of matter which can possess no interest for the general reader; so that, without in any way trenching upon their province, it may be useful to give here a brief summary, in "language to be understooded of the people," of the most important provisions of the laws which govern railway companies in their daily dealings with the public. It has been said that a little law, like a little knowledge, is a dangerous thing; and it has been likewise remarked that "the man who is his own lawyer has a fool for his client"; but all this proverbial philosophy must be taken *cum grano*, and it may well be that a little intelligent appreciation of the state of the law on a given subject may suffice to keep a man out of the law courts when a resort to litigation could only end in the loss of time, temper, and money.

The law as affecting railways is defined in various ways. There are, first, the provisions of the special Acts authorising the making of the several railways; secondly, the various public Acts which have been passed from time to time for the regulation of railways; thirdly, there is what is known as common law, or the custom of the realm; and in addition to all these, there is a great body of what is called "case law," that is, the recorded decisions which have been given by the Courts at different times upon disputed questions involving the interpretation of Acts of Parliament. In the remarks that follow, we shall treat all these authorities as one for our purpose, and merely attempt to give the reader some idea of what, in the present state of the law, he has a right to demand from the railway companies in his dealings with them, and what, on the other hand, they are entitled to expect from him.

In considering railway law, nearly every thing appears to turn upon the great question of what constitutes a "common carrier," and if this point is once clearly established in a given case, the rights, liabilities, and immunities of a common carrier are pretty clearly defined by the authorities. We learn, then, that a "common carrier" is one who undertakes the conveyance of goods or passengers for hire or reward, and therefore stands in the light of a bailee. He must exercise the business of carrying as a public employment, and must undertake to carry all persons, or the goods of all persons, as the case may be, indiscriminately. Having become a common carrier, as thus defined, the law places upon him the *duty to carry*, according to his profession, though there may be no specific agreement as to the performance of the service, or the price to be charged for it, and, with certain reservations, which will be noticed hereafter, he becomes an *insurer*, and is liable for loss or damage, unless such loss or damage arises from the act of God or the Queen's enemies.

Legally speaking, railway companies are not common carriers unless they choose to constitute themselves as such. The Railway Clauses Consolidation Act of 1845 provides that it *shall be lawful* for a railway company to employ engines and carriages and convey passengers and goods, but it does not say that they *shall* do so. Thus some of the earlier railway companies simply allowed other people to run their own engines and carriages over the railway on payment of tolls, and they were not common carriers; but so soon as a railway company exercises its discretion under the Act of 1845, and holds itself out to the world as a common carrier, it comes within the operation of all the provisions of carrier's law, which, with some variations, applies equally to all other means of conveyance, whether by land or water.

A railway company is not entitled to make any charges for the services it performs, in excess of the charges specified in the Acts relating to its undertaking.

From this point it will be convenient to divide the remarks which follow under two heads, viz., (*a*) as to the law affecting the carriage of merchandise (in which term is included coal and other minerals, and live stock); and (*b*) as to the law affecting the conveyance of passengers and their luggage.

## (*A.*)—As to the Law affecting the Carriage of Merchandise.

(1.) A common carrier, as a general rule, is bound by the common law to receive and carry, to those places which he holds himself out as carrying to, all goods offered to him for that purpose, from all persons alike upon the tender of payment for his hire; and if he refuses to do this, an action is maintainable against him. It must, however, be proved that he had the *means* of carrying the goods; that, in the case of goods of great value, he had the means of carrying them *securely*, and that they were offered to him at a reasonable time.

He is only liable to carry to such places as he holds himself out to be a common carrier to and from, and then only to carry such descriptions of goods as he professes to carry. As will be seen hereafter, there are certain articles of which railway companies are not, and decline to be, common carriers.

(2.) A carrier may refuse to take the custody of goods unless he is previously paid the price of their carriage. Railway companies, as a matter of practice, charge the carriage forward, if so desired, and collect it from the consignee, and in some cases they allow ledger accounts and collect their freight charges monthly; but, in so doing, they waive their rights in order to meet the convenience of their customers.

(3.) The responsibility of a carrier commences on the delivery of the goods to him and continues until he has delivered them or tendered them for delivery to the consignee. Many actions at law have turned upon the question of what constitutes "delivery" to a carrier, and the point is one of some delicacy ; but, speaking generally, it may be said that the goods must be delivered by the sender or his accredited agent actually into the hands of the carrier, or some person who can be shown to be his agent, for the purpose of receiving them ; for instance, his carman or the keeper of one of his receiving offices.

(4.) Goods delivered to a carrier must be properly and securely packed, and if any injury arises to them during their conveyance from their being, unknown to the carrier, improperly or insufficiently packed, the carrier is absolved from liability.

(5.) If any fraud or deceit be practised on the carrier whereby the real value of goods is concealed from him, and he is induced to regard them as of comparatively trifling value, he is not liable in case they be lost or stolen from him.

(6.) Railway companies are not bound to carry articles of a dangerous nature, such as gunpowder or other explosives, or lucifer matches ; and if a person sends such articles by railway without declaring their true nature, he is liable to a penalty. The company may refuse to accept any package which they have reason to suspect contains goods of a dangerous nature, or to require that the package shall be opened so as to ascertain the facts.

Railway companies are not common carriers of articles of this description, and only convey them by arrangement with the senders, and under proper regulations.

(7.) At common law a carrier is in the nature of an insurer, and is bound to keep and carry goods entrusted to his care safely, and is liable for all losses, and in all events save only, as before mentioned, those resulting from the act of God or the Queen's enemies; and this holds good notwithstanding that there may have been no actual negligence on his part, and that the injury or loss may have been occasioned by the act of a third party. The "Act of God" has been defined as being something in opposition to the act of man, as for example, winds and storms, lightning, earthquake, inundations, or sudden illness or death, the consequences of which could not by any reasonable precautions on the part of the carrier have been prevented. "The Queen's Enemies" means *foreign* enemies, who are such by open declaration of war; not domestic enemies, as in the case of insurrection or riot, where the carrier, if made liable, would have his remedy in turn against the county.

(8.) The carrier is liable for the loss of goods occasioned by fire while in his possession as a carrier, notwithstanding that the fire may not have originated on his premises, or been caused by his negligence; but if the carrier is merely acting in the capacity of a warehouseman for the owner of the goods, the liability of a common carrier will no longer attach to him.

(9.) A carrier is not liable for losses or damage arising from the ordinary deterioration of goods in quantity or quality during transit, or from their inherent tendency to decay or deteriorate, or from accident occurring to any animal through its own inherent vice.

(10.) At a very early period in the history of railways, viz., in 1830, an Act was passed, which, although at the time intended for the protection of coach proprietors, mail contractors, and other carriers by road, was, by the 89th section of the Railways Clauses Consolidation Act of 1845, extended to railway companies in their capacity as common carriers. This Act (I. Will. IV. cap. 68) is popularly known as the "Carriers' Act," and it has a very important bearing upon the liability of a railway company for loss of, or damage to, valuable goods entrusted to its care.

The principle of the Act is contained in the first and second clauses, which provide that no common carrier by land for hire shall be liable for the loss of, or injury to, any articles of the following descriptions, viz.:—

| | |
|---|---|
| Gold or silver coin. | Writings. |
| Gold or silver in a manufactured or unmanufactured state. | Title deeds. |
| | Paintings. |
| | Engravings. |
| Precious stones. | Pictures. |
| Jewellery. | Gold or silver plate or plated articles. |
| Watches. | |
| Clocks and timepieces. | Glass. |
| Trinkets. | China. |
| Bills. | Silks, manufactured or unmanufactured, and whether wrought up with other material or |
| Bank notes. | |
| Orders, notes or securities for payment of money. | |
| Stamps, English or Foreign. | Furs. [not. |
| Maps. | Lace. |

whether delivered to be carried for hire or to accompany the person of a passenger by any public conveyance, when the value of such article exceeds ten pounds, unless at the time of delivery to the carrier the nature and value of such articles shall have been declared by the sender, and he shall have paid, or agreed to pay, such additional charge, over and above the ordinary rate of carriage, as the carrier shall, by notice, demand as compensation for the greater risk and care to be taken for the conveyance of the articles. In plain terms, the carrier is not liable unless the sender declares the value and pays the charge for insurance fixed by the carrier, and railway companies give effect to this Act by fixing an *ad valorem* scale of insurance for the articles named in the Act, this scale being duly advertised in their time tables and by other means.

By an amending Act, passed in 1865, it was enacted that the term "lace" should be construed so as not to include machine-made lace. It should also be mentioned that the Act of 1830 limits the carrier's liability to the declared value of the goods, plus the additional charge for insurance, but does not preclude the carrier from reducing this liability by proving that the declared value exceeds the actual value, if such be the case. Further, as the intention of the Act, as stated in its preamble, was to protect the carrier from the risk of depredation of articles of great value in small compass, it very properly provided that, where such depredation was committed by the servants of the carrier, he should be liable notwithstanding any of the provisions of the Act.

(11.) When railway companies first commenced to carry horses, cattle, sheep, and other live stock, they were in the habit of giving notice to the senders that they were not common carriers of live stock, and that they only conveyed it on the understanding that the owners took the entire risk, and this notice, being printed on the ticket, was held by the courts to be a special contract, and legal and binding upon both parties; but by an Act passed in 1854, entitled, "An act for the better regulation of the traffic in railways and canals," it was provided that in future all conditions limiting the liability of railway companies should be void unless they were reasonable, and were signed by the consignor, with a further proviso limiting the liability of railway companies for loss of, or injury to, animals and live stock committed to their care, to the following amounts:—

| For any horse, | | not exceeding £50. | |
|---|---|---|---|
| " | neat cattle, per head | " | 15 |
| " | sheep or pigs, per head | " | 2 |

The companies are exempted from liability for any greater sums than these, unless the sender shall declare the value of the animals at the time of delivery to them, and pay a reasonable charge for insurance, to be fixed by the company, over and above the ordinary rate of carriage. In point of fact, the principle of the "Carriers' Act" is, with certain limitations, applied to the conveyance of live stock.

(12.) By an Act passed in 1845 the railway company is empowered, in any case where they fail to recover the charges payable for the carriage of goods, to detain and sell the goods, and to retain out of the profits of the sale the amount due to them for freight, rendering up the surplus, if any, to the owner of the goods. The carrier may, however, sue for his carriage and is not obliged to rely entirely upon his lien on the goods where they are not equivalent in value to the amount of the freight.

(13.) A railway company is also entitled to retain possession of the goods until the amount due for freight has been paid.

(14.) We have seen in clause 3 that the liability of a

carrier terminates only on the goods being delivered up out of his custody to their owner, but this requires a little elucidation. The law provides that if the terms of the carrier's contract with the sender necessitate his transferring the goods to another company or conveyance in order to complete their transit, he is liable throughout, and the company or person to whom he hands them at the termination of their transit over his own railway is looked upon as his agent; but where, by the terms of the contract, his own duty is complete and the goods have passed out of his hands, the liability is transferred to the third person, until the delivery of the goods is completed.

Practically, this means that if the goods are booked and the carriage paid *throughout*, the contracting company, in the absence of any special condition to the contrary, is liable for the whole journey; but if the contracting company book the goods and are paid the carriage from A to B only, and there, by the instructions of the sender, hand them over to another company or carrier to convey from B to C, the liability for the latter portion of the journey rests with the carrier from B to C.

(15.) It is the duty of a carrier to deliver the goods within a *reasonable time* according to the usage of trade, the ordinary course of business, or the terms of the contract.

(16.) We have seen that the responsibility of the carrier continues until he has effected delivery of the goods to the consignee, but much litigation has from time to time arisen as to what constitutes a good delivery. The point is one involving some difficulty, but the following principles have been laid down:—

(*a.*) The carrier is bound to deliver the goods at the place of business, or residence of the consignee, provided it be known to him, and that he has been paid a charge which includes delivery from the receiving station to the consignee's address.

(*b.*) If the carrier tenders the goods for delivery at consignee's residence or place of business, and the latter is not in a position to pay for their carriage, the carrier's liability is at an end, as he is not bound to bring them a second time. The consignee must fetch them away when he is in a position to pay the carriage.

(*c.*) Where it is not part of the duty of the carrier to deliver the goods to the consignee's residence, as in the case of goods carried at station to station (*i.e., not carted* rates), or where the consignee's residence or place of business is beyond the recognised limits of delivery, the carrier is bound to give notice to the consignee of the arrival of the goods ; and when a reasonable time for their removal has elapsed, the liability of the carrier for loss or damage ceases, and he is, in law, held to have effected a constructive delivery.

(17.) If the carrier delivers goods to any other than the person entitled to receive them, he is liable to the proper owner for their value.

(18.) The sender of goods has a right of what is called "stoppage in transitu," which may be exercised in the following circumstances:—If goods are sold upon credit and delivered to a carrier to be conveyed to the buyer, and if, while the goods are in transit, the buyer, not having paid the whole of the purchase money, becomes bankrupt, or fail, or stop payment, the sender may countermand the consignment, and require the goods to be re-delivered to himself, of course upon payment of the carriage.

(19.) When goods have been delivered to a carrier for conveyance the property in them is vested in him for the time being, and he is not obliged to give them up again until he has been paid his charges. Even if the sender changes his mind and does not require them to be forwarded, the carrier may still demand his hire, because by taking the goods into his custody he has already incurred risks. The carrier, while he is liable to the owner for the safety of the goods, may maintain an action at law in his own name against a third party who takes them out of his possession or damages them, just in the same way as a letter while in transit through the post, is held to be, at law, the property of the Postmaster-General.

(20.) When goods are directed to be left with the carrier until called for, and the consignee does not remove them within a reasonable time, the carrier is entitled to make a charge for warehousing them.

(21.) In an action against a carrier for loss of goods the amount to be recovered depends upon the extent of the carrier's liability, *i.e.*, upon whether he is liable for the whole value of the goods, or whether his liability has been limited by Act of Parliament (as, for instance, in the case of a horse carried at the uninsured rate), or by any special contract. If no special damage can be proved, the plaintiff cannot recover beyond the value of the goods.

In the case of the non-delivery of goods, a plaintiff is entitled to recover the value of the goods at the place of delivery, at the time at which they ought to have been delivered, so that, in the case of goods sent to a market, the plaintiff is entitled, not merely to the cost price, but to the market value; and in the case of delay in delivery, he is entitled to recover any difference between the market value at the time when the goods ought to have been delivered and at the time when they were actually delivered.

In other cases, special damages for delay may be recovered even when the article delayed has suffered no deterioration in value, as, for instance, when the company has accepted the goods with notice that their non-delivery by a specified date will defeat the object with which they are sent; but only such damages can be recovered as must be taken to have been within the contemplation of the parties to the contract of carriage when such contract was entered into, and as might reasonably be expected to result from a breach of such contract.

## (*B.*)—As to the Law affecting the Conveyance of Passengers and their Luggage.

(1.) A railway company, having constituted itself a carrier of passengers, is bound to convey upon its railway all such passengers as may offer themselves for that purpose, without unreasonable delay, and without partiality, and if a railway company issues time-tables and advertises that a train will run at a particular time, this amounts to a contract on their part to run the train and convey all persons who offer themselves as passengers, provided they are prepared to pay the usual fare, and that there is room in the train.

(2.) The passenger must be in a fit and proper state as to sobriety, health and conduct, so as not to cause offence or danger to the other passengers. A railway company is not compelled to convey upon their railway a person who is intoxicated or insane, or who is suffering from an infectious disease. A passenger is also bound to submit to all reasonable regulations which may be adopted for the convenience, safety and comfort of the public.

(3.) By an Act passed in 1883, called the "Cheap Trains Act," it is provided that if at any time the Board of Trade have reason to believe that upon any railway or system of railways, whether belonging to one company or more than one, but which forms a continuous mode of communication, a due and sufficient proportion of the accommodation provided is not available for passengers at fares not exceeding one penny per mile, or that upon any passenger railway proper and sufficient workmen's trains are not provided for workmen going to and returning from their work at such fares and at such times between 6 p.m. and 8 a.m. as appear to the Board of Trade to be reasonable and necessary, they may hold an enquiry, and, if called upon to do so by any railway company concerned, may refer the matter for the decision of the Railway Commissioners. If the result of the enquiry is to prove to the satisfaction of the Board of Trade or of the Railway Commissioners that such proper accommodation is not provided, then the Board or the Railway Commissioners, as the case may be, may order the company to provide such accommodation, and at such fares as seem to them reasonable.

As a matter of fact, this power has, on several occasions, been exercised by the Board of Trade since the passing of the Act.

(4.) A railway company, in carrying passengers, is not subject to the same liabilities as apply to a common carrier of goods. It has been shown in the first portion of this chapter, that as to goods the carrier is in the position of an insurer, and is liable in all events except the act of God or the Queen's enemies, but he is not called upon absolutely to *warrant* the safety of the passengers. He only undertakes that so far as human care and foresight can go he will provide for their safe conveyance ; he is to use the utmost care and diligence, and is responsible for the consequences of the slightest neglect on his part, but his liability goes no further. Thus, in a case where an accident occurred through the breaking-down of a bridge the Court held that if the bridge was constructed by a competent engineer, and of reasonable and proper strength for the purpose, and was maintained with due care and skill, the company was not liable.

(5.) A railway company is responsible for the negligence or default of its servants *within the scope of their legitimate employment* as if their acts were its own. Thus, if a signalman causes an accident by giving a wrong signal, the company is liable ; but if a porter or telegraph boy were to mischievously, or without authority, interfere with the signals, or with an engine and cause an accident, the company would not be liable.

(6.) A railway company is bound to carry free, with each passenger, his personal luggage to an amount fixed by the Acts of Incorporation of the several railway companies, according to the class of carriage in which the passenger travels. This amount varies in different Acts, but, in practice, the railway companies carry free 120 lbs., 100 lbs., and 60 lbs., for 1st, 2nd, and 3rd class passengers respectively, and the company's liability with respect to passengers' luggage is the same as that with respect to goods entrusted to it for conveyance, so long as the passenger's luggage is under the charge of the company. If, however, the passenger takes the luggage under his own control, the company's liability is diminished, and only arises where negligence is shown on the part of its servants.

(7.) The question of what constitutes personal luggage has been the subject of many judicial decisions, but, broadly speaking, personal luggage may be defined as consisting of such articles as the passenger requires for his own use or personal convenience upon or in connection with his journey, although more recent decisions have included articles which might not perhaps fall strictly within that definition.

As a negative definition, however, it may be said that personal luggage does not include merchandise and materials intended for trade purposes.

(8.) The provisions of the Carriers' Act apply equally to passengers' luggage as to goods, and the foregoing remarks upon the subject of that Act may be taken as referring to both, with the additional observation that, though the Act protects the carrier from loss or damage under the circumstances stated, it does not protect him from the consequences of delay, unless the delay is such as to practically amount to a loss even though the articles are eventually recovered.

(9.) If a passenger travels upon a railway without paying his fare, or travels a greater distance than that for which he has paid, and there is evidence that he has acted with a fraudulent intent, he is liable to a penalty, and may be detained by any officer of the company, or by any peace officer, until he can be brought before a justice for the purpose of punishment. If there is no evidence of fraud, the company have no right to detain the individual or to use force to expel him from the train after he has commenced his journey ; their proper course is to exercise the right, which they possess, of lien on his luggage for payment of the fare, or to sue him in a court of justice.

(10.) Under the bye-laws of railway companies which they are by Act of Parliament empowered to make, and which are legal and binding, a passenger is bound to show his ticket when requested to do so by any servant of the company.

(11.) In an action against a railway company for refusing to carry, or for not carrying, a passenger within a reasonable time, the plaintiff, on proof of negligence, is entitled to recover any extra expense he may have reasonably incurred in reaching his destination by other means, and he may also, within certain limits, recover damages for any loss or expense which he may have sustained by reason of the delay ; but the extent to which these special, or consequential, damages may be recovered involves the consideration of many intricate questions of law which would be beyond the scope of this chapter, although the principles already laid down with regard to the recovery of special damages for delay to goods may be taken as generally applicable.

In an action for loss of, or injury to, the luggage of a passenger, or for delay in delivery, the damages will be assessed upon the same principles which apply to goods.

(12.) Railway companies are also liable for the negligence of their servants, resulting in death or personal injury to any person. In the case of death no action was maintainable until the passing, in 1846, of the Act known as Lord Campbell's Act, under which an action can now be brought for the benefit of the parents, grand parents, children, grandchildren or stepchildren of the deceased person (but not on behalf of any other relative or person), provided the action be brought within twelve months of the death of the deceased. In any such action, actual pecuniary loss must be shown to have been sustained by the persons for whose benefit the action is brought.

In an action for personal injury the plaintiff is entitled to recover, not only the pecuniary loss sustained by him by reason of the accident, such as loss of salary, wages or business profits, and any expenses incurred for medical fees, extra nourishment, nursing, change of air, assistance in business, and the like, but also compensation for bodily pain and suffering. The claim may, furthur, include compensation for losses or expenses to be incurred before the plaintiff may have completely recovered from the effects of the accident, or for any permanent injury which he may have sustained.

## CHAPTER XVII.

### ON THE RAILWAYS AS A MEANS OF DEFENCE.

IT can hardly be necessary to insist upon the obvious importance of the railway system when considered in relation to the means of warfare, and more particularly in connection with any scheme for the defence of the country in the event of invasion. Thanks to our insular position and to the admirable and powerful navy with which England keeps the narrow seas, it may safely be said that the possibility of an invader ever being able to set foot on our shores, is more or less remote; but there have not been wanting those of late who have not hesitated to discuss this contingency as one within the regions of practicability, and, whether it be remote or otherwise, it is only prudent to reckon with it.

If a calamity so great should at any time overtake us, it is quite evident that the prospect of our being able to repel the invader and maintain inviolate our hearths and homes would to a very great extent depend upon the perfect equipment and efficient working of the network of railways which now covers these islands. The Government have been fully alive to this fact, and many years ago a step was taken which would probably turn out to be a very prudent one if ever an emergency should arise. A Corps was constituted which is termed the "Engineer and Railway Volunteer Staff Corps," and which is composed of a certain number of engineers, several of the great contractors, and the general managers of most of the principal railways, the contractors forming what is called the "Labour Branch" of the Corps. The intention is that in case of an invasion the officers of this corps would superintend the working of the railways, as they do in time of peace, but acting then under the directions of the military commanders. The railways of the country, so far as might be necessary, and wholly if need be, would have to be, for the time being, given up to the service of the State, as was recently done in Western France, when the experiment was tried of mobilising certain Army Corps, and by thus utilising the means and appliances which are at all times available, and making a free use of the perfect organization and large resources of the great railway companies, it is believed that no difficulty need be anticipated in concentrating a considerable body of troops within a brief period of time upon any part of our shores that might be threatened by a foe.

From the time when railways began to assume their present prominence as a potent factor in the life of the community in all European countries, it became evident that the invention of the locomotive steam engine must revolutionize the conditions of modern warfare very much as it had revolutionized everything else, and it came to be obviously a matter of the very first importance that the organization of military transport by railways in time of war should be carefully thought out and planned beforehand, so as to have everything prepared in the event of an emergency arising. No European State of any consequence has failed to grasp the importance of this question, and, briefly put, the problem they had to solve was this:—the railways of the country being such as they are, what are their relations to the State to be in time of peace and war, so far as regards their place in any scheme of national defence, and by whom, and under what conditions should they be worked in time of actual warfare, so as to develop their resources to the utmost extent, and to secure uniformity of action and control, and so that the greatest amount of benefit may be derived from them in the carrying out of whatever operations may become necessary? The different European Governments have endeavoured to solve this problem in various ways.

In Germany, most of the railways being owned by the State, a central bureau has been established, assisted by four local bureaux, and by this means the entire rolling stock of the railways is regulated and controlled in time of peace and for ordinary commercial purposes, even the private railway companies being brought within the same system, and paid at a mileage rate for the use of their wagons. The effect of this would be in time of war to place the carriage and wagon stock of the country absolutely in the hands of the Government, together with the organized machinery for its control. A law passed in 1871 divides the railways into large groups or lines of communication for military purposes in time of war, and defines precisely the relations which are then to exist between the civil and military Officers who would have to carry out the transport arrangements, all the lines being placed at the disposal of the Army and worked by the staff of the Army for its own purposes. Periodical courses of practical instruction, held at the stations, and lasting two and a half months, have been established, and are attended by Officers and non-commissioned officers of all arms, and those who have undergone this course of training would be detailed, in the event of mobilization, to take over the management of the railways.

In Austria-Hungary, in time of peace, the railways, both Government and private, are combined into groups, for each of which a central bureau or office controls the distribution of rolling stock, as in Germany, and keeps an account of its whereabouts. There is a convention, approved by law, between the War Office and the various railways, providing for their use in time of war, for the terms of user, and for the common utilization of wagon stock as required. What is termed a "Line Commission" is appointed for each main line or group of lines, consisting of a military General Officer and a railway man of some standing. They are called respectively the "Line Commandant" and the "Line Commissary." These "Line Commissions" are responsible to the central military organization for all transport arrangements in time of war.

In France, the plan of a central control of the common rolling stock in time of peace, as in Germany and Austria, has not yet been brought about, owing to difficulties which have arisen in dealing with the private railways, but the Government has power by law, in the event of mobilization, to take possession of the private railways at a specified rate of payment, and some of the railways are already State railways. A Military Commission exists, its President being the Chief of the Headquarters Staff, and this Commission would be charged with the superintendence of the rolling stock, and with all the arrangements for the transport of troops and stores. In time of peace there is a Special Committee for each of the seven railway systems, viz., the six private railways and the Government railways, each such Committee comprising a military Staff Officer and a practical railway engineer, and these Committees in time of war would work the railways under the instructions of the Military Commission, while, if the operations extended beyond the frontier, they would assume, also, the control of the railways in the occupied territory.

In Italy, the military organization of the railways is very similar to that of France, but the railways belong to the Government, and are worked by two large companies, the distribution and control of the rolling stock of each company being in the hands of a central bureau. A civilian element also is introduced into the Military Commission in time of war by the fact of its including the managers of the two companies.

In the case of Switzerland, most of the principal railway companies have combined to place the control and distribution of their common rolling stock in the hands of a central bureau, which makes a daily distribution of the vehicles, and keeps accounts as between the companies, and this organization would be utilized in time of war to facilitate transport operations. There is, in time of peace, what is called the "Consulting Commission," composed of representatives of the railways, with the War Minister as President, and the duties of this Commission are very similar to those of the French "Military Commission." In time of war, a special "Central Direction" of five members is organized, and takes the place of the "Consulting Commission." This body receives instructions from the Chief of the Staff as to the transport required, and is responsible for carrying them out, and it, in fact, takes over the entire management and control of the Swiss railways, both for military and commercial purposes, for the time being. It is not very clear as to how this body is constituted, or whether the military or the civilian element prevails, but in all probability the " Central Direction " is really the " Consulting Commission " under a different title and with a new *status*.

This brief digest will be sufficient to show that all European Governments attach great importance to the question of railway transport, and have done their best to organize it; but in Great Britain, where the whole of the railways have been constructed by private enterprise, and where the number of Companies, great and small, is so large, it is obvious that the antecedent conditions differ so widely from those existing in most Continental States that any such arrangements as those which have been devised in Germany, Austria, France, or Italy, would be inapplicable here. The writer's view is that in time of war, when, in accordance with the provisions of the National Defence Act of 1888, the railway companies may be called upon by the Secretary of State for War to suspend, so far as may be necessary, the ordinary traffic, and to devote the railways, in priority, to military purposes, the principal railway officials should become, for the time being, the servants of the State, and the railways should be worked and controlled, under the direction of the Headquarters Staff, by the Officers of the Engineer and Railway Volunteer Staff Corps, who are the managers of the leading railway companies ; that is to say, that the Headquarters Staff would instruct them as to the transport required, and they would be responsible for providing it. The smaller railways should, for the time being, for all purposes connected with military transport, be affiliated to the other leading railways whose managers are Lieutenant-Colonels of the Railway Staff Corps, so that in fact all the railways of the country would be divided into a certain number of groups or sections, each of which would be under the direct management of an Officer of the Railway Staff Corps, these Officers in turn acting in conjunction with the Council of the Corps. Each Officer in charge of a group should be able to requisition stock, if required, from any of the other groups or sections; but this should be done through the medium of the Council, whose business it would be, with a full knowledge of the operations contemplated, and their extent, to regulate the distribution and supply of rolling stock throughout the area affected.

As to the payment ultimately to be made by the Companies for the use of rolling stock other than their own, the Railway Clearing House already provides complete machinery for keeping an account and arranging for payment as between one Company and another, on a system of mileage charges.

As regards the grouping of the lines into sections, the details have been gone into, but it is not necessary to trouble the reader with them at any length. It will be sufficient for the purpose of illustration to say that one group would comprise the Great Eastern, Great Northern, and Manchester, Sheffield, and Lincolnshire Railways for transport on the East Coast between the Thames and the Humber. Another group would include the London and North Western Railway from London to Carlisle and Holyhead, the Great Western

Railway from London to Chester, the North Staffordshire Railway, and a portion of the railways in Wales, and so on throughout the country. For each section there would be a Committee, composed of the General Managers of the lines included in the section, assisted by the principal engineers, locomotive engineers, passenger superintendents, and goods' managers, the President of the Committee being the Lieutenant-Colonel of the Engineer and Railway Volunteer Staff Corps whose railway was included in the section. In the event of the transport requiring the co-operation of two or more sections of the railways, the Committees of such sections would act in unison, under the directions of the Council of the Railway Staff Corps. Routes, way-bills, and invoices would have to be sent with all troops and stores conveyed over the railways, with a view to a record being kept and the Companies being ultimately remunerated for the services performed.

As to the rules and regulations for the working of the lines, these are now uniform on all railways, and they would, of course, be the same in time of war as in time of peace.

An important provision would be to appoint for each section or group of railways a military Officer of rank, with power to arrange for the supply of food, forage, and water for the troops and horses *en route*, and this Officer should be also able to command the services of the Royal or Volunteer Engineers to assist the ordinary railway staff in the erection of temporary platforms, landings, or sidings in emergencies when required. He should co-operate with and assist in every way in military matters the Committee of Section having charge of his district, but should nor interfere with the working of the railways or the movement of the traffic.

This is a very brief outline of the scheme, and there are numerous details to be filled in, but in its general effect it has met with the approval of the Council of the Engineer and Railway Volunteer Staff Corps, who have been invited by the War Office to consider the whole question, and, if ultimately adopted and elaborated as it might be, it would probably represent the manner in which the perfect organization and ample appliances of the existing railways could be utilized to the greatest advantage for the benefit of the State in time of war.

There can be little doubt that this plan, which is somewhat akin to the one adopted in Switzerland, is greatly preferable to the system of organization which has found favour in France, Italy and Germany, as the latter would have the effect of taking the actual working of the railways, at a period when the greatest strain was put upon them, out of the hands of the experienced officials who control them at ordinary times, and placing it in the hands of military Officers, whose only practical knowledge had been gained by occasional exercises and periods of training. It would, in fact, be very much like taking the command of a great ship from her experienced Captain during a storm and entrusting it to an amateur yachtsman!

The Continental States attach great importance to the possession of strategical lines of railway, both for purposes of attack and for the defence of the frontier, and an able writer in the *Times*, treating of the military situation in Northern Europe, has recently shown the great advantage which has been gained by Germany and Austria-Hungary by the construction of such lines, as compared with Russia, who does not possess them to the same extent. He points out that there are no less than eleven German railways leading to the Russian frontier, while in Austria, there are six through lines of railway leading into Galicia; but Russia has no such railways as yet, and the result is that she is forced to maintain enormous masses of troops in her frontier provinces, at great distances from their homes, and from their base of supplies, because she cannot rely upon bringing them rapidly to the front upon the alarm being given. Happy the nation that has no frontier! England has none; or, rather, her frontier is the sea, and her first line of defence is the powerful Navy with which she patrols it. Her Government has no necessity to construct strategical railways, for private enterprise has already covered the country with a complete network of railways which would amply fulfil every requirement of any scheme of national defence.

Since railways first became an important factor in military operations, there have been in Europe but three opportunities of testing their value, and putting to the proof the arrangements made for working them under the strain of warlike operations. An able writer in the *Russian Military Magazine* (Colonel A. von Fendrikh), has usefully summarized the lessons to be drawn from the Austro-Prussian War of 1866, the Franco-German War of 1870-71, and the Russo-Turkish War of 1877-78, and the result goes to show that, although, as might have been expected, the railways played an important part in the operations which were undertaken, and their use or abuse contributed largely to the results which were arrived at, many mistakes were made, and many failures have to be recorded which a wiser forethought might have avoided. In short, those who played the great game of war had, since they had last engaged in it, become possessed of a new and powerful weapon, but had not yet learned to use it with the dexterity which only comes of practice. Colonel von Fendrikh's article has appeared in an English translation in the Journal of the Royal United Service Institution, and it will not, therefore, be necessary to do more than just touch briefly upon its conclusions.

In the war of 1866, as we learn, although the general organization of the transport by the German railways was good, there was a great want of free communication between the higher military authorities and those charged with the management of the railways, the consequence being that trains were frequently run on slight occasions for the conveyance of small parties of men, or small quantities of stores, involving a great waste of resources. There was no controlling body having a complete grasp of the rolling stock of the country, and of the arrangements for the vehicles being well distributed, promptly unloaded, and returned empty to be used again, so that, at one time, there were nearly a thousand wagons standing under load in one part of the country, while in another there was a great dearth of rolling stock. This is one of the greatest mistakes that can be made. If wagons are restricted to mere conveyance, and unloaded promptly on arrival at their destination and returned, they can be used again and again, whereas if they are kept under load, they not only block up the sidings, which should be free for other purposes, but they are liable to fall into the hands of the enemy in the event of a reverse or a strategical retreat, and meanwhile they are altogether diverted from their legitimate use as vehicles of conveyance.

In 1870, when the German armies were launched upon the French frontier, the Germans showed that they had profited somewhat from the lessons of 1866, for the arrangements for railway transport were extremely methodical and worked fairly well. The entire German railway system was divided into nine main lines of communication for the concentration of troops towards the frontier—one of these being allotted to every two or three army corps. The Line Commissions, who were charged with the management of the transport, had each attached to them a special bureau for the control and distribution of the rolling stock, but still the mistake was made of having no *central* bureau having a grasp of the whole, so that each separate bureau worked —so to speak—for its own hand, and a certain loss of efficiency was the result. There was also still a want of sufficient promptitude in unloading and returning the wagons, and there proved to be a great need for some supreme central administration of the transport of stores during the progress of the operations. Stores were handed over to the railways by the contractors indiscriminately, sometimes in less, and sometimes in greater, quantities than were required, and in the latter case the capacities of the receiving dépôts were often overtaxed; the wagons could not be unloaded, and remained uselessly at the dépôt, there being a want of temporary magazines in which to store the goods until they were required. The Germans, however, as practical people, soon learned the lessons of failure, and began to set their house in order. For instance, we learn that for the 1st and 2nd Armies, quartered near Metz, trains of supplies, in large numbers, arrived at the station at Remilly, but, owing to the want of siding room at that station, and others in the rear, and of magazines into which to unload the stores, something like a deadlock at one time resulted, there being upwards of 2,000 wagons containing supplies for these armies, under load. This had the effect of hampering the military operations all along the line to Sarbrücken ; but soon a remedy was applied. Magazines were formed at several places, into which the wagons were unloaded, the empties returned, and the sidings cleared, and from that time forward a regular daily supply of food and forage was maintained for the whole Army of occupation. Here we have in a nutshell a great mistake and the remedy. It is obviously useless to despatch vast quantities of stores and munitions to the front without securing that at the point of arrival there shall be ample sidings to receive the wagons, magazines in which to store the goods until required for use, plenty of manual labour to unload them promptly, and adequate means of distributing them to the points where they are needed.

On the side of the French, although there was a complete system of railways directed upon the frontier, and a plentiful supply of rolling stock, and the railway companies displayed the greatest energy in carrying out the task laid upon them, their best efforts were frustrated by the want of a proper understanding between their officers and the military authorities, and between the Headquarters Staff and those who commanded at the front. Contradictory orders were given, countermanded, again given, and again countermanded, and the utmost confusion prevailed, the result being that for weeks, in the neighbourhood of Metz, not only all the sidings, but the main lines and the lines leading to the locomotive sheds were blocked up with loaded wagons, which ultimately fell into the hands of the Germans. Our author sums up the mistakes of the French in this campaign under so many different heads that there is not space to quote them all, but the most serious defects appear to have been the want of some special bureau of control on the lines of communication, which should have every day the accurate details for regulating the movement of troops and supplies, and of rolling stock; and the strained relations between the military element and the civilian railway staff throughout the campaign.

In the case of the Russo-Turkish War of 1877-78, it would appear from Colonel v. Fendrikh's account that no great advantage was derived from railway transport, for in addition to the available lines being few in number, badly equipped in every respect, and poorly supplied with rolling stock, every mistake was made which it was possible to make, and as the result the greatest confusion prevailed, no proper organization of transport was attempted, and the military operations were greatly hampered in consequence.

These are valuable lessons for us in the art of "how not to do it," and it behoves us to take them to heart and profit as far as may be from the failures of others.

One good and sufficient reason for our seeking to derive what benefit we can from the experiences of other nations is that, happily for us, we have had no such experiences of our own, the most recent warlike operations in these islands having been conducted at a period long anterior to the introduction of railways. It it true that we have had from time to time to deal with Autumn Manœuvres and Volunteer Reviews, but there

## RAILWAYS AS A MEANS OF DEFENCE. 355

is hardly any comparison between such occasions as these and the emergency which would arise in the presence of actual warfare. The number of men engaged is comparatively small, and as regards the Volunteers at any rate, they travel to and fro without much baggage or equipment, and are really almost as easily dealt with by the railway companies as an equal number of holiday excursionists.

What does really afford, however, some indication of what the English railway companies can accomplish in the way of dealing with large masses of people within a brief space of time is a glance at what is done by means of excursion trains on the occasion of the bank holidays, when the special facilities offered to the public by the companies tempt an immense number of people to flock from the large towns into the country, or from one town to another. For example, on the occasion of a recent August bank holiday the London and North Western Company, alone, carried between various points within their system, on the two days, Saturday and Monday, 165,000 excursion passengers. The number of excursions, special, and relief trains run on the two days was 1,027, which were composed of about 10,500 vehicles. When it is borne in mind that all this was done on only one of the railways of this country, while all the rest were equally well employed, and that it was all over and above the usual everyday traffic, and was accomplished, so far as the North Western Company at any rate were concerned, without material interruption to the regular running of the ordinary passenger and goods trains, it will be apparent that the resources of the English railway companies are very great, and that the task of transporting to the scene of operations the largest army which this country could put into the field, and keeping it supplied with provisions and munitions of war, is not one by which their powers would be unduly taxed.

Of course, it is perfectly obvious that to convey 165,000 excursionists is a very different undertaking to transporting an equal number of troops. The excursionists take with them little or no luggage, and all you have to do is to provide sufficient trains for their conveyance and to take proper measures to avoid confusion on the platforms and at the booking offices. The troops, on the contrary, carry with them large quantities of baggage, horses, carriages, guns, and a host of other *impedimenta*, and all this must be provided for ; but, on the other hand, it may be taken for granted that in an emergency there would be no hesitation in partially or wholly suspending the ordinary traffic, while, if necessary, the companies would co-operate one with another in carrying on the transport upon a given line of communication where two or more routes existed, so that there is little doubt that our railways as a whole would prove perfectly competent for any task that might be set them.

Of the great number of excursion passengers referred to, very large bodies were directed upon certain points. For example, there were carried to and from Llandudno, during the two days, including ordinary passengers, 21,000 people, the number of trains run being 182, composed of 1,822 vehicles. To and from Blackpool, a great and favourite resort of excursionists from the industrial centres of Lancashire and Yorkshire, the London and North Western and Lancashire and Yorkshire Companies carried on the same two days no less than 100,000 passengers, for whose conveyance upwards of

480 trains were employed, composed of nearly 6,000 vehicles.

Such an invading army as this can only be efficiently dealt with by means of ample accommodation, judiciously laid out, and the most perfect arrangements for working, otherwise the result would be a complete deadlock. In Plate XXXIII. will be found a diagram showing the manner in which the stations and sidings at Llandudno are constructed, and it will not, perhaps, be out of place at this stage to give some idea of the manner in which the accommodation is utilized, as this has a somewhat important bearing upon the question of detraining troops at the point of arrival.

It will be observed that there are at that station four of the lines which are called platform lines or bays, that is, lines which run immediately alongside platforms, and these are numbered from 1 to 4. Two of these, Nos. 3 and 4, are reserved for the ordinary traffic, the other two, Nos. 1 and 2, being appropriated on busy days entirely to the excursion traffic. The trains, as they arrive, come in on the line marked A, and run either into No. 3 or No. 4 platform line, as the case may be, and as soon as the trains are empty the engines propel them backwards over the line A, into the large group of standing sidings which is marked B on the plan, where they stand for the rest of the day. These standing sidings, ten in number, are nearly two miles in aggregate length. There is no engine-shed at Llandudno itself, but there is a large one at Llandudno Junction, three miles away, and the engines therefore cross to the up main line through the points C, and run back to the junction, where they turn, take coal and water, and prepare for the return trip. When the time arrives for getting the excursionists away on their homeward journey, the engines run from the junction as far as the signal cabin, at the south end of the excursion sidings, where each one is turned into the siding in which its train is standing, and propels it forward to one of the platforms, and is ready to go away on the up main line as soon as the passengers have taken their seats.

A striking evidence of what great things can be accomplished in the way of transport within the space of a few hours will be within the experience of any one who has happened to be at the Great Northern Station at Doncaster on the day of the St. Leger. On this great "day of days" to the good folks of Yorkshire, an immense concourse of people is directed upon Doncaster from all parts of the country, and by no less than six different railway routes, viz., those of the Great Northern, Manchester, Sheffield, and Lincolnshire, London and North Western, Lancashire and Yorkshire, Midland, and North-Eastern Companies, all these people being brought to Doncaster and taken back to their homes again within the space of a single long day of about eighteen hours. The Great Northern Company, who own the station, knowing the sort of deluge they have to expect, make their preparations accordingly. Doncaster being a great locomotive centre of theirs, they have there a large number of sidings, used ordinarily for locomotive purposes, in connection with the engine sheds and shops, and they have also a tolerably extensive goods yard. By six o'clock in the morning of the St. Leger day, all these sidings are cleared out, the goods traffic being, for the time being, suspended, and each siding is prominently numbered, certain groups of sidings being allotted to the trains of each Company. Soon after six o'clock, the long lines of excursion trains— many of which have started at midnight—begin to arrive, every train carrying on the engine a number corresponding to the number of one of the sidings, which has been set apart for its reception, and into which it runs. For such a mass of people, and for one day only, it would be all but impossible to provide platforms for the trains to run to, and, accordingly, the passengers alight without them, on the ballast, and make their way by a bridge across the station to the race ground. As for the trains, each one remains where it is during the day, but the engines get round the carriages by means of convenient crossings, turn on an engine turntable, take in fuel and water, and are placed in front of the trains ready to go away on the return journey. By-and-bye, when the excursionists begin to troop back over the bridge, there is no need for confusion or bewilderment, or enquiries as to where the trains start from, for every excursionist knows the time his train leaves, knows its number, if he has taken the trouble to remember it, and knows also that he will find it exactly where he left it in the morning. The only drawback to all this is that he has to scramble into the train from the ballast as best he can, but race-going folks make little difficulty about this. Meanwhile, the station, with its platforms, waiting-rooms, and conveniences, is kept quite free from the excursion traffic, and the ordinary trains run to and fro as usual.

On the last St. Leger day, there were carried into and out of Doncaster, between morning and night, 99,000 passengers, who travelled in 216 trains, composed of nearly 2,500 vehicles, and yet this enormous number of people were brought together and dispersed to their homes again with practically no confusion or delay, and with but little interruption to the ordinary traffic.

It will thus be seen that, with ample accommodation and a proper system of roads and sidings, laid out in such a way as exactly to provide for the operations required, the working of the largest traffic becomes a matter of the utmost simplicity, but with inadequate accommodation, or injudicious and ill-adapted arrangements, the wildest confusion is likely to arise, and this is the lesson which is to be drawn, for our present purpose, from the working of the excursion traffic. Give an experienced railway superintendent all that he asks for in the way of accommodation at both ends, and an ample staff, and he will face the biggest " rush " with perfect equanimity.

Our object in describing the mode of laying out and working these stations is to impress upon the reader the fact that at the point of detrainment of troops, if accommodation of the description referred to did not already exist, it would be essential for it to be provided.

Probably, in matters of this kind, one good plain illustration is worth a great deal of vague generalization, and therefore the writer proposes to show what he, as a railway manager, after a careful study of the subject, believes would be the arrangements it would be necessary to make in order to transport a body of troops, with all its *matériel* of war, to a given scene of operations by railway within the shortest possible space of time. To commence with, it will be assumed that a somewhat alarming state of things has arisen, that is, that a foreign invader has succeeded in baffling the vigilance of our Fleet, and has commenced to land, or is about to land, troops on the Essex coast, somewhere between Shoeburyness and Southend. Mr. Stanhope, in his speech on introducing the Army Estimates, in March, 1890, foreshadowed what our present resources would enable us to do in such an emergency, and that by utilizing some battalions of Militia we should be in a position to immediately place in the field as our first line of defence about 110,000 men of all arms, divided into three complete Army Corps, leaving the Volunteer Army to occupy certain strong defensive positions as the second line of defence. It will be assumed that the three Army Corps, consisting of regular troops and Militia, have been mobilized, and that the object of the moment is to concentrate them with the least possible loss of time upon the line of Stanford-le-Hope and Chelmsford, occupying what is known to military men as the Basildon position ; but for our present purpose it will be sufficient to consider the movements of one of the three Army Corps, which it will be supposed has been mobilized at or near the military centre on Lichfield Common and Cannock Chase. Supposing now that the writer or any practical railway manager were called upon to undertake the task of transporting this particular Army Corps to the scene of operations, he would probably set about it somewhat in the following manner. In the first place, he would endeavour to avoid the common error of over-estimating even the greatest resources, and taking too sanguine a view of what could be accomplished by their means, than which nothing can be more fatal to success. If, for instance, it be imagined that trains can be made up and despatched from a given point every twenty minutes, and it turns out in practice that they take half-an-hour to load, the result will be confusion and disaster, but if it be assumed that the trains can only be despatched once an hour, and it proves that they could be loaded in less than that time, the only effect would be that the scheme laid down would work with so much the greater smoothness. By all means, therefore, let us in all things under-estimate rather than over-estimate our resources.

In considering the problem set before us, the first point is to ascertain the limits of the task to be performed; in other words, what does an Army Corps consist of? So far as one can gather, a complete English Army Corps, on a war footing, consists of 3 Divisions, or 21 battalions of infantry, with 3 regiments of divisional cavalry, 9 batteries of divisional field artillery, 3 companies of Royal Engineers, 3 reserve ammunition columns, 3 companies of the Commissariat Transport Corps, and other miscellaneous details, together with the Divisional Staff. But, in addition, there will be the general Staff of the Army Corps, with a brigade of cavalry (3 regiments), 3 batteries of Royal Horse Artillery, 2 field batteries, a corps of Royal Engineers, and $2\frac{1}{2}$ companies of the Commissariat Transport Corps.

To sum up all this and to drop, for our present purpose, the technical distinction between the divisional cavalry and artillery and the troops of those and other arms attached to the Army Corps, it is found that what we have to deal with is as follows:—

    21 Battalions of infantry.
     6 Regiments of cavalry.
    11 Batteries of field artillery.
     3 Batteries of horse artillery.
     4 Companies of Royal Engineers with pontoon troop and telegraph battalion.

## RAILWAYS AS A MEANS OF DEFENCE. 363

    6½ Companies of Commissariat Transport Corps.
    7 Field hospitals.
    1 Bearer company.
      Military police.
      Postal and Veterinary Departments.

The whole comprising—

    33,292 Non-commissioned officers, rank and file, drivers, servants, &c.
    1,234 Commissioned Officers.
    12,934 Horses and mules of all kinds.
    1,362 Wheeled vehicles, exclusive of gun carriages.
    90 Guns.

With, of course, a large quantity of personal baggage and other *impedimenta*.

Looking at a railway map, it will be seen that the natural route from Lichfield to the imaginary scene of operations is over the Trent Valley Railway to Rugby; thence viâ Market Harborough to Peterborough, and from there over the Great Eastern line by way of Cambridge. With a view as nearly as possible to give a clear run for the troop trains, without interruption from the ordinary traffic (supposing that the emergency was not yet so great as to necessitate the entire suspension of the latter), it would probably be found necessary to devote the Trent Valley Railway between Lichfield and Rugby and the branch between Rugby and Peterborough exclusively to military purposes, working all the ordinary trains from north to south, and *vice versâ*, round by way of Coventry and Birmingham, while for Peterborough they would have to go round by way of Northampton.

It would be desirable to use for entraining the troops two stations, Lichfield and Tamworth, loading the infantry, as far as possible, from one station, and the cavalry and artillery and military train from the other, so as to keep these separate and avoid confusion. Both the stations are of fair size and not deficient in accommodation for ordinary purposes; but probably, to enable them to meet such a strain as would be put upon them, it would be necessary to supplement the permanent accommodation by erecting temporary platforms and laying down temporary sidings, such as could easily be constructed in a few hours. It is understood that the troops themselves can entrain and detrain, if need be, without platforms, and it is well known to those who are experienced in such matters that in the absence of regular loading banks, guns and baggage wagons can be loaded by means of ramps or inclined planes, which can be improvised in a very short time and carried with the trains for use when required, but for loading horses there must be proper landings or loading banks, and these would be constructed with ballast and old sleepers in a few hours. Horses could, however, be unloaded, and even loaded in an emergency, by means of portable ramps or landings, such as are used by railway companies for dealing with cattle at stations where there are no proper cattle landings; and Plate XXXIV shows one of these portable landings, and the manner in which it would be placed in position and made use of.

While upon the subject of the loading of horses, it may be observed that a suggestion has more than once been made that the cattle-trucks used for this purpose should have the ends made to let down, so that the portion of the train composed of these trucks would form a continuous platform, the horses being walked from the

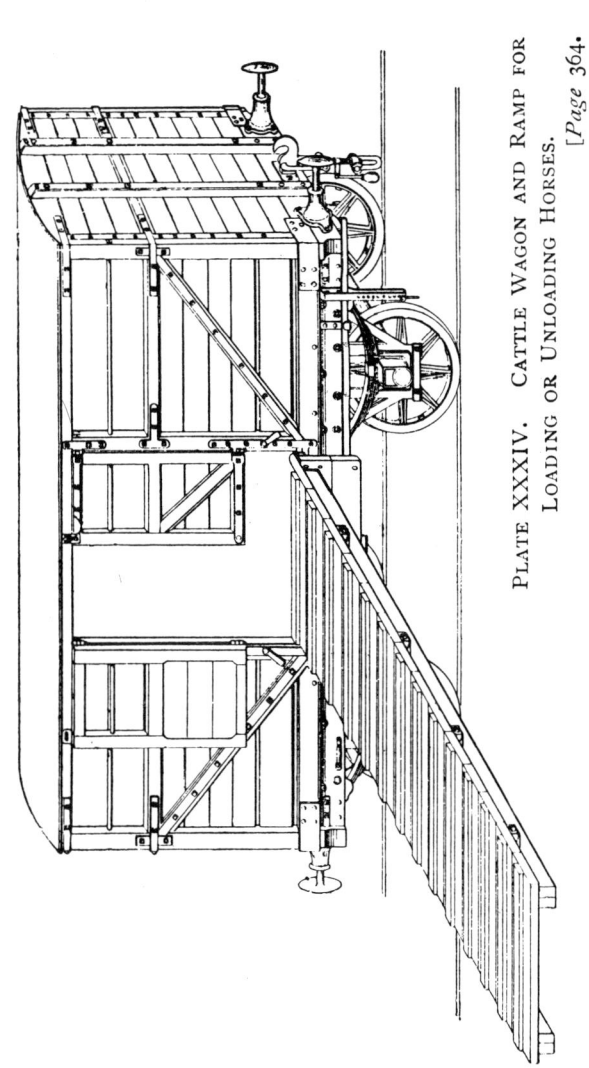

PLATE XXXIV. CATTLE WAGON AND RAMP FOR LOADING OR UNLOADING HORSES.

[*Page* 364.

end of the train to the most forward truck. When the first truck was full, the end would be raised to its proper position, and the second truck would be filled in like manner, and so on, the same principle being suggested for the loading of wheeled vehicles. It is, however, open to serious doubt whether the method suggested would prove to be a practicable one, and, in any case, it could not be adopted unless the entire stock of cattle-trucks and carriage-trucks throughout the country were altered as to their mode of construction, since no English railway company constructs its vehicles in this fashion.

It may be mentioned that at the City Station at Lichfield the London and North Western Company have an important goods station, with every convenience for dealing with a large traffic, and no doubt a great deal of the heavy baggage and camp equipment, such as would not necessarily be carried actually with the troops, as well as stores and ammunition, would be despatched from the station in the same way as ordinary traffic in time of peace.

The chief superintendent of the line, with his principal assistant, would be present, and direct the operations in person, and an ample staff of inspectors, foremen, porters, shunters, guards, and others would be concentrated upon the spot. The two stations, Lichfield and Tamworth, would be connected by telephone or telegraph with each other, and with the points of detrainment at the other end, and it would be probably advantageous for a similar communication to be established between all the stations concerned in the operation and the Headquarters Staff.

By the use of the telegraph, an ample supply of

rolling stock of all descriptions would be assembled in the rear, at Stafford and Crewe, and, in the extensive sorting sidings which exist at those places, all the trains would be marshalled and made up and forwarded to Lichfield and Tamworth as required, care being taken not to block up those stations with empty trains before they were wanted, but at the same time always keeping one or two in reserve, so as to guard against any momentary hitch in the arrangements for supplying them.

It would be desirable to make up long trains, consisting of from twenty-five to thirty vehicles, and run them at a moderate rate of speed, say twenty-five miles an hour, including two or three necessary stoppages on the way, and to haul such heavy weights, at even so low a rate of speed, it would be best to employ the largest and most powerful type of goods or coal engine. The principal object in running such heavy trains would be to preserve the tactical units complete as far as possible, as it can easily be imagined that if this were done, it would save a vast amount of confusion and delay. For instance, it is not possible to carry an entire battalion of infantry, with all its baggage, horses, and vehicles, by one train, but each battalion could be taken by two trains, the two following each other at a short interval, say of fifteen minutes, so that, practically, they would arrive at their destination together, could be detrained as a whole, and march away from the station to their camping-ground with all their belongings as a complete battalion.

In the same way each battery of artillery would be carried by two trains following each other at the same interval, but the cavalry would be less easy to deal with, as, probably, each regiment would require more than four trains, that is, two regiments would occupy about nine trains, and all that could be done would be to proceed methodically, that is to complete the sending away of one entire regiment before commencing on a second. Of course the military authorities would assist in this, and in the avoidance of confusion and overcrowding, by marching the troops to the points of entrainment in proper order, and not before the trains were ready for them, the latter being a point of great importance.

The necessity for long trains being admitted, the low rate of speed becomes imperative, and it is equally obvious that the most powerful type of engine must be employed.

Another point to be borne in mind is that each engine must carry with it a sufficient supply of coal to last it on the return, as well as the outward, journey, as there will probably be no facilities for re-coaling at the other end. It would be best for the same engines and engine-drivers to work the trains throughout, the Great Eastern Company providing pilotmen to join the trains at Peterborough, as the North Western drivers would not be familiar with the lines and signals.

About forty men could be placed in each vehicle as an average, but every vehicle should be conspicuously lettered to show the number of men who should occupy each compartment, so as to avoid confusion. Third class carriages would be used as far as possible, but failing these, we should fall back upon second class carriages or what are called composites, and seeing that the men would take with them into the carriages their kits and accoutrements, forty men per vehicle is probably as many as could be reckoned on. The Officers' chargers would travel in horse-boxes, but the troop-horses and baggage animals would be loaded in covered cattle-trucks, about six or seven in a truck, each animal being secured by the head, and the ends of the wagons being protected with sheets. The guns and baggage-wagons and other vehicles would be carried on low-sided carriage-trucks.

So far as can be judged from a very careful calculation, it is believed that the entire Army Corps, with its complete equipment, could be carried in about 150 trains such as have been described, and it would not be safe to assume that these trains could be despatched at one end or received and liberated at the other end at less intervals than one hour for each train, except that, as has been said, in the case of infantry, two trains could depart each hour, following each other at a short interval of, say, fifteen minutes. This calculation, of course, only represents an average, for it is said by those who have had practical experience in such matters, that while half a battalion of infantry can be entrained in about twenty minutes, a train of cavalry, owing to the restiveness and nervousness of the horses, will sometimes occupy considerably over an hour.

With the block telegraph system in operation there is no difficulty in passing trains over a railway at intervals of five or ten minutes; but the measure of the capacity of the line is of course the rate at which the trains can be got ready and despatched at one end, and unloaded and released at the other end; it will, therefore, only be assumed that by using two stations at each end, and working both by night and day, we should succeed in transporting the whole body to the scene of operations within seventy-two hours, or, roughly speaking, within three days; that is to say that—the distance being about 186 miles—the first train would arrive in eight hours, and the remainder at the rate of two per hour— one at each station—or, in the case of infantry, four per hour, or two at each station. Of course this is assuming that the railway companies, by utilizing all the resources at their command and by employing a system of reliefs with regard to the staff, would have no difficulty in carrying on the operations continuously, both by day and night, until the whole task was accomplished.

In a journey of this length probably two stoppages would be required, one of which would be of sufficient duration to enable the troops to be supplied with food and the horses with forage and water. The trains should not all stop at the same places, but should be alternated so as not to overtax the resources provided at any one point of stoppage; for instance, if the first train made its principal stoppage at Market Harborough, the second would make it at Peterborough, and so on. The arrangements at these stopping places would, of course, be undertaken by the military Officer who it has been suggested should be appointed for each group or district of railways to attend to the wants of the troops and horses in the matter of food, forage, and water *en route*, and he would require to have at his command a staff of helpers and all the necessary appliances.

But now, supposing that all the arrangements for entraining the troops are matured and work smoothly, and that the trains safely reach their destination at the hours appointed, we approach the most difficult part of the problem—and yet the one upon which most depends. At such stations as exist at or near the assumed scene of operations, it is not to be expected that permanent sidings, platforms, landings, and other accommodation of the character required to conduct such extensive operations would be found existing, and it would be necessary to supply the deficiencies by works of a temporary nature, but carefully planned, so as to meet all the requirements of the business in hand.

It will not be forgotten that three Army Corps have been supposed to be making their way simultaneously to the proposed line of defence, while we have only been concerning ourselves with the movements of one; but it would be a matter of the first importance to fix upon different stations for the detrainment of the three Army Corps, as any attempt to concentrate them all at one or two stations could only result in a complete dead-lock. It would therefore be necessary to appropriate Brentwood and Chelmsford stations for the detrainment of the Army Corps coming from Lichfield, leaving a second, which would probably be coming from the direction of Aldershot, to be dealt with at the various stations on the Tilbury and Southend Railway, and the third, coming probably by the East Coast lines, at some other Great Eastern Stations in the district, such as Ingatestone and Shenfield. In detraining it would be essential to preserve the same distinction as at the point of entrainment, appropriating one of the two stations to cavalry and artillery, and the other, as far as possible, to infantry. The same class of superior officials and the same ample staff of foremen, porters, shunters, &c., would be required as at the point of departure; but the first and most important step to be taken would be at the very outset to despatch to the places of detrainment a staff of platelayers, artisans, and labourers, with an ample supply of rails, sleepers, points, and crossings and other materials, so that they might, as quickly as possible, and working night and day, provide all that was necessary in the way of temporary landings and platforms for unloading guns, baggage, stores, and horses, and sidings into which the numerous trains might run with convenient crossings to enable the engines to run round the carriages and draw out the empty trains for the return journey. Sufficient siding room should also be provided for standing a certain number of empty trains in the vicinity, which should be kept on hand in the event of their being required for the conveyance of the sick and wounded to the rear. Another important requirement would be to establish at a convenient point on the railway, near the camp, a large temporary goods station, with unloading banks, sidings, steam cranes, and cart approaches, so as to deal in the most convenient manner with the supplies of goods, ammunition, and stores, which would be daily coming to the front so long as the Army was in the field. Probably for this purpose there would be nothing more suitable than the temporary arrangements which it is customary for the railway companies to make in connection with the meetings of the Royal Agricultural Society from year to year.

It would also be necessary for the engineers to make sure of an adequate supply of water for the locomotives and for other purposes; and, if this did not already exist, it would be absolutely essential to meet the deficiency by running a temporary service from the nearest available source.

All the sidings, landings, and other conveniences should be located, not, perhaps, necessarily actually at the stations which have been named, but as near to them as possible, and on level ground adjoining the railway, so as to avoid extensive earthworks, and thus minimize the labour and loss of time. For carrying on the work during the hours of darkness it would be found advantageous to use the "Wells" light—a patent, by means of which a powerful light is obtained from crude petroleum or shale oil. This is commonly used now by railway and other contractors for carrying on their works during the night.

On the arrival of a troop train at the point of detrainment, the energies of all concerned would at once be concentrated upon the purpose of unloading the horses, baggage wagons, &c., with the least possible loss of time, and the troops should be formed up and marched off the ground as quickly as possible, so as to leave the way clear for the arrival of the next train. The engine would meanwhile have taken in fuel and water, and got round the train so as to be ready to start back with it as soon as it was empty.

It will have been gathered that the difficulties most to be feared are those connected with the deficiency of permanent accommodation at the points of detrainment, but, no doubt, by the display of energy and determination on the part of all concerned, and by the lavish use of the large resources which would undoubtedly be at command, these difficulties would be overcome, and the task would be accomplished with promptitude and efficiency.

The writer has thus attempted, very briefly, and perhaps very imperfectly, to give a mere outline sketch of what he conceives would be the proper way in which to carry out such an operation as that which has been contemplated. As it stands, it is of course a mere skeleton, and numberless details would require to be considered and filled in—difficulties, some of them quite unforeseen, would doubtless arise from time to time, and would have to be met and overcome; but what has been said will perhaps suffice to indicate the magnitude of the task which would have to be undertaken, and the careful and methodical arrangements which would be necessary in order to avoid confusion and disaster. It may also serve to demonstrate that it would be an act of worse than folly, at such a crisis, to dream of taking the management of the railways out of the hands of the skilled experts who have passed their lives amidst the practical working of them, and placing it even partially under the control of military men, who, at best, can only possess a theoretical knowledge of the subject. The object of localising the operations, and assuming a certain state of things has been merely to make the matter more intelligible, but it will, of course, be understood that what has been laid down as necessary for the transport of an Army Corps from Lichfield to Chelmsford would be equally applicable to the movement of a similar body of troops from one point to another anywhere within Great Britain.

Of course, in the event of this country being engaged in warfare on the continent of Europe, or elsewhere abroad, either independently or in conjunction with some other power, the advantages which in a war of defence would be derived from the perfection of our railway system would no longer be available, or if they existed, they might be used against us. For instance, when the Germans invested Paris in the war of 1870-1, not only did they avail themselves of the railways around the city, but they took possession of the extensive locomotive works of the Northern of France Railway, and were thus enabled to repair the rolling stock and plant required to work the railways of which they were in possession, even seeking out and impressing into their service many of the artizans employed in the works, although it must be said to their credit that they honourably paid these men for their labour. Mention of this fact recalls a somewhat amusing incident related to the writer by M. Banderali, the able Locomotive Superintendent of the Northern of France Railway, and which was a striking proof of the extent to which the courtesies of nations are sometimes displayed in modern warfare. M. Banderali occupied a comfortable and well-furnished residence at St. Denis, and when, on the approach of the German army, he was forced to retreat with the Northern army to Lille, taking with him, as far as possible, the rolling stock and other *personnel* of the railway, he had no time to dismantle his house, or remove any of his goods and chattels. He accordingly left behind him a letter addressed to any officers of the German army who might be quartered in his house, politely begging them to make free use of everything they found there, but expressing a hope that they would do as little damage as possible. But the Teuton was not to be beaten in courtesy by the Gaul, for on M. Banderali's return, after the evacuation, he found everything just as he had left it, and upon the piano in his drawing-room was a volume of Schubert's songs subscribed to their courteous, though involuntary, host by the officers of the German army who had been his guests!

Colonel H. M Hozier, who recently read a paper

before the members of the Royal United Service Institution on the "Equipment and Transport of Modern Armies," enlarged upon the importance, to military commanders, of having the control of an efficient railway corps able to move with an army, to construct or repair railways in advancing, and to dismantle and break them down when necessary to cover a retreat. There is no doubt that in such a case, it would be of the greatest assistance to those who were conducting such operations, to be able to command the services not only of trained Engineer officers, but of artificers, engine drivers, firemen, and men of all the various crafts connected with the making, repairing, and working of railways ; and it is satisfactory to add that the need of such a body of men has not been lost sight of by the War Office, and that the nucleus of a force of the kind has already been formed. At the locomotive works of the London and North Western Company at Crewe, where something like 6,000 men are employed, a Volunteer force was embodied in the early part of the year 1887, under the title of the 2nd Cheshire (Railway) Engineer Volunteers, which comprises at present an effective force of 642 men, of whom 24 are officers, 519 are non-commissioned officers and men, and 99 are first-class Army Reserve men who are employed in the works, and are attached to the corps as supernumeraries. The corps is composed almost entirely of men who, in their ordinary avocations, are smiths, fitters, firemen, etc., and they are undergoing, in addition to the ordinary infantry drill, a course of instruction in military engineering. The corps having been incorporated upon the ordinary volunteer principle, is at present only liable to be called out in case of invasion, but such men as these would be invaluable in case of a war on the continent, or elsewhere, in which we might be engaged, and the War Office, recognising this fact, have arranged that a certain proportion of the men comprising each company should enlist in the Royal Engineers, as a matter of form, for one day, and then be placed in the first-class Army Reserve for six years, in which case they would receive pay, and their services would be available in case of need either at home or abroad. A considerable number of men have already come forward, and if the movement proves successful, the example will doubtless be followed in other large railway works throughout the country.

The Crewe Volunteers were reviewed by H.R.H. the Duke of Cambridge, on the occasion of his opening the Crewe Park, on the 9th June, 1888, when he complimented them very highly on their efficiency, and spoke of their probable value to the country in the event of war; at the same time expressing the hope that the example so well set at Crewe would be followed elsewhere.

NOTE.—Since the foregoing chapter was written, the author has published an article which appeared in the *United Service Magazine* of April, 1892, in which he has demonstrated how, in an extreme emergency, such as a sudden invasion, it would be practicable, by stopping ordinary traffic, using duplicate routes, pushing forward the fighting strength and guns, and leaving all heavy baggage and equipment behind, for an army of 90,000 men to be concentrated upon a given line of defence well within *forty-eight hours*.—EDITOR.

## CHAPTER XVIII.

RECENT PROGRESS IN WORKING AND MANAGEMENT.

IN the world of railways there is no such thing as finality. To a visitor from another planet, at this end of the nineteenth century, the wonderful organisation of a great English railway, bending to its own uses all the resources of modern science and of civilisation, might well appear to represent something like the perfection of means to an end; but the world does not stand still, neither do the railways. Every fresh discovery, every new invention, every new idea, is pressed into their service, either to improve their working or to effect economy; and, as an illustration of this fact, it may be mentioned that, while the horseless carriage, or motor-car, the latest child of science, is still in its infancy, one railway company at least is already experimenting with it as a substitute for the ordinary parcel cart.

Bearing in mind this tendency to continual change and improvement, it becomes obvious that any book which purports to give some description of the means adopted for working an English railway stands in need of constant revision to keep it abreast of the times, for what is perfectly true to-day may be obsolete in a year or two. Inventors and experts of all kinds are continually experimenting, inventing, and discovering, and the would-be historian of their achievements toils panting in their rear.

The object, therefore, of the notes which follow is—without, for the present, reprinting the whole of the book—to record briefly the changes which have taken place since the fifth edition was issued, in 1894, shortly after Sir George Findlay's lamented death.

## THE STAFF (Chapter III.)

*Superannuation.*—In Chapter III. an account is given of the Superannuation Fund, established in 1853, for the benefit of the salaried officers and clerks of the London and North-Western Company, but the advantages of this fund have since been greatly improved. For many years past, the members, and even the Company's chief officers, had felt strongly that, having regard to the enormous accumulated balance of the fund, amounting at the present time to not far short of a million sterling, and to the fact that, although the fund had been in operation for forty-five years, the income was sufficient to cover the present outgoings without touching the balance, the time had arrived when the benefits might with safety be increased. The official actuaries, however, could not be induced to take the same view, and for a long time the agitation proceeded without tangible result. At length, in the year 1896, the directors boldly cut the knot by sanctioning an increase in the benefits, practically, if not legally or ostensibly, upon their guarantee; and the substantial nature of this increase may be gathered by a comparison of the following table, which has been in force since April 1896, with the one which appears at page 76 of this edition :—

| Years of Contribution completed. | Superannuation in percentage of average Salary. | Years of Contribution completed. | Superannuation in percentage of average Salary. | Years of Contribution completed. | Superannuation in percentage of average Salary. | Years Contribution completed. | Superannuation in percentage of average Salary. |
|---|---|---|---|---|---|---|---|
| 10 | 22¾ | 19 | 43¼ | 28 | 64½ | 37 | 86½ |
| 11 | 25 | 20 | 45¾ | 29 | 66¾ | 38 | 89¼ |
| 12 | 27¼ | 21 | 48 | 30 | 69¼ | 39 | 91¾ |
| 13 | 29½ | 22 | 50¼ | 31 | 71¾ | 40 | 94½ |
| 14 | 31¾ | 23 | 52¾ | 32 | 74 | 41 | 97¼ |
| 15 | 34¼ | 24 | 55 | 33 | 76½ | 42 | 100 |
| 16 | 36½ | 25 | 57¼ | 34 | 79 | 43 | 103 |
| 17 | 38¾ | 26 | 59¾ | 35 | 81½ | 44 | 106 |
| 18 | 41 | 27 | 62 | 36 | 84 | 45 & upwards | 109 |

It will be seen that an individual joining the service as a lad of 14 or 15, and retiring at the age of 60, will in future be entitled to a pension equal to considerably more than his average salary during the period of his membership.

*Insurance Fund.*—The coming into operation of the 'Workmen's Compensation Act of 1897' has entirely revolutionised the relations between the railway companies and their wages staff in respect of accidents occurring to the latter in the discharge of their duties. The Employers' Liability Act of 1880 provided for an injured man being compensated by his employer in cases where the accident was due to the employer's neglect, but not otherwise; and under this law very few cases could be brought home to the employer. At p. 77 is given some account of the London and North-Western Insurance Society, to which the men paid a small subscription, the Company contributing largely, and the men receiving, in case of injury while on duty, a weekly allowance during disablement, and a sum payable to their families in case of death. The men accepted the benefits of this Society in lieu of their rights under the Employers' Liability Act, and, in fact, contracted themselves out of the Act. The Workmen's Compensation Act altogether changed the position of affairs, for it provided that a man injured or killed on duty should be compensated (or his relatives should be so compensated, as the case might be) whether the employer was to blame or not, unless there was wilful neglect or misconduct on the part of the man; but, on the other hand, the Act did not provide for cases in which disablement continued for less than two weeks. Most of the railway companies, the London and North-Western included, decided, in this new state of things, to accept their liability under the Act, and to make no attempt to contract the men out of it, although the Act afforded a loophole for doing so; and accordingly the North-Western Company's Insurance Fund came to an end. At the request of a large majority of the men, however, a new Society was constituted under the same title, which is supported entirely by the men's own contributions, and membership of which is no longer compulsory. The men subscribe 2*d*. or 3*d*. per week, thus becoming first or second class members at their option; boys at wages of less than 12*s*. per week subscribing 1*d*. per week. In cases of disablement lasting not more than two weeks, for which the Act does not render the Company liable, the Society pays first-class members 24*s*. per week, second-class members 16*s*., and boys 8*s*. Besides this, in cases lasting more than two weeks, the Society supplements the compensation payable by the Company under the Act to the extent of 9s., 6s., or 3s. per week, according to class. The reason for this latter provision is that, in cases of temporary disablement, the amount of compensation payable under the Act is not equal to the allowance formerly paid by the Insurance Society, and the men desired to make it equal in this way. There is, nevertheless, a provision in the rules that the allowance from the Society and the compensation payable by the Company are not in the aggregate to exceed the man's ordinary weekly wages, this stipulation being considered necessary in order to avoid any inducement to "malingering."

## PERMANENT WAY (Chapter IV.)

*Metal Sleepers.*—At page 94 (Chapter IV.) it was stated that some years ago the experiment was tried on the London and North-Western Railway, of laying down a certain number of steel sleepers, but that a sufficient length of time had not elapsed to fairly test their durability. It may now be stated that up to the end of 1888 about 100,000 steel sleepers were laid down, but about half of these have been since taken up, and the remainder will be replaced by timber sleepers as fast as they wear out. The average life of a steel sleeper under a main line of rails over which heavy trains pass at a high rate of speed is found to be not more than about $8\frac{1}{3}$ years. On branch lines, where the traffic is lighter, they last on the average about $11\frac{1}{2}$ years, while in some exceptional places, where the atmospheric conditions are unusually favourable, they may last a few years longer; but seeing that the life of a wooden sleeper is twenty years or thereabouts, that its first cost is less than that of a steel sleeper, and that it costs less to maintain, it may be taken that the result of the experiment of using steel sleepers has not been very favourable. The London and North-Western Company, at any rate, have no intention of pursuing it further.

*Signals and Interlocking.*—One of the most important developments in railway working is in connection with the working of the points and signals, for it amounts to nothing less than the substitution of electric power for manual power for effecting the necessary movements of the levers. This system, in various forms, has been in use on some of the railways in the United States for some time past, but the London and North-Western Company have recently been experimenting with it to some small extent, and it is shortly to be applied by them on a scale of considerable magnitude at Crewe. Very extensive works for the rearrangement and enlargement of the Crewe station, sidings, and junctions, are now in progress; and when these are complete, it is intended that a system of electric power working shall be applied to the whole of the sixteen signal cabins at Crewe, containing in all about 1,250 levers.

The power is generated in the ordinary way by a steam engine and dynamo, and the same installation can of course be utilised for the production of the electric light for lighting the station and shunting yards. The points are worked by electro-motors and the signals by electro-magnets; small levers are introduced into the cabin, which are mechanically interlocked, and by a suitable arrangement of carbon switches the electric current is transmitted from the interlocking apparatus to the motors and magnets as required.

The advantages of the system are obvious, and are very great at a large and busy station, where several cabins are required. Many thousands of movements of the levers are necessary within twenty-four hours, and many of these levers, actuating points and signals at a distance, involve great exertion on the part of even a powerful man to pull them over. On the other hand, by the power system, the levers can be manipulated by a child, like the stops of an organ, so that the saving in manual power is enormous; besides which the power levers can be worked so much more quickly that one man can, with ease, perform the work which would otherwise require the services of three men. There is, also, a considerable gain in space, for while a manual locking frame containing, say, 60 levers, is 30 feet in length, an electric power frame of equal capacity would only be about 9 feet in length, so that the work is more concentrated. This saving of space would be a great advantage in a signal cabin, like the one which controls the entrance to Euston Station, for example, which contains no less than 288 levers, this being the largest locking frame ever constructed at the Crewe works. There is no doubt that the important experiment which is about to be tried at Crewe will be followed with the greatest interest by railway engineers throughout the United Kingdom.

ROLLING STOCK—ENGINES (Chapter VII.)

At page 184, an Appendix to Chapter VII. gives in a tabulated form the details of construction of the various types of engine in use on the London and North-Western Railway. Since the issue of the fifth edition, this appendix has been revised, and now includes particulars of seventeen, instead of the original fourteen, distinct types of engines.

The following are more detailed particulars of the three types which have been added, and these will doubtless prove of interest to the expert in engine building and others, who, for various reasons, have devoted a certain amount of attention to this important subject :—

## 6-FEET EIGHT-WHEELED COMPOUND PASSENGER LOCOMOTIVE, "JOHN HICK" CLASS.

The first engine of this class was built at Crewe in February 1894. In principle it is the same as the other compound locomotives previously built by Mr. Webb, but the details and design have been altered and improved. It is carried on four pairs of wheels, the leading pair being 3 feet 9 inches diameter, and fitted with Mr. Webb's arrangement of radial axle box with central controlling spring. The high and low pressure driving wheels are placed in front of the firebox, the back end of the engine being carried on a pair of wheels, 3 feet 9 inches diameter, placed close behind the firebox. The barrel of the boiler is 18 feet 6 inches long. The tubes in the boiler are divided into two lengths by a combustion chamber placed in the length of the barrel, the tubes extending from the firebox to the combustion chamber being 5 feet 10 inches long, and those forming the front group are 10 feet 1 inch long. The combustion chamber itself is 2 feet $8\frac{1}{2}$ inches long, having an opening at its base large enough for a man to get through, to which is attached a hopper for getting rid of any ashes which may accumulate in the chamber.

AN ENGLISH RAILWAY, PAGE [384].

CREWE WORKS, *Dec.* 22, 1898.

## DESCRIPTION OF TYPES OF ENGINES IN USE ON THE LONDON AND NORTH-WESTERN RAILWAY.

| PARTICULARS. | GOODS ENGINES. | | | | PASSENGER ENGINES | | | | | | COMPOUND PASSENGER ENGINES. | | | | | | COMPOUND GOODS ENGINE. |
|---|---|---|---|---|---|---|---|---|---|---|---|---|---|---|---|---|---|
| | 5 ft. Six Wheels Coupled Special D.X. Class. | 5 ft. Six Wheels Coupled 18 in. Goods Class. | 4 ft. 3 in. Six Wheels Coupled (Coal Trains). | 4 ft. 3 in. Six Wheels Coupled Coal Side Tank Engine. | 7 ft. 6 in. "Lady of the Lake" Class. | 6 ft. 6 in. Straight Link Engine. | 6 ft. Straight Link Engine. | 5 ft. 6 in. Side Tank Engine. | 4 ft. 6 in. Side Tank Engine (Eight Wheeled) | 4 ft. 6 in. Side Tank Engine (Six Wheeled). | 7 ft. Compound Engine (Eight Wheeled) | 7 ft. Compound Engine (Six Wheeled). | 6 ft. 6 in. Compound Engine. | 6 ft. Compound Engine. | 6 ft. Compound Pass. Engine (eight-wheeled) "John Hick" Class. | 7 feet Compound Pass. Engine (four wheels coupled) "Black Prince" Class. | 4 ft. 3 in. Compound Goods Engine (eight wheels coupled). |
| Cylinders—Diameter | 17 in. | 18 in. | 17 in. | 17 in. | 16 in. | 17 in. | 17 in. | 17 in. | 17 in. | 17 in. | 2 High Pressure Cylinders 15 in. diameter 24 in. stroke. | 2 High Pressure Cylinders 14 in. diameter 24 in. stroke. | 2 High Pressure Cylinders 13 in. diameter 24 in. stroke. | 2 High Pressure Cylinders 14 in. diameter 24 in. stroke. | 2 High Pressure Cylinders 15 in. diameter 24 in. stroke. | 2 High Pressure Cylinders 15 in. diameter 24 in. stroke. | 2 High Pressure Cylinders 15 in. diameter 24 in. stroke. |
| Stroke | 4 in. | 24 in. | 24 in. | 24 in. | 24 in. | 24 in. | 24 in. | 24 in. | 20 in. | 20 in. | 1 Low Pressure Cylinder 30 in. diameter 24 in. stroke. | 1 Low Pressure Cylinder 26 in. diameter 24 in. stroke. | 1 Low Pressure Cylinder 30 in. diameter 24 in. stroke. | 1 Low Pressure Cylinder 30 in. diameter 24 in. stroke. | 1 Low Pressure Cylinder 30 in. diameter 24 in. stroke. | 2 Low Pressure Cylinders 20½ in. diameter 24 in. stroke. | 1 Low Pressure Cylinder 30 in. diameter 24 in. stroke. |
| Diameter of Driving Wheels | 5 ft. | 5 ft. | 4 ft. 3 in. | 4 ft. 3 in. | 7 ft. 6 in. | 6 ft. 6 in. | 6 ft. | 5 ft. 6 in. | 4 ft. 6 in. | 4 ft. 6 in. | 7 ft. | 7 ft. | 6 ft. 6 in. | 6 ft. | 6 ft. | 7 ft. | 4 ft. 3 in. |
| Wheel Base | 15 ft. 6 in. | 15 ft. 6 in. | 15 ft. 6 in. | 21 ft. 3 in. | 15 ft. 5 in. | 15 ft. 8 in. | 15 ft. 8 in. | 22 ft. 5 in. | 21 ft. 3 in. | 14 ft. 6 in. | 23 ft. 8 in. | 18 ft. 1 in. | 17 ft. 7 in. | 18 ft. 1 in. | 23 ft. 8 in. | 23 ft. 2 in. | 17 ft. 3 in. |
| Heating Surface Tubes | sq. ft. 980·0 | sq. ft. 980·0 | sq. ft. 980·0 | sq. ft. 980·0 | sq. ft. 981·4 | sq. ft. 980·0 | sq. ft. 980·0 | sq. ft. 980·0 | sq. ft. 886·8 | sq. ft. 886·8 | sq. ft. 1,381·2 Firebox and Combustion Chamber. 159·7 | sq. ft. 1,241·3 | sq. ft. 980·0 | sq. ft. 1,241·3 | sq. ft. 1,381·2 | sq. ft. 1,241·3 | sq. ft. 1,374·3 |
| Fire Box | 94.6 | 103·5 | 94·6 | 94·6 | 87·3 | 103·5 | 103·5 | 94·6 | 84·8 | 84·8 | | 159·1 | 103·5 | 159·1 | 159·7 | 159·7 | 114·7 |
| Total | 1,074·6 | 1,083·5 | 1,074·6 | 1,074·6 | 1,068·7 | 1,083·5 | 1,083·5 | 1,074·6 | 971·6 | 971·6 | 1,540·9 | 1,400·4 | 1,083·5 | 1,400·4 | 1,540·9 | 1,401 | 1,489 |
| Grate Area | 17·1 ft. | 17·1 ft. | 17·1 ft. | 17·1 ft. | 15 ft. | 17·1 ft. | 17·1 ft. | 17·1 ft. | 14·2 ft. | 14·2 ft. | 20·5 ft. | 20·5 ft. | 17·1 ft. | 20·5 ft. | 20·5 | 20·5 | 20·5 |
| Weight in Working Order | tons cwts. 31  0 | tons cwts. 35  4 | tons cwts. 29  11 | tons cwts. 43  0 | tons cwts. 29  6 | tons cwts. 32  15 | tons cwts. 33  4 | tons cwts. 50  10 | tons cwts. 45  18 | tons cwts. 38  4 | tons cwts. 52  15 | tons cwts. 45  10 | tons cwts. 37  15 | tons cwts. 42  10 | tons cwts. 52  0 | tons cwts. 53  18 | tons cwts. 49  5 |
| Weight on Driving Wheels | 31  0 3 pairs coupled. | 35  4 3 pairs coupled. | 29  11 3 pairs coupled. | 33  11 3 pairs coupled. | 11  10 1 pair | 22  10 2 pairs coupled. | 22  17 2 pairs coupled. | 28  18 2 pairs coupled. | 26  16 2 pairs coupled. | 28  8 2 pairs coupled | 32  0 2 pairs *not* coupled. | 31  0 2 pairs *not* coupled | 27  7 2 pairs *not* coupled. | 30  0 2 pairs *not* coupled. | 32  0 2 pairs *not* coupled. | 34  2 2 pairs coupled. | 49  5 4 pairs coupled. |

engine. The opposite end of this lever engages with a cross-head fixed to the front end of the high-pressure valve spindle, which thereby receives its motion from the low-pressure valve spindle. Thus only one set of motion is used for working the two valves. An important object which has been aimed at in the design of this engine has been to get all the bearing surfaces as large as possible throughout.

This engine ran its first trip on August 2, 1897, and on the following October it commenced running on alternate days the "Up Dining Saloon Express," which left Crewe at 5.2 P.M., running through to Willesden without a stop, a distance of $152\frac{1}{2}$ miles, and returning to Crewe the same night with the "Scotch Sleeping Saloon Express," leaving Euston at 11.50 P.M., running through to Crewe without a stop.

## 4 FEET 3 INCHES EIGHT-WHEELED COMPOUND GOODS ENGINE.

This class of engine was designed principally for working the heavy mineral traffic over the South Wales District, but it is now also largely used in working the ordinary goods traffic.

The first engine was built in 1893, and has three cylinders, two high-pressure and one low-pressure, all placed in line and bolted together, the low-pressure being placed immediately under the smoke box, and the high-pressure cylinder on each side outside the frames, the steam chests being within the frame.

All the cylinders drive on to one axle, the second from the front, the two high-pressure cylinders being connected to crank pins in the wheels set at right angles

This class of engine is principally used in working the heavy express passenger trains between Crewe and Carlisle.

## 7-FEET FOUR-WHEELED COUPLED COMPOUND PASSENGER ENGINE, "BLACK PRINCE."

This engine was built from the designs of Mr. F. W. Webb in July 1897, and differs in one or two points from other compound engines previously built at Crewe. It has two high- and two low-pressure cylinders, all being in line and driving on to one axle, this axle being coupled to the trailing axle behind the firebox. The leading end of the engine is carried on a double radial truck, the centre of which is fitted with the radial box and central controlling spring. This arrangement permits of 1 inch side play, and gives greater freedom to the truck when passing round curves than is possible in the ordinary type of bogie with a rigid centre pin. Another distinctive feature of this engine is the method devised for working the slide valves, two sets of valve gear only being required for working the four valves. This is accomplished in the following manner:—

The valve motion used is Joy's, which is applied to the low-pressure cylinders in the usual way. The valve spindle of the low-pressure valve is prolonged through the front of the steam chest, and on the end of this spindle a cross-head is fixed, having a loose phosphor bronze bush, which is free to turn in the cross-head. This cross-head engages with a lever of the first order, which is pivoted in such a position as to give the necessary length of travel to the high-pressure valve, the pivot being firmly secured to the frame of the to each other, the low-pressure being connected to a centre crank set at an angle of 135° with the high-pressure crank pins.

The ordinary curved link motion is used for the high-pressure cylinders, and for the low-pressure Mr. Webb's single eccentric motion is used.

In April 1894 some interesting trials were made with one of this class of engine, and another exactly similar in all other respects, except that it was non-compound. The trials consisted in running trains, each composed of fifty-two loaded coal wagons, and three brake vans, between Crewe and Stafford, the total weight of each train being as nearly equal as possible, viz. 695 tons 13 cwt. 2 qrs. 14 lbs. for one, and 690 tons 16 cwt. 1 qr. 21 lbs. for the other.

The results of the trials, which were very carefully carried out, were distinctly in favour of the compound engine, and since that time large numbers of this class of engine have been built.

### ROLLING STOCK—CARRIAGES (Chapter VIII.)

*Dimensions of Carriages.*—In Chapter VIII. it is stated that the longest carriages in use on the London and North-Western Railway, at the time this chapter was written, were 42 feet in length; but these comparatively modest dimensions have since been left far behind, for railway carriages, like ocean steamships, exhibit a tendency to get larger and still larger. The North-Western Company have now in use about 150 carriages which are 45 feet in length, and about 250 which are 50 feet long; besides which they have a considerable number of dining and sleeping saloons which are no less than 65 feet 6 inches in length. Upwards of 500 50-feet carriages are now being built, and it may be assumed that this length will be for the present taken as the standard for the North-Western Railway.

These long vehicles are built on bogie frames, and their greater weight and increased dimensions are found to ensure smoother and easier riding, and greater stability in the train.

*Heating of Carriages.*—At page 188 a description is given of the system of warming the carriages during the winter by means of foot-warmers, hitherto generally in use on all railways. But it seems probable that this device, which was doubtless of a somewhat primitive character to be in use at the end of the nineteenth century, will, before long, be completely superseded on the railways of the United Kingdom. Most of the principal companies have, during the last three or four years, been experimenting with various systems of heating the carriages by means of steam from the engine. The system which has found favour upon the London and North-Western Railway is known as the "Consolidated Direct Steam-Storage Heating System," in which the apparatus made use of comprises two cylinders, one within the other, with an air space between the two, the inner chamber being filled with acetate of soda. One of these double cylinders is placed under the seat of each compartment, and the whole are connected by a steam pipe running the length of the train, with couplings between the carriages, so that steam can be injected by the engine by means of the main pipe throughout the train, and into each cylinder. The steam is admitted into the space between the outer and inner chambers, and part of it is at once radiated from the outer surface of the cylinder to warm the carriage, while the remainder is absorbed and held in storage by the acetate of soda in the inner chamber, so as to maintain the temperature of the compartment when steam is not being injected by the engine.

Up to the present time the London and North-Western Company have about 650 carriages fitted with the steam-heating apparatus, and its application to the whole of their stock is probably only a question of time. The experience gained as the result of the experiment is wholly favourable, and the increased comfort of the steam-heated carriages during cold weather seems to be greatly appreciated by the travelling public.

*Lighting of Carriages.*—In Chapter VIII. something has been said as to the probability that electric lighting would, sooner or later, supersede all other means of lighting railway carriages, and particulars have been given of certain very tentative experiments made by the London and North-Western and other companies in that direction. Since these lines were written, the question has almost passed out of the region of experiment, and the electric lighting of trains is rapidly becoming an accomplished fact. The system which the London and North-Western Company have commenced to adopt, and are gradually extending, is that known as "Stone's," in which the electric current is generated by the motion of the vehicle, acting upon a dynamo connected with the axle of one of the wheels, the apparatus being self-contained in each vehicle. Each carriage carries, also, an accumulator, which stores the excess of current for use when the vehicle is stationary. The light compares very favourably with gas, and as the cost is little, if at all, in excess of the cost of gas, the change is one which will probably become general in course of time.

## THE WORKING OF THE TRAINS (Chapter X.)

*Fog Signalling.*—In Chapter X. (pp. 216–221) an account has been given of the system of fog signalling adopted on English railways, and some idea perhaps has been conveyed of the difficulties under which the necessary operations are carried on, and the hardship and danger to be encountered by the men engaged in conducting them. During the last few years, however, a very ingenious and useful apparatus has been brought into use on the London and North-Western Railway for carrying on fog signalling by mechanical means, with a minimum of risk to the men employed, and in such a way as greatly to diminish the expense, while reducing the amount of delay to the trains. This apparatus, which is the invention of Mr. E. Woodhead, a gentleman engaged in the engineering department of the London and North-Western Railway, consists of a frame and levers, which can be fixed in any convenient and safe spot by the side of the line, and an arrangement of cranks and rods, by means of which the fog-signalman can cause the detonators to be placed on the rails and taken off again at will without leaving the spot where he is stationed. The apparatus is, of course, specially valuable at places where there are three or four or more lines of rails to be crossed, because it was at such places that the greatest amount of risk was formerly incurred by the fog-signalmen ; but apart from the question of safety, many advantages are claimed for the invention, the principal amongst them being the following :—

(1) If the semaphore signal goes to "danger," and a detonator is placed on the line, but the semaphore drops just as a train is due to pass, the detonator can be removed in an instant. Under the old system the man would not have had time to remove the signal, or would not have run the risk, and it would have been uselessly exploded, and would have unnecessarily delayed the train.

(2) There is less delay to the trains, because they are only brought to a stand if it is really necessary, *i.e.* if the signal is actually at danger when they reach it. Under the old plan they were frequently slowed down unnecessarily, merely because there was not time to remove the detonators.

(3) Economy in detonators, because they are only exploded when actually required, and may be put on the line and taken off again many times before being destroyed.

(4) Economy in staff, for one man can "fog" two or more lines of rails from the side of the line.

A record which was taken of the working of a couple of these machines at the north end of Willesden station during five days of continuous fog, showed that in the period in question detonators were placed on the lines 884 times, but only on 174 occasions were they exploded, for on the remaining 710 occasions the semaphore arms dropped, and the detonators were removed before trains approached. During the same period there were upwards of a thousand occasions on which, under ordinary circumstances, the fog-signalmen would have had to cross the intervening lines of rails to place in position or remove the detonators, but were saved the necessity of doing so by the use of the apparatus.

There are at the present time upwards of 400 of these machines in operation on the North-Western system, and their use is being gradually extended.

## THE RELATION OF THE STATE TO RAILWAYS
(Chapter XIV.)

*Powers of the Board of Trade.*—The tendency of modern legislation, as affecting the railways of this country, is to confer upon the Board of Trade and the Railway Commissioners increased powers of interference with the working of the lines and the responsibility of the executive. This fact has been recently exemplified by the passing of an Act entitled the "Railway Regulation Act, 1893," which was an Act to amend the law relating to the hours of labour of railway servants. The passing of this Act was the outcome of the sitting of a Parliamentary Committee appointed in 1891 to consider certain allegations of systematic overwork on railways, and while the Committee in their report agreed that a general charge of this nature could not be sustained, it appeared there were some cases (chiefly on the minor railways) in which sufficient effort had not been made by the companies to keep the hours of the men within reasonable limits.

The Act of 1893 provides that if it be represented to the Board of Trade that the hours of duty of any of the servants of a railway company are excessive, the Board of Trade shall enquire into the allegation, and if they find reason to believe that there is ground for the complaint, they may call upon the company concerned to submit a revised schedule of hours for the servants in question, such as will, in the opinion of the Board, bring such hours within reasonable limits. If the railway company fail to comply, the Board of Trade, if they think fit, may report the facts to the Railway Commissioners, who will go through the same procedure as regards calling for a revised schedule of hours, but if the company still remain obdurate the Commissioners have the power to enforce their decision by imposing heavy penalties upon the company.

During the five years that have elapsed since this Act became law, the intervention of the Board of Trade has been invoked in a great number of cases. In some of these the Board has not seen its way to interfere, in many others it has been satisfied with the explanations given by the companies, and in a certain number of cases the companies have agreed to reduce the hours, but up to the present time there has been no case in which the Board has taken the extreme step of calling for the intervention of the Railway Commissioners.

## Passenger Traffic (Chapter XV.)

*The Relations of the Classes.*—It has been shown in Chapter XV. that one of the problems which have rather perplexed railway managers during the past twenty years has been the rapid diminution of the second-class traffic, and that there has been much controversy as to the proper course to pursue in the circumstances, some of the companies having abolished second class altogether, while others, although believing in its utility and loth to abandon it, have deplored its gradual disappearance. The London and North-Western Company have recently, as they believe, solved the problem to a certain extent by adopting, since May 1897, a revised scale of second-class fares throughout their system, the example having been followed by the Lancashire and Yorkshire Company. The difference of fare between third and second class had, before this change, amounted to about 25 per cent., but it has now been reduced to as nearly as possible 10 per cent., the object, of course, being to induce people to travel second class instead of third. So far, the experiment has proved an entire success, for, in the year ending June 30, 1898, the London and North-Western Company carried about three-quarters of a million more second-class passengers than they did in the previous year, and this without reducing the proportion of first-class passengers, or affecting the average receipts for passengers all round. It is thus clear that the increment of second-class traffic has been drawn from the third class and not from the first, and that the reduction in the second-class fares has been compensated for by the number of passengers transferred from third to second class. No doubt, when the change has attained greater publicity, its effect will be even more marked, for the experiment is at present only in its infancy, but the public are evidently beginning to appreciate the advantages of travelling in greater comfort, and with a certain sense of social distinction, for a very small addition to the third-class fare.

# APPENDIX.

Paper read at the Society of Arts, February 14th, 1890.

## ON MODERN IMPROVEMENTS OF FACILITIES IN RAILWAY TRAVELLING.

### By George Findlay, Assoc. Inst. C.E.
*General Manager, London and North-Western Railway.*

In the autumn of last year, I had the honour to act as Reporter for the English railway companies at the International Railway Congress, which was held in Paris, and in discharge of that office, to read a paper relating to a certain group of questions arising in connection with the conduct of the railway passenger traffic in England. These questions had reference, mainly, to the relation of the classes one to another, their relative power of earning revenue, the fares charged, and the composition, weight, number, and speed of trains. It was shortly afterwards suggested by your Secretary that I should read this paper at a meeting of your Society, which I was not at all unwilling to do; but, on reviewing the matter, it appeared to me that the paper I read in Paris, being addressed to an audience exclusively composed of experts, if I may call them so, in railway matters, and being, moreover, encumbered with a large amount of statistical matter only interesting to such an audience, would scarcely be quite suitable on the present occasion, and I have therefore judged it better to approach the subject from a somewhat different point of view, and, without going quite so much into statistics, to present to you such facts bearing upon the question as will be most likely to prove interesting to those who are good enough to give me their attention this evening.

On coming to consider the subject upon which I have undertaken to address you, and which I have ventured to describe as "Modern Improvements of Facilities in Railway Travelling," one can nardly refrain from devoting some little contemplation, at the outset, to the beneficial revolution which has been brought about in the life of the country, during a comparatively recent period of time, by the invention of the locomotive steam-engine, with which the rugged genius of the great North-countryman, Stephenson, startled the world in the early part of this century, and in contemplating that revolution, there is nothing more striking than the extreme rapidity with which it has been accomplished, a rapidity, one would almost say, eminently characteristic of the nature of the agency itself. For if we consider any of the other great social movements of equal importance, we shall find that they were the slow and gradual growth, not of a few years but of generations, and sometimes of centuries, and that they have not arrived at anything like their ultimate development until most of those who were entitled to the credit of their inception have long passed away from the scene of their labours, leaving others to take up their work and carry it on. In this case, however, the child has so quickly grown to almost the perfection of manhood, that many of those who were actually present at his birth are with us still, and are able, within their own individual recollection, to compare the old state of things with the new. I should like you to fully realise this simple and striking fact, that the great system of railways which covers this country to-day is, after all, but a mere bantling, so to speak, of little more than half a century's growth, and that there must be many persons still living whose memories can carry them back to the time, prior to the era of railways, when Manchester and Cornwall, or London and Aberdeen, were, in effect, as widely separated as London and Rome, or Madrid, are to-day ; when a journey from London to the far north of Scotland was as momentous an undertaking as it is now considered to cross the Atlantic between the old world and the new ; when, in country places, thousands of people were born, lived their lives, and died without any wider knowledge of the outer world than could be gathered from a visit to the nearest market town. To us, looking back upon those days, it seems as if the want of speedy locomotion must have laid a paralysing hand upon all the affairs of man, whether of pleasure or of commerce, and we almost seem to feel the impatience of their slow methods, which we fancy our progenitors must have felt. But, doubtless, they knew nothing of this feeling, and were well content with such fruits of progress in civilisation as they had already realised, and with the limited facilities for trade and commerce which at that time they possessed, so that, on the principle that ignorance is bliss, and that a man cannot be said to miss what he never possessed, perhaps we need not waste too much pity on our predecessors who never knew the advantages of railways.

And now, in less than 60 years from the day when the first primitive locomotive drew the first rude train from Manchester to

## APPENDIX. 379

Liverpool, what have railways accomplished for our benefit and for the benefit of those who will come after us? If I were to attempt to answer that question in detail, and merely to enumerate the many boons for which we have to thank the invention of railways, I fear I should exhaust the limits of space accorded to this paper, but in these fortunate days we are apt to take so much as a matter of course that it is, perhaps, worth while to mention, very briefly, just a few of the advantages we enjoy as compared with an earlier generation.

I wonder whether—say in the year 1820—paterfamilias was much in the habit of taking his family to the seaside in the summer months? I should say probably not, for although the fashionable world drank the waters at Bath or Cheltenham, the idea of transporting a large family, with all its *impedimenta*, to the seaside would have offered a prospect of trouble, difficulty, and expense calculated to appal the stoutest heart. But now it is easily within the resources even of the humble clerk or shopman, with a little saving and self-denial, to take his wife and children to the sea to spend their holidays, and the undertaking is one which involves but a moderate expense, and no difficulties whatever. Emphatically, it is the railways that have made the seaside watering-places what they are.

In former times, when young people of either sex left their homes to push their fortunes in distant towns they were practically exiled, for their small means would rarely permit of their affording more than once a year or so to revisit the paternal roof, whereas now the young folks so situated are enabled to spend their holidays, however short, amidst the family circle, and are thus retained to a much greater extent within the sphere of the parents' influence.

Formerly those employed in towns and cities were forced to dwell there, for the loss of time in going to and fro between their business and the suburbs would have been too great to be faced, to say nothing of the fact that the roads were at night not always of the safest. Now, a great city like London is, at night or on Sundays, like a deserted village, for comparatively few live in it with the exception of caretakers. The multitudes who make up its busy throng are able to make their homes in the pleasant suburbs, north, south, east and west, or even fifteen or twenty miles in the country; and the trains run so frequently, and at such speed, that the clerk, who at five o'clock may be hard at work in Fleet Street, at six o'clock may be sitting at his tea in his pleasant little villa at Watford, or Dulwich, or elsewhere. I leave you to judge how incalculable must be the effect of this change upon the mental and physical welfare of the commercial community connected with large centres of business, and of their families.

Why is it that letter-writing as an art has died out? Broadly speaking, it is because places in all parts of the United Kingdom are now brought so closely together in point of time that if we have more to say to anyone than will come within the compass of a telegram or a brief note, it will usually keep until we can spare a few hours to go and see them. Thus, too, the merchant has the great advantage of personally seeing the people he does business with, instead of having to trust to agents or to correspondence.

I have but named a few of the advantages we have derived from the introduction of railways, but, generally, it may be said, without undue enthusiasm or exaggeration, that this great invention has imported a stimulus and a vital energy into all the affairs of man, whether connected with business or pleasure ; has multiplied in a manifold degree our capacities and opportunities of enjoyment ; has vastly increased the volume of trade and manufactures in the country ; and has in a thousand ways contributed more to the happiness and welfare of our race than any other discovery or invention that could be named. There are not wanting, indeed, certain philosophers of the pessimistic school who are wont to deplore the fact that, in these lightning days of steam and electricity, we live at express speed—that we live too fast, in fact, and crowd into a few years the emotions and experiences that might well serve for a lifetime.

There may be just a grain of truth in this ; but, to my thinking, the life of the full and flowing river is preferable to that of the stagnant pool, and I have faith that in the course of time, and in obedience to a natural law, the race of mankind has gradually learnt to adapt itself to the novel conditions of its being, and is enabled to lead a richer and a fuller life without in any way shortening its duration.

Up to this point I have been rather led into contrasting the state of things which exists to-day with that which obtained at a period anterior to the introduction of railways, and the train of thought is one which might be pursued far ; but here I am reminded that my more immediate object in addressing you is rather to impress upon you the fact that the railway system as we have it to-day is the child of evolution, like most other things, and has grown up to be what it is from very rude beginnings.

So much has been said and written about the Liverpool and Manchester Railway that most people are now aware that this was the first public passenger railway, and that it was opened for traffic in the summer of 1830. It was originally projected to carry goods only, and the conveyance of passengers was an afterthought ; but the directors soon found the latter a most important branch of their business, and they set themselves to cultivate it accordingly, although their notions of cultivation would hardly fit in with the ideas of 1890, and a glance at some of the old prints of the period will serve to show us the kind of accommodation which was provided at the outset, and for some time afterwards, for the conveyance of passengers. There appear to have been two classes of trains, which were run separately. The first-class trains consisted of small vehicles on four wheels, very much resembling the old road coaches, from which they were doubtless designed, and each of these vehicles bore a name, such as " The Wellington " or " The Victory " (reminiscences, these, of recent warlike times) in the same way as the coaches they had succeeded. The lower class of passengers, conveyed by what were termed "second-class trains," were accommodated in vehicles very much resembling a modern cattle-truck, having no seats or partitions, but with a light awning over head and sides about three feet high. In short, the prevailing idea seemed to be that the only thing required was by any means to transport the passenger from one place to another, without consideration of inconvenience or discomfort, it being probably thought that as he had been accustomed to travel outside the coaches without protection from the weather, nothing more was necessary when he travelled by the trains. It should have been remembered, however, that even the outside passenger by coach had a seat provided for him; and some idea of the conditions under which the luckless "second-class" passenger travelled at this time may be gathered from the fact that as we learn there were frequent cases of their overbalancing themselves and falling out of the trucks or carriages while the trains were in motion.

The travelling, too, would be far from smooth or agreeable, and must have been very different from the easy, gliding motion to which we are accustomed, for the imperfectly constructed permanent way, laid, not upon wooden sleepers, but upon rigid stone blocks, was continually getting out of order, while the speed of the trains at first was, under the most favourable circumstances, not more than twenty miles an hour, and only exceeded by about one-third the speed of the fastest coaches which had been running previously.

The Liverpool and Manchester directors, pioneers as they were, of the new movement, had many discouragements and difficulties to overcome in establishing their enterprise in public favour, and they and their able first chairman, Mr. Charles Lawrence, are entitled to great credit for the energy and perseverance they displayed in meeting these difficulties one by one, and profiting by the lessons of failure. For a long time their great trouble was the supply of locomotive power. When the line was projected, the question of motive power was left an open one, and it was not without hesitation and misgiving that they at length committed themselves, in spite of ridicule and opposition, to the adoption of their great engineer's invention. For a long time, reading between the lines of their early reports, it is easy to see that the subject was one of great anxiety to them, and at one time they made an almost piteous appeal to the ingenuity of the country to come to their aid with suggestions and improvements. The truth is that, although Stephenson had got his idea, in which he never lost faith, it required a great deal of perfecting before really serviceable engines could be produced, and at one time a rumour was actually circulated, although it was promptly denied by the directors, that they had decided to give up the steam-engine, and revert to the use of horses for drawing their trains. We hear of the tubes and fire-boxes rapidly wearing out, and burning away, and Stephenson and his assistants were perpetually changing the material and altering and experimenting in every way, the directors being, in the meantime astonished and somewhat dismayed at the heavy cost incurred for repairs. It was thought that a veritable triumph had been achieved when, in February, 1831, a new engine, called the "Sampson," conveyed a train weighing 150 tons, from Manchester to Liverpool, but she was assisted up the heavy incline from St. Helens Junction to Rainhill by three other engines, and the directors in their report of the occurrence gravely admit that this engine was of extraordinary size and capacity, and perhaps too powerful for ordinary use. One cannot help wondering what they would have thought of one of the coal engines now in use on the leading railways which draw with ease trains weighing from 500 to 600 tons.

As the engines became heavier and more powerful, a fresh trouble arose, for now the greater weight and wear and tear proved too much for the frail permanent way, and the rails at first laid down had to be as soon as possible removed and replaced by others weighing 60 lbs. to the lineal yard, the stone blocks having long since had to disappear and make way for wooden sleepers. It may be mentioned in this connection that the fine steel track in use all over the London and North-Western system to-day is composed of rails weighing 90 lbs. to the lineal yard; each 30 foot rail resting on ten sleepers, to which it is secured by twenty chairs each weighing 45 lbs.

Our indefatigable pioneers, having at last got workable engines, and a permanent way which would bear their weight, had still new troubles in store, for they were next confronted by a strike of their engine drivers, and their places having to be filled with inexperienced men, a plentiful crop of accidents resulted. Some of the strikers, it may be interesting to recall, having signed time agreements with the company, which they disregarded, were promptly brought before the magistrates and committed to Kirkdale Gaol.

However, the Liverpool and Manchester directors, being first in the field, had everything to learn, but they frankly admitted and profited by their failures and mistakes, and in time were rewarded by seeing their enterprise develop itself into something more like what we understand a railway to be at the present day. Meanwhile their success, comparative as it was, had had its inevitable effect, and new railways were, in the next ten years, rapidly projected and constructed all over the country, and as the promoters of these new undertakings were able to profit by the experience or the first comers, and to begin, as it were, where the latter had left off, the standard of improvement was carried on, and each new railway was an advance, in some degree, upon the one which had last preceded it.

Amongst other results of this forward movement, the companies began to cater to some extent for the comfort and convenience of their patrons, and even with regard to the hitherto neglected third-class passenger (or rather second-class, for in those days there were only two classes) after one company, in daring innovation, had raised the open sides of their carriages, so as to prevent the passengers from falling out, another company actually went the length of covering in the vehicles altogether, and providing rude seats. Surely the passengers of that day must have thought they had nothing left to sigh for !

The speed of the trains was meanwhile gradually improving, although nothing like the standard of the present day had been reached, and passengers of the lower class were only conveyed by trains stopping at every station.

I have recently been favoured by Messrs. Blacklock & Co. with a copy of a very interesting little book, which is well worth perusal, as it presents a picture, so to speak, of the railway system of this country just fifty years ago. It is nothing less than a reprint of one of the earliest issues of "Bradshaw's Guide," published in October, 1839, and it is a tiny duodecimo volume of just twelve pages, the price of which was sixpence. If you will compare this in your imagination with the familiar "Bradshaw" of the present day, it will convey to your minds more forcibly than any words of mine could do, what fifty years of progress have done for us in the extension of our railway system.

In those days there was a railway between London and Birmingham, and one between Liverpool and Manchester, besides which there was the Grand Junction from Birmingham to Warrington and Newton Bridge, joining the Liverpool and Manchester at the latter place. The North Union Railway from Newton, through Wigan to Preston, had been constructed, as well as the lines from Manchester and Kenyon to Bolton, and from what is now called Widnes to St. Helens. From Manchester to Leeds passengers enjoyed the advantage of a railway as far as Littleborough, near Rochdale, but the remainder of the journey had to be performed by coach. The Midland Railway existed from Birmingham to Derby and Nottingham, and the Great Western Railway, which has now the longest mileage of any railway in the kingdom, at that time was open only from London to Twyford, a distance of thirty-one miles, although it had been authorised, and was in course of construction, onwards to Bath and Bristol, while the London and South-Western had been made as far as Basingstoke, and the Brighton line as far as Reigate. In the north, what is now the North-Eastern Railway existed from Newcastle to Carlisle,

and from Leeds to York and Selby, and with the addition of a
short branch from Sheffield to Rotherham, this was all. Scotland,
Wales, Ireland, Devon and Cornwall, and the Eastern counties
were a blank, and the mountains of Wales and the highlands of
Scotland must have been almost as much a *terra incognita* to the
average Englishman as in the days of Rhoderick Dhu and
Cadwallader.

A few illustrations, taken at random from this record of the
time-tables of the past, will afford some idea of the extent of the
accommodation provided in those days on the railways which did
exist, as compared with what the public enjoy to-day.

Between Liverpool and Manchester there were eleven trains
each way per day, but five of these in each direction were restricted
to first-class passengers. The time occupied is not stated—probably it could not be guaranteed—but it was something like an
hour and a half. The London and North-Western Company are
now running about twenty express trains a day, in each direction,
and the Lancashire and Yorkshire and Cheshire lines Committee
an even greater number by each of their lines, the journey being
performed in about forty minutes.

Between Birmingham and Liverpool there were, at that time,
seven trains in each direction, while now there are thirteen ; and
whereas in 1839 the journey, even by the first-class and mail trains
occupied four hours, and by the second-class trains five hours and
a quarter, it is now performed in about two hours and a half, or
two hours and three-quarters. The fares were 21s. first-class, and
17s. second-class ; but now the first-class traveller pays only 13s.,
the second-class 10s., and the third-class 7s. 6d., while other fares
have been correspondingly reduced.

Between London and Birmingham, although there were in 1839
nine trains per day in each direction, three of these were restricted
to first-class passengers, and even these latter were five hours and
a half performing a journey that is now accomplished in two hours
and three-quarters, while the mixed trains—that is, those which
carried second-class passengers—took six hours. At this period,
it will be seen, the passengers who paid the higher fares gained
not much in speed, but a good deal in comfort. The first-class
coaches held four or six passengers inside, according to the amount
of fare paid. Thus, the first-class single fare from London to Birmingham was 30s. if the passenger travelled in a carriage holding
five other passengers, but if he liked to pay 2s. 6d. more, or 32s. 6d.,
he could travel in a carriage holding four passengers only, so that
he got more space for the extra money. The second-class carriages
were closed and protected from the weather at night, but by the
day trains they were open at the sides, without divisions, linings,
or cushions, although the fact is carefully noted in the time-tables
that "each carriage carries a small roof lamp by day and night."
The second-class fare was 20s. by day and 25s. by night, the third-

class fare, which now corresponds to it, being 9s. 5d. only, while the first-class is 17s. 4d.

It is not necessary that I should trace, step by step, the gradual improvement that took place in the speed and comfort of railway travelling for some thirty years after the period wh ch I have chosen for illustration. The improvement was continual, if rather slow, but it is during the last twenty years that the most rapid progress has been made, and down to about the year 1870 the only material change in the position of affairs was that the whole country had been gradually covered with a network of railways, so that it was already becoming difficult to point to any spot upon the map on which a new railway was required.

Prior to the year 1872, the general practice of English railway companies had been to convey by the mail and the principal fast passenger trains only first and second-class passengers, third-class passengers travelling by less important trains calling at a greater number of stations, or by the Parliamentary trains, so called, which stopped at every station, and which the companies were bound by statute to run over their lines at least once a day in each direction. For example, in 1872 the Parliamentary train from Euston to Liverpool, a distance of $201\frac{3}{4}$ miles, started at 7.40 a.m., stopped at every station on the route, and reached its destination at 6.35 p.m., thus occupying nearly eleven hours on a journey which the more fortunate third-class passenger of to-day is enabled to perform in $4\frac{1}{2}$ hours. The fares charged at that period averaged 2d. per mile for a first-class passenger, $1\frac{1}{2}$d. per mile for second-class, and 1d. per mile for third-class by Parliamentary trains, while fares at a little over 1d. per mile were charged for third-class passengers conveyed by a few fast trains of a secondary character to which third-class carriages were attached. At this time the third-class carriages were not upholstered in any way, and still contained nothing more than plain wooden seats, but were, of course, covered in as a protection from the weather.

The second-class compartments were fitted up very much in the same way as the third-class are to-day, while the first-class were very much like the second-class of to-day, with the addition of armrests. Foot-warmers were at this time supplied in the winter months only to first-class passengers, and to a limited extent to the second-class.

In the year 1872, the Midland Company adopted the practice (immediately, and of necessity, followed by all the other leading railway companies) of conveying third-class passengers by all their trains, while three years later, on the 1st January, 1875, they introduced the further innovation of abolishing second-class and running only two classes, which they termed, rather paradoxically, first and third, at the same time reducing the first-class fares to about $1\frac{1}{2}$d. per mile. The other companies did not, at the time, follow the Midland Company's policy of abolishing second-class, although one or two of them have since done so to a partial extent, but all were at once compelled to place themselves on an equality with the Midland Company as regarded the readjustment of their fares, and this was effected by reducing the first-class to 1½d. per mile, making the second-class 1¼d., and the third-class 1d.

As regards the classes, most of the companies have hitherto held the opinion that society in Great Britain, and probably in most civilised countries, except, perhaps, in the United States, where there is a greater striving after equality, resolves itself naturally into three classes, and that the comfort and convenience of the travelling public are most effectually promoted by the general practice of having three classes of accommodation.

The effect of the new departures of 1872 and 1875 upon the earnings of the principal railways from passenger traffic was very striking indeed, and it must be admitted, and may be broadly stated at the outset, that of the many improvements in the facilities for railway travelling of which the public have had the benefit within the last twenty years, there is not one which has not been gained entirely and directly at the expense of the railway shareholder, and which does not represent a greater or less diminution of the profit which Parliament has authorised him to reap from his investments. I am not at all sure that the public fully realise this fact, or give the companies sufficient credit for it; and, indeed, it can hardly be denied that in these modern times the demands made upon railway companies on behalf of the public, not only for reduction of fares but for increased speed, more frequent trains, and superior accommodation have increased, and continue to increase, in such ratio as to render it exceedingly difficult for the companies to keep pace with them, while still preserving any reasonable margin of profit for their shareholders. There is, in fact, too great a tendency to look upon them as monopolists—a reproach to which, in these days of unrestricted competition, but few of them are open—and to bring to bear upon them every sort of influence, whether social or legislative, to exact from them new concessions without any regard to their profit or loss in carrying on the business. The public benefit, indeed; but the railway shareholder finds himself at times occupying the somewhat unprofitable position of a philanthropist, whose capital is invested for the advantage of the community at large.

It cannot be doubted that if it had not been for the fall, during recent years, in the value of materials, and more especially of coal, and some other favourable circumstances, " the bitter cry of the railway shareholder" would have been heard in the land ere this, and if there should be, at any time, a material rise in prices, or loss upon the working of the goods traffic by reason of bad times, or if there should be any considerable reduction of the Parliamentary powers of the companies, which are now undergoing revision at the hands of the Board of Trade, the outlook for those whose capital is invested in railways may be a somewhat serious one.

I need hardly apologise for this digression, as it relates to a subject which is of great importance to the railway interest, with which every class of the community is more or less directly or indirectly concerned.

The immediate result of the adoption of the practice of conveying third-class passengers by all trains, coupled with the reduction of fares, was to largely increase the third-class traffic and the receipts therefrom, but to greatly diminish the receipts from the first and second classes. On the London and North-Western Railway (from which, I must confess, my illustrations are mainly drawn) in the year 1871, the gross earnings from first-class passenger traffic were £728,779, or 13·59d. per passenger train-mile (*i.e.*, each mile run by passenger trains); but in 1888, the earnings from that class were only £480,780, or 5·81d. per train-mile. From second-class traffic in 1871, we earned £867,099, or 16·17d. per train-mile; but in 1888, only £328,771, or 3·97d. per train-mile. On the other hand, while in 1871 the receipts from third-class were only £999,051, or 18·46d. per train-mile, in 1888 they had grown to £2,433,485, or 29·38d. per train-mile. The net result of this wholesale transfer of passengers from the superior classes to the third-class was that the total passenger receipts per train-mile from all three classes combined fell from 48·22d. in 1871, to 39·16d. in 1888, this diminution representing, of course, a very serious loss of revenue when applied to a train-mileage of upwards of 20,000,000 of miles per annum.

During the past twenty years there has been a very marked increase in the speed of trains in this country, and more particularly in that of the express trains, which are now open to all classes of travellers. For example, in 1872, the fastest trains between London and Liverpool, a distance of 201¾ miles, performed the journey in 5¼ to 6 hours, while now it is accomplished in 4½ hours. Between London and Manchester, 188¾ miles, the shortest time occupied was 5 hours, while now the distance is covered in 4¼ hours. Between London and Birmingham, 113 miles, one train ran in 3¼ hours, but the others were much longer on the road, while to-day all the fast trains perform the journey in 2¾ hours. But the most remarkable development in the rates of speed is found in the running of the express trains between London and Scotland; and as regards these, it will be a sufficiently striking illustration to mention that the 10 a.m. Scotch Express from London, which in 1872 reached Edinburgh at 9.10 p.m. and Glasgow at 9.30 p.m., now starts from London at the same hour, but is timed to reach Edinburgh at 6.30, and Glasgow at 6.45. The journey to Edinburgh is thus performed in 8½ hours, and to Glasgow in 8¾ hours, but even this rate is sometimes exceeded, for during the tourist season of 1888 the journey to Edinburgh was accomplished in less than 8 hours, the distance being 401 miles, giving a speed throughout of 50 miles an hour, including all stoppages.

Messrs. E. Foxwell and T. C. Farrer have recently published a valuable work entitled "Express Trains, English and Foreign," to which I am indebted for some very interesting figures with regard to the comparison of the speed of express trains on the principal railways in this country and abroad. The facts they adduce are very striking, and should go far to convince English readers that they have every reason to be proud of their railways, and, whether with regard to speed or other considerations, they have little cause for envy in contemplating those of their continental neighbours.

As regards English railways, it appears that so far as speed is concerned, the Great Northern Company, doubtless owing to the straight course and easy gradients of a great portion of their railway, are entitled to the pride of place, for, notwithstanding their small mileage, as compared with their more powerful neighbours, they can boast of no less than 77 express trains daily running at an average speed of nearly 44 miles an hour throughout, inclusive of all stoppages; while the Midland Company have a large number of express trains running at a speed, according to time-table, only a trifle less than that of the Great Northern expresses. To save repetition, I may say that all the rates of speed I am about to refer to include stoppages—that is to say, that they represent the time occupied by the trains from departure to arrival, and the actual running speed would of course be considerably higher, and would vary on different portions of the route.

The London and North-Western Company have not hitherto made it their primary object to run their trains at the highest attainable rate of speed. In these days, journeys must be accomplished quickly, in order to keep pace with the times, and to meet the growing requirements of the travelling public, but the highest speed is not always the most compatible with safety and punctuality, and these latter essentials are certainly not the least important to be secured in the working of a great passenger traffic. In speaking of this question of punctuality, however, it must be borne in mind that, even on the most efficiently managed railway, there must always be a percentage of late arrivals, especially at certain periods of the year, from causes which are quite unavoidable, and the utmost foresight and good management can do no more than reduce this percentage to a minimum. For instance, in the summer months the passenger traffic is abnormally increased by the influx of tourists proceeding to seaside and other holiday resorts, taking with them enormous quantities of luggage, which add to the weight of the trains, and to the difficulty of getting them promptly away from the stations. Again, in the winter months, the trains are frequently delayed by adverse weather, to say nothing of the greatest enemy of railway companies, the fogs which often descend over the whole country in an hour, and blot out the entire system of visible signals, so that the speed of the trains must, of necessity, be reduced, and more or less delay is inevitable, in the interests of safety, which is of course an even greater consideration than punctuality.

While upon the subject of punctuality, I may perhaps be excused for digressing for a moment to refer to a noticeable piece of good work in this direction recently accomplished by the companies who unite in forming what is known as the west coast route between Aberdeen and London. By an arrangement between the companies, the Christmas cattle from Scotland to the metropolis is carried in alternate years by the east and west coast routes; and this year, it being the turn of the west coast route, the bulk of the cattle was brought up on the 13th December in four trains, each conveying 30 wagons, about $24\frac{1}{2}$ hours being allowed for the journey, or an average of about 21 miles an hour throughout. It must be borne in mind that these were special trains, having to thread their way through the ordinary traffic at a time, just before Christmas, when it is abnormally heavy, yet of the four trains two came in a minute or two before time, one was only a few minutes behind, and only one of the four was a couple of hours late. The west coast companies may well look upon this as a piece of good work.

However, to return to the comparison of speed, if the London and North-Western do not, as I have said, claim to run their trains at the greatest possible speed, they can still, according to our authors, point to a good record in the way of express running, for they have no less than 135 trains daily running at an average speed of $41\frac{1}{2}$ miles, inclusive of stoppages, and the large majority of these trains run absolutely to time.

But it is not only the three or four leading companies who can lay claim to an honourable record in the way of improving the speed of their trains, for taking England and Scotland throughout, we are told that the time-tables show a total of 670 trains daily, with a mileage of 62,904 miles, having an inclusive speed of upwards of 41 miles per hour, whereas 20 years ago, or say in the year 1871, on the 10 leading railways of England, there were no more than 57 trains run at a speed exceeding 39 miles an hour, while none of the lesser railways could boast of any such trains.

If we now turn from the English railways to their neighbours on the Continent we shall find that the lengths to which the English companies have proceeded, under the stress of competition, in making concessions to the public, have had the effect of placing railway travellers in Great Britain in a most favoured position, as compared with the public who use the continental railways.

It is not too much to say that trains running at anything like the rates of speed in vogue on the best English railways are practically unknown in any other country of Europe. The nearest approach to them is shown in France, where the Northern Railway have a certain number of trains running at an average speed of 36 miles an hour, the Eastern Railway have a few at 34½ miles an hour, and the Orleans Railway have twelve trains between Paris and Bordeaux at 35½ miles an hour. The so-called express trains of the other French companies are run at an average speed of less than 32 miles an hour, and the express trains of Belgium at precisely the same average speed, while those of Holland very slightly exceed it. On the railways of North Germany there are some forty trains which attain a speed of between 34 and 35 miles an hour, but the remainder, even those which claim the title "express," do not exceed an average speed of 32 miles an hour, while many do not exceed 29 miles. On the South German and Austrian railways the speed of the express trains varies from 29 to 34 miles an hour, with very few exceptions. On the Italian lines there are no trains which exceed an average speed of 31 miles an hour, and in Russia the highest limit is 29 miles. Even the Orient express, one of the most famous of continental trains, although it runs through France at a speed of 37 miles an hour, travels at so much slower a rate on the other portions of the route that the entire journey from Paris to Constantinople is only accomplished at an average throughout speed of 27 miles an hour; whereas if it travelled at 40 miles an hour, a speed commonly exceeded on English railways, there would be a saving of no less than twenty-two hours in the journey. In the same way, it has been calculated that if a passenger travelled from London to Berlin, *viâ* Calais, at a speed of 40 miles an hour, exclusive, of course, of the sea-passage, there would be a saving of between ten and twelve hours as compared with the existing service.

It must be borne in mind, moreover, that all express trains on the Continent are not open to third-class passengers, while many of the best trains are actually restricted to first-class only, and the unhappy third-class passenger must put up with a rate of speed which would be perfectly intolerable to English travellers of the present day. Again, while the English companies place the most luxurious accommodation in their trains at the disposal of the first-class passenger for a very trifling sum in addition to the ordinary fare, and in some cases without any addition whatever, for the use of the *trains de luxe*, abroad an extra charge is made so high as to be prohibitive to any but the wealthiest class of travellers. For instance, from London to Perth a sleeping berth costs 5s. over and above the fare, the distance being 450 miles, while on the journey from Paris to Avignon, a distance of 461 miles, the same accommodation would cost from 36s. to 48s.

As regards the speed of the trains, it is an undoubted fact that the type of permanent way generally in use on the continental railways, which is of a lighter description than that adopted by English railway companies, and of a method of construction long discarded by English engineers, is unsuitable to bear the enormous strain of long and heavy trains running over it at the high rates of speed which prevail with us, but if it be asked generally, what is the reason that the continental railways are so much behind our own, not only in speed but in progress, in studying the interest of the public, and more particularly of the masses? the answer will undoubtedly be found in the wide difference in the conditions under which the railways have been constructed and are worked. Most of the railways in Germany, Austria, and Belgium are either State railways or are controlled by the State, and are worked not only for the benefit of the travelling public but with a view to the improvement of the State revenue, and in France, although the principal railways have been constructed by private companies, it has been done upon a system of territorial concession for a period of time, the State reserving a control over the fixing of the rates and charges, so that the question of competition seldom arises. In England, on the contrary, the Legislature has fostered the principle of competition by sanctioning the construction of alternative routes between most points of importance, and it must be confessed that a great deal of the readiness of English railway companies to yield to the increasing demands of the public, and to proceed rapidly from one concession to another, has no doubt arisen from the peculiar nature of the traffic of a country of limited extent, and where the business is so extremely competitive. For instance, between London and Liverpool, Manchester, Leeds, Edinburgh, Glasgow, Perth, or Aberdeen, and between Liverpool and Manchester, there are no less than three rival routes open to the intending traveller; between London and most of the principal places in the West of England, two routes; and so on, more or less throughout the country. Thus, between all the principal towns there are running daily large numbers of express trains by the different routes, very often at the same hours, or nearly so, and in most cases at the same speed and fares, so that the traffic is acutely competitive, and the general conditions being so equal, it requires but the smallest inducement to influence the travelling public in their choice of route, so that there is a constant temptation to the competing companies to make fresh concessions, in order to attract business from their rivals.

A careful series of statistics which have recently been prepared, but with the details of which I will not trouble you, has shown that the practice adopted for the first time, as I have said, in 1872 of attaching third-class carriages to all trains has had the effect of causing the trains as a whole to be less profitably utilised as to sapce; and as the trains cannot be indefinitely increased in length and weight, this has entailed the running of an amount of additional mileage out of all proportion to the natural increase in the business. For instance, on the London and North-Western Railway, during the eighteen years which elapsed between 1870 and 1888, the amount of revenue derived from passenger traffic increased by 44 per cent., but the passenger-train mileage increased by 61 per cent. This increase of mileage, added to the greater weight and higher rate of speed of the trains, has had the effect of very seriously increasing the cost of locomotive power, so much so, indeed, that I find that during the eighteen years in question the amount of fuel consumed on the London and North-Western Railway has increased by 142 per cent., or in more than double the ratio of the increase of train mileage, showing the unmistakable effect of the increased speed and the heavier weights to which motive power has to be applied, and this notwithstanding the improvements in engine building, and in the methods of economising fuel, which have been effected.

The exceptionally high rates of speed adopted on English railways add to the cost of working in more ways than one; in fact, they have a tendency to increase almost every item of working expenses. In the first place, there is greater wear and tear of the engines and vehicles, and more frequent repairs and replacements become necessary. Secondly, the engines must be worked at much higher pressure, and be of greater capacity, and the increased consumption of fuel, to which I have already referred, is a very serious item. Mr. Webb, our locomotive engineer, tells me that with one of his compound passenger engines, drawing a train weighing 321 gross tons, he is able to haul 1 ton of dead weight 1 mile, at a speed of 24 miles an hour, with the expenditure of 1·26 oz. of coal, but if the speed be increased to 44 miles an hour, 2·06 oz. of fuel will be required to perform the same task, so that it will be seen at a glance that speed is a very important element in calculating the cost of working. Then, again, to permit of heavy trains being run with safety at such high rates of speed, the permanent way must be proportionately strengthened, and becomes more expensive to provide and keep in repair, for it must be maintained in the most absolutely perfect condition, and the moment a rail shows signs of wear it must be taken out and replaced by a new one. The great speed at which the trains are run also necessitates a most elaborate and complicated system of signalising and interlocking, to admit of the traffic being conducted with safety and efficiency, and all this adds to the cost of the service. As an illustration, however, of how much is now demanded from railway companies, it may be mentioned that, notwithstanding all they have done, and the large sums they have expended within recent years in introducing the block telegraph system of working, in the interlocking of points and signals, the adoption of continuous brakes, and the multiplication of safety appliances, they are still considered not to have done enough; and an Act passed in the last session of Parliament conferred upon the Board of Trade new powers of control, by means of which still greater sacrifices may be imposed upon them. In virtue of those powers, the Board of Trade are now proposing to issue an order which would render it obligatory upon the companies to adopt the absolute block system upon all their lines (except very short single lines worked by the train staff or by one engine) within twelve months, and within eighteen months to interlock every station and siding upon the most improved modern principles, and to adopt continuous brakes upon every train conveying passengers, coupled with such restrictions as would practically preclude the running of mixed trains. The railway companies, as a body, have ventured to deprecate the issue of such an absolute order as this, on the ground that although the measures indicated are such as they are willing and indeed anxious to adopt, it would be almost a physical impossibility to carry them out within the limited period specified, to say nothing of the great pecuniary burden which would thus be imposed upon some of the railway companies.

There has been during recent years a very striking increase in the size and weight of the carriages employed for the conveyance of passengers, arising in great measure from the popular demand for improved accommodation, and the extent to which that demand has been conceded, and the same causes have led to a marked improvement in the arrangements for the comfort and convenience of the travelling public who use the vehicles. The standard third-class carriage of 1872 on the London and North-Western Railway, for example, was 30½ feet long and weighed about 10 tons, but the standard third-class carriage of 1889 is 42 feet in length and weighs upwards of 18 tons. The carriage of 1872 was capable of seating 50 passengers, but that of 1890 only seats 20 more or 70 in all, so that the weight of the vehicle has increased in double the ratio of the accommodation provided. To take another illustration, the standard composite carriage built by the same company in 1872, 30 feet 6 inches in length, weighed 10 tons 8 cwt., but those of the latest type, built recently, measure 42 ft. in length and weigh from 18 to 19 tons. Of course the modern type of vehicle being longer, wider, and higher, than those formerly used, gives the passenger a great deal more elbow room, and being well upholstered and of handsome proportions, is more spacious and comfortable in every way.

The typical composite carriage in use upon the leading railways at the present time furnishes indeed a striking contrast to the primitive vehicles in use 50 years ago, and may be taken as representative of the latest development of the carriage builders' art in these modern times. Upwards of 40 feet in length, with accommodation for three classes of passengers and for their luggage, provided with lavatories for first-class passengers mounted upon the easiest of springs, well lighted by gas, and warmed during the winter, adorned with ornamental woods, and the handsomest upholsterers' work, and replete with every convenience and comfort throughout, it embodies in fact in a high degree the latest development of modern civilisation as exemplified in railway travelling.

But in these matters there appears to be no finality, and at the present time the principal companies are going even a step further, and are building carriages for their leading long journey trains which will provide lavatory accommodation for second and third as well as first-class passengers. Our carriage-builder, Mr. Park, has furnished me with particulars of one of these vehicles now being constructed by the North-Western Company, which he informs me will weigh 19½ tons, will cost about £860, and yet will only furnish seats for 33 passengers of all classes. It is probable that some of our ingenious friends who talk learnedly upon the subject of a "ton of freight and a ton of passengers" and found all sorts of theories upon the difference of charge for the two, overlook the fact that a ton of freight means simply a ton, with a reasonable allowance for the dead weight of the wagon, whilst a ton of passengers means not merely 2,240 pounds of living freight, but something like 10 tons of dead weight in addition.

The effect of the great increase in the weight of the vehicles is seen if we come to compare the length and weight of the trains as they are running to-day with the dimensions of the corresponding trains run some years ago, and, of course, when trains under ordinary circumstances are of such great weight and length they cannot be easily strengthened to meet any abnormal increase of traffic or sudden pressure, and it becomes necessary, instead, to run extra or duplicate trains, thus adding in another way to the working expenses. The increase of speed has also had the indirect effect of adding considerably to the number of trains run and to the amount of train mileage; in order, for example, to enable a train to run from London to Edinburgh, in the autumn of 1888, in 8 hours, it became not only necessary to maintain a high rate of speed throughout, but very few stoppages could be permitted, and other trains had to be run to serve the stations where the stoppages were dispensed with, and to enable the passengers from those stations to get on to other stations at which the train did stop.

Another innovation which, while it has had the effect of greatly increasing the weight and bulk of the trains, has largely promoted the comfort and convenience of railway travellers, or such of them as can afford to pay first-class fares, is the introduction of saloon carriages of various descriptions. Sleeping saloons, each of which is in charge of an attendant, are now run on all the more important night trains, a small fee being charged for each berth in addition to the first-class fare. Drawing-room saloons, fitted up in the most luxurious manner, are run on some of the principal day trains without any extra charge, and also luncheon and dining cars, for the use of which there is no extra charge beyond the fare and the cost of the meals supplied. With regard to the drawing-room saloons, however, it is remarkable that these are not patronised by the public to the extent which would be naturally expected, and I believe the Midland Company have had the same experience in respect to the sumptuous Pullman Parlour Cars, which they run on their day express trains. It seems to be a fact that there is something in the semi-privacy of the ordinary compartment which appeals more to the taste of the British travelling public, and induces them to prefer it to the open saloons, notwithstanding their superior comfort and convenience, and the absence of any extra charge for their use. Saloon carriages are also run for family parties on any of the trains on payment of six first-class fares, or their equivalent, and also saloons for picnic parties and for invalids and their attendants. All these vehicles are of exceptional weight and dimensions; they add immensely to the weight of the trains, and are very expensive to build and maintain, and yet they accommodate but a limited number of passengers. For instance, a sleeping saloon 42 feet in length, weighing $22\frac{1}{2}$ tons, and costing about £1,300, only contains berths for 16 individuals. The invention of sleeping carriages is, without doubt, a very great boon to travellers, and more particularly to business men, with whom time is an object of the first importance. If, for example, in former times a London merchant wished to transact a day's business in Glasgow, Edinburgh, or elsewhere in the North, it must have been necessary for him to allot three days to the trip, as he would want a day to go and a day to return; while even if he exposed himself to the fatigue and discomfort of night travelling, a great part of the following days must necessarily be devoted to repairing the effects of the journey. Under existing circumstances he can leave London, say on Monday night, may sleep in the train as comfortably almost as if he were in his own bed at home, devote Tuesday to his business, and leave again on Tuesday night, arriving back in London on Wednesday morning, after a good night's rest, ready for the day's business. He will thus practically have only been absent from his London office for a single day.

The provision of lavatory accommodation in trains is, perhaps, one of the greatest boons that has ever been bestowed upon railway passengers, as everyone must admit who can recall the miseries of a long journey by train on a hot summer's day, after a spell of dry weather, and with no opportunity of removing the stains of travel before reaching their destination. This great convenience to the public, however, entails upon railway companies a heavy sacrifice in space and in the haulage of dead weight, in proof of which it will be sufficient to mention the fact that a first-class carriage of the largest size, 42 feet in length, which under ordinary circumstances would provide seats for forty passengers, when the necessary space for lavatories has been abstracted, only affords accommodation for 28 passengers, so that practically one-third of the seat space is lost, and the weight of the train is correspondingly increased.

To keep pace with the increased weight of the vehicles, the power and weight of the engines employed to draw them has had to be correspondingly augmented. The most powerful passenger engines in use on the London and North-Western Railway in 1872, having driving wheels 7 ft. 6 in. in diameter, weighed, without tenders, 27 tons 1 cwt. ; but the compound engines now being made by Mr. Webb, at the Crewe Works, having triple cylinders and driving-wheels 6 ft. in diameter, weigh $42\frac{1}{2}$ tons ; while an even more powerful type of engine, on the compound system, having 7 ft. driving-wheels, weighs no less than $45\frac{1}{2}$ tons, or with the tender attached upwards of 70 tons.

There are many minor additions which have been made to the comfort and convenience of those who travel on railways, to which we have so soon become accustomed that we are apt to forget that we did not always enjoy them. Amongst these may be reckoned foot-warmers, curtains to exclude the sun (what little we see of him), doors and windows so constructed as to exclude, and not to admit, draughts, nets in which we can deposit our parcels and other small *impedimenta*, instead of nursing them or thrusting them under the seats as we once had to do, and racks for our hats. All these little privileges, too, are bestowed not merely on the first-class passenger, as would once have been the case, but upon all classes alike.

Another institution is the luncheon basket. It is not every traveller who is constitutionally fitted to grapple with the difficulties of a luncheon consumed in a railway refreshment-room during the few minutes that the train can be allowed to stop for the purpose, but by the device of the luncheon basket the traveller who so wishes can procure at any of the larger stations a substantial luncheon, either hot or cold, with wine or beer and all the necessary conveniences, and this he can consume at his leisure as he speeds on his journey, putting out the empty basket at any station at which the train stops afterwards.

Another very great convenience is the railway family omnibus. Anyone who has lived in a country place, or in the suburbs of a large town, before the era of the railway omnibus, must have experienced the difficulty and expense of procuring conveyances to take them and their luggage to and from the railway station, while even in large towns, where the harmless necessary "growler" is readily procurable, a family party bound for the seaside, with large quantities of luggage, would frequently require two or three vehicles to convey them all to the station. But now all that is necessary is to send a telegram or post-card to the station-master, and punctually at the appointed hour a roomy and commodious vehicle, vastly more comfortable than any four-wheeled cab, makes its appearance, and for an extremely moderate charge—so moderate, indeed, as to be barely remunerative—takes the entire party, with all its *impedimenta*, and deposits them at the station, while on their return journey a similar conveyance can meet them at their journey's end and take them to their home.

There is one respect in which the travelling public of to-day have an inestimable advantage over that of an earlier generation, and that is in the greater immunity from accident that they enjoy. It is hardly possible to exaggerate the importance of this point, for although speed and comfort may be very desirable, yet safety of life and limb is, after all, the paramount consideration.

It is often said that figures may be made to prove anything, but certainly if there is anything that figures do prove beyond the possibility of a doubt it is that railway travelling has, during the last twenty years, become in a remarkable degree safer than it was, and may, indeed, be said to be now the safest mode of progression known to mankind, there being more danger actually in crossing the streets of a large town than in riding in an express train. This result has been achieved, of course, by means of the multiplication of safety appliances, the block telegraph system, the interlocking of points and signals, and the application of powerful continuous brakes to trains, and it should be borne in mind that it has been brought about in spite of the increase in the speed of the trains, which might be thought to tend in the opposite direction. In the year 1888 there were carried upon the railways of the United Kingdom upwards of 742,000,000 of passengers, exclusive of the enormous number of journeys performed by season ticket holders. During the year, 11 persons, only, lost their lives by reason of accidents to trains, and 594 were injured from the same cause, so that only about one passenger in 67,000,000 was killed, and one in about 12,500,000 was injured. Now, if we turn back to the year 1870, the first year in which the Board of Trade returns were published in their present complete form, we shall find that although the number of passengers carried was less than half—say about 307,000,000—the number killed in train accidents was 90, besides 1,094 injured; so that one passenger in about 4,700,000 was killed, and one in about 280,000 was injured. These figures speak highly for the improved safety of railway travelling, but almost as significant a result is obtained if we come to compare the amounts paid by railway companies for compensation for personal injury or loss of life with the sums paid by them under the same head at an earlier period; and Mr. Haggard, of Tunbridge Wells, a gentleman who is very much interested in railway statistics, has recently favoured me with some calculations of his bearing upon this subject which it may be worth while to quote here.

In 1868, Mr. Haggard finds that the railway companies of the

United Kingdom paid in compensation £306,442, while in 1888 this amount had fallen to £102,727, or just about one-third. But in the meantime the passenger train mileage run upon railways had grown from less than 75,000,000 of miles to upwards of 155,000,000, or in other words had more than doubled, so that the average payment for every 100,000 miles run was reduced in the twenty years from £409 to £66.

Although the result shown by these figures is extremely gratifying, yet railway companies are far from taking the view that nothing more can be done to reduce railway accidents to a minimum. On the contrary, the subject is one of the greatest anxiety to them at all times, and whenever a mishap does unfortunately occur, the circumstances attending it are most keenly inquired into, in the hope that out of evil may come good, and that some lesson may be learned from the calamity which may be taken to heart and used to prevent a recurrence.

There are many ways in which railway companies, in the natural desire to increase their business and improve their revenue, confer very substantial benefits upon the community, and not the least important of these is the universal practice of issuing season tickets. The object the companies have in view is, of course, to build up and encourage a residential traffic in connection with all the large towns upon their systems; but the advantage to the city merchant or clerk in being able to escape from the smoke and din amidst which his business is pursued, and to pass his hours of rest and leisure amidst the purer and healthier surroundings of the country or suburbs, is very great indeed, and but for the concession of the season ticket this would be a thing impossible for any but those possessing large incomes, since the cost of daily railway travelling, paying the ordinary fares, would constitute an addition to their expenses not to be contemplated.

Another great boon to the public is the tourist ticket—the advantages of which to those who, in the holiday season, seek health and recreation at the many places of resort around our coasts and elsewhere are very great. In many cases tickets are issued for what are known as "circular tours," and the nature of these can best be described by means of an illustration. For a sum of just over £4 a passenger can obtain a ticket entitling him to travel from London to Carmarthen, thence to Tenby and back, then northwards to Aberystwith, thence to Dolgelly and Barmouth, thence to Portmadoc and Carnarvon, Carnarvon to Bangor, Bangor to Chester, and so back to London. This is what is called the "North, South, and Mid-Wales Circular Tour," and practically it means that the holiday-maker for about £4 gets a free run over nearly all the railways throughout Wales, with all its glories of sea, mountain, and river for two months. If anyone were to perform such a tour as this and to pay the ordinary fares from point to point, he would be in a position to appreciate the pecuniary advantages of the tourist programme, especially if the fares paid were not for a solitary passenger but for a family party.

Then, again, in order to bring holiday travelling for shorter periods within even the modest means of the toiling millions, excursion trains at extremely low fares, are run frequently during the summer, and at Easter and Whitsuntide, between all the large towns and from large centres of population to the seaside resorts, and as these trains are for the most part run during the night, they enable the artisan who can, perhaps, only afford to lose a single day's wages, to spend the whole of that day at the seaside, or amongst his friends in some far distant town. It will afford some idea of the extent to which advantage is taken of these exceptional facilities, to mention the fact that during nine months of last year the London and North-Western Company alone carried considerably more than 1,500,000 excursion passengers.

Although perhaps not quite germane to my subject, it may not be out of place to refer to one respect n which the railway companies render a great service to the public, although like many other things, it has come to be looked upon as very much a matter of course. I allude to the marvellous facility with which the railways enable the Post-office to perform its functions. You post a letter or a parcel in London, say, at 6 o'clock this evening, and to-morrow morning your friend in Carlisle, Edinburgh, or Glasgow, finds it on his breakfast table. When one thinks of the many long miles between the sender and the receiver, and how long it would once have taken to cover them, this seems almost to resemble a conjurer's feat, and certainly it can only be beaten by electricity itself. The manner in which the duties of the Post-office are performed in this country is a theme of common admiration, and deservedly so, but few of those who eulogise the Post-office, and the way in which its work is carried on, realise that it is only the perfection of our railway system that has enabled such splendid results to be attained, and that indeed it is only the existence of that system that has rendered the postal service, as we know it, a possibility at all. Mr. W. M. Acworth, in his recent work, entitled " The Railways of England," has given so graphic a picture of the manner in which the mail service is conducted ; of the innumerable cross-country trains which join the great trunk mail routes at the appointed junctions in the dead of night, and safely and punctually exchange their precious freight ; of the ingenious apparatus by which mail bags are taken on board or cast off at the various stations and junctions while the trains speed on their journey without pausing for an instant ; and of the busy interiors of the mail carriages where the clerks perform their duties of sorting and making up the bags while the trains are on the way, that I could not hope by any words of mine to improve upon it. But the " proof of the pudding is in the eating," and it can hardly be gainsaid that the mail train service of this country, as performed by the railway companies, as a whole, furnishes results which leave little to be desired, and which could hardly be much improved upon.

The parcel post, compared with its elder brother the letter post, is as yet but in its infancy, but it has almost at a bound become one of the great institutions of the country, and has clearly justified its inception. This service again, which is evidently so highly appreciated by the public, would be impossible but for the facilities afforded by the railway system, and the railway companies, so far from showing any unworthy jealousy of a new establishment which they might not unreasonably expect to rob them of a lucrative branch of their business, have from the outset given it a loyal support, and done their best to contribute to its success, although it has had the effect of greatly adding to the weight and bulk of their trains and the difficulty of getting them away from the stations and junctions with punctuality. This it will not be difficult for you to believe when I mention the fact that during the past year the railway companies of the United Kingdom have carried for the Post-office something like 34,000,000 parcels. Indeed, one effect of this great influx of parcels, as far as the London and North-Western Railway is concerned, has been that the time-honoured "limited mails" have had to be disestablished as passenger trains, and since July, 1885, have been run as postal trains exclusively, other trains having been run in lieu of them for the conveyance of passengers to and from Scotland.

In addition to the special postal trains to and from Scotland, which travel between London and Carlisle at an average speed of 46 miles an hour, the London and North-Western Company run no less than four other important mail trains daily to Scotland, and two in the opposite direction, besides the two up and two down Irish mails, and numerous other mail trains, but at exceptionally busy times even these are found to be inadequate, and at Christmas, when the parcels post business, to say nothing of the mails, is swollen to abnormal proportions, it becomes necessary to adopt extraordinary measures to cope with the emergency which arises. The up and down special postal trains are duplicated throughout, as well as some of the other trains, extra vehicles are attached to all the more important mails, the timing of the trains has to be altered, and generally the whole of the service throughout the system has to be strengthened and re-arranged, so as to meet the great strain that is imposed upon it, and which taxes to the utmost extent the resources both of the company and the Post-office.

I am far from believing that my subject is exhausted, for there is much remaining that might be said; but I have already exceeded the limits of the time and space allotted to me and must draw to a close, but before doing so, I may perhaps be allowed to point the moral of my tale—if moral there be.

# APPENDIX.

Railway companies are, beyond a doubt, about the best abused body in the community, not excepting even that universal scapegoat, the metropolitan police. There is a great tendency to regard them as grasping monopolists, pursuing only their own selfish advantage, at the expense of the community ; but all this is hardly deserved. Monopolists, as I have just shown they are not, and cannot be, except in isolated cases, and although it is perfectly true that they pursue their own advantage, which as business men they are quite justified in doing, it is an elementary fact, to which no one is more fully alive than they are, that in the long run the public interest is theirs, or, rather, the two are inter-dependent. It is the object of the merchant not only to sell his wares to the best advantage, but to sell as many of them as possible, and it is the same with the railway companies. Whatever will induce people to travel more frequently, and will promote the circulation of goods traffic throughout the country, increases their revenue, and the profits of their shareholders, and advantages judiciously offered to the public within reasonable limits are as the seed that produces the harvest.

It is said to be an Englishman's privilege to grumble, and certainly he exercises this privilege without stint, so far as the railway companies are concerned. The merchant whose goods are a few hours late in delivery, roundly abuses the railway company, unheeding of the fact that they have arrived punctually nine times out of ten, and not knowing that, perhaps, the train which carried them on this particular occasion may have had to grope its way for hundreds of miles through a dense fog, or that they may have lain in the hold of a steamer which has fought its way across the channel in the teeth of a violent storm. The passenger whose train is half-an-hour late in reaching its destination on one occasion in ten is unsparing of his censure, although, if he only knew it, the delay has arisen from some perfectly unavoidable cause, or has been incurred from a due regard to his safety, and that of his fellow passengers.

The policy of railway companies finds many critics, but on the whole it is probable that if the circumstances were as well understood by the public as they are by themselves, it would be apparent that, after all, they know more of their own business than could be taught them by some, at least, of their censors.

If I have made use of the opportunity thus afforded me to such effect as to induce you to realise more fully the advantages which are derived from the railway system by the population of this country, and to bring you to believe that John Bull, after all, has cause to be proud of his railways, especially when he looks abroad and compares them with those of his neighbours, my object will have been sufficiently attained, and I shall not have addressed you in vain.

# INDEX.

ABSOLUTE BLOCK TELEGRAPH, Introduction of, 138
—— Various Descriptions of, in use, 139
—— Mode of Working, 140
ACCIDENTS to Railway Servants, Insurance against, 77
—— And Mishaps which occur on Railways, 113
—— Regulations as to Reporting to Board of Trade, 281
—— Greater Immunity from, in Modern Times, 394
ACCOMMODATION Works, Mode of Authorisation of, 65
ADMINISTRATION of a Great Railway, 58, 60
ADVANTAGES Derived from Introduction of Railway Travelling, 44, 379
AGENTS at Stations, Duties of, 61
ALTERATIONS of Trains, Method of Dealing with, 66
AMERICA, Introduction of Railways into, 53
ARBITRATION as a Means of Settling Disputes between Railway Companies, 267
AUSTRO-PRUSSIAN War of 1866, Organisation of Military Transport, 350
AUTHOR, Biographical Sketch of, 1
AUTOMATIC Vacuum Brake, Description of, 172


BESSEMER Process of Converting Iron into Steel, 165
BIOGRAPHICAL Sketch of Author, 1
BLOCK TELEGRAPH, Various Descriptions of, in use, 138, 139
—— "Tell Tale" Apparatus in Connection with, 140, 144

BLOCK Mode of Working, 140
—— Apparatus for Single Lines, 144
—— Combined Indicator and Bell System, 142
BOARD Meetings, Business Transacted at, 59
BOARD OF TRADE, Definition of their Powers of Control over Railways, 281
—— Inspection of New Railways by Officers of, 281
—— All Accidents to be Reported to, 281
BOILERS, Application of Steel to the Manufacture of, 168
BOYS, Employment and Training of, 72
BRADSHAW'S Guide in 1839, 380
BRAKE Power, various Descriptions of, in Use, 172
—— Description of Automatic Vacuum, 172
BRASSEY, MR., Character of, 15
BRICK-MAKING Plant at Crewe Works, 168
BRIDGE Rails, Early Use of on Great Western Railway, 88
BROAD STREET Station, Description of Construction and Working of, 240


"CALLING ON" Signals on Home Signal Posts, 130
CARRIAGES, Rude Type of, in Use Half a Century Ago, 176
—— Improved Type of, in Use at Present Time, 177
—— Proportions of Accommodation for various classes of Passengers, 178

CARRIAGES, Abolition of Second Class by Midland Company in 1875, 178
—— London and North-Western Company's Practice of Building their Own, 180
—— of the Saloon Type, 179
—— Works at Wolverton, description of, 180
——— Description of Methods of Construction of, at Wolverton Works, 180
—— Examination, Washing, Greasing, &c., of, 186
—— Heating of, 188
—— Lighting of by Gas, 189
—— Lighting of by Electricity, 192
—— Increase in size and Weight of, 305, 390
CARRIERS' Act of 1845, Provisions of, 329, 338
CATTLE, Mode of Dealing with at Holyhead, 254
(*See also* Live Stock.)
CHAIN Drag for Arresting Runaway Waggons, 235
CHAIRS (Railway) Type of in use, 92
CHANNEL Tunnel Railway Projected in 1833, 50
CHEAP TRAINS Act of 1883, Provisions of described, 336
CHECK Rails for Crossings, 100
CLAIMS, Mode of Settling Disputes between Railway Companies as to, 268
CLASSES of Passenger Traffic, relation of, to each other, 297
CLASSIFICATION of Merchandise Traffic, 263
COACHES, Introduction of, in 17th century, 41
——— Mail, Introduction of, in 18th century, 42
COAL, Consumption of by Engines, 313, 389
—— Supply, rapid exhaustion of, in Great Britain, 55
COMMITTEES of the Board, Functions and Composition of, 58

COMMON Carriers, Rights and Responsibilities of, 326
COMMUNICATION between Passengers and Guards, 282
COMPARTMENTS, Practice of Reserving for Passengers, 308
COMPENSATION, Striking Decrease in Amount Paid for, 395
COMPETITION, Effect of upon Rates and upon Earnings of Railways, 265, 388
——— Means Adopted for Avoiding Excessive, 266
——— When pushed to Extremes not to ultimate Advantage of Public, 267
——— Undue, upon English Railways, with regard to Passenger Traffic, 388
COMPOUND Engines, Description of, 154
CONCENTRATION of Troops, in event of Invasion, by means of Railway Transport, 341
CONFERENCES of Officers, Constitution and Functions of, 61
——— Of Railway Companies to Agree upon Rates and Fares, 265
CONSIGNMENT Notes for Goods, Utility of, 246
CONTINENTAL RAILWAYS — Relation of to the State, 278
——— Disadvantages of State ownership of, 294
——— Inferiority of, to English Railways, 317
——— Organisation of, in times of mobilisation, 343
——— Type of Permanent Way in use upon, 388
CORRIDOR Trains, 180
COTTAGES for Company's Servants, 220
CREWE Locomotive Works, Description of, 158
CROSS-CHANNEL Traffic with Ireland, Mode of Conducting, 252
CROSSINGS and Points, 97
——— (Diamond) Effect of, 97
——— ——— Construction of, 97

CURVES, Super-elevation of Outer Rails on, 101
——— Avoidance of Severe, 102
——— Effect of on Speed of Trains, 107, 108
——— of Adjustment, 110


DEBTS and Goods Claims Committee, Functions of, 59
DEFENCE of the Country, Importance of Railway System Considered in Relation to, 26, 341
DELAYS to Passengers, Liabilities of Railway Companies with Respect to, 339
DELIVERY of Goods to and by a Carrier, What Constitutes, 326, 333
DERAILMENTS at Crossings, 98
DETECTOR Locks and Bars, 127
DIAGRAMS of Engine Working, 203
DIRECTORS, Qualification and Functions of, 58
DISC Signals, 121
DISPUTES between Railway Companies settled by Arbitration, 267
DISTANT Signals, **120**
DISTRICT Officers, Duties and Responsibilities of, 60
DIVISION of Traffic between Railway Companies in Percentages, 266
——— Of Traffic in Mileage Proportions of a Through Route, 270
DONCASTER RACES, Organisation of Traffic on Occasion of, 358
DRAINAGE of Permanent Way, System of, 94
DUPLICATION of Lines on Crowded Railways, 204, 281
DWELLINGS for Company's Servants, 220


EARLESTOWN Waggon Works, Description of, 198

EARNINGS of the various classes of Passengers, 301, 314
EDGE HILL Gridiron Sidings, described, 229
ELECTRIC Signal Repeaters and Light Indicators, 145
——— Locks for Sidings, 146
——— Lighting of Carriages, 192
——— Staff Working for Single Lines, 216
EMPLOYERS' Liability Act, 77
ENGINES, Primitive Type of, in Use on Early Railways, 150
——— Early Difficulties with Regard to, 151, 153
——— Trial of, at Rainhill in 1829, 152
——— Various Types of in use at Present Time, 154
——— "Webb's Compound," Description of, 154
——— Advantages of, 155
——— Special Types of, for Narrow Gauge and for Station Yards, 157
——— Number of, Constructed at Crewe Works, 162
——— Methods of Building at Crewe Works, 162
——— Interchangeability of Parts, 163
——— Increase in Power and Weight of, 305, 393
ENGINE DRIVERS, Selection and Training of, 74
ENGINE WORKING, Diagrams for Regulating, 203
ENGINE HEAD LIGHTS, System of Distinctive, 209
ENGINEER and Railway Volunteer Staff Corps, Constitution and Functions of, 342
——— Volunteers, Enrolment of, at large Railway Works, 375
ENTRAINMENT of Troops, 364
EUSTON STATION in the Tourist Season, 223
EXCURSION Traffic, what Railway Companies accomplish in connection with, 355
——— Arrangements, great advantage to the Public of, 396

# INDEX.

CURVES, Super-elevation of Outer Rails on, 101
—— Avoidance of Severe, 102
—— Effect of on Speed of Trains, 107, 108
—— of Adjustment, 110

DEBTS and Goods Claims Committee, Functions of, 59
DEFENCE of the Country, Importance of Railway System Considered in Relation to, 26, 341
DELAYS to Passengers, Liabilities of Railway Companies with Respect to, 339
DELIVERY of Goods to and by a Carrier, What Constitutes, 326, 333
DERAILMENTS at Crossings, 98
DETECTOR Locks and Bars, 127
DIAGRAMS of Engine Working, 203
DIRECTORS, Qualification and Functions of, 58
DISC Signals, 121
DISPUTES between Railway Companies settled by Arbitration, 267
DISTANT Signals, 120
DISTRICT Officers, Duties and Responsibilities of, 60
DIVISION of Traffic between Railway Companies in Percentages, 266
—— Of Traffic in Mileage Proportions of a Through Route, 270
DONCASTER RACES, Organisation of Traffic on Occasion of, 358
DRAINAGE of Permanent Way, System of, 94
DUPLICATION of Lines on Crowded Railways, 204, 281
DWELLINGS for Company's Servants, 220

EARLESTOWN Waggon Works, Description of, 198

EARNINGS of the various classes of Passengers, 301, 314
EDGE HILL Gridiron Sidings, described, 229
ELECTRIC Signal Repeaters and Light Indicators, 145
—— Locks for Sidings, 146
—— Lighting of Carriages, 192
—— Staff Working for Single Lines, 216
EMPLOYERS' Liability Act, 77
ENGINES, Primitive Type of, in Use on Early Railways, 150
—— Early Difficulties with Regard to, 151, 153
—— Trial of, at Rainhill in 1829, 152
—— Various Types of in use at Present Time, 154
—— "Webb's Compound," Description of, 154
—— Advantages of, 155
—— Special Types of, for Narrow Gauge and for Station Yards, 157
—— Number of, Constructed at Crewe Works, 162
—— Methods of Building at Crewe Works, 162
—— Interchangeability of Parts, 163
—— Increase in Power and Weight of, 305, 393
ENGINE DRIVERS, Selection and Training of, 74
ENGINE WORKING, Diagrams for Regulating, 203
ENGINE HEAD LIGHTS, System of Distinctive, 209
ENGINEER and Railway Volunteer Staff Corps, Constitution and Functions of, 342
—— Volunteers, Enrolment of, at large Railway Works, 375
ENTRAINMENT of Troops, 364
EUSTON STATION in the Tourist Season, 223
EXCURSION Traffic, what Railway Companies accomplish in connection with, 355
—— Arrangements, great advantage to the Public of, 396

# INDEX.

HEAD LIGHTS for Engines, System of Distinctive, 209
HEATING of Carriages, 188
HOLYHEAD Goods Station and Harbour, Construction, and Working of, 252
HOME SIGNALS, 120
HORSES, Loading and Unloading of, for Military Purposes, 364
HOUSES for Company's Servants, 220

IMPROVED Facilities for Railway Travelling, 377
INSPECTION, System of Periodical, 63
—— of Permanent Way, Daily, 112
—— of Railways by Board of Trade, 281
INSPECTORS, Duties of, 60
INSURANCE Fund for Railway Servants, 77
—— of Goods by Railway Companies, 325, 327
INTERLOCKING of Points and Signals, First Introduction of, 118
—— Theory and Practice of, 123
—— of Siding Points by Means of "Keys," 128
—— Apparatus, Maintenance and Repair of, 133
INVASION, Value of Railways in the Event of, 26, 341
IRISH Cross-Channel Traffic, Mode of Conducting at Holyhead, 252
—— Railways, Administration of and Policy with regard to, 23
IRON Sleepers, Use of, Experimentally, 94

JUNCTIONS, Formation of, 101
—— Signals at, 134

KEY, Interlocking, for Siding Points, 128

LAND, Compulsory Powers for Purchase of, for Railway Purposes, 280
—— Extravagant Prices formerly paid for, 280
LAVATORY Accommodation for Passengers in Trains, 391, 392
LAW, as between Railway Companies and the Public, 323
—— Affecting Railway Companies, Where and How Defined, 324
LEGISLATION Hostile to Railway Companies, 285
LEVEL CROSSINGS, Board of Trade Powers with regard to, 282
LIGHT Indicators for Signals, 145
LIGHTING of Signals by Gas and Oil, 132
—— of Carriages by Electricity, 192
LITIGATION, Railway Companies' avoidance of, as between themselves, 267
LIVERPOOL AND MANCHESTER RAILWAY, projection of, 46
—— Opposition offered to, 46
—— Construction and Opening of, 48
—— Mode of Construction and Working, 48, 377
—— Great Success of, 49, 379
—— Type of Permanent Way in use on, 90, 378
LIVE STOCK, Conditions on which Railway Companies carry, 330
(*See also* Cattle)
LLANDULAS Viaduct Washed away by Flood in 1879, 114
LLANDUDNO, Arrangements for Excursion Traffic, 357
LOCKING Bars for Points, 127
LOCOMOTIVE Engines (*See* Engines)
—— Committee, Functions of, 58
—— Department: Societies for Benefit of Staff, 82
LONDON AND BIRMINGHAM RAILWAY, Projection and Construction of, 50

## INDEX.

LONDON AND NORTH-WESTERN RAILWAY, Various Companies Amalgamated under Title of, 50
——— Statistics of, 51, 203
LOST LUGGAGE, The Railway Clearing House as a Means of Tracing, 277
LUGGAGE, Law affecting the Conveyance of, 337, 339
LUNCHEON BASKETS, Convenience of, 393

MAILS, Expeditious Conveyance of, by Railway, 396
——— Description of Method of Conveyance, 225
MAINTENANCE AND REPAIR of Permanent Way, 111
——— of Signals and Interlocking Apparatus, 113
——— of Telegraph Apparatus, 147
MANAGEMENT of a Great Railway, 58
——— General Principles Laid Down for, 67
MARSHALLING of Goods Trains, 227
MERCHANDISE, The Law affecting the Conveyance of, 326 (*See also* Goods)
MILITARY Operations, Railways considered in Relation to, 341
MODERN Improvements of Facilities for Railway Travelling, 377

NATIONAL DEFENCE, Railways as a means of, 341
NEW WORKS, Mode of Dealing with Proposals for, 65

OFFICERS, District, Duties and Responsibilities of, 60
——— Attending Periodically at Head Quarters, 63
——— Hints to, for Economising Time, 69

OFFICERS, Selection and Promotion of, 73
——— Conference, Business Transacted at, 61 .
OIL GAS, Use of, for Lighting Carriages, 189
OMNIBUSES (Family), Provided by Railway Companies, 393

PARCELS POST Act of 1882, 397
PARLIAMENTARY Powers for Construction of Railways, 279
——— Procedure in the Matter of New Railways, 279
PASSENGER Communication with Guards and Drivers, 282
——— Traffic, Conduct of, 297
——— Traffic, Revenue earning Powers of, 300, 302, 308, 384
——— Traffic, Working Expenses and Net Profits of, 312.
PASSENGERS, The Law Affecting the Conveyance of, 335
——— Conditions on which Railway Companies are not bound to Carry, 336
——— Travelling on Railways without Paying their Fares, 384
——— Must Show their Tickets on Demand, 339
——— Luggage (*See* Luggage)
PENSION AND PROVIDENT Funds, Constitution of, 79
PERCENTAGE, Divisions of Traffic amongst Railway Companies, 266
PERMANENT WAY Committee, Functions of, 58
——— Improved Type of, as compared with Earlier Railways, 84
——— The "Bridge" and "Vignoles' Rails, 88
——— Various Forms of, formerly in use, 88
——— Introduction of Fish Plates, 90
——— Improved Sectional Area of Rails, 90

## INDEX.

PERMANENT WAY, Introduction of Steel Rails, 90
——— Type of in use at present time, 92
——— Essentials of a Sound and Good, 94
——— Arrangements for Maintenance and Repair of, 111
——— Daily Inspection of, 112
——— Type of in use on Continental Railways, 388
PERMISSIVE, Block Telegraph Working, 139
PERSONAL Injuries to Passengers, Mode of Assessing Damages for, 340
POINTS AND CROSSINGS, Various Descriptions of, 97
POINT Rod Compensators, 127
——— Rods, Construction of, 132
POPE'S Oil Gas for Lighting Carriages, 189
POSTAL TRAINS Between London and Scotland, 304
POST OFFICE (Parcels) Act of 1882, 276, 397
——— Great Services Rendered by Railways to, 396
PROVIDENT and Pension Fund, Constitution of, 79
PROMOTION by Merit to Higher Ranks of Service, 74
PUNCTUALITY of Trains, Difficulties in Maintaining, 205, 385
PURCHASE of Railways by the State Discussed, 289

QUEEN'S TRAIN, Description of Mode of Working, 26, 222

RADIAL Axle Boxes for Engines 156
RAIL Making, 166
RAILS, "Fish Bellied," as used in 1789, 88
——— "Bridge," 88
——— "Vignoles," 88
——— "Double-headed," 88
——— Steel, Introduction of, 90
——— Long, for Special Purposes, 94

RAILWAYS, a Subject of Interest to all Classes, 37
——— State of Things Existing prior to introduction of, 39
——— Advantages of, Enumerated, 44, 378
——— First dawn of Conception of, 45
——— Rapid Development of, since their Origin, 378
——— Relation of the State to, in Great Britain, 278
——— Purchase of, by the State Discussed, 289
——— And their relation to the Trade of the Country, 283
——— Increasing Demands made upon, 298
——— As a Means of National Defence, 341
——— Their Liability to Adverse Criticism, 398
——— Statistics of, in United Kingdom and in the World, 51

RAILWAY and Canal Traffic Act of 1873, Provisions of, 282
——— Ditto of 1888, Provisions of, 263, 285
——— Companies' Arbitration Act of 1859, 268
——— Commissioners' Court, Constitution and Powers of under Act of 1873, 282
——— Commissioners' Extended Powers under Act of 1888, 285
——— Rates Committee of 1882, Conclusions of, 288
——— Transport of Troops at Home and Abroad, 341
——— Travelling, Improved Facilities for, in Modern Times, 377

RAILWAY CLEARING HOUSE Origin of, 272
——— Functions of, 274
——— Statistics of, 272
——— Methods and Machinery of, 274
——— Various Conferences held at, 276

RAILWAY CLEARING HOUSE, As a Means of Tracing Lost Poperty, 277
RATES and Fares Committee, Functions of, 58
―― and Fares, Mode of Calculating, 262
―― Effects of Competition upon, 264
―― Conferences of Railway Companies to agree upon, 263
―― Demand that the State should be empowered to fix, 283
RECEIPTS and Expenses of Passenger Traffic, 300, 302, 308
RESPONSIBILITY, Chain of, throughout Railway Service, 61
―― of Railway Companies, as regards Carriage of Goods, where it begins and ends, 326
―― of Railway Companies for the Acts of their Servants, 337
RETURNS to be Submitted by Railway Companies to Board of Trade, 282
ROADS, Condition of in Middle Ages, 39
―― Improvement of after 16th Century, 40
"ROCKET," the, Trial of at Rainhill in 1829, 152
RODS for Working Points, 132
ROUTE INDICATORS (Electric) for Junction Cabins, 146
ROYAL TRAIN, description of Mode of Working, 26, 222
RULES AND REGULATIONS for Working Railways, 64
RUNAWAY Waggons, Chain Drag for Arresting, 235
RUSSO-TURKISH War of 1877-8, Organisation of Military Transport, 350

SALOON CARRIAGES, 179, 307, 391
SEASON Tickets, Advantages of, 395

SECOND Class, Abolition of, on Some Railways, 178, 301, 382
SHEFFIELD Colliery Tramway of 1776, 86
SHUNTING Indicators for Station Yards, 146
―― and Marshalling of Goods Trains, 227
―― of Slow Trains to allow Fast Trains to Pass, 206
―― Sidings, Various Systems of, in Use, 228
―― Footner's Plan of Gridiron Sidings for, 229
SIDINGS, for Marshalling Waggons, Various Systems of Laying Out, 228
―― Footner's System of Gridiron, 229
SIDINGS, Control of, by Electric Locks, 146
SIGHTING of Signals, Rules for, 134
SIGNALS, Concentration of, 120
―― Various Descriptions of, in Use, 120
―― Home, 120
―― Distant, 120
―― Starting, 120
―― Disc, 121
―― Construction of, 129
―― Fitting Establishment at Crewe, 129
―― Lighting of, 132
―― Maintenance and Repair of, 133
―― Rules for Sighting of, 134
―― for Junctions, 135
―― Electrical Repeating of, 145
SIGNAL Cabins and Apparatus, 123
SIGNALMEN, Training and Examination of, 72
SIGNALLING and Interlocking, System of, 116
―― Earlier Methods of, 117
SINGLE-LINE Block Telegraph Apparatus, 144
SINGLE Lines, Working of, by Train Staff and Ticket System, 211
―― Lines, Various Modes of Working, 211, 212, 213

# INDEX.

SINGLE Lines, Train Tablet System for Working, 213
—— Lines, Working of, by Electric Staff System, 214
SLEEPERS, Type of, Now in Use, 92
—— Stone, Formerly in Use, 88
—— Iron and Steel, Experiments with, 94
SLEEPING SALOONS, Advantages of, 179, 307, 392
SOAP, Manufacture of, from Refuse Oil and Grease from Engines, 168, 170
SOCIETIES for the Benefit of the Staff, 75
SPEED of Trains, Great Increase in, 303
—— of Trains, the result of competition, 106
—— of Trains, English and Foreign, 386
—— of Trains. Effect of, Upon Working Expenses, 389
STAFF, Number of Men Employed, 71
—— Training and Examination of, 72
STARTING Signals, 120
STATE, The Relation of Railways to, in Great Britain, 278
—— The Relation of Railways to, in Different Countries, 278
—— Purchase of Railways Discussed, 289
STATION MASTERS, Duties of, 61
STATISTICS of the London and North-Western Railway, 51, 203
STEAM as a Motive Power, First Introduction of, 45
STEAMERS for Cross-Channel Traffic with Ireland, 252
STEEL RAILS, first Introduction of, 90
STEEL SLEEPERS, Experimental Introduction of, 94
STEEL Making Plant at Crewe Works, 165
STEEL, Use of, for Boiler Making, 168

STOCKTON & DARLINGTON Railway, Construction of in 1821, 45
STONE SLEEPERS, Early Use of, 88
STOPPAGE of Goods, "*in transitu*," Law of, 333
STRATEGICAL Lines of Railway for National Defence, 349
SUPERANNUATION Fund for Clerks, 75
SUPER-ELEVATION of Outer Rail on Curves, 101
SUPERVISION, Elaborate Arrangements for, 68
SWITCHES, Description of, 101

TELEGRAPHY, Various Uses of, in Working Railways, 137
TELEGRAPHS, Various Descriptions of "Block," in Use, 138
—— for Speaking purposes, Extensive Use of, 147
—— Arrangements for Maintenance and Repair of, 147
—— Wires, Relative Advantages of Iron and Copper, 149
—— Wires, Description of, in Use, 149
TELEGRAPH Statistics relating to, 147
TELEGRAPH Batteries, description of in use, 149
TELEGRAPH, (*See also* Block Telegraph)
TELEGRAPHING Progress of trains from Point to Point, 207
TELEPHONES, Use of in Railway Working, 147
"TELL TALE" Instruments for Telegraph Working, Block 140, 144
THIRD CLASS Passengers formerly only carried by Slow Trains, 299, 382
—— Traffic, enormous increase of, 316
THROUGH Booking of Traffic by Railways which connect: Power of Railway Commissioners to require, 282
TICKETS must be Shown by Passengers on demand, 339

# INDEX.

TIME-TABLES, Compilation and Revision of, 66
—— of 50 years ago, 380
TOURIST TICKETS, Advantages of, 395
TRAFFIC Committee—Functions of, 59
—— Receipts, Agreements for Division of, between Railway Companies, 266
TRAIN Alterations, Method of Dealing with, 65, 66
—— Starting Indicators, electric, 146
—— Diagrams for Regulating Engine Working, 203
TRAIN Staff and Ticket System for Single Lines, 211
—— Tablet System for Single Lines, 213
TRAINS, Various descriptions of, to be accommodated on same Line of Rails, 202
—— Difficulties in Attaining Absolute Punctuality, 205, 385
—— On the Corridor System 180
—— Increase in Length, Weight and speed of, 210, 306
—— Composition, Speed and Weight of, 297, 377
—— Increase in Speed of, 303, 384
—— Run between Same Points by Various Routes, 319
—— Great Increase in Number of, in Recent Years, 381
—— Speed of English and Foreign Compared, 386
—— Effect of High speed Working Expenses, of, on ——
—— Training of ——es, 383
TRANSPORT of —— t Staff, 72
—— Troops by Railway at Home and Abroad, 26, 341
TRAVELLING, before Introduction of Railways, 43
TROOPS, Transport of, by Railway at Home and Abroad, 26, 341
—— Entrainment and Detrainment of, 364

"UNDUE PREFERENCE," what Constitutes, 287
UNITED STATES, Introduction of Railways into, 53

VACUUM Brake (Automatic), Description of, 172
VALUABLE Articles, Liability of Carriers with Regard to, 329
"VEHICLE ON LINE," Electric Indicators, 146

WAGGONS, Ownership of, by Railway Companies, 194
—— Belonging to Private Owners, Difficulties with Regard to, 195
—— Belonging to Private Owners, Specification for Construction of, 195
—— Examination and Greasing of, 197
—— Minimum Dimensions of Axles and Tyres, 197
—— Number and Description of, in use, 198
—— Works at Earlestown for Construction of, 198
WAR, Working of Railways in time of, 341
WARS, Lessons drawn from Events of Recent European, 351
WAREHOUSES, Methods of Construction and Working of, 257
WATER TRO——GHS, to enable Trains in Motion to take Water, 158
WHEELS for Passenger Carriages— Mode of Construction, 183
WIDENING of Railways, 204, 281
WOLVERTON Carriage Works, Description of, 180
WORKS, Mode of Dealing with Applications for New, 65
WORKING of the Trains, Difficulties with Regard to, 201
—— Expenses of Passenger Traffic, 312
WORKMEN'S Trains, Board of Trade powers to Enforce Running of, 282, 336